# 30

## MOCK TEST SERIES

for

## Olympiad

English | Mathematics
Science | General Knowledge
Cyber | Logical Reasoning

**8**

Class

**Comprehensive MCQ with detailed solutions covering all the Olympiad Exams.**

- **Corporate Office :** 45, 2nd Floor, Maharishi Dayanand Marg, Corner Market, Malviya Nagar, New Delhi-110017

  Tel. : 011-49842349 / 49842350

**Typeset by Disha DTP Team**

**Printed at Repro Knowledgecast Limited, Thane**

**DISHA PUBLICATION**




**For further information about the books from DISHA,**

Log on to **www.dishapublication.com** or email to **info@dishapublication.com**

# CONTENTS

## English



## Mathematics



## Science

# ENGLISH

## OLYMPIAD Mock Test  1

Name : __________

Max. Marks : 50

Number of Questions : 50

Time : 2 Hours

**There is no negative marking in the test.**

**DIRECTIONS (Qs. 1 to 21):** Choose the best option to complete each sentence.

1. The _______ that I want to read from the book includes a description of the fall of the Roman Empire.
   (a) example    (b) excerpt
   (c) words      (d) books

2. He was caught _______ book from the shop.
   (a) packing    (b) gifting
   (c) eating     (d) pilfering

3. After the wrestling match, the wrestler had run out of steam. He was _______________.
   (a) more energised
   (b) completely out of energy
   (c) fuming with anger
   (d) in a mood to conciliate

4. It proved to be a great ______ experience for Brian.
   (a) teaching   (b) learning
   (c) picking    (d) trying

5. The reporter provided a/an __________ account of the whole incident.
   (a) dramatic    (b) arbitrary
   (c) detailed    (d) enthusiastic

6. The exact ______ of this civilisation is not known.
   (a) local       (b) origin
   (c) site        (d) king

7. Mr. Abrol's character was quite __________. He didn't seem to succumb to any challenge.
   (a) solid
   (b) stolid
   (c) unimpressive
   (d) patronising

8. That lady is very elusive. She is as slippery as a/an __________.
   (a) orange     (b) eel
   (c) book       (d) flower

9. She was not well ______ she went for the party.
   (a) but        (b) yet
   (c) and        (d) while

10. Ten kilometres __________ a long distance to walk.

    (a) is              (b) are

    (c) were            (d) none of these

11. He has the habit of ________to conclusions.

    (a) listening

    (b) speaking

    (c) jumping

    (d) making

12. I want to ______the actress.

    (a) meet            (b) stumble

    (c) adjoin          (d) cross

13. "You ______ go back home now", said the teacher.

    (a) may             (b) might

    (c) could           (d) would

14. __________ children, parents also attended the party.

    (a) Beside          (b) Besides

    (c) Alongwith       (d) With

15. It was a terrible earthquake, but the lady was __________ unhurt.

    (a) clearly

    (b) meticulously

    (c) miraculously

    (d) terribly

16. David drives his car ______.

    (a) softly          (b) carefully

    (c) definitely      (d) cooly

17. I must leave now because I have to be at my workplace______ 11 o' clock.

    (a) until           (b) by

    (c) after           (d) later

18. Not ______people came for the show.

    (a) any             (b) some

    (c) many            (d) most

19. ________ ozone layer will continue to deplete, if we don't find a way to stop its depletion.

    (a) A               (b) An

    (c) The             (d) None of these

20. The Façade Stadium ________ has been in existence for more than fifty years, is now in shambles.

    (a) that            (b) which

    (c) who             (d) whom

21. Which spelling is correct?

    (a) Endevour        (b) Endeavour

    (c) Endeavor        (d) Endeavor

**DIRECTIONS (Qs. 22 to 24):** Choose the antonym of the underlined word in each sentence.

22. <u>Affluence</u> and illiteracy are two of the greatest social evils.

    (a) Cheap           (b) Poverty

    (c) Paucity         (d) Dusk

23. He is quite <u>agile.</u>

    (a) aged            (b) dull

    (c) active          (d) young

24. He was very <u>curt</u> to me.

   (a) rude

   (b) brief

   (c) argumentative

   (d) polite

**DIRECTIONS (Qs. 25 & 26):** Choose the most appropriate option to fill the blanks.

25. A government run by a dictator is known as _______.

   (a) oligarchy　(b) autocracy

   (c) mobocracy　(d) plebiscite

26. A person in charge of a museum is called a _______.

   (a) museologist

   (b) curator

   (c) museogist

   (d) mercenary

**DIRECTIONS (Qs. 27 to 31):** Select the option that changes given sentences into passive form.

27. The delivery man will deliver the parcel today by the delivery man.
   (a) The parcel will be delivered today by the delivery man.
   (b) The parcel is delivered today.
   (c) The parcel has been delivered today.
   (d) The delivery man has delivered the parcel today.

28. The earthquake destroyed the building.
   (a) The building was destroyed by the earthquake.
   (b) The earthquake was the destroyer of the building.
   (c) The building got destroyed by the earthquake.
   (d) The earthquake got the building destroyed.

29. He makes mats.

   (a) He is making mats.

   (b) He has made mats.

   (c) Mats are made by him.

   (d) He has been making mats.

30. The manager has given her a notice.

   (a) The manager will give her a notice.

   (b) She will get a notice by the manager.

   (c) The manager has been given a notice by her.

   (d) She has been given a notice by her manager.

31. The teacher did an experiment.

   (a) An experiment was done by the teacher.

   (b) The teacher is doing an experiment.

   (c) The teacher has done an experiment.

   (d) The teacher has doing experiments.

**DIRECTIONS (Qs. 32 to 36):** Read the passage given below and answer the questions that follow.

Buddhism, as a religion, gained prominence in the ancient kingdom of Magadha (now in Bihar). It was based on the teachings of Siddhartha

Gautama, who was deemed as "Buddha"("Awakened One"). Even though the practice of Buddhism, as a distinct and organised religion, lost influence after the Gupta reign and declined from the land of its origin, it continued to prosper in several parts of South Asia located at the crossroads of significant routes; Bamiyan emerged as a major hub for Buddhist activities. The artistic and architectural remains of Bamiyan valley are a testimony to the interchange of Indian, Hellinistic, Roman and Sasanian influence as the basis for the development of a particular artistic expression on the Gandharan School. The region exemplified a cultural landscape and a significant period in Buddhism. The Buddha statues of Bamiyan coexisted with numerous stupas; scattered in the Afghan mountains were built to house relics of the Buddha and later saints.

The statues were destroyed by dynamites over several weeks, starting on March2, 2001. Initially, the statues were fired at for several days using anti-aircraft guns and artillery. This caused severe damage, but did not topple them. Later, the Taliban placed anti-tank mines at the bottom, so that when fragments of rock broke off from artillery fire, the statues would crumble. In 2003, the UNESCO declared the valley a world heritage site and archaeologists flocked to it. What they found were two enormous empty caverns and a pile of debris littered with unexploded mines.

32. Which of the following is false?
    (a) Buddhism lost is influence after the Gupta reign.
    (b) It prospered in several parts of South Asia.
    (c) Stupas were built to house the travellers.
    (d) Bamiyan emerged as a major hub of Buddhist activities.

33. What method was used to destroy the statues?
    (a) Dynamite
    (b) Anti-tank mines
    (c) Anti-aircraft guns
    (d) All of these

34. What do you understand by artillery?
    (a) Tanks
    (b) Munitions
    (c) Heavy weaponry
    (d) Army

35. What did the archaeologists discover at Bamiyan?
    (a) Buddha statues
    (b) Empty caverns and debris
    (c) Mines
    (d) Relics of Buddha and later saints

36. What is the meaning of caverns?
    (a) Tunnel       (b) Corridor
    (c) Gallery      (d) A small cave

**DIRECTIONS (Qs. 37 to 41):** Look at the table given below and answer the questions that follow.

## INFREQUENT FLYERS

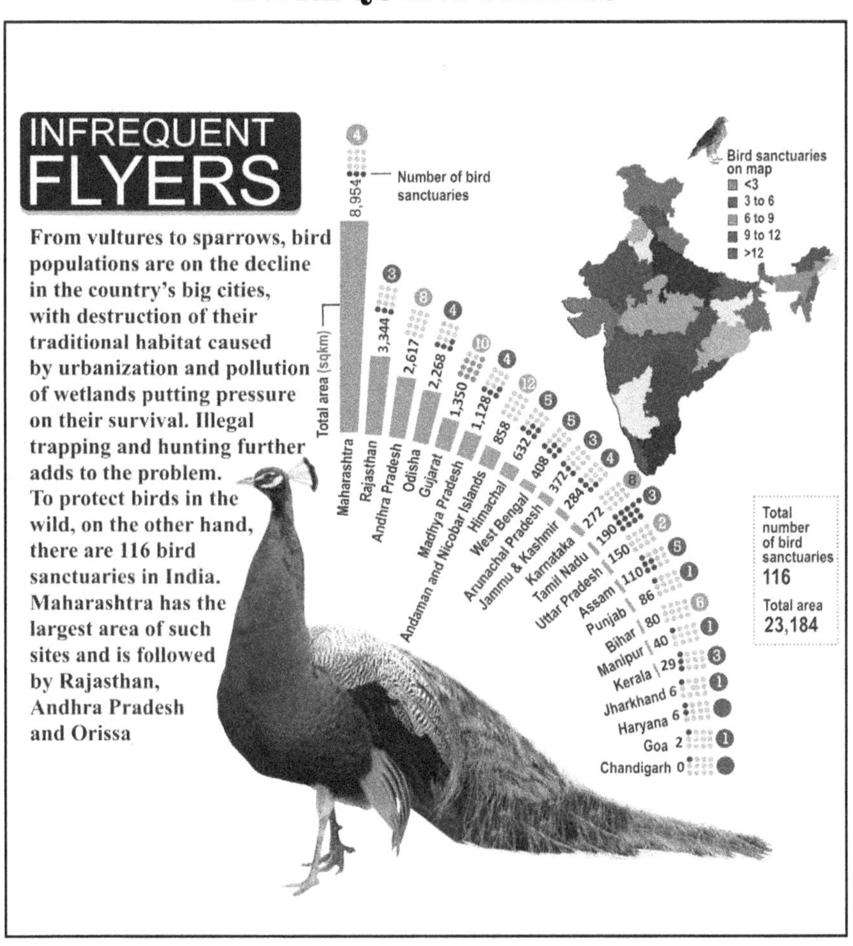



37. What is causing destruction of habitat for birds?
    (a) Urbanisation
    (b) Pollution of wetlands
    (c) Illegal trapping and hunting
    (d) All of these

38. How many bird sanctuaries are there in India?
    (a) 116    (b) 118
    (c) 8,954    (d) 23,184

39. Which of the following statements is false?
    (a) Six states have less than 12 bird sanctuaries.
    (b) Total area under bird sanctuaries is 23,184.
    (c) Maharashtra has the largest area for bird sanctuaries.
    (d) Andhra Pradesh has eight bird sanctuaries.

40. What is the source of the information given here?
    (a) Department of Bird Management
    (b) Ministry of Bird Management
    (c) Board of Directors for Management of Bird Migration
    (d) Ministry of Environment Forest & Climate Change

41. Why do we need to have bird sanctuaries?
    (a) To protect bird population.
    (b) To provide habitat to the birds.
    (c) To help them against the onslaught by hunters and trappers.
    (d) All of the above

**DIRECTIONS (Qs. 42 to 44):** Choose the correct beginning for each of the following sentences from the four options given below.

42. ___________ That I could paint.
43. ___________ She has left the world.
44. ___________ We won the world cup.
    (a) Alas!          (b) Oh!
    (c) Terrific news!
    (d) Terrible news.

**DIRECTIONS (Qs. 45 to 50):** Complete the conversation from the options given below.

45. Harris: Have you ever heard her singing?___________
    Clement: Even I enjoy when she sings.
    (a) How well she sings!
    (b) It's quite boring.
    (c) Don't do that.
    (d) I sing better than her.

46. Ruff: Are you left with any money to buy a new pair of shoes? They are on discount.
    Ginny:___________
    Ruff: Oh!
    (a) I wish I hadn't spent all my pocket money.
    (b) Yes, let's go and buy.
    (c) No, I don't want to buy.
    (d) Yes, but I am not too keen.

47. Roli: Please lend me your cycle for tomorrow.
    Devi:___________
    (a) I can't as I have to go out.
    (b) Sure! You can take it tomorrow.
    (c) You can take it after Sunday.
    (d) No, I am not into habit of sharing things.

48. Keerti: Oh no! I have lost my favourite hairband.
    Hema: ___________
    (a) Why didn't you take care of it?
    (b) Don't worry; I'll help you find it.
    (c) Don't worry, they are meant to be lost.
    (d) Why did you buy a hairband?

49. Arnie: Let's go for a movie tomorrow.
    Samson:___________
    (a) No, we can't. I don't like watching movies.
    (b) Sure, but we'll go and watch a movie of my choice.
    (c) Fine, which one would you like to see?
    (d) Fine, let's go to the zoo.

50. Rekha: Are you free today? Let's go shopping.
    Amita:___________
    (a) The shops will be crowded.
    (b) No, the shops are closed.
    (c) Okay, let's go to the mall.
    (d) It's too hot to stay in the market.

# OLYMPIAD
# Mock Test 2

Name : _________

Number of Questions : 50

**There is no negative marking in the test.**

Max. Marks : 50

Time : 2 Hours

**DIRECTIONS (Qs. 1 to 21):** Choose the best option to complete each sentence.

1. That university is a/an_________ university. It does not have to follow the government policies.
   (a) reliant        (b) autonomous
   (c) dependant (d) Indian

2. He has won ____________for creating an inexpensive water treatment plant for his school science project.
   (a) desire        (b) accolades
   (c) happiness (d) prize

3. He knew how to ________ someone to the height of a mountain.
   (a) raise        (b) push
   (c) exalt        (d) send

4. This organisation _________of all the major countries of the world.
   (a) collects        (b) comprises
   (c) divides        (d) has

5. The foreign tourist was ______at the state of poor people in India.
   (a) appalled     (b) glared
   (c) seized        (d) attracted

6. He is not going to tolerate any _______ in his office.
   (a) constructions (b) restrictions
   (c) obedience        (d) contraction

7. He has ______power from the king.
   (a) used        (b) snatched
   (c) usurped     (d) caught

8. The secret agent ______his country's plans of invading our country.
   (a) unveiled     (b) spoiled
   (c) instructed  (d) understood

9. Don't be _______ sighted; look to the future.
   (a) far        (b) near
   (c) star        (d) gloomy

10. The ________ caused by floods is going to push the area back by a decade or more.
    (a) destruction
    (b) paucity
    (c) overproduction
    (d) pollution

11. It was widely _______that the rural population of the country was neglected.
    (a) seen        (b) glimpsed
    (c) perceived     (d) forecasted

12. Where _______the silver cutlery which was kept here?
    (a) is        (b) are
    (c) were        (d) was

13. _______for future is very important.
    (a) Listening     (b) Planning
    (c) Talking     (d) Speaking

14. I _______ to tell the car owner about the crash.
    (a) could        (b) should
    (c) ought        (d) must
15. You forgot to tell me _______ you went to the hospital.
    (a) this         (b) why
    (c) who          (d) where
16. They _______ wished me good luck in my exams.
    (a) sincerely    (b) carefully
    (c) hesitantly   (d) forcefully
17. Dennis fell _______ his bicycle and broke his right arm.
    (a) on           (b) from
    (c) near         (d) along
18. You can't rest _______ you have met her and resolved the matter with her.
    (a) until        (b) before
    (c) after        (d) by
19. We've got to far away from our key goals. We need to get back to _______.
    (a) originals    (b) basics
    (c) elementary   (d) fundamentals
20. He saw _______ animal that looked like a goat.
    (a) an           (b) a
    (c) the          (d) none of these
21. One of the students _______ I approached to ask for the way to Principal's office was on duty outside his office.
    (a) whom         (b) who
    (c) which        (d) that

**DIRECTIONS (Qs. 22 to 24):** Choose the antonym of the underlined word in each sentence.

22. He was <u>flustered</u>.
    (a) rejoiced     (b) amazed
    (c) agitated     (d) calm

23. The opposition party was not able to <u>wrest</u> power from the ruling party.
    (a) renounce     (b) give
    (c) control      (d) snatch
24. He gave me a very <u>lucrative</u> offer.
    (a) absurd       (b) valuable
    (c) precious     (d) unnecessary

**DIRECTIONS (Qs. 25 to 26):** Choose the most appropriate option to fill the blanks.

25. A man who has no money is called a _______.
    (a) frugal       (b) pauper
    (c) beggar       (d) filthy
26. A sleep enjoyed in the afternoon is _______.
    (a) nap
    (b) after noon sleep
    (c) noon sleep
    (d) siesta

**DIRECTIONS (Qs. 27 to 31) :** Select the option that changes given sentences into passive form.

27. I keep all the fruits in the fridge.
    (a) All the fruits are being kept in the fridge.
    (b) All the fruits will be kept in the fridge.
    (c) All the fruits are kept in the fridge.
    (d) Fruits are kept in the fridge.
28. They have written a new editorial.
    (a) They might have written a new editorial.
    (b) A new editorial was written by them.
    (c) They will write a new editorial.
    (d) A new editorial has been written by them.
29. The teacher gave the notebooks back to the students.
    (a) The notebooks were given back to the students by the teacher.

(b) The students got their notebooks back from their teacher.

(c) The teacher has given back the notebooks to the students.

(d) The students will get their notebooks back from their teacher.

30. They selected her as the captain of the team.

(a) She was selected as the captain of the team.

(b) She has been selected as the captain of the team.

(c) She is selected as the captain of the team.

(d) She is being selected as the captain of the team.

31. Can they repair my computer?

(a) Can my computer be repaired?

(b) My computer can be repaired?

(c) Will my computer get repaired?

(d) Is my computer being repaired?

**DIRECTIONS (Qs. 32 to 36):** Read the passage given below and answer the questions that follow.

With two Mars orbiters sent into space last year, including India's MOM probe, traffic has picked up around the Red Planet so much that NASA has bolstered its traffic monitoring process to avoid spacecraft collisions. The US space agency has beefed up a process of traffic monitoring, communication and manoeuvre planning to ensure that Mars orbiters do not approach each other too closely.

The new traffic system in space is handled by NASA's Jet Propulsion Laboratory (JPL) which hopefully will keep accidents and collisions from happening. JPL will alert the handlers of other orbiters if the spacecraft comes too close towards each other's range. With communication facilities in the US, Spain and Australia, the system utilises a global antenna network designed to assist interplanetary spaceflight. The system will also help NASA keep track of Mars Global Surveyor, an orbiter sent in 1997, which has since stopped working.

32. What is the meaning of bolster used in the above passage?

(a) Increase      (b) Decrease

(c) Strengthen (d) Modify

33. What do you understand by 'beefed up the process'?

(a) To strengthen

(b) To speed up

(c) To make it short

(d) To start up

34. Who is going to handle the new traffic system?

(a) NASA

(b) JPL

(c) The government

(d) Spanish government

35. What was the name of the orbiter sent in 1997?

(a) Mars Global Surveyor

(b) Jet Propulsion Laboratory

(c) Spacecraft

(d) MOM

36. Where is the traffic supposed to get managed?

(a) In America

(b) In Spain

(c) Around Mars

(d) US space agency

**DIRECTIONS (Qs. 37 to 42):** Read the table below and answer the questions that follow.

India's IT industry is often lauded across the world. However, data on internet and broadband penetration rates in the country shows a gloomy picture. In many of these indicators of access to information technology, India ranks lower even than countries of sub-Saharan Africa. As for the development world, in 2013, about 90% of the UK's population was using the internet compared to India's 15.1%. Similarly 36% of Uk residents had fixed broadband connections against India's abysmally low 1.2%. In mobile broadband penetration and household ownership of computers as well, India has a lot of catching up to do.

## Digital Penetration In Major Economic

| Data in % | | Internet Users | Fixed broadband Subscriptions | Active mobile broadband subscriptions |
|---|---|---|---|---|
| 1 | United Kingdom | 89.9 | 35.7 | 87.2 |
| 2 | Japan | 86.3 | 28.8 | 120.5 |
| 3 | United States | 84.2 | 28.5 | 92.8 |
| 4 | Germany | 84 | 34.6 | 44.7 |
| 5 | France | 81.9 | 38.8 | 57.1 |
| 6 | Spain | 71.6 | 25.6 | 67.1 |
| 7 | Russian Federation | 61.4 | 16.6 | 60.1 |
| 8 | Italy | 58.5 | 22.3 | 64.8 |
| 9 | Brazil | 51.6 | 10.1 | 51.5 |
| 10 | South Africa | 48.9 | 3.1 | NA |
| 11 | China | 45.8 | 13.6 | 21.4 |
| 12 | India | 15.1 | 1.2 | 3.2 |

37. What is the meaning of the word lauded?
   - (a) Happy      (b) Proud
   - (c) Criticised    (d) Appreciated
38. Which of the following statements is false?
   - (a) 90% of the UK's population was using internet in 2013.
   - (b) India has the lowest number of people using internet.
   - (c) Japan leads in active mobile broadband subscribers.
   - (d) South Africa has more active mobile broadband subscribers than India.
39. What is meant by 'India has lot of catching up to do'?
   - (a) India will have to catch up internet users.
   - (b) India will have to increase the number of internet users.
   - (c) India will catch up all the mobile users worldwide.
   - (d) India will have to work hard to reach up to the international standards.
40. This data is based on a survey done in______.
   - (a) 2015      (b) 2013
   - (c) 2014      (d) 2012
41. What is this data indicative of?
   - (a) Digital penetration
   - (b) Access to information technology
   - (c) Development of a country
   - (d) Mobile users in every country
42. This data has been done per__________ of population.
   - (a) hundred      (b) thousand
   - (c) lakh      (d) ten

**DIRECTIONS (Qs. 43 to 45):** Choose the correct beginning for each of the following sentences from the four options given below.

43. _______broke the world record?
   - (a) Who      (b) Whose
   - (c) Whom      (d) What
44. _________I could not win the race.
   - (a) How terrible!
   - (b) Oops!
   - (c) How disappointing!
   - (d) Wow!
45. ______________view we have of the city from here!
   - (a) What a terrible
   - (c) What a fantastic
   - (c) What an awful
   - (d) What a pitiable

**DIRECTIONS (Qs. 46 to 49):** Match the sentences in column I with responses in column II to make different conversations.

|  | Column I |  | Column II |
|---|---|---|---|
| 46 | I am very happy with your score. | a | Yes, but it's only a trial test. |
| 47 | Don't you have a test today? | b | I feel sick. |
| 48 | Please don't drive so fast. | c | I have a race tomorrow. |
| 49 | Why are you practicing so hard? | d | Thanks ma'am. |

50. Gautam was writing an email to his team leader. How should he end?
   - (a) With regards      (b) Yours sincerely
   - (c) Yours truly      (d) Hope to see you soon.

Name : __________

Number of Questions : 50

Max. Marks : 50

Time : 2 Hours

There is no negative marking in the test.

**DIRECTIONS (Qs. 1 to 19):** Choose the best option to complete each sentence.

1. A lot of _________ improves one's vocabulary.
   (a) reading        (b) listening
   (c) seeking        (d) speaking

2. I _________ to tell you the truth, but I am scared.
   (a) should        (b) could
   (c) may        (d) ought

3. A place where coins are made is called
   (a) ostler        (b) mint
   (c) kiln        (d) creche

4. The thief stood _________ in the police station.
   (a) charmingly   (b) silently
   (c) cruelly        (d) happily

5. He was trying hard to put the baggage_________ the trolley.
   (a) in        (b) on
   (c) near        (d) under

6. We spotted Sam and chatted with him _________ the rehearsal.
   (a) while        (b) during
   (c) until        (d) by

7. There is so _________ to tell that I don't know where to begin from.
   (a) many        (b) few
   (c) much        (d) little

8. We have a _________ argeement with them and we must respect it.
   (a) hidden        (b) valid
   (c) binding        (d) severe

9. This is the highway on _________ the accident happened.
   (a) which        (b) where
   (c) that        (d) who

10. You always leave late for work _________ I tell you to leave early.
    (a) therefore    (b) even though
    (c) since        (d) whenever

11. He drove very fast _________ he could reach the airport on time.
    (a) therefore    (b) so that
    (c) but        (d) because

12. It is futile suggesting anything to him _________ he always does what he thinks is right.
    (a) because        (b) but
    (c) therefore    (d) since

13. The reports of widespread infection are not _________.
    (a) flexible        (b) accurate
    (c) inflexible    (d) negotiable

14. He had to change our plan at the _________ hour because of sudden onset of fever.

   (a) eleventh
   (b) last
   (c) time and again
   (d) tenth

15. His fickle-mindedness ________ the entire class.
   (a) amazed     (b) bewildered
   (c) confused    (d) encouraged

16. He was a brave, honest man and we all ________ him.
   (a) honoured    (b) disdained
   (c) encouraged (d) led

17. My car crashed into a ________ jeep.
   (a) stationary   (b) stationery
   (c) stalemate   (d) none of these

18. Hitin is a restless child. He doesn't remain ________ in class.
   (a) attentive    (b) attention
   (c) relaxing    (d) relaxed

19. I haven't seen Ram ________ last Friday.
   (a) while      (b) when
   (c) during    (d) since

**DIRECTIONS (Qs. 20 to 24):** Choose the correct meaning from the given options.

20. What do you understand by 'Red letter day'?
   (a) A day when every letter posted is red.
   (b) A day when all the stationery used is red.
   (c) An important day.
   (d) A day when a battle was fought.

21. I ________ a faint sound and realised that there was someone listening to the whole conversation.
   (a) listened    (b) heard
   (c) made      (d) cried

22. Choose the opposite of the bold word in each sentence.
It was a **desolate** place.
   (a) fertile      (b) uninhabited
   (c) solitary    (d) lonely

23. He is quite **susceptible** to falling.
   (a) vulnerable  (b) acceptable
   (c) capable    (d) immune

24. It is **imperative** that you restrict everything that can make you sick.
   (a) insignificant (b) important
   (c) vital       (d) burning

**DIRECTIONS (Qs. 25 to 29):** Change the following sentences into passive form.

25. I know your strong points.
   (a) Your strong points are known to me.
   (b) Strong points of yours are known by me.
   (c) Your points that are strong are known by me.
   (d) Your strong point is known by him.

26. (a) Harry kept his schedule busy.
   (b) Harry's schedule was kept busy.
   (c) Harry's schedule will be busy.
   (d) Harry's schedule is being kept busy.
   (e) Harry's schedule is busy.

27. They gave her a gift.
   (a) A gift was given to her.
   (b) A gift has been given to her.
   (c) She has got a gift.
   (d) A gift is being given to her.

28. They sent me a parcel.
   (a) A parcel was sent to me.
   (b) They have sent me a parcel.
   (c) I got a parcel.
   (d) A parcel was received by me.

29. This dog has bitten a lot of people.
    (a) A lot of people have been bitten by this dog.
    (b) A lot of people are been bitten by this dog.
    (c) This dog has been biting a lot of people.
    (d) This dog has been bitten a lot of people.

**DIRECTIONS (Qs. 30 to 32):** Read the passage given below and answer the questions that follow.

Cloud seeding is a technique of spreading dry ice (silver iodide aerosols), into the upper part of clouds to try and stimulate the precipitation process and form rain. The first cloud seeding experiment was conducted in 1946 by Irving Langmuir Laboratories in New York. Cloud seeding is most commonly done by airplanes. Aircrafts fly into select cloud formations and release packets of microscopic silver iodide particles using flares. When the particles meet cool moisture in the clouds, they trigger the formation of ice crystals and rain drops. The amount of silver iodide is small ensuring that there is no risk of pollution.

30. What is dry ice ?
    (a) Ice that is dried
    (b) Silver iodide aerosols
    (c) Dry clouds
    (d) Carbon dioxide

31. The first cloud seeding experiment was conducted in __________.
    (a) 2011          (b) 1946
    (c) 1900          (d) 1889

32. Why is only a small amount of silver iodide added to clouds ?
    (a) Because it is very expensive
    (b) Because of fear of flooding
    (c) To avoid risk of pollution
    (d) None of these

**DIRECTIONS (Qs. 33 to 35):** Read the notice given below and answer the questions that follow.

33. This notice seems to be issued by a __________.
    (a) A swimming pool authority
    (b) A beach authority
    (c) A jungle authority
    (d) A minister

34. Why shouldn't we swim after a heavy rainfall ?
    (a) Because we tend to get wet
    (b) Because of the fear of drowning
    (c) Because bacteria levels are higher
    (d) None of these

35. We should________ swallow beach water.
    (a) always          (b) never
    (c) sometimes     (d) at times

**DIRECTIONS (Qs. 36 to 39):** Read the editorial given below and answer the questions that follow.

A new study by European Environmental Agency (EEA) evaluates how European ecosystems were affected by acidifying and eutrophying air pollutants in the past decades, and projects the levels of impacts in the near future under a scenario where the 2012 amended Gothenburg Protocol under the convention on Long Range Transboundary Air Pollution (LRTAP) is assumed to be fully implemented by 2020. The deposition of acidifying air pollutants causes acidification of surface waters (lakes, rivers and streams) and forest soils leading to loss of nutrients such as potassium and magnesium from soils and the release of toxic aluminium into soils and waters.

36. What is meant by protocol ?
    (a)  An agreement
    (b)  A treaty
    (c)  Understanding between countries
    (d)  All of these
37. What does the acidifying of air lead to?
    (a)  Loss of nutrients from soils
    (b)  Release of toxic elements into soils and water
    (c)  Acidification of lakes and streams
    (d)  All of these
38. EEA stands for
    (a)  European Ecosystem Agency
    (b)  European Environment Agency
    (c)  European Environmental Agency
    (d)  None of these
39. What do you understand by an ecosystem ?
    (a)  Physical environment of an area constitutes an ecosystem.
    (b)  All the living beings regardless of the environment constitute an ecosystem.
    (c)  A system formed by the interaction of the organisms with their physical environment.
    (d)  All of these

**DIRECTIONS (Qs. 40 to 44):** Rearrange the following five sentences in proper sequence to form a meaningful paragraph, then answer the questions given below.

(A) The history of mankind is full of such fightings between communities, nations and people.
(B) From the primitive weapon of warfare, man has advanced to the modern nuclear weapons.
(C) Ever since the dawn of civilisation, man has been fighting with man.
(D) A modern war is scientific in character, but the effect is the same, wiping human existence out of this earth.
(E) The only difference now seems to be in the efficiency of the instruments used for killing each other.

40. Which of the following should be the first sentence ?
    (a)  A            (b)  B
    (c)  C            (d)  D

41. Which of the following should be the second sentence ?
    (a) A      (b) B
    (c) C      (d) D

42. Which of the following should be the fourth sentence ?
    (a) A      (b) B
    (c) C      (d) D

43. Which of the following should be the third sentence ?
    (a) A      (b) B
    (c) C      (d) D

44. Which of the following should be the fifth sentence ?
    (a) A      (b) B
    (c) C      (d) E

**DIRECTIONS (Qs. 45 to 46):** Complete the following conversation using appropriate sentences.

45. It is a _________ tragedy.
    (a) terrible      (b) fantastic
    (c) great      (d) memorable

46. _________ The floor is slippery.
    (a) Oops! I will fall!
    (b) Alas!
    (c) Walk carefully!
    (d) How disappointing!

**DIRECTIONS (Qs. 47 to 50):** Choose the best option which can complete the incomplete sentences correctly and meaningfully.

47. Unless you work harder, you will fail means _________
    (a) if you fail, you will work harder.
    (b) you must at least plan well, then you will not fail.
    (c) hardly you will fail, if you do not desire so.
    (d) if you do not put more efforts, then you will fail.

48. "You are thinking very highly about Ravi but he is not so" means _________
    (a) Ravi is as good as you think about him.
    (b) you have a good opinion about Ravi but he is not as good as you think.
    (c) your view about Ravi is philosophical, keep it up.
    (d) you have a good opinion about Ravi but he does not have a good opinion about you.

49. Owing to the acute power shortage, the people of our locality have decided to _________
    (a) resort to abundant use of electricity for illumination.
    (b) off-switch the electrical appliance while not in use.
    (c) explore other avenues for utilising the excess power.
    (d) resort to use of electricity only when it is inevitable.

50. "The food in this hotel is no match to what were forced at late hours in Hotel Kohinoor" means _________.
    (a) the food in this hotel is quite good compared to what we ate at Kohinoor.
    (b) hotel Kohinoor served us good quality food than what we get here.
    (c) both hotels have maintained good quality of food.
    (d) both hotels serve poor quality of food.

**Name :** __________

**Number of Questions : 50**

**Max. Marks : 50**

**Time : 2 Hours**

**There is no negative marking in the test.**

---

**DIRECTIONS (Qs. 1 to 21):** Choose the best option to complete the sentences given below.

1. __________ for more than 8 hours is not good for health.
   - (a) Sleeping
   - (b) Wandering
   - (c) Eating
   - (d) Walking

2. You __________ not yell at me like that ever again.
   - (a) may       (b) must
   - (c) could     (d) would

3. We didn't arrange to meet. It was __________ coincidence that I saw him.
   - (a) clear      (b) pure
   - (c) great      (d) very

4. The mischievous kids__________ threw the wrappers out of the window .
   - (a) trustingly
   - (b) deliberately
   - (c) thoughtfully
   - (d) sincerely

5. It is quite hot today; the temperature seems to be __________ forty five degrees.
   - (a) below      (b) on
   - (c) above      (d) at

6. He got up twice __________we were having breakfast.
   - (a) during     (b) by
   - (c) until      (d) while

7. Our principal is going away for __________ weeks.
   - (a) some       (b) much
   - (c) a few      (d) most

8. This is __________ story about a king who used to disguise himself.
   - (a) a          (b) an
   - (c) the        (d) None of these

9. It is not difficult to find a person __________ has suffered in the similar manner.
   - (a) whom       (b) whose
   - (c) who        (d) that

10. His brain __________ methods explained in his easily read book are being employed in colleges and business offices.
    - (a) spoiling
    - (b) storming
    - (c) thundering
    - (d) effective

11. A collection of poems is called an
    _______.
    (a) elegy           (b) anthology
    (c) epitaph         (d) fatal
12. I found __________ of the movies
    interesting.
    (a) either          (b) or
    (c) neither         (d) nor
13. Keep the keys under the doormat
    __________ locking the door carefully.
    (a) after           (b) before
    (c) because         (d) whenever
14. Two wrongs do not __________
    (a) make you leap.
    (b) help on the other side.
    (c) make the sun shine.
    (d) make a right.
15. My car __________ failed on the
    highway.
    (a) breaks          (b) brakes
    (c) steering        (d) wheels
16. After the landslide the tourists
    were left in a __________ condition.
    (a) pitiful         (b) pitiable
    (c) mountainous     (d) doubtful
17. Let's go to the _______ and collect
    some sea shells.
    (a) river           (b) ground
    (c) seashore        (d) park
18. I think iodine is best for wounds.
    The doctor advised that any
    wound or cut should be __________
    cleaned.
    (a) never           (b) perpetually
    (c) gradually       (d) thoroughly
19. My father has __________ a surgery
    for the removal of his gallbladder.
    (a) underwent       (b) undergone
    (c) went            (d) going

20. Her presentation at the seminar
    was so good that she received
    many __________ .
    (a) complements
    (b) compliments
    (c) complimants
    (d) none of these
21. The singer was mobbed by a
    __________ of fans.
    (a) heard           (b) band
    (c) herd            (d) tribe

**DIRECTIONS (Qs. 22 to 24):** Choose
the word that means the same of the
bold word in each sentence.

22. The soldiers were **deplored** going
    for war every now and then.
    (a) condemned  (b) adored
    (c) merry           (d) rejoice
23. The king could not **discern** that
    there was disappointment among
    the people.
    (a) doubt           (b) confuse
    (c) forget          (d) judge
24. It is a **contagious** disease.
    (a) transmittable
    (b) harmless
    (c) viral
    (d) non-communicable

**DIRECTIONS (Qs. 25 to 29):**
Change the following sentences into
passive form.

25. Please keep standing. Do not start
    running.
    (a) You are pleased to stand and
        not to run.
    (b) You are requested to remain
        standing and not to start
        running.

(c) You are requested to stand and not to start running.

(d) You are requested to stand up and stop running.

26. His sister gave him an interesting novel to read.

(a) An interesting novel was given by his sister to him to read.

(b) His sister is giving him an interesting novel to read.

(c) An interesting novel is being given to him to read by his sister.

(d) His sister has given him an interesting novel to read.

27. My father bought me a pair of binoculars.

(a) I was given a pair of binoculars by my father.

(b) A pair of binoculars was given by my father to me.

(c) I got a pair of binoculars from my father.

(d) A pair of binoculars was bought by my father for me.

28. Mr. Rahim teaches us Math.

(a) Math is taught by Mr Rahim to us.

(b) Mr. Rahim has been teaching us Math.

(c) Mr. Rahim was teaching us Math.

(d) Mr. Rahim is teaching us Math.

29. Do they read the newspaper every day?

(a) Is the newspaper read by them every day?

(b) Was the newspaper read every day?

(c) Is the newspaper being read every day?

(d) Newspaper is been read every day?

---

**DIRECTIONS (Qs. 30 to 34):** Read the passage given below and answer the questions that follow.

The Indian rupee has touched a two-year low of 66 per US dollar recently. The last time it fell to this level was on September 6, 2013.

In 2015, the rupee fell in sync with global currencies. In fact, the rupee is still among the top five best performing currencies in the world since the beginning of this year. Till date, the rupee has fallen less than four per cent which is nothing when compared to the bruising that other emerging market currencies have taken. In other words, the rupee is better off compared with most emerging markets.

30. When was it the last time that the dollar's cost was ₹66?

(a) 2012          (b) 2013
(c) 2015          (d) 1999

31. Find the word that has the same meaning as working together.

(a) Sync
(b) Fallen
(c) Better
(d) Emerging

32. Rupee is among the top __________ currencies of the world.

(a) ten           (b) five
(c) three         (d) hundred

                                    

33. The fall of rupee is less than ______per cent.
    (a) two
    (b) five
    (c) four
    (d) eight

34. Find out a word from the above passage that is the opposite of **dying**.
    (a) Imerging
    (b) Compared
    (c) Global
    (d) Bruising

**DIRECTIONS (Qs. 35 to 39):** Read the table given below and answer the questions that follow.

## Story on '65 war on Sept 1?
## WAR HEROES
Indian soldiers killed in wars, conflicts & operation

| World War-I (1914-1918)\|Over 60,000 | World War-II (1939-1945) \| Over 36,000 | J&K operations (1947-1948) \| 1,140 | China war (1962) \| 3,250 | Pakistan war (1965) \| 3,264 | Bangladesh Liberation war (1971) \| 3,843 |
|---|---|---|---|---|---|

| IPKF'S Operation Pawan in Sri Lanka (1987) \| 1,157 | Siachen Glacier-Salton Ridge (since1984) \| Over 36,000 | Counter-insurgency operations Over 8,000 (1962) \| 3,250 | UN peacekeeping missions (since 1950) \| Over 140 |
|---|---|---|---|

| THE FORGOTTEN SOLDIER India stil does not have a dedicated National War Memorial, first mooted in 1960, to honour the soldiers killed after 1947 | India Gate constructed in 1931 to remember 84,400 indian soldiers killed defending the British empire from 1914-1921 | Amar Jawan Jyoti built under arch of india Gate in 1972 as a tribute to soldiers killed in 1971 Indo-Pak war |
|---|---|---|

35. Which of the following statements is false?
    (a) The number of Indian soldiers killed in the First World War was 60,000.
    (b) India lost more soldiers in war with China than in war with Pakistan.
    (c) The number of Indian soldiers died in the Second World War was lower than in the First World War.
    (d) Almost 8,000 soldiers have lost their lives in counter-insurgency operations.

36. Why was India Gate constructed?
    (a) To remember total number of soldiers who lost their lives in various wars.
    (b) To remember Indian soldiers who were killed defending the British Empire.
    (c) To commemorate the visit of the British King.
    (d) To commemorate the Kargil causalities.

37. What is a glacier?
    (a) Moving river of ice
    (b) Passes between mountains
    (c) Land that slides away from mountains
    (d) None of these

38. What is meant by insurgency?
    (a) Any kind of disturbance
    (b) A revolt against the government
    (c) A memorial
    (d) A war

39. Find out a word from the above table that means the opposite of definite.
    (a) Moot          (b) Defend
    (c) Counter       (d) Dedicated

40. Complete the conversation using appropriate options.
    ________ were the first Asian Games held?
    (a) In which year (b) Where
    (c) How            (d) Why

**DIRECTIONS (Qs. 41 & 42):** In the passages given below, complete the conversation using appropriate options.

41. Mr. Nayyar to the carpenter: Why haven't you repaired my chair?
    The carpenter: _________
    (a) Because I don't have time.
    (b) Because it cannot be repaired.
    (c) Because we need to change the machine.
    (d) Because you have not paid me.

42. Mr. Nayyar: Why don't you buy the machine?
    The carpenter: __________
    (a) The market was closed today. I will buy one tomorrow.
    (b) I don't have time to change it.
    (c) I don't know the market.
    (d) Why don't you go?

**DIRECTIONS (Qs. 43 to 48):** Complete the conversation from the options given below.

43. Jasmine to her mother: 'What have you made for dinner?'
    Mother:______
    (a) Today we will not eat dinner.
    (b) I have made your favourite dish.
    (c) Why don't you cook dinner today?
    (d) I don't know, let's go and eat outside.

44. Mrs. Ramamurthy to her driver: Why is there a dent on the car?
    The driver: _________
    Mrs. Ramamurthy: Where did the accident take place?

(a) I don't know.
(b) You need to call the cops to investigate.
(c) Get it repaired.
(d) It met with a small accident.

45. Siya: Which game do you like the most?
    Gauri:______
    (a) I don't like playing games; I just like to watch movies.
    (b) I like to watch football; I don't miss any match.
    (c) Why do you want to know that?
    (d) I am not sure myself.

46. Harris to James: What gift will you buy for your parents?
    James: ______
    (a) I don't believe in gifts.
    (b) What do you think I should buy?
    (c) I want to buy a microwave for them.
    (d) My parents don't like gifts.

47. Raj to his friend: Why don't you review my new novel?
    Friend:______
    (a) Why do you want me to review your novel?
    (b) Sure, let me first finish reading it.
    (c) Sure, but I will not review anybody's novel.
    (d) Why don't you do the job?

                                        

48. Geetima: Would you like to take a lift?

    Seeta:______

    (a) I will go by bus.
    (b) Why do you ask me that?
    (c) I don't know the way.
    (d) Which way are you going?

---

**DIRECTIONS (Qs. 49 & 50):** Sentence below consist of a word which is bold. It is followed by four words. Select the word which is closest to the OPPOSITE in meaning of the bold word.

---

49. Poets often prefer **ambiguity** to
    (a) clarity
    (b) certainty
    (c) rationality
    (d) perversity

50. Like poverty, **affluence** can sometimes create its own problems.
    (a) indigence
    (b) opulence
    (c) sorrow
    (d) exuberance

# OLYMPIAD
# Mock Test 5

Name : _________      Max. Marks : 50

Number of Questions : 50      Time : 2 Hours

**There is no negative marking in the test.**

---

**DIRECTIONS (Qs. 1 to 21):** Choose the best option to complete the sentences given below.

1. _______ is also an art, which many people do not have.
   (a) Speaking    (b) Listening
   (c) Sleeping    (d) Pulling

2. Ma'am, ________ I ask a question?
   (a) can    (b) should
   (c) must    (d) could

3. Don't ______ the hand that feeds you.
   (a) bite    (b) bend
   (c) burn    (d) bark

4. It was_______ very cold today in the afternoon.
   (a) surprisingly (b) intentionally
   (c) interestingly (d) happily

5. I' am afraid her husband has got a ______ addiction to gambling.
   (a) regular    (b) interesting
   (c) chronic    (d) dangerous

6. Hitler wrote 'Mein Kampf'_____ his stay in the prison.
   (a) while    (b) during
   (c) until    (d) by

7. Mr. Smith's office is the________ one from the right.
   (a) only    (b) first
   (c) a little    (d) much

8. There was ________ programme on TV about dangers to environment.
   (a) a    (b) an
   (c) the    (d) none of these

9. One who compiles a dictionary is a
   (a) lexicographer
   (b) obstetrician
   (c) philanderer
   (d) philogynist

10. India is projected to________ China's population by 2022.
    (a) suppress    (b) surpass
    (c) assimilate    (d) adjust

11. Choose the best option to complete the sentence given below.

    He was ________and sent to lifetime imprisonment.
    (a) acquitted    (b) discharged
    (c) convicted    (d) committed

12. He was________ the award for his efforts for promoting world peace.
    (a) offered    (b) conferred
    (c) withdraw    (d) proposed

13. Thomas Edison tried more than a thousand experiments before he _______ a successful incandescent lamp.
    (a) developed      (b) made
    (c) evolved        (d) grew

14. She is usually very chirpy, _____ today she is tired.
    (a) although       (b) since
    (c) but            (d) and

15. Our class teacher is the _______ of many students.
    (a) idle           (b) ideal
    (c) god            (d) teacher

16. It's an absolutely_______ idea! It is not going to work.
    (a) ridiculous     (b) marvellous
    (c) ridicule       (d) progressive

17. The number of participants who are participating in this event is quite _______.
    (a) motivating     (b) impressive
    (c) countless      (d) low

18. We were supposed to write the _______ idea of this poem.
    (a) central        (b) gist
    (c) canvas         (d) main

19. Sameer could not understand the basic _______ of physics.
    (a) principals     (b) principles
    (c) idea           (d) base

20. He can't decide right now, give him_______ more time to think.
    (a) a few          (b) a little
    (c) much           (d) little

21. You have not done the right thing; now you _______
    (a) face the music.
    (b) don't put off for tomorrow.
    (c) there is no use crying.
    (d) go for song.

**DIRECTIONS (Qs. 22 to 24):** Choose the opposite of the word underlined in each sentence.

22. He <u>vilified</u> the whole incident.
    (a) favoured       (b) abused
    (c) rip down       (d) cursed

23. He was full of <u>disdain</u> for all the poor people.
    (a) dislike        (b) flattery
    (c) scorn          (d) respect

24. He came out as a <u>disgruntled</u> man.
    (a) contented      (b) dislike
    (c) flattered      (d) courageous

**DIRECTIONS (Qs. 25 to 29):** Change the following sentences into passive form.

25. The bank gave him some money on loan.
    (a) Some money was given as loan.
    (b) Some money was given to him as loan by the bank.
    (c) Some money is given to him as loan.
    (d) Some money is being given to him by the bank as loan.

26. Did Kamal draw this picture?
    (a) Was this picture drawn by Kamal?
    (b) Was Kamal drawing this picture?
    (c) Is this picture drawn by Kamal?
    (d) Is this picture being drawn by Kamal?

27. Put all the books away.
    (a) Let all the books be put away.
    (b) Books should be put away.
    (c) Books are to be put away.
    (d) Let's put all the books away.
28. You should eat your meals at regular times.
    (a) Meals should be eaten at regular times.
    (b) Meals should be eaten by you at regular times.
    (c) Meals are to be eaten by you at regular times.
    (d) Meals are eaten by you at regular times.
29. Please send us the mail as soon as possible.
    (a) The mail may kindly be sent to us as soon as possible.
    (b) The mail should please be sent to us as soon as possible.
    (c) The mail may please be sent to us as soon as possible.
    (d) The mail should be please sent to us as soon as possible.

---

**DIRECTIONS (Qs. 30-34):** Read the advertisement given below and answer the questions that follow.

---

# TIMES APPOINTMENTS

# REQUIRED

For a Leading Coaching Institute

## For Drawing, Design & Architecture

Entrance Exam Preparation Classes

Full Time / Part Time / Visting basis

**(For Delhi Centre:Malviya Nagar, Preet Vihar, Rajouri Garden, Gurgaon)**

### DESIGN FACULTIES
### DRAWING FACULTIES

Eligibilty: Graduate & Postgraduate from NID / NIFT / IIT-Delhi / SPA / DCA / MSU /Othern Design & Fine Art Collage (Ex.Faculties or Alumni can apply)

Salary : 3 lac to 8 per annum

### HEAD OF DEPARTMENT
### COUNSELLOR

Eligibilty: Graduate, Fluent in English / Hindi

Salary : 3 lac to 6 Lac per annum

30. What does the above advertisement require?

    (a) Students to study

    (b) Teachers

    (c) A clerk

    (d) Receptionist

31. What is the eligibility for design faculty?

    (a) Graduate in any discipline

    (b) Post graduate in any discipline

    (c) Graduate and post Graduate from NID/NIFT/IIT, etc.

    (d) None of these

32. How can one send their resume for any requirement?

    (a) Through courier

    (b) Through e-mail

    (c) Through Post

    (d) All of them

33. If one has to send a resume to a company for employment how will one end it?

    (a) Bye, dude!

    (b) Regards.

    (c) See you soon.

    (d) Cheers!

34. What do you understand by post-graduation?

    (a) A post held after doing graduation.

    (b) Any office joined after graduation.

    (c) Any office that qualifies you for any post.

    (d) A degree obtained after graduation.

**DIRECTIONS (Qs. 35-40):** Determine the meaning of the expressions in bold.

35. After going to the zoo, the mall and the movies, Ridhima was sick of **bending our back words** to entertain her cousins.

    (a) Doing very little

    (b) Making small efforts

    (c) Trying very hard

    (d) Not trying at all

36. Occasionally **accidents will happen.**

    (a) Things will get broken

    (b) Things will spill

    (c) Things take place often

    (d) Things will ximply occur

37. Kusum would have gone home, if she hadn't **burned her bridges.**

    (a) Ended her relationships

    (b) Burned her house down

    (c) Lost her way

    (d) Been angry

38. **In the end,** the prisoner confessed the both crimes.

    (a)  Finally

    (b)  Towards the end

    (c)  By the end

    (d)  At the end

39. If you **give me a hand**, I'll be able to go out with you.

    (a)  Lift me up

    (b)  Help me

    (c)  Hold my hand

    (d)  Take my hand

40. Whenever Sakina used internet, her mother **kept an eye on** her.

    (a)  Considered

    (b)  Checked on

    (c)  Closely observed

    (d)  Looked at

**DIRECTIONS (Qs. 41 to 44):** Complete the conversations using the correct option.

41. Wilson to Francis: Which plane has been hijacked?

    Francis: ______

    (a)  Ask the President.

    (b)  I was not in that plane.

    (c)  The one which was flying from Indonesia to Delhi.

    (d)  Let's read the newspapers.

42. Wilson: What do the hijackers want?

    Francis: ________

    (a)  They want to get the terrorists released.

    (b)  They want to go globe trotting.

    (c)  They want to party in the plane.

    (d)  I can't tell.

43. Ravi: Do you know Mr. Sharma?

    Ela: I think ______

    (a)  I have met him once before.

    (b)  No, he is an unknown person

    (c)  Why should I?

    (d)  What made you ask me this?

44. Sameer: Hope you had a nice weekend in Goa.

    Ram:________

    (a)  Yes, but we could not go out.

    (b)  Yes, we did. We went to the beach and enjoyed.

    (c)  Yes, but it was raining so not much

    (d)  No, it was very tiring.

**DIRECTIONS (Qs. 45 to 50):** In questions given below, choose the option which can be substituted for the given sentences.

---

45. One who is bad in spellings -
    (a) Cacographer
    (b) Choreographer
    (c) Curator
    (d) Graphologist

46. A person appointed two parties to solve a dispute -
    (a) Auditor
    (b) Arbitrator
    (c) Amateur
    (d) Dextrous

47. One who feeds on human flesh -
    (a) Omnivore
    (b) Carnivore
    (c) Cannibal
    (d) Herbivore

48. A person having a sophisticated charm
    (a) Debonair
    (b) Connoisseur
    (c) Chauvinist
    (d) Epicure

49. One who believes in fate -
    (a) Astrologer
    (b) Fortune-teller
    (c) Fatalist
    (d) Clairvoyant

50. Someone who leaves one's country to settle in an other -
    (a) Emigrant
    (b) Migrate
    (c) Hibernate
    (d) Traveller

# MATHEMATICS

## OLYMPIAD
# Mock Test 1

Name : _________

Number of Questions : 50

There is no negative marking in the test.

Max. Marks : 50

Time : 2 Hours

1. If $\dfrac{a}{2} + b = 0.8$ and $\dfrac{7}{a + \dfrac{b}{2}} = 10,$ then $(a, b)$ is

   (a) $(0.2, 0.4)$   (b) $(0.3, 0.5)$

   (c) $(0.4, 0.6)$   (d) $(0.4, 0.5)$

2. Let 'K' be the greatest number that will divide 1305, 4665 and 6905, leaving the same remainder 25 in each case. Then sum of the digits of 'K' is

   (a) 7   (b) 5

   (c) 6   (d) 8

3. The measure of an angle, if six times its complement is 12° less than twice its supplement, is

   (a) 58°   (b) 48°

   (c) 38°   (d) 78°

4. Find out the missing number.

   240, ?, 120, 40, 10, 2

   (a) 120   (b) 240

   (c) 40   (d) 10

5. In an examination a student was asked to find $\dfrac{3}{14}$ th of a certain number. By mistake, he found $\dfrac{3}{4}$ of it. His answer was 150 more than the correct answer. The number is

   (a) 290   (b) 280

   (c) 240   (d) 180

6. If $\sqrt{0.04 \times 0.4 \times a} = 0.4 \times 0.04 \times \sqrt{b},$ then value of $\dfrac{b}{a}$ is

   (a) 0.016   (b) $\dfrac{125}{2}$

   (c) 0.16   (d) None of these.

7. If $(a+b):(b+c):(c+a) = 6:7:8$ and $a + b + c = 14$, then the value of '(a + b)' is

   (a) 8   (b) 7

   (c) 6   (d) 12

8. If the area of the three adjacent faces of a cuboidal box are 120 cm$^2$, 72 cm$^2$ and 60 cm$^2$ respectively. The volume of the box is

(a) 720 cm$^3$      (b) 780 cm$^3$

(c) 728 cm$^3$      (d) 798 cm$^3$

9. Factorise : $x^2 + \dfrac{4}{x^2}$

(a) $\left(x + \dfrac{2}{x}\right)\left(x + \dfrac{2}{x}\right)$

(b) $\left(x - \dfrac{2}{x}\right)\left(x + \dfrac{2}{x}\right)$

(c) $\left(x + \dfrac{2}{x} + 2\right)\left(x + \dfrac{2}{x} - 2\right)$

(d) None of these

10. A clock loses $\dfrac{1}{2}$% on true time during one week and gains $\dfrac{1}{4}$% on true time during the next week. If it is set right at 12 O'clock on Saturday morning, what time will it indicate at the end of second week ?

(a) 11 : 34      (b) 11 : 48

(c) 12 : 15      (d) 13 : 02

**11.** Area of the field shown in the figure given below is:

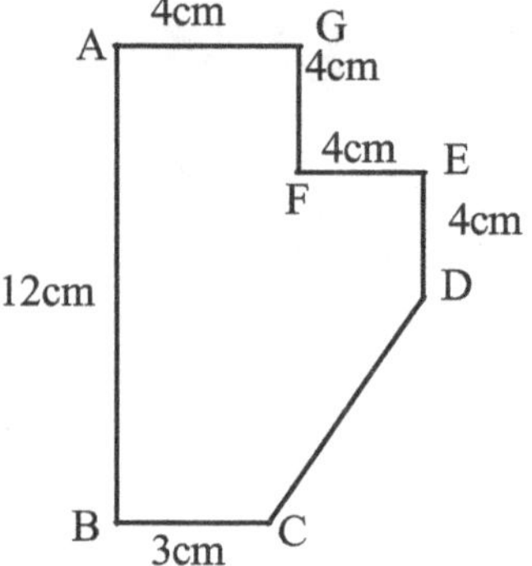


(a) 68 cm$^2$      (b) 70 cm$^2$

(c) 72 cm$^2$      (d) 75 cm$^2$

12. A businessman allows two successive discounts of 20% and 10%. If he gets ₹ 108 for an article, then its marked price is

(a) ₹ 124      (b) ₹ 140

(c) ₹ 150      (d) ₹ 170

13. What number should replace the question mark?

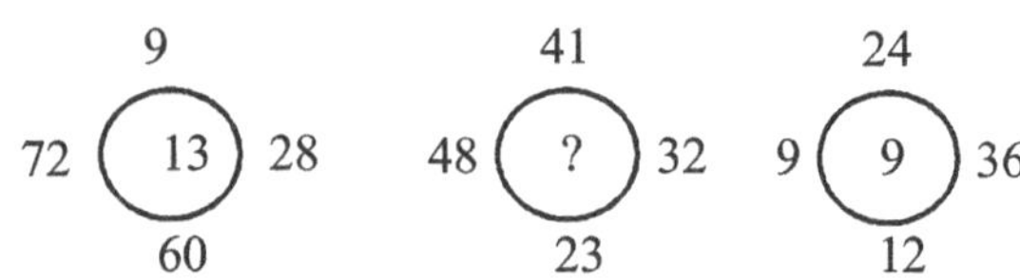


(a) 12      (b) 15

(c) 17      (d) 18

14. One day, Ravi left home and cycled 10 km southwards, turned right and cycled 5 km and turned right and cycled 10 km and turned left and cycled 10 km. How many kilometres will he have to cycle to reach his home straight?

(a) 10 km      (b) 15 km

(c) 20 km      (d) 25 km

15. The product of two numbers is 1936. If one number is 4 times the other, the numbers are

    (a) 16, 121　　　　(b) 22, 88

    (c) 44, 44　　　　(d) None of these

16. If a number increased by 8% of itself gives 135, then that number is

    (a) 112　　　　(b) 100

    (c) 125　　　　(d) None of these

17. If $(a + b + c) = 0$ then value of

    $$\frac{(b+c)^2}{3bc} + \frac{(c+a)^2}{3ac} + \frac{(a+b)^2}{3ab} \text{ is}$$

    (a) 3　　　　(b) 1

    (c) $\dfrac{1}{3}$　　　　(d) 2

18. What number should replace the question mark ?

    $$27, 27, 30\frac{1}{4}, 23\frac{3}{4}, 33\frac{1}{2}, 20\frac{1}{2}, 36\frac{3}{4},$$
    $$17\frac{1}{4}?$$

    (a) 30　　　　(b) 20

    (c) 40　　　　(d) 10

19. From his house, Lokesh went 15 km to the North. Then he turned West and covered 10 km. Then, he turned South and covered 5 km. Finally , turning to East, he covered 10 km. In which direction is he from his house?

    (a) East　　　　(b) West

    (c) North　　　　(d) South

20. The radius of a sphere is increased by P%. Its surface area increase by

    (a) P%　　　　(b) P²%

    (c) $\left(2P+\dfrac{P^2}{100}\right)\%$　(d) $\dfrac{P^2}{2}\%$

21. The least multiple of 7 which leaves remainder of 4, when divided by 6, 9, 15 and 18 is

    (a) 74　　　　(b) 94

    (c) 184　　　　(d) 364

22. If $\dfrac{a(x-b)}{a-b} + \dfrac{b(x-a)}{b-a} = 1$, then

    x =

    (a) a　　　　(b) b

    (c) 1　　　　(d) ab

23. The volumes of two cubes are in the ratio 343 : 1331, the ratio of their edges, is

    (a) 7:10　　　　(b) 7 : 11

    (c) 7 : 12　　　　(d) None of these

24. Seventy eight is divided into two parts such that five times the first part and four times the second part are in the ratio 15 : 14. The first part is

    (a) 32　　　　(b) 36

    (c) 42　　　　(d) 46

25. A chess board contains 64 equal squares and the area of each square is 6.25 cm². A border round the board is 2 cm wide. The length of the side of the chess board is

    (a) 18 cm　　　　(b) 21 cm

    (c) 24 cm　　　　(d) 28 cm

26. HCF of first 200 prime numbers which are of the form $10p + 1$ is

    (a) 10                  (b) 7

    (c) 6                   (d) None of these

27. If 'x' is any natural number, then

    $x^2 + \dfrac{1}{x^2}$ will always be greater than or equal to

    (a) 1                   (b) 2

    (c) 3                   (d) 4

28. Which number lies opposite the face 4, if the four different positions of a dice are as shown in the figures given below.

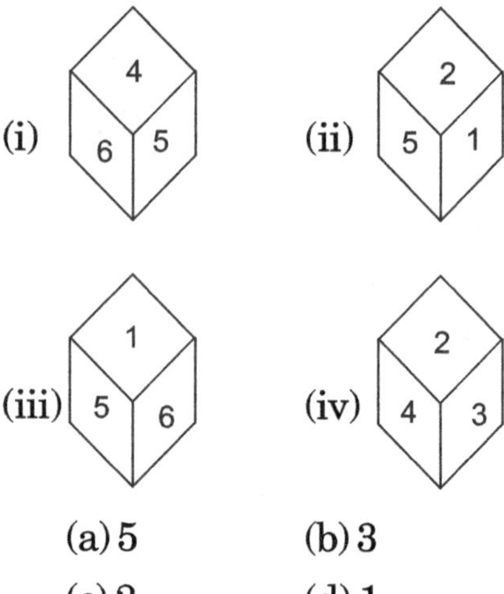


    (a) 5                   (b) 3

    (c) 2                   (d) 1

29. Read all the conclusions and then decide which one of the given conclusions logically follows from the three given statements, disregarding commonly known facts.

    **Statements–**

    Some ice are ring. No ring is paint. Some rings are gold

**Conclusions –**

I.   No gold is paint

II.  No ice is gold

III. Some rings are paints

IV.  All gold are rings

    (a) Only I and III follow

    (b) Only I and II follow

    (c) Only III and IV follow

    (d) None of these

30. Find the mean of 50 observations. It is given that the mean of 32 of them is 28 and the mean of the remaining 18 observations is 30.

    (a) 30.24               (b) 28.72

    (c) 24.82               (d) 30.32

31. In the given figure, value of x is

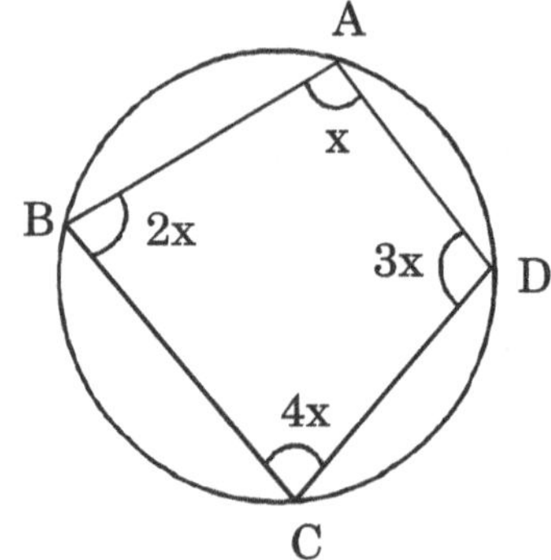


    (a) 36°                 (b) 108°

    (c) 72°                 (d) 144°

32. Find the value of x, if median of the following observations arranged in ascending order is 25.

    11, 13, 15, 19, x + 2, x + 4, 30, 35, 39, 46

    (a) 23.5                (b) 22

    (c) 22.5                (d) 24

33. Rekha sold a watch at a profit of 15%. She had bought it at 10% less and sold it for ₹ 28 less. She would have gained 20%. The C.P. of the watch is

(a) ₹250
(b) ₹400
(c) ₹425
(d) ₹450

34. A hemisphere of radius 6 cm is cast into a right circular cone of height 75 cm. The radius of the base of the cone is

(a) 2.4 cm
(b) 2.8 cm
(c) 3.5 cm
(d) 3.8 cm

35. The denominator of a rational number is greater than its numerator by 8. If the numerator is increased by 17 and the denominator is decreased by 1, the number obtained is $\dfrac{3}{2}$. Then the rational number is

(a) $\dfrac{13}{20}$
(b) $\dfrac{20}{13}$
(c) $\dfrac{21}{13}$
(d) $\dfrac{13}{21}$

36. The edges of three iron cubes are 6 cm, 8 cm and 10 cm, respectively. A new cube was made by melting them. Find the edge of the new cube.

(a) 8 cm
(b) 12 cm
(c) 14 cm
(d) 10 cm

37. If $3 + 5 = 16$ ; $7 + 9 = 64$ ; $10 + 12 = 121$, then $11 + 3 = ?$

(a) 56
(b) 48
(c) 49
(d) 196

38. The speed of a car increases by 2 kilometer after every one hour. If the distance travelled in the first one hour was 35 kilometers, then the total distance travelled in 12 hours was

(a) 460 km
(b) 552 km
(c) 483 km
(d) 572 km

39. If $\dfrac{3^x}{1+3^x} = \dfrac{1}{9}$, the value of $\dfrac{9^x}{1+9^x}$ is

(a) $\dfrac{1}{27}$
(b) $\dfrac{1}{64}$
(c) $\dfrac{1}{65}$
(d) None of these

40. Which of the following picture is the correct for the given net ?

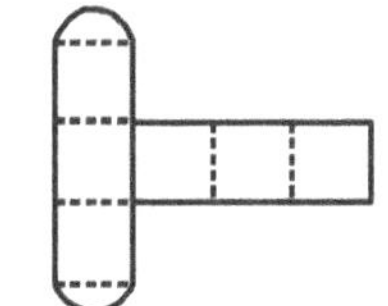

(a) 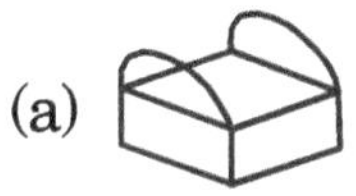
(b) 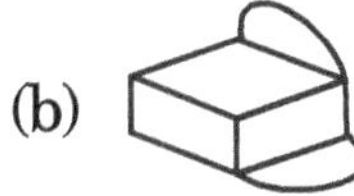
(c) 
(d) 

41. What number should replace the question mark ?

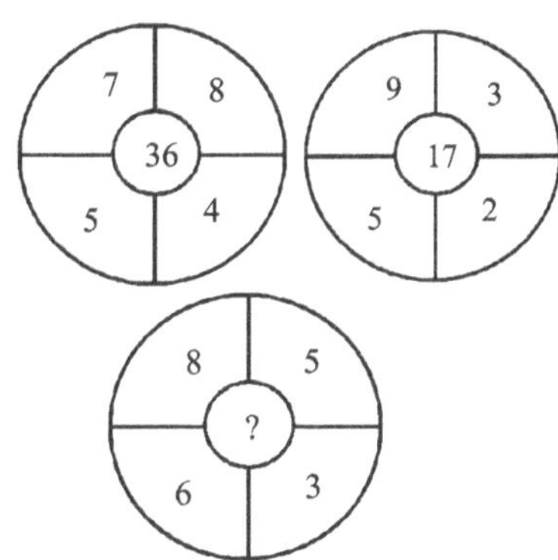

(a) 18

(b) 22

(c) 36

(d) 19

42. If the radius of a circle is increased by 1 cm, its area increases by 22 cm$^2$, then original radius of the circle is

(a) 4 cm

(b) 3 cm

(c) 3.5 cm

(d) 5 cm

43. Find the value of $\left[\left(\sqrt[n]{x^2}\right)^{n/2}\right]^2$ is equal to:

(a) 0

(b) $x^2$

(c) $x$

(d) $1/x$

44. In measuring the sides of a rectangle errors of 5% and 3% in excess are made. The error percent in the calculated area is

(a) 7.15%

(b) 6.25%

(c) 8.15%

(d) 8.35%

45. In $\triangle ABC$, AD is a median. Also, G is a point on AD which divides it in the ratio 2 : 1 and is located 12 units from A. Find AD.

(a) 16

(b) 18

(c) 24

(d) 36

46. Mean of the following frequency distribution

| Class Interval | 90-100 | 80-90 | 70-80 | 60-70 | 50-60 |
|---|---|---|---|---|---|
| Frequency | 10 | 15 | 14 | 12 | 9 |

is

(a) 74.8

(b) 75.8

(c) 72.6

(d) 73.5

47. A sum of money, put out at compound interest, becomes ₹672 in two years and ₹714 in three years. The rate of interest is :

(a) 5% per annum

(b) 6% per annum

(c) $6\dfrac{1}{4}$% per annum

(d) $7\dfrac{1}{2}$% per annum

**DIRECTIONS (Qs. 48-50) :** Study the following graph carefully and answer the questions based on it.

Production of rose in various states

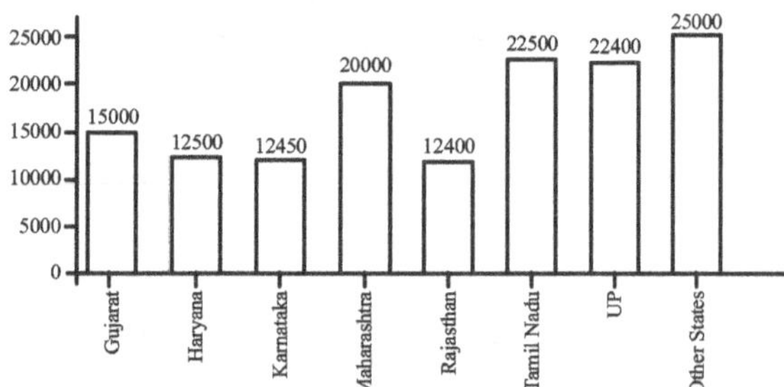


48. Which of the following state(s) contribute(s) less than 10 per cent in the total rose production?

(a) Only Rajasthan

(b) Rajasthan, Karnataka

(c) Rajasthan, Karnataka, Haryana

(d) Rajasthan, Karnataka, Haryana and Gujarat

49. What is the approximate average production of roses (in thousands) across all the states?

(a) 21

(b) 20

(c) 19

(d) 18

50. If total percentage contribution of the states having production of roses below twenty thousand is considered, which of the following statements is true?

(a) It is little above 40%

(b) If is exactly 35%

(c) It is below 35%

(d) None of these

# OLYMPIAD
# Mock Test 2

Name: _________

Number of Questions : 50

There is no negative marking in the test.

Max. Marks : 50

Time : 2 Hours

1. If $x^2 + \dfrac{1}{x^2} = 27$, then value of $x + \dfrac{1}{x}$ is

   (a) 9      (b) 29

   (c) $\sqrt{29}$      (d) 3

2. If HCF $(a, b) = 12$ and $a \times b = 1800$, then LCM $(a, b) =$

   (a) 900      (b) 150

   (c) 90      (d) 3600

3. PQRS is a parallelogram. Then, y equals:

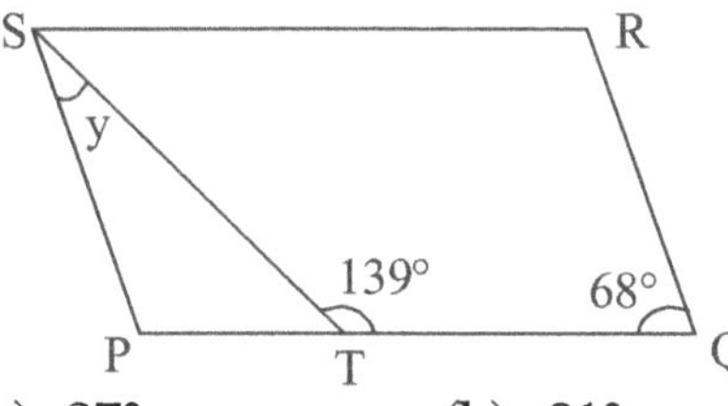


   (a) 27°      (b) 61°

   (c) 41°      (d) 28°

4. What number should replace the question mark ?

   4322 : 48

   4172 : 56

   7615 : ?

   (a) 336      (b) 210

   (c) 49      (d) 52

5. The mean of 21 observations is 59. If each number is multiplied by 4, the new mean is

   (a) 486      (b) 244

   (c) 236      (d) 224

6. The smallest number by which 18432 must be divided so that quotient is a perfect cube, is

   (a) 2      (b) 36

   (c) 12      (d) None of these

7. In the following questions, a sequence or groups of letters and numbers is given with one term missing as shown by (?). Find the missing term in the series

   EJO, TYD, INS, XCH, ?

   (a) NRW      (b) MRW

   (c) MSX      (d) NSX

8. One card is drawn from a pack of 52 cards, each of the 52 cards being equally likely to be drawn. The probability that the drawn card is either red or king is

   (a) $\dfrac{7}{13}$  (b) $\dfrac{1}{13}$

   (c) $\dfrac{27}{52}$  (d) $\dfrac{1}{2}$

9. If 'a' is prime and 'b' is a composite number such that a + b = 31. Their LCM is 220. Then the value of 'a' and 'b' is

   (a) 17, 14  (b) 13, 18

   (c) 11, 20  (d) None of these

10. The numerator of a fraction is 4 less than its denominator. If the numerator is decreased by 2 and the denominator is increased by 1, then denominator is eight times the numerator. The fraction is

    (a) $\dfrac{9}{13}$  (b) $\dfrac{5}{9}$

    (c) $\dfrac{3}{7}$  (d) None of these

11. The cost of levelling and turfing a square lawn at ₹4.00 per m$^2$ is ₹6400. The cost of fencing it at ₹10 per metre is

    (a) ₹1600  (b) ₹400

    (c) ₹160  (d) None of these

12. The sides of a triangle are in the ratio $\dfrac{1}{2} : \dfrac{1}{3} : \dfrac{1}{4}$ and its perimeter is 104 cm. The length of the longest side is

    (a) 48 cm  (b) 32 cm

    (c) 26 cm  (d) 52 cm.

13. On January 12, 1980, it was Saturday. The day of the week on January 12, 1979 was –

    (a) Saturday  (b) Friday

    (c) Sunday  (d) Thursday

14. LCM of $1\dfrac{1}{4}$, $1\dfrac{2}{3}$, $2\dfrac{1}{2}$ is

    (a) $\dfrac{5}{12}$  (b) 5

    (c) $\dfrac{125}{12}$  (d) 125

15. A number is multiplied by $\dfrac{1}{3}$ times itself and 18 is added to the result. If the final result is 2901, the number is

    (a) 54  (b) 93

    (c) 83  (d) 84

16. A person sells two watches for ₹ 500 each. On one watch, he lost 10% and on the other he gained 10%. His gain or loss % is

    (a) 1.5% gain  (b) 1.5% loss

    (c) 1% loss  (d) 1% gain

17. In what time will ₹ 72 become ₹81 at $6\frac{1}{4}\%$ p.a. SI?

  (a) $1\frac{1}{2}$ year     (b) $2\frac{1}{2}$ years

  (c) 2 years     (d) None of these

18. At what compound interest rate will a sum be 16 times of itself in 4 years?

  (a) 20%     (b) 25%

  (c) 50%     (d) 100%

19. If $(x-1)$ is the HCF of $(x^2-1)$ and $px^2 - q(x+1)$, Then

  (a) $q = 2p$     (b) $p = 2q$

  (c) $2q = 3p$     (d) $3q = 2p$

20. The LCM of polynomials $2x^2 - 3x - 2$ and $x^3 - 4x^2 + 4x$ is

  (a) $x(x-2)^2(2x+1)$

  (b) $x(x-2)(2x+1)^2$

  (c) $x(x-2)(2x+1)$

  (d) $x^2(x-2)^2(2x+1)^2$

21. If the given interchanges namely: signs + and ÷, numbers 2 and 4, are made in signs and numbers respectively, then which one of the following four equations would be correct?

  (a) $2 + 4 \div 3 = 3$    (b) $4 + 2 \div 6 = 1.5$

  (c) $4 \div 2 + 3 = 4$    (d) $2 + 4 \div 6 = 8.$

22. 3 chairs and 2 tables cost ₹700 and 5 chairs and 3 tables cost ₹1100. The cost of 2 chairs and 2 tables is

  (a) ₹800     (b) ₹600

  (c) ₹900     (d) ₹1000

23. Which of the following picture is the correct for the given net ?

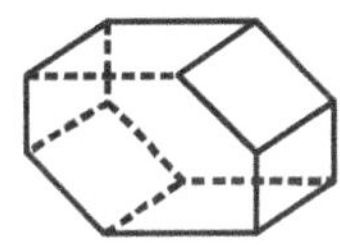

  (a) 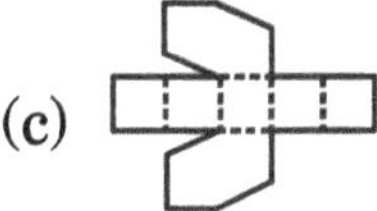     (b)

  (c)     (d)

24. Two cubes each of 10 cm edge are joined end to end. The surface area of the resulting cuboid is

  (a) 400 sq.cm     (b) 300 sq .cm

  (c) 1000 sq.cm     (d) 800 sq.cm

25. A train does a journey without stopping in 8 hours. If it had travelled 5 km an hour faster, it would have done the journey in 6 hours 40 min, its slower speed is

  (a) 32 km/hr     (b) 25 km/hr

  (c) 28 km/hr     (d) 40 km/hr

26. Find the missing number in the following sets of number around the circle from the choice given below :

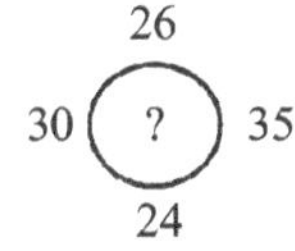
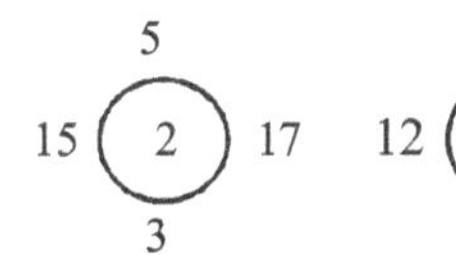

  (a) 4     (b) 5

  (c) 6     (d) 7

27. The radius of wheel is 1.4 decimeter. How many times does it revolve during a journey of 0.66 km?

  (a) 500     (b) 750

  (c) 900     (d) 950

28. If 10 masons can build a 50 meters long wall in 25 days of 8 hours each, then in how many days of 6 hours each will 15 masons build a 36 metres long wall?

    (a)  15 days        (b)  24 days

    (c)  18 days        (d)  16 days

29. What must be subtracted form $3a^2 - 6ab - 3b^2 - 1$ to get $4a^2 - 7ab - 4b^2 + 1$    ?

    (a)  $-a^2 + ab + b^2 - 2$

    (b)  $a^2 + ab + b^2 + 2$

    (c)  $a^2 - ab - b^2 + 2$

    (d)  $a^2 - ab - 4b^2 - 2$

30. Match the entries in column I with entries in column II.

    | Column-I | Column-II |
    |---|---|
    | A. Product of $\left(\sqrt{5}-\sqrt{3}\right)$ and $\left(\sqrt{5}+\sqrt{3}\right)$ is | (p) a prime number |
    | B. 2 is | (q) $\dfrac{12}{21}$ |
    | C. A rational number equivalent to $\dfrac{4}{7}$ is | (r) a rational number |
    | D. Reciprocal of $\dfrac{21}{12}$ is | (s) $\dfrac{8}{14}$ |

    (a)  (A) - (p, r), (B) - (p, r), (C)- (q, r, s), (D) - (p, q)

    (b)  (A) - (q, r), (B) - (q, r), (C)- (r, q), (D) - (r, s)

    (c)  (A) - (p, r), (B) - (p, r), (C)- (q, s, r), (D) - (q, r)

    (d)  (A) - (p, r), (B) - (q, r), (C)- (q, r, s), (D) - (q, r)

31. The HCF of two numbers obtained in three steps of division is 7. The first three quotients are 2, 4 and 6 respectively. The numbers are

    (a)  175, 392        (b)  189, 392

    (c)  168, 385        (d)  None of these

32. In $\triangle ABC$, AD bisects $\angle BAC$ and $AD = DC$.

    If $\angle ADB = 100°$, then value of $\angle ABD$ is

    (a)  40°                    (b)     50°

    (c)  30°                    (d)     35°

33. If $A:B:C = 2:3:4.$ then $\dfrac{A}{B}:\dfrac{B}{C}:\dfrac{C}{A}$ is equal to

    (a)  $4:9:16$        (b)  $8:9:12$

    (c)  $8:9:16$        (d)  $8:9:24$

34. A cloth merchant decides to sell his material at the cost price, but measures 80 cm for a metre. His gain % is.

    (a)  15%             (b)  18%

    (c)  20%             (d)  25%

35. If A is to the south of B and C is to the east of B, in what direction is A with respect to C ?

    (a)  North-east    (b)  North-west

    (c)  South-east    (d)  South-west

36. When the following figure is folded to form a cube, how many dots would lie opposite to the face bearing five dots ?

(a) 1

(b) 2

(c) 3

(d) 4

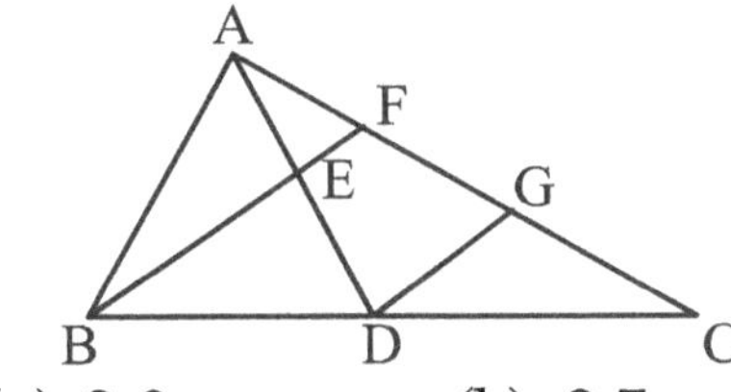

37. In the adjoining figure, a $\triangle ABC$ has been given in which AD is its median, E is the mid-point of AD, BE produced meets AC at F and DG || EF, meets AC at G . If AC = 5.4 cm then the length of AF is

(a)  3.6 cm       (b)  2.7 cm

(c)  1.8 cm       (d)  10.8 cm

38. Jatin leaves his house and walks 12 km towards North. He turns right and walks another 12 km. He turns right again, walks 12 km more and turns left to walk 5 km. How far is he from his home and in which direction ?

(a) 7 km East      (b)  10 km East

(c) 17 km East    (d)  24 km

39. Which one of the following explains correctly?

(a) A number is divisible by 11, if the difference of the sum of the alternative digts is zero or a multiple of 11.

(b) A number is divisible by 11, if the last digit of that number is odd.

(c) If the sum of the digits of a given number is divisible by 11, then that number is divisible by 11.

(d) Given number is divisible by 11, if it is divisible by both 3 and 7.

40. If 20% of 60% of a number is 144, then the number is

(a)  1200       (b)  2880

(c)  8640       (d)  None of these

41. If $(3x - 4)(5x + 7) = 15x^2 - ax - 28$, then a = _________ .

(a)  1         (b)  $-1$

(c)  $-2$       (d)  none of these

42. Find the SI on ₹ 1800 from 21st Feb 2003 to 12th April 2003 at 7.3% rate per annum.

(a) ₹18.25      (b) ₹18.00

(c) ₹18.50      (d) ₹18.75

43. Which of the following statements is incorrect :

(a) Every parallelogram is a quadrilateral

(b) Every rectangle is a parallelogram

(c) Every rhombus is a parallelogram

(d) Every trapezium is a parallelogram

44. The radii of two cylinders are in the ratio of 2 : 3 and their heights in ratio of 5 : 3, their volumes will be in ratio of

    (a) 4 : 9         (b) 27 : 20

    (c) 20 : 27       (d) 9 : 4

45. The slant height of a cone is increased by P%. If radius remains same, the curved surface area is increased by

    (a) P%            (b) $P^2\%$

    (c) 2P%           (d) None of these

46. Area of a square field is 22500 m². A man cycles along its boundary at 15 km/ hr. The time will be taken by a man to return to starting point, is

    (a) 2 min 24 sec.  (b) 3 min 12 sec.

    (c) 4 mins.        (d) None of these

**DIRECTIONS (Qs. 47-50):** The following given pie chart here shows the spending of a country on various sports during a particular year. Study the graph and answer the following four questions that follow:

47. The ratio of total amount spent on football to that spent on hockey is

    (a) 1 : 15        (b)    1 : 1

    (c) 15 : 1        (d)    3 : 20

48. If the total amount spent on sports during the year was ₹ 1, 20,000, the amount spent on basketball was :

    (a) ₹ 9,500       (b) ₹ 10,000

    (c) ₹ 12,000      (d) ₹ 15,000

49. Graph shows that the most popular game of the country is

    (a) Hockey        (b) Football

    (c) Cricket       (d) Tennis

50. Out of the following, the country spent the same amount on

    (a) Hockey and Tennis

    (b) Golf and Basketball

    (c) Cricket and Football

    (d) Hockey and Golf

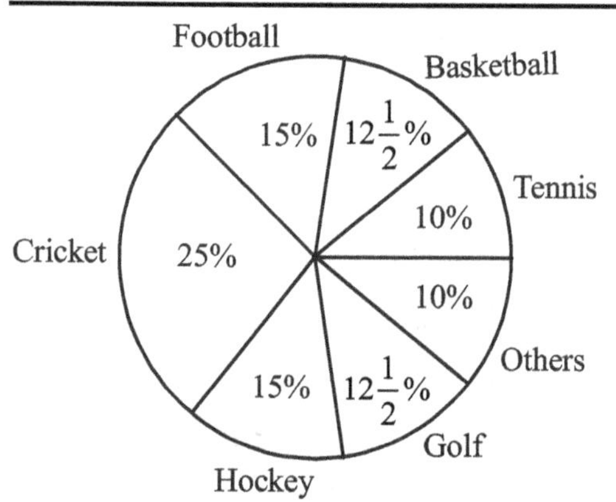

**Name:** __________                                              **Max. Marks: 50**

**Number of Questions : 50**                          **Time : 2 Hours**

**There is no negative marking in the test.**

1. If N is a natural number then, when $N^3$ is divided by 9, it leaves a remainder 'r'. What can you say about 'r'?
   (a) It is a perfect cube
   (b) It is a perfect square
   (c) It is equal to N
   (d) None of these.

2. If $\sqrt{3^n} = 81$. Then, n is equal to
   (a) 2            (b) 4
   (c) 6            (d) 8

3. Find the value of
   $$\frac{2}{3} \times \frac{3}{\dfrac{5}{6} \div \dfrac{2}{3} \text{ of } 1\dfrac{1}{4}}.$$
   (a) $\dfrac{1}{2}$            (b) $\dfrac{2}{3}$
   (c) 1            (d) 2

4. What number should replace the question mark?

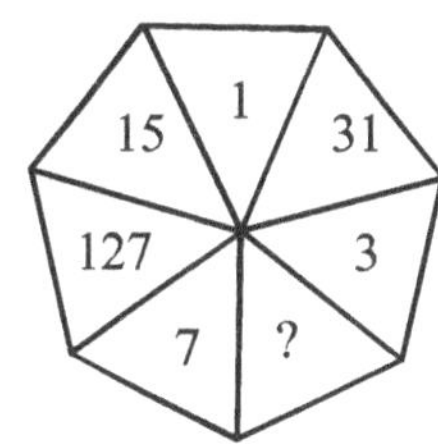

   (a) 64            (b) 63
   (c) 72            (d) 78

5. It is given that AB = BC and AD = EC. Then $\triangle ABE \cong \triangle CBD$ by ________ congruency.

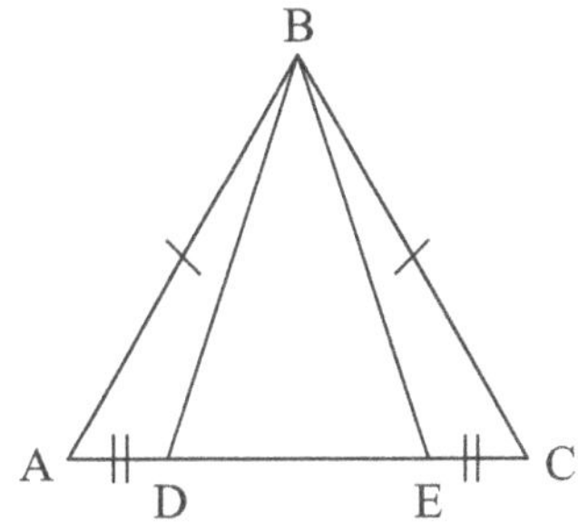

   (a) SSS            (b) ASA
   (c) SAS            (d) AAS

6. If angles A, B, C, D of a quadrilateral ABCD taken in order are in the ratio 3 : 7 : 6 : 4, then ABCD is a
   (a) rhombus
   (b) parallelogram
   (c) trapezium
   (d) kite

7. If the diagonals of a rhombus are 24 cm and 10 cm, then the area and perimeter of the rhombus are respectively
   (a) 120 sq cm, 52 cm
   (b) 240 sq cm, 52 cm
   (c) 120 sq cm, 64 cm
   (d) 240 sq cm, 64 cm

8. A solid cube with an edge 10 cm is melted to form two equal cubes. The ratio of the edge of the smaller cube to the edge of the bigger cube is:

(a) $\left(\dfrac{1}{3}\right)^{\frac{1}{3}}$      (b) $\dfrac{1}{2}$

(c) $\left(\dfrac{1}{2}\right)^{1/3}$      (d) $\left(\dfrac{1}{4}\right)^{1/3}$

9. What number should replace the question mark ?

(a) 10878      (b) 10899
(c) 10879      (d) 12879

10. The L.C.M. of two numbers is 28 times of their H.C.F. The sum of their L.C.M. and H.C.F. is 1740. If one of the numbers is 240, find the other number.

(a) 240      (b) 620
(c) 540      (d) 420

11. The digit in the units' place in the square root of 15876 is

(a) 8      (b) 6
(c) 4      (d) 2

12. The factors of $x^4 + 4$ are

(a) $(x^2 + 2)^2$
(b) $(x^2 + 2)\,(x^2 - 2)^2$
(c) $(x^2 + 2x + 2)\,(x^2 - 2x + 2)$
(d) $(x^2 - 2)^2$

13. A profit of ₹ 6000 is to be distributed among A, B and C in the ratio 3 : 4 : 5, respectively. How much more will C get than B?

(a) ₹500      (b) ₹1200
(c) ₹2000      (d) ₹2500

14. If the price of a book is first decreased by 25% and then increased by 20%, the net change in the price of the book is

(a) 10% decrease (b) 5% decrease
(c) No change      (d) 5% increase

15. If the simple interest for 6 years be equal to 30% of the principal, it will be equal to the principal after

(a) 10 years      (b) 20 years
(c) 22 years      (d) 30 years

16. Find the wrong letter in the below given series. X S N I C Y

(a) Y      (b) C
(c) S      (d) I

17. There are four prime numbers written in ascending order. The product of the first three is 385 and that of last three is 1001. Find the first number.

(a) 5      (b) 7
(c) 11      (d) 17

18. In a school, $\dfrac{3}{7}$ of the students are girls and the rest are boys. $\dfrac{1}{4}$ of the boys are below ten years of age and $\dfrac{5}{6}$ of the girls are also below ten years of age. If the number of students above ten years of age is 500, then find the total number of students in the school.

(a) 600      (b) 1000
(c) 900      (d) 1100

19. If $a + b + c = 11$ and $ab + bc + ca = 20$, then the value of the expression $a^3 + b^3 + c^3 - 3abc$ will be

  (a) 121           (b) 341

  (c) 671           (d) 781

20. Factors of $x^4 + 5x^2 + 9$ are:

  (a) $(x^2 + 2x + 3)(x^2 + 3x + 3)$

  (b) $(x^2 - x + 3)(x^2 - x - 3)$

  (c) $(x^2 - x - 3)(x^2 + x + 3)$

  (d) $(x^2 - x + 3)(x^2 + x + 3)$

21. 78, 79, 81, ?, 92, 103, 119

  (a) 88           (b) 85

  (c) 84           (d) 83

22. $\sqrt{(0.798)^2 + 0.404 \times 0.798 + (0.202)^2}$ + 1 is equal to

  (a) 0           (b) 2

  (c) 1.596           (d) 0.404

23. Find the greatest number of five digits which when divided by 4, 6, 14 and 20 leaves respectively 1, 3, 11 and 17 as remainder

  (a) 99930           (b) 99960

  (c) 99997           (d) 99957

24. If $a = 0.1039$, then the value of $\sqrt{4a^2 - 4a + 1} + 3a$ is:

  (a) 0.1039           (b) 0.2078

  (c) 1.1039           (d) 2.1039

25. $(4)^{0.5} \times (0.5)^4$ is equal to

  (a) 1           (b) 4

  (c) $\dfrac{1}{8}$           (d) $\dfrac{1}{32}$

26. By selling 100 pencils, a shopkeeper gains the S.P. of 20 pencils. His gain percent is

  (a) 25%           (b) 20%

  (c) 15%           (d) 12%

27. The ratio of two numbers is $a : b$. If first of them is $x$, then second is

  (a) $\dfrac{ab}{x}$           (c) $\dfrac{b}{ax}$

  (c) $\dfrac{b}{a+b}x$           (d) $\dfrac{bx}{a}$

28. If $\div$ means $+$, $-$ means $\div$, $\times$ means $-$ and $+$ means $\times$, then

$$\frac{(36 \times 4) - 8 \times 4}{4 + 8 \times 2 + 16 \div 1} = ?$$

  (a) 0           (b) 8

  (c) 12           (d) 16

29. The sum of the numerator and the denominator of a fraction is 11. If 1 is added to the numerator and 2 is subtracted from the denominator, it becomes $\dfrac{2}{3}$. The fraction is:

  (a) $\dfrac{5}{6}$           (b) $\dfrac{3}{8}$

  (c) $\dfrac{4}{7}$           (d) $\dfrac{1}{10}$

30. A man buys an article for ₹ 80 and marks it at ₹ 120. He then allows a discount of 40%. What is the loss or gain %?

  (a) 12% gain           (b) 12% loss

  (c) 10% gain           (d) 10% loss

31. What is the compound interest on an amount of ₹ 4800 at the rate of 6 percent p.a. at the end of 2 years?

(a) ₹ 544.96  (b) ₹ 576.00

(c) ₹ 593.28  (d) ₹ 588.00

32. If 5 spiders can catch 5 flies in 5 minutes, how many flies can 100 spiders catch in 100 minutes?

(a) 100  (b) 500

(c) 1000  (d) 2000

33. If $a + b + c = 9$ and $ab + bc + ca = 26$, then the value of $a^3 + b^3 + c^3 - 3abc$ is:

(a) 27  (b) 29

(c) 495  (d) 729

34. A,B,C and D are playing cards. A and B are partners D faces towards North. If A faces towards west, then who faces towards south?

(a) B  (b) C

(c) D  (d) Data inadequate

35. The sides of a triangle are 5, 12 and 13 units. A rectangle of width 10 units is constructed equal in area to the area of the triangle. Then, the perimeter of the rectangle is:

(a) 30 units  (b) 26 units

(c) 13 units  (d) 15 units

36. Select from the alternative, the box that can be formed by folding the sheet shown in figure (X)

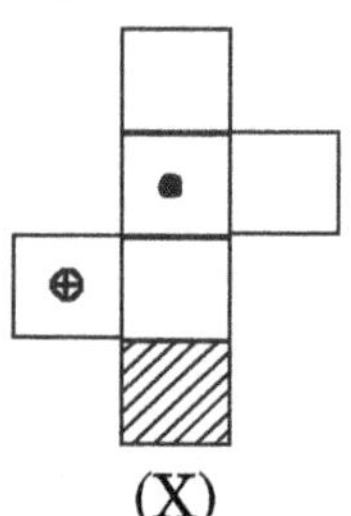

(X)

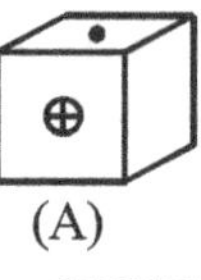
(A)

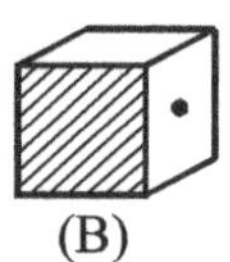
(B)

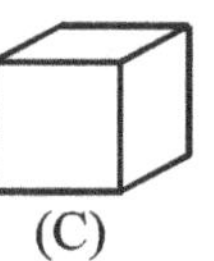
(C)

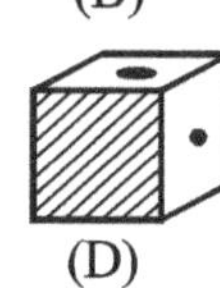
(D)

(a) A only

(b) A and C only

(c) A, C and D only

(d) A, B, C and D

37. Sobha was facing East. She walked 20 metres. Turning left she moved 15 metres and then turning right moved 25 metres. Finally, she turned right and moved 15 metres more. How far is she from her starting point?

(a) 25 metres  (b) 35 metres

(c) 50 metres  (d) 45 metres

38. The area of the figure ABCEFGA is 84 m². AH = HC = AG = AB = 6 m and CE = HF = 4 m. If the angles marked in the figure are 90° and ABCH is a parallelogram then the length of DB will be

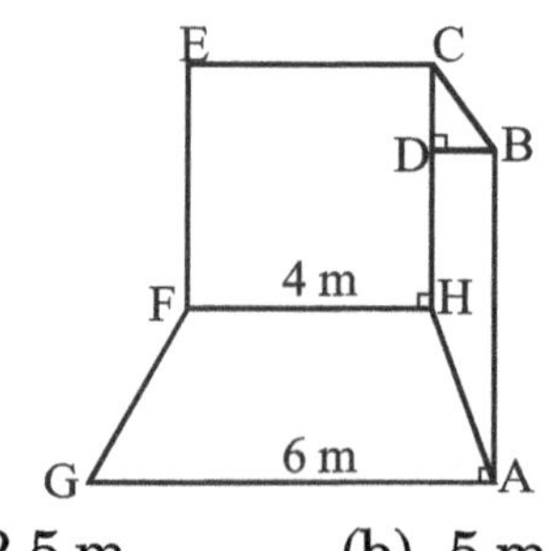

(a) 2.5 m  (b) 5 m

(c) 6 m  (d) 12 m

39. A rectangular tank 25 cm long and 20 cm wide contains 4.5 litres of water. When a metal cube is lowered in the tank, the water level rises to a height of 11 cm. Find the length of each edge of the cube?

(a) 15 cm      (b) 5 cm
(c) 11 cm      (d) 10 cm

40. If A stands for +, B stands for –, C stands for ×, then what is the value of $(10\,C\,4)\,A\,(4\,C\,4\,)\,B\,6$ ?

(a) 60      (b) 56
(c) 50      (d) 46

41. If $64^a = \dfrac{1}{256^b}$, then 3a + 4b equals

(a) 2      (b) 4
(c) 8      (d) 0

42. The value of $64a^3 + 48a^2 b + 12ab^2 + b^3$ at a = 1 and b = –1 is:

(a) 25      (b) 125
(c) 27      (d) 54

43. If Dennis is $\dfrac{1}{3}$ rd the age of his father Keith now and was $\dfrac{1}{4}$ th the age of his father 5 years ago, then how old will his father Keith be 5 years from now?

(a) 20 years      (b) 45 years
(c) 40 years      (d) 50 years

44. The roots of the equation $2x^2 - 11x + 15 = 0$ are:

(a) $3, \dfrac{5}{2}$      (b) $5, \dfrac{3}{2}$
(c) $-3, -\dfrac{5}{2}$      (d) None of these

45. In a trapezium ABCD, AB || DC, AB = AD, ∠ADC = 64° and ∠BCD = 54°. Find ∠DBC.

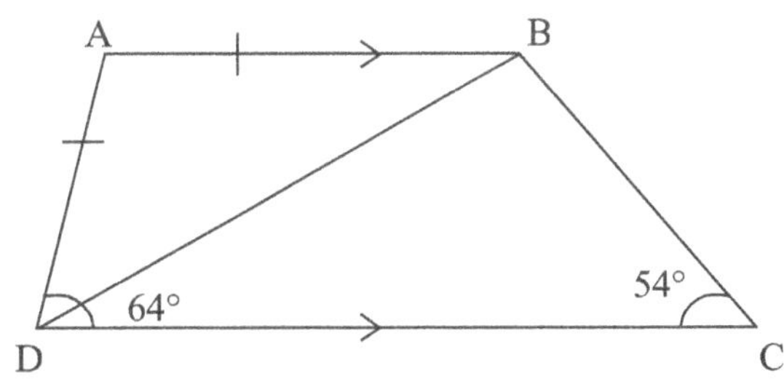


(a) 64°      (b) 72°
(c) 94°      (d) 116°

46. If the volume of a right circular cylinder with its height equal to the radius is $25\dfrac{1}{7}$ cm³, then the radius of the cylinder is equal to:

(a) 1 cm      (b) 3 cm
(c) 4 cm      (d) 2 cm

47. The pie chart given below shows the expenses incurred and saving by a family in a month. What is the percentage of expenses incurred on account of recreation?

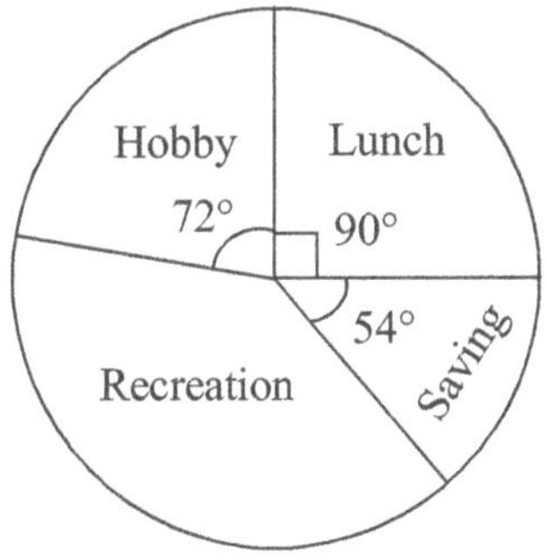


(a) $\dfrac{800}{17}$%      (b) 20%
(c) 35%      (d) 40%

                                     

48. In a single throw of two dice, what is the probability of getting a total of 11?

(a) $\dfrac{1}{9}$      (b) $\dfrac{1}{18}$

(c) $\dfrac{1}{12}$      (d) $\dfrac{35}{36}$

49. The population of four towns A, B, C and D as on 2011 are as follows:

| Town | Population |
| --- | --- |
| A | 6863 |
| B | 519 |
| C | 12185 |
| D | 1755 |

What is the most appropriate diagram to present the above data?

(a) Pie chart

(b) Bar chart

(c) Histogram

(d) Line graph

50. The angles of a pentagon in degree are $x°$, $(x + 20)°$, $(x + 40)°$, $(x + 60)°$ and $(x + 80)°$. What is the measure of the largest angle?

(a) 78°      (b) 148°

(c) 68°      (d) 158°

**Name :** _________

**Max. Marks : 50**

**Number of Questions : 50**

**Time : 2 Hours**

**There is no negative marking in the test.**

1. When N is divided by 4, the remainder is 3. What is the remainder when 2N is divided by 4?

    (a) 2  
    (b) 3  
    (c) 4  
    (d) 8

2. Evaluate: $\dfrac{1\frac{1}{7} - \frac{2}{3} + \dfrac{\frac{2}{5}}{1 - \frac{1}{25}}}{1 - \frac{1}{7}\left(\frac{1}{3} + \dfrac{\frac{2}{5}}{1 - \frac{2}{5}}\right)}$.

    (a) $\dfrac{3}{4}$  
    (b) $\dfrac{24}{25}$  
    (c) 1  
    (d) $1\dfrac{1}{24}$

3. What number should replace the question mark?

| 3C | 2B | 4A |
|----|----|----|
| 27A | ? | 64B |
| 9C | 4A | 16B |

    (a) 8C  
    (b) 12C  
    (c) 16C  
    (d) 18C

4. The smallest number that must be added to 680621 to make the sum a perfect square is:

    (a) 4  
    (b) 5  
    (c) 6  
    (d) 8

5. If $x + \dfrac{1}{x} = 3$, then the value of $x^6 + \dfrac{1}{x^6}$ is:

    (a) 927  
    (b) 414  
    (c) 364  
    (d) 322

6. The difference between the simple interest received from two different sources on ₹ 1500 for 3 years is ₹ 13.50. The difference between their rates of interests is:

    (a) 0.1%  
    (b) 0.2%  
    (c) 0.3%  
    (d) 0.4%

7. The side of a rhombus is 10 cm and one diagonal is 16 cm. The area of the rhombus is:

    (a) 96 cm²  
    (b) 95 cm²  
    (c) 94 cm²  
    (d) 93 cm²

8. I am facing south. I turn right and walk 20 m. Then I turn right again and walk 10 m. Then I turn left and walk 10 m and then turning right walk 20 m. Then I turn right again and walk 60 m. In which direction am I from the starting point

   (a) North      (b) North-west

   (c) East      (d) North-east

9. Give the next number in this series:

   220, 200, 100, 80, 40, 20, ?

   (a) 20      (b) 10

   (c) 30      (d) 40

10. $(64)^{\frac{-2}{3}} \times \left(\dfrac{1}{4}\right)^{-3}$ equals

    (a) $\dfrac{1}{4}$      (b) 1

    (c) 4      (d) 16

11. A person spends $\dfrac{1}{3}$ of the money with him on clothes, $\dfrac{1}{5}$ of the remaining on food and $\dfrac{1}{4}$ of the remaining on travel. Now, he is left with ₹100. How much did he have with him in the beginning?

    (a) ₹200      (b) ₹250

    (c) ₹300      (d) ₹450

12. ₹ 2010 are to be divided among A, B and C in such a way that if A gets ₹5, then B must get ₹12 and if B gets ₹4, then C must get ₹5.50. The share of C will exceed that of B by

    (a) ₹620      (b) ₹430

    (c) ₹360      (d) ₹270

13. ABCD is a rectangle. Find x.

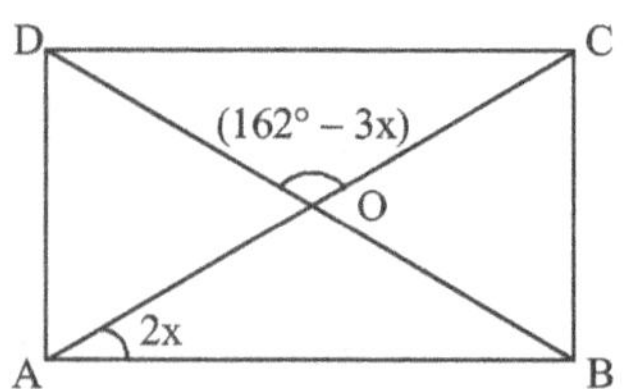


    (a) 54°      (b) 36°

    (c) 24°      (d) 18°

14. The volume of a right circular cylinder whose height is 40 cm and the circumference of its base is 66 cm is

    (a) 55440 cm³    (b) 34650 cm³

    (c) 7720 cm³    (d) 13860 cm³

15. What number should replace the question mark?

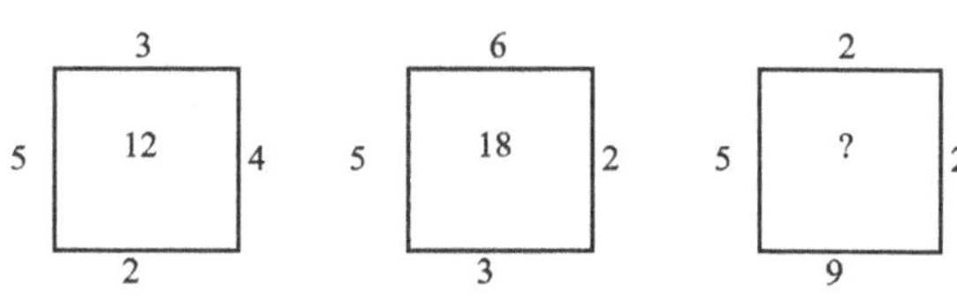


    (a) 15      (b) 16

    (c) 17      (d) 18

16. What is the sum of two numbers whose difference is 45 and the quotient of the greater number by the lesser number is 4?

    (a) 100      (b) 90

    (c) 80      (d) 75

17. A man first sold $\frac{2}{3}$rd of his total quantity of rice and 100 kg. Again he sold $\frac{1}{2}$ of the remaining quantity and 100 kg. If the total remaining quantity of the stock is 150 kg. Then, what was the original stock of rice?

    (a) 2100 kg          (b) 1800 kg

    (c) 2400 kg          (d) 2000 kg

18. Find the greatest number of five digits which become exactly divisible by 10, 12, 15 and 18 when 3769 is added to it.

    (a) 99819          (b) 99911

    (c) 99900          (d) 99111

19. If $3a = 4b = 6c$ and $a + b + c = 27\sqrt{29}$, then $\sqrt{a^2 + b^2 + c^2}$ is:

    (a) $3\sqrt{29}$          (b) 81

    (c) 87          (d) 29

20. What number comes next ?

    1, 1, 3, 6, 5, 11, 7, ?

    (a) 16          (b) 18

    (c) 20          (d) 22

21. $\left(\frac{1}{64}\right)^0 + (64)^{\frac{-1}{2}} + (32)^{\frac{4}{5}} - (32)^{\frac{-4}{5}}$ is equal to

    (a) $16\frac{1}{8}$          (b) $17\frac{1}{8}$

    (c) $17\frac{1}{16}$          (d) $-17\frac{1}{16}$

22. The factors of $625a^{12} - 81b^{12}$ are:

    (a) $(25a^6 + 9b^6)(5a^3 - 3b^3)(5a^3 + 3b^3)$

    (b) $(5a^3 + 3b^3)^2 (5a^3 - 3b^3)^2$

    (c) $(5a^3 - 3b^3)^4$

    (d) $(25a^6 - 9b^6)^2$

23. If I would have purchased 11 articles for ₹10 and sold all the articles at the rate of ₹ 11 for 10, the profit per cent would have been

    (a) 10%          (b) 11%

    (c) 21%          (d) 100%

24. A rectangular field is half as wide as it is long and is completely enclosed by x metre of fencing. What is the area of the field?

    (a) $\frac{x^2}{2} m^2$          (b) $2x^2 m^2$

    (c) $\frac{2x^2}{9} m^2$          (d) $\frac{x^2}{18} m^2$

25. The cross-section of a canal is in the shape of trapezium. The canal is 15 m wide at the top and 9 m wide at the bottom. If the area of the cross-section is $720 \, m^2$, then the depth of the canal is:

    (a) 58.4 m          (b) 58.6 m

    (c) 58.8 m          (d) 60 m

26. Simplify: $\dfrac{\left(x^{2^{n-1}} + y^{2^{n-1}}\right)\left(x^{2^{n-1}} - y^{2^{n-1}}\right)}{x^{2^n} - y^{2^n}}$

    (a) $(xy)^{mn}$          (b) $x^n$

    (c) 1          (d) $(7)^{mn}$

27. If $20 - 10$ means 200, $8 \div 4$ means 12, $6 \times 2$ means 4 and $10 + 12$ means 5 then

    $100 - 10 \times 1000 \div 1000 + 100 \times 10 = ?$

    (a) 0         (b) 20

    (c) 1000        (d) 1900

28. A cube having each side of unit length is cut into two parts by a plane through two diagonals of two opposite faces. What is the total surface area of each of these parts?

    (a) $3 + \sqrt{2}$ sq. units

    (b) $2 + \sqrt{3}$ sq. units

    (c) $3\sqrt{2}$ sq. units

    (b) 3 sq. units

29. If a clock strikes 12 in 33 seconds, it will strike 6 in how many seconds?

    (a) $\dfrac{33}{2}$        (b) 15

    (c) 12         (d) 22

30. Which of the following numbers is the least?

    $(0.5)^2$, $\sqrt{0.49}$, $\sqrt[3]{0.008}$, 0.23

    (a) $(0.5)^2$        (b) $\sqrt{0.49}$

    (c) $\sqrt[3]{0.008}$      (d) 0.23

31. Find the least number which when divided by 12, 24, 36 and 40 leaves a remainder 1, but when divided by 7 leaves no remainder.

    (a) 361        (b) 1080

    (c) 721        (d) 371

32. The remainder obtained on dividing the polynomial $3x^4 - 4x^3 - 3x - 1$ by $(x - 1)$ is:

    (a) 0         (b) 5

    (c) –5        (d) 6

33. Factorise: $a^4 - 20a^2 + 64$.

    (a) $(a + 2)(a - 2)(a + 4)(a - 4)$

    (b) $(a - 2)^2 (a - 4)^2$

    (c) $(a - 2)^2 (a + 4)^2$

    (d) None of these

34. My grandfather was 8 times older to me 16 years ago. He would be 3 time of my age 8 years from now. Eight years ago, what was the ratio of my age to that of my grandfather?

    (a) $1:2$        (b) $1:5$

    (c) $13:18$       (d) $11:53$

35. Find a if $a - 3 = \dfrac{10}{a}$.

    (a) $\sqrt{7}, 7$       (b) $5, -2$

    (c) $-5, 2$       (d) $-\sqrt{7}, 7$

36. The price of an article is reduced by 25% but the daily sale of the article is increased by 30%. The net effect on the daily sale receipts is:

    (a) $2\dfrac{1}{2}\%$ decrease

    (b) $2\dfrac{1}{2}\%$ increase

    (c) 2% decrease

    (d) 2% increase

37. If $\sqrt{1296} = 36$, then find the value of

$$\sqrt{12.96} + \sqrt{0.1296} + \sqrt{0.001296} + \sqrt{0.00001296}$$

  (a) 3.9956       (b) 3.9996

  (c) 39.996       (d) 399.96

38. The principal that amounts to ₹4913 in 3 years at $6\frac{1}{4}\%$ per annum compound interest compounded annually is:

  (a) ₹4096       (b) ₹4085

  (c) ₹4076       (d) ₹3096

39. In the given figure, OA = OB, OC = OD, ∠AOB = ∠COD. Which of the following statements is true?

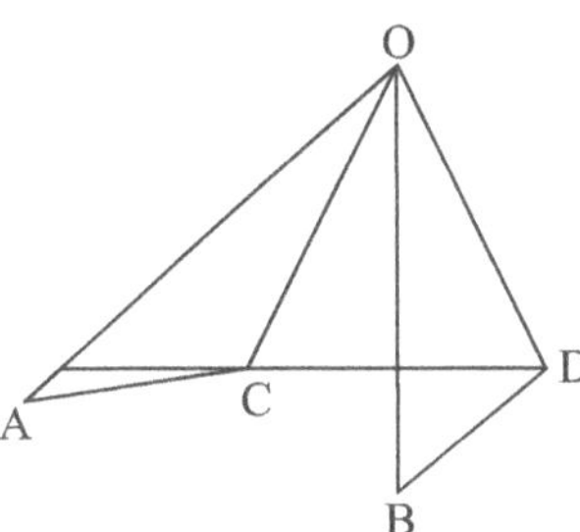

  (a) AC = CD

  (b) OA = OD

  (c) AC = BD

  (d) ∠OCA = ∠ODC

40. ABCD is a rhombus.

  ∠DAB = 2x + 15°,

  ∠DCB = 3x − 30°, ∠BDC equals

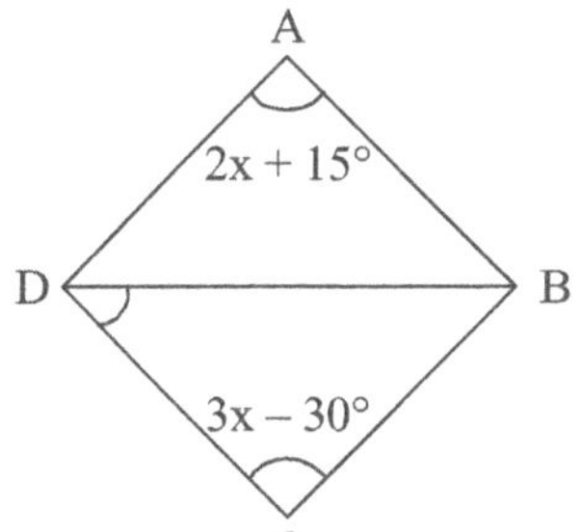

  (a) 45°       (b) 35°

  (c) 37.5°       (d) 42.5°

41. A three centimetre cube has been painted red on all its sides. It is cut into one centimetre cubes. How many cubes will be there with only one side painted red?

  (a) 4       (b) 6

  (c) 1       (d) 9

42. The sum of the length, breadth and height of a cuboid is 19 cm and the diagonal is $5\sqrt{5}$. Its surface area is:

  (a) 361 cm²       (b) 125 cm²

  (c) 236 cm²       (d) 256 cm²

43. Going 50 m to the south of her house, Radhika turns left and goes another 20 m. Then turning to the North, she goes 30 m and then starts walking to her house. In which direction is she walking now?

  (a) North-west   (b) North

  (c) South east   (d) East

44. A result of a survey of 1000 persons with respect to their knowledge of Hindi (H), English (E) and Sanskrit (S) is given below.

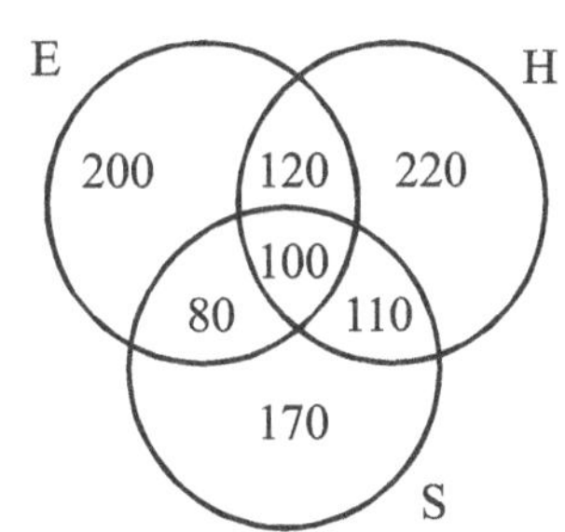

What is the ratio of these who know all the three languages to those who do not know Sanskrit?

(a) $\dfrac{1}{9}$

(b) $\dfrac{1}{10}$

(c) $\dfrac{10}{17}$

(d) $\dfrac{5}{27}$

45. A solid cube with an edge 10 cm is melted to form two equal cubes. The ratio of the edge of the smaller cube to the edge of the bigger cube is:

(a) $\left(\dfrac{1}{3}\right)^{\frac{1}{3}}$

(b) $\dfrac{1}{2}$

(c) $\left(\dfrac{1}{2}\right)^{\frac{1}{3}}$

(d) $\left(\dfrac{1}{4}\right)^{\frac{1}{3}}$

46. The height and radius of a cone are 3 cm and 4 cm respectively. Its curved surface area must be

(a) $62\dfrac{6}{7}$ sq. cm

(b) $57\dfrac{3}{4}$ sq. cm

(c) $6\,\text{cm}^2$

(d) $12\,\text{cm}^2$

47. If $2A = 3B = 4C$, then $A : B : C$ is

(a) $2 : 3 : 4$

(b) $4 : 3 : 2$

(c) $6 : 4 : 3$

(d) $3 : 4 : 2$

48. Calculate the mean of weekly wages from the following frequency distribution:

| Wages (in ₹) | No. of workers |
| --- | --- |
| 30-40 | 10 |
| 40-50 | 20 |
| 50-60 | 40 |
| 60-70 | 16 |
| 70-80 | 8 |
| 80-90 | 6 |

(a) 52

(b) 43

(c) 48

(d) 56

49. In a test, the marks obtained by 15 students are 34, 37, 44, 39, 45, 46, 35, 42, 48, 40, 39, 33, 43, 47, 44. The probability that a pupil chosen at random passed the test, if the passing marks are 40 is

(a) $\dfrac{8}{15}$

(b) $\dfrac{3}{5}$

(c) $\dfrac{7}{15}$

(d) $\dfrac{11}{15}$

**DIRECTION:** Study the chart and give the answer of following questions.

Selling of the car in UK according to the colours

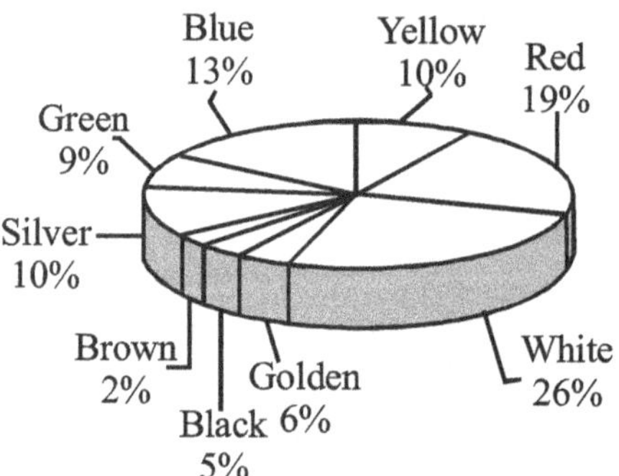


50. If in a certain period the total production of all cars was 95400 then how many more blue cars were sold than green?

(a) 2580

(b) 3618

(c) 2850

(d) 3816

# OLYMPIAD
# Mock Test 5

Name: _________

Number of Questions : 50

There is no negative marking in the test.

Max. Marks : 50

Time : 2 Hours

1. The simplest answer for $\sqrt{9a^4 b^8}$ is:

   (a) $9a^2 b^4$

   (b) $3a^2 b^4$

   (c) $81a^8 b^{16}$

   (d) $3ab^2$

2. In the matrix given below, the value of A, B and C are

   | 9 | A | 12 |
   |---|---|----|
   | B | 10 | 7 |
   | 8 | C | 11 |

   (a) A = 13, B = 11, C = 9

   (b) A = 13, B = 9, C = 11

   (c) A = 9, B = 11, C = 13

   (d) A = 9, B = 13, C = 11

3. If 1156 students in a school are to form a square pattern on the field for the mass drill function on the Sports Day, how many students will form each side of the square?

   (a) 31      (b) 24

   (c) 29      (d) 34

4. Divide $(38a^3 b^3 c^2 - 19a^4 b^2 c)$ by $19a^2$ bc.

   (a) $2ab^2 c - a^2 b$    (b) $2ab^2 - 3ac^2$

   (c) $ab^2 c - a^2 b$    (d) $2ab^2 c + a^2 b$

5. Factorise $10xy - 5y + 8 - 16x$.

   (a) $(2x - 1)(5y - 6)$

   (b) $(2x - 1)(5y - 8)$

   (c) $(x - 1)(y - 30)$

   (d) $(5x - 1)(2y - 6)$

6. If $4^{\sqrt{x}^{\sqrt{x}}} = 256$ then the value of x is

   (a) 2      (b) 16

   (c) 4      (d) $\sqrt{2}$

7. The digit in the units' place in the cube root of 21952 is:

   (a) 8      (b) 6

   (c) 4      (d) 2

8. The common root of the equations $x^2 - 7x + 10 = 0$ and $x^2 - 10x + 16 = 0$ is:

   (a) –2      (b) 3

   (c) 5      (d) 2

9. ₹1000 invested at 5% p.a. simple interest. If the interest is added to the principal after every 10 years, the amount will become ₹2000 after

(a) 15 years      (b) $16\frac{2}{3}$ years

(c) 18 years      (d) 20 years

10. How much should a sum of ₹16000 approximately amount to in 2 years at 10% p.a. compounded half yearly?

(a) ₹17423      (b) ₹18973

(c) ₹19448      (d) ₹19880

11. A job can be completed by 12 men in 12 days. How many extra days will be needed to complete the job, if 6 men leave after working for 6 days?

(a) 10 days      (b) 12 days

(c) 8 days      (d) 24 days

12. If the following series is written in the reverse order, which number will be fourth to the right of the seventh number from the left ?

7, 3, 9, 7, 0, 3, 8, 4, 6, 2, 1, 0, 5, 11, 13

(a) 0      (b) 5

(c) 9      (d) 11

13. Of a certain sum, $\frac{1}{3}$ rd is invested at 3%, $\frac{1}{6}$ th at 6% and the rest at 8%. If the SI for 2 years from all these investments amounts to ₹600. Then the original sum was

(a) ₹2000      (b) ₹3000

(c) ₹4000      (d) ₹5000

14. The perimeter of a rhombus is 40 cm. If the length of one of its diagonals be 12 cm, then the length of the other diagonal is:

(a) 14 cm      (b) 15 cm

(c) 16 cm      (d) 12 cm

15. In how many years will ₹4000 amount to ₹5324 at 10% p.a. compounded annually?

(a) $2\frac{3}{4}$ years      (b) 3 years

(c) $3\frac{1}{2}$ years      (d) 5 years

16. Sindhu is 40 years old and Smita is 20 years old. How many years ago was Sindhu three times as old as Smita?

(a) 9      (b) 6

(c) 10      (d) 8

17. Sanjay sold his old dining table set at a loss of 20%. If he had sold it for ₹800 more, he would have received a profit of 5%. The cost price is:

(a) ₹1730      (b) ₹2150

(c) ₹2600      (d) ₹3200

18. Ahmed repaid an amount of ₹9125 to the bank which includes an interest of ₹625. What was the money that he borrowed from the bank?

(a) ₹7860      (b) ₹8400

(c) ₹8500      (d) ₹9250

19. If + means × . × means –, ÷ means + and – means ÷, then which of the following gives the result of

$175 - 25 \div 5 + 20 \times 3 + 10$ ?

(a) 77      (b) 160

(c) 240      (d) 2370

20. $\sqrt[3]{\sqrt[3]{a^3}}$ is equal to:

   (a) a               (b) 1

   (c) $a^{\frac{1}{3}}$            (d) $a^3$

21. Find x, if $8^{x-2} \times \left(\dfrac{1}{2}\right)^{4-3x} = (0.0625)^x$.

   (a) 0               (b) 4

   (c) 2               (d) 1

22. ₹53 are divided among A, B and C such that A gets ₹7 more than B and B gets ₹8 more than C. What is the ratio of their shares?

   (a) 16 : 9 : 18     (b) 25 : 18 : 10

   (c) 18 : 25 : 10    (d) 15 : 8 : 30

23. In a medical certificate, by mistake a candidate gave his height as 25% more than the actual. In the interview panel, he clarified his height was 5 feet 5 inches. Find the percentage correction made by the candidate from his stated height to his actual height.

   (a) 28.56         (b) 20

   (c) 25             (d) 24

24. A plot of land is in the form of a quadrilateral, where one of its diagonals is 230 m long. The two vertices on either side of this diagonal are 60 m and 70 m away. What is the area of the plot of land?

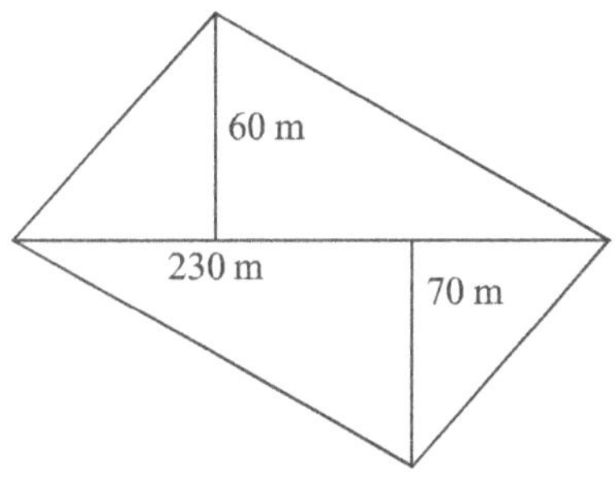


   (a) 21426 sq. m.   (b) 14950 sq. m.

   (c) 12616 sq. m.   (d) 10928 sq. m.

25. A godown has dimension 7 m × 4.5 m × 2 m. How many cartons of dimension 70 cm × 22.5 cm × 40 cm can be stored in it?

   (a) 1120          (b) 1108

   (c) 1040          (d) 1000

26. The total surface area of a box of length 8 cm and breadth 6 cm is 208 sq. cm. Find the height of the box.

   (a) 4.0 cm        (b) 3.6 cm

   (c) 5.2 cm        (d) 4.8 cm

27. The area of an equilateral triangle is $36\sqrt{3}$ sq. m. Find the length of its sides.

   (a) 17.2 m        (b) 16 m

   (c) 14 m          (d) 12 m

28. Find the missing character in the following questions.

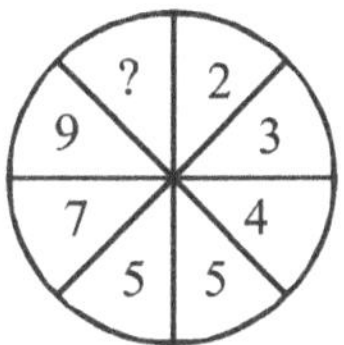


   (a) 10             (b) 11

   (c) 12             (d) 13

29. If A's salary is 50% more than B's, then by what % B's salary is less than A's salary?

(a) $33\dfrac{1}{3}$

(b) $23\dfrac{1}{3}$

(c) 33

(d) 30

30. The volume of a wall, 5 times as high as it is breadth and 8 times as long as it is high is 18225 m$^3$. Find the breadth of the wall.

(a) 32.5 m

(b) 5 m

(c) 4.5 m

(d) 3.5 m

31. If $2x - 5y = 3$ and $xy = 4$, then the value of $8x^3 - 125y^3$.

(a) 387

(b) 423

(c) 486

(d) 507

32. Simplify :

$$\frac{3x^2 - 6x - 105}{5x^2 - 125} \div \frac{x^2 - 12x + 35}{x^2 - 5x}.$$

(a) $\dfrac{2x}{2(x-6)}$

(b) $\dfrac{3x}{5(x-5)}$

(c) $\dfrac{x}{5(x-5)}$

(d) $\dfrac{2x}{5x-25}$

33. If $x = 2a - 1$, find the value of 'a' from the equation

$$\frac{1}{3}(4x + 5) - \frac{1}{2}(5a - 3) = \frac{1}{6}.$$

(a) 21

(b) 10

(c) $-10$

(d) $-16$

34. In a two digit number, ten's digit is twice the unit's digit. The number formed by interchanging the digits is 36 less than the original number. Find the number.

(a) 48

(b) 70

(c) 72

(d) 84

35. In the adjoining figure, find the value of x.

(a) $32°$

(b) $46°$

(c) $27°$

(d) $70°$

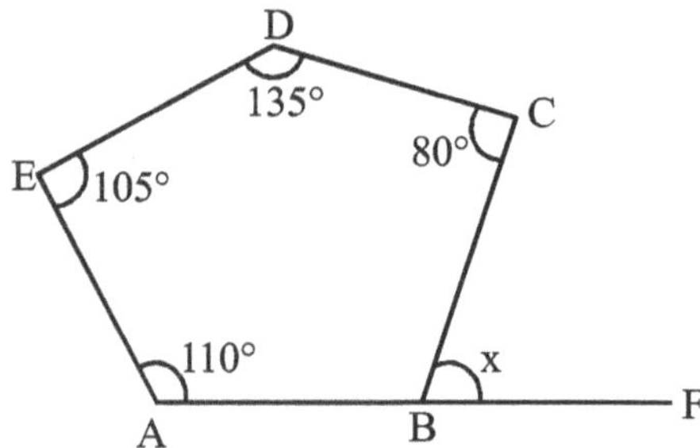


36. A water tap fills a tank in p hours and the tap of the bottom of the tank empties it in q hours. If p is less than q and when both the taps are open, the tank is filled in r hours. Then

(a) $\dfrac{1}{r} = \dfrac{1}{p} + \dfrac{1}{q}$

(b) $\dfrac{1}{r} = \dfrac{1}{p} - \dfrac{1}{q}$

(c) $r = p + q$

(d) $r = p - q$

37. One pendulum ticks 57 times in 58 sec, while another ticks 608 times in 609 sec. If they started together, then how often will they tick together in the first hour ?

(a) 47

(b) 53

(c) 57

(d) 67

38. If an article is sold for ₹178 at a loss of 11%, what should be its selling price in order to earn a profit of 11%?

    (a) ₹222.50        (b) ₹267

    (c) ₹222           (d) ₹220

39. In how many years will a sum of ₹800 at 10% per annum compound interest, compounded semi-annually become ₹926.10?

    (a) 1 year         (b) 3 years

    (c) 2 years        (d) $1\frac{1}{2}$ years

40. In the given figure, AD = BC, AC = BD. Then $\triangle$PAB is:

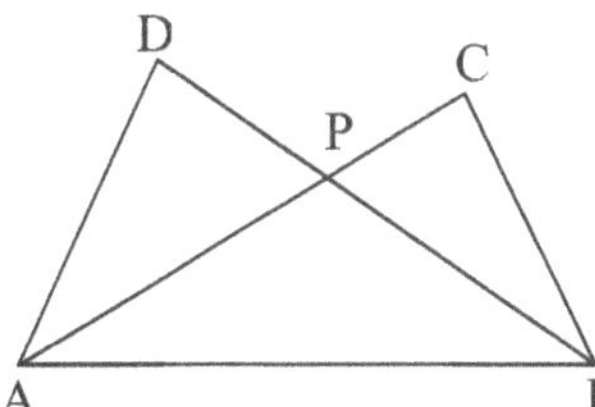

    (a) equilateral    (b) right angled

    (c) scalene        (d) isosceles

41. The area of the given field is 3500 m². AF = 25 m, AG = 50 m, AH = 75 m and AB = 100 m. The rest of the dimensions are shown in the figure. Find the value of x.

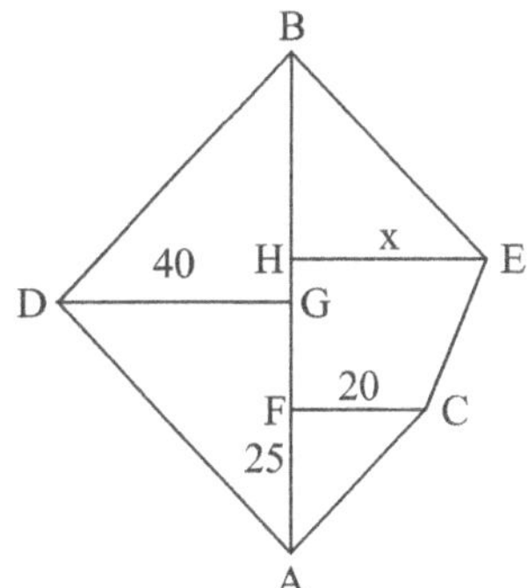

(a) 17 m              (b) 20 m

(c) 22 m              (d) 25 m

42. A water tank is 30 m long, 20 m wide and 12 m deep. It is made up of iron sheet which is 3 m wide. The tank is open at the top. If the cost of the iron sheet is ₹ 10 per metre, then the total cost of the iron sheet required to build the tank is:

    (a) ₹6000          (b) ₹8000

    (c) ₹9000          (d) ₹10000

43. The curved surface area of a cylindrical pillar is 264 m² and its volume is 924 m³. Find the ratio of its diameter to its height.

    (a) 3 : 7          (b) 7 : 3

    (c) 6 : 7          (d) 7 : 6

44. P,Q,R,S, T and U are points on the circle shown below and the length of arc PQR is 6 cm. Then length of arc STU is

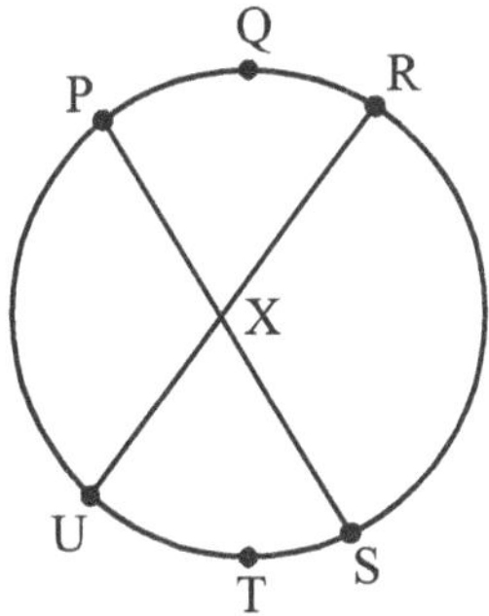

(a) 12 cm

(b) 6π cm

(c) 6 cm

(d) cannot be determined from the given data

45. The statistical data are of two types. These types are

    (a) technical data and presentation data

    (b) primary data and secondary data

    (c) primary data and personal data

    (d) None of the above

46. If the mean of x and 1/x is M, then the mean of $x^2$ and $1/x^2$ is

    (a) $M^2$

    (b) $M^2/4$

    (c) $2M^2 - 1$

    (d) $2M^2 + 1$

**DIRECTIONS (Qs. 47-49):** Read the following passage and answer the questions that follow.

### PASSAGE

Miss Neha asked the children in her class, 'What is your favourite colour?' Her results are shown on the bar chart.

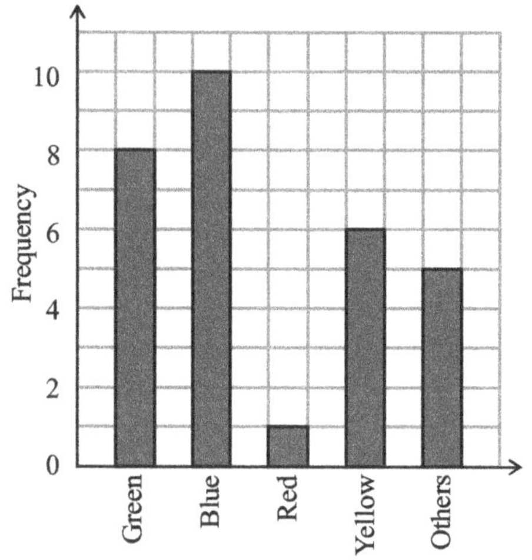


47. How many children are in her class?

    (a) 30

    (b) 42

    (c) 28

    (d) 37

48. What is the mode of the distribution?

    (a) Green

    (b) Blue

    (c) Red

    (d) Yellow

49. Above given information is also to be represented in a pie-chart. Calculate the angle of the sector representing yellow.

    (a) 90°

    (b) 60°

    (c) 52°

    (d) 72°

50. A card is drawn from a well shuffled deck of playing cards. Find the probability of drawing a face card

    (a) $\dfrac{16}{53}$

    (b) $\dfrac{4}{13}$

    (c) $\dfrac{13}{15}$

    (d) $\dfrac{4}{52}$

# SCIENCE

## OLYMPIAD
# Mock Test  (1)

**Name :** _________

**Number of Questions : 50**

**There is no negative marking in the test.**

**Max. Marks : 50**

**Time : 2 Hours**

### PHYSICS

1. When a net force acts on an object, the object will be accelerated in the direction of the force with an acceleration proportional to
   (a) the force on the object
   (b) the velocity of the object
   (c) the mass of the object
   (d) the inertia of the object

2. To weigh roughly two-thirds less than what you do on Earth, which planet would you be on?
   (a) Uranus
   (b) Mars
   (c) Venus
   (d) Jupiter

3. Four children were asked to arrange forces due to rolling, static and sliding frictions in a increasing order. Their arrangements are given below. Choose the correct arrangement.
   (a) Rolling, Static, Sliding
   (b) Static, Rolling, Sliding
   (c) Rolling, sliding, static
   (d) Sliding, Static, Rolling

4. The best conductor of electricity is
   (a) Distilled water
   (b) Tap water
   (c) Rain water
   (d) Sea water

5. The strength of force is expressed by
   (a) weight
   (b) mass
   (c) magnitude
   (d) longitudinal force

6. We can never see the backside of the Moon from the Earth. Why ?
   (a) The Moon completes one rotation on its axis as it completes one revolution around the Earth.
   (b) The back and front side of the Moon are the same.
   (c) The backside of the moon is little further away.
   (d) The backside of the Moon is dark.

7. Voice of which of following is likely to have minimum frequency?
   (a) Baby girl         (b) Baby boy
   (c) A man             (d) A woman

8. Choose the wrong statement.
   (a) A concave mirror can form a magnified real image.
   (b) A concave mirror can form a magnified virtual image.
   (c) A convex mirror can form a diminished virtual image.
   (d) A convex mirror can form a diminished real image.

9. A train at rest tends to move from the platform and it attains a velocity of 100 km/h within a few second. While trying to come in motion it has to overcome the frictional force; that frictional force is:
   (a) Static friction
   (b) Rolling friction
   (c) Sliding friction
   (d) Kinetic friction

10. A vehicle slows down after applying brakes because of
   (a) magneticforce
   (b) frictional force
   (c) electric force
   (d) none of the above

11. In order to reduce the loudness of a sound we have to
   (a) decrease its frequency of vibration of the sound
   (b) increase its frequency of vibration of the sound
   (c) decrease its amplitude of vibration of the sound
   (d) increase its amplitude of vibration of the sound

12. An electroscope is a device which is used to find
   (a) presence and magnitude of charge.
   (b) magnetic field.
   (c) free of cracks.
   (d) electric field.

13. Name the gases which are formed during lightning.
   (a) Sulphur dioxide and Sulphur trioxide
   (b) Nitric oxide and Nitrogen dioxide
   (c) Carbon monooxide and carbon dioxide
   (d) Nitrogen trioxide and Sulphur dioxide

14. Which of the following solutions will not make the bulb in Fig. glow?

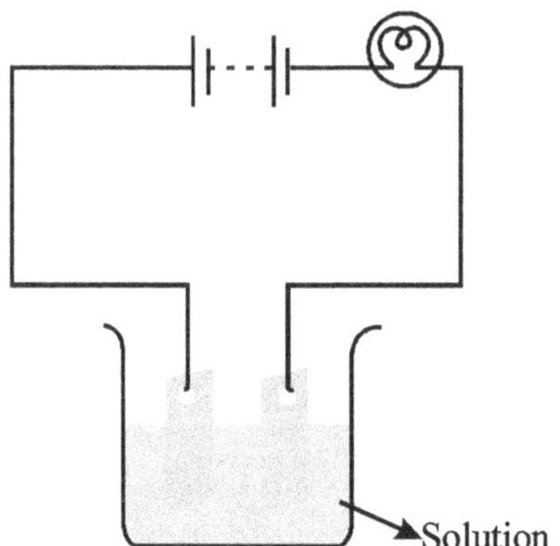


   (a) Sodium chlorides
   (b) Copper sulphate
   (c) Silver nitrate
   (d) Sugar solution in diluted water

15. Ear drum is a part of:
   (a) sound producing organ
   (b) skeletal system
   (c) hearing organ
   (d) reproductive organ

16. When sound travels through air, the air particles ______.

    (a) vibrate along the direction of wave propagation

    (b) vibrate but not in any fixed direction

    (c) vibrate perpendicular to the direction of wave propagation

    (d) do not vibrate

17. Pascal is a unit of

    (a) pressure

    (b) force

    (c) linear momentum

    (d) energy

18. Which of the following statements are correct?

    (i) Sound is produced by vibrations.

    (ii) Sound requires a medium for propagation.

    (iii) Light and sound both require a medium for propagation.

    (iv) Sound travels slower than light.

    (a) i & ii only

    (b) i, ii & iii only

    (c) ii, iii & iv only

    (d) i, ii & iv only

19. Which one of the following is not used to reduce friction?

    (a) Oil          (b) Ball bearings

    (c) Sand          (d) Graphite

### CHEMISTRY

20. Which statement is true for cotton clothes?

    (a) It absorbs water efficiently and burns at a moderate speed.

    (b) It does not absorb water efficiently but burns at a moderate speed

    (c) It does not absorb water efficiently and does not burn at a moderate speed.

    (d) It absorbs water efficiently but does not burns at a moderate speed.

21. Which one of the following properties would you consider when choosing a material for food containers?

    (i) Able to resist high temperatures

    (ii) A good insulator of heat

    (iii) Non-corrosive

    (iv) Can be made into various shapes

    (a) (i) and (iv) only

    (b) (ii) and (iii) only

    (c) (i), (ii) and (iv) only

    (d) All of the above

**DIRECTIONS :** *On the basis of following diagram / picture answer the questions given below :*

22. Four experimental set-ups are shown in the given figure.

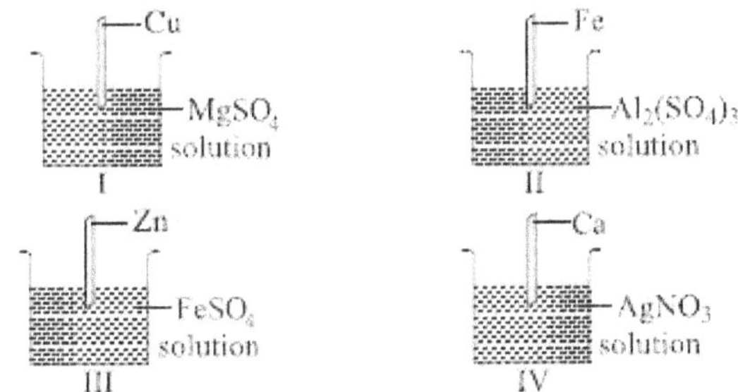


No reaction will take place in beaker(s)

    (a) II only

    (b) I and IV only

    (c) I and II only

    (d) III and IV only

23. Choose the correct sequence of components of crude oil after fractional distillation of petroleum from top to bottom.
    (a) Residue, Gasoline, Petroleum gases, Kerosene, Diesel oil.
    (b) Petroleum gases, Gasoline, Diesel oil, Kerosene, Residue.
    (c) Petroleum gases, Gasoline, Kerosene, Diesel oil, Residue.
    (d) Petroleum gases, Kerosene, Gasoline, Diesel oil, Residue.

24. Coal is fossil fuel and it cannot be prepared in a laboratory or industry because the formation of coal
    1. is a very slow process.
    2. needs very low pressure and low temperature.
    3. needs very high pressure and high temperature.
    4. causes air pollution.
    Select the correct alternative
    (a) 1 and 2          (b) 2 and 4
    (c) 1 and 3          (d) 4 and 3

25. Swati tries an experiment with five different metals namely sodium, magnesium, zinc, iron and copper in five different test tubes.

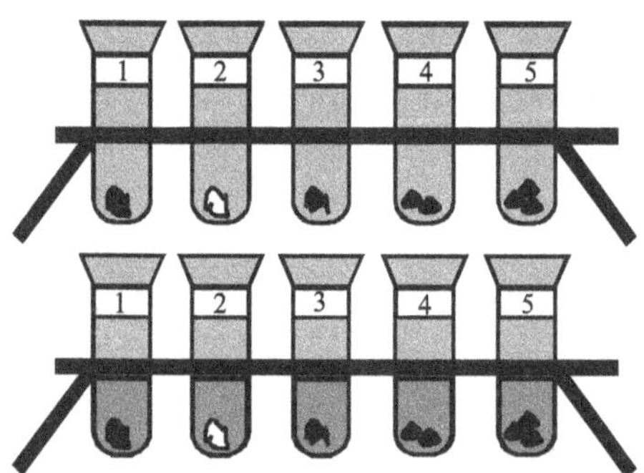

She added 5 ml of water in each test tube. Swati observed that hydrogen gas is evolved in test tube 3, only when it was boiled. Test tube 3 contains only ______.
    (a) Zn              (b) Na
    (c) Mg              (d) Cu

26. Students were carrying out an experiment in the laboratory. However, the teacher strictly instructed the students not to heat alcohol directly on flame. Why do you think the teacher gave such an instruction?
    (a) The temperature of the flame is not high enough to heat alcohol.
    (b) Alcohol is highly inflammable.
    (c) The heat of the flame is sufficient enough to overcome the ignition temperature of alcohol and it can easily catch fire.
    (d) Both (b) and (c)

27. Divya sets up an electric circuit by using copper wire.
    She repeated the experiment with different objects :
    I → Aluminium foil, II → Iron nail, III → Coal, IV → Graphite.
    In which cases the bulb will light up?

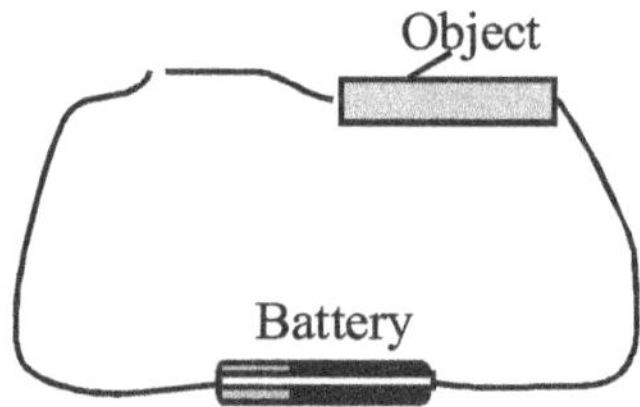


    (a) I and II only   (b) II and IV only
    (c) I, II and IV    (d) All of these

28. Polycot is obtained by mixing
    (a) nylon and wool
    (b) polyester and wool
    (c) nylon and cotton
    (d) polyester and cotton

29. Match the items given in column A with those given in column B.

| **Column-A** | **Column-B** |
|---|---|
| (i) Present in Natural gas | (p) $CO_2$ |
| (ii) Carbon dioxide gas | (q) $CH_4$ |
| (iii) Present in chalk,marble and limestone | (r) Obtained by heating sodium bicarbonate |
| (iv) Used as 'dry ice' | (s) Carbon and oxygen |

(a) (i) - (q), (ii) - (r), (iii) - (p), (iv) - (s)
(b) (i) - (q), (ii) - (r), (iii) - (s), (iv) - (p)
(c) (i) - (r), (ii) - (q), (iii) - (p), (iv) - (s)
(d) (i) - (p), (ii) - (r), (iii) - (s), (iv) - (q)

30. When you introduce a glass plate into the luminous zone of a candle flame for a few seconds, the observation is as shown in figure (b).

What does the observation indicate?

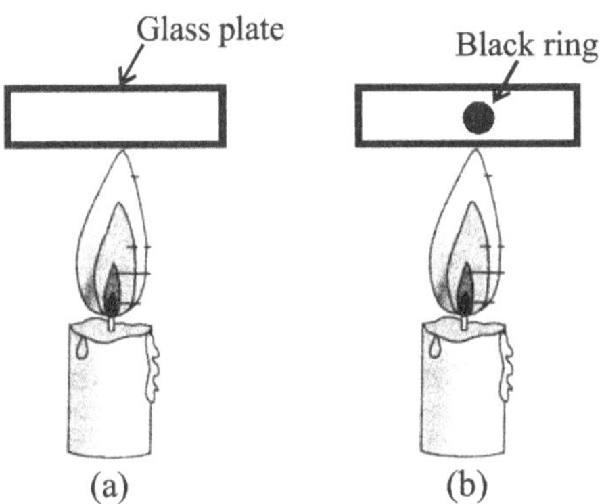


(a) Deposition of burnt $CO_2$ particles present in the air around the flame.

(b) Deposition of unburnt carbon particles in the luminous zone of the flame.

(c) Deposition of molten wax.

(d) All of these

31. The substances which have very low ignition temperature will

(a) Catch fire easily

(b) Will not catch fire

(c) Catch fire after some time

(d) None of these

## BIOLOGY

32. The term 'aquaculture' means:

(a) Aspergillosis

(b) Marine fisheries

(c) Inland fisheries

(d) (b) and (c) both

33. Buffer stock refers to

(a) the grains stocked for emergencies.

(b) the grains to be exported.

(c) the grains having high nutritive value.

(d) the grains having low nutritive value.

34. The practice of growing a cereal crop and the pulse crop alternately in the same field in successive season is called ....................

(a) crop rotation

(b) harvesting

(c) winnowing

(d) threshing

35. Which practices are examples of an integrated cultivation system?

(i) Breeding livestock in oil palm plantations.

(ii) Breeding small fishes in paddy fields.

(iii) Planting many types of crops in a small area.

(a) (i) and (ii)

(b) (i) and (iii)

(c) (ii) and (iii)

(d) (i), (ii) and (iii).

36. Which of the following characteristics is/are true for a virus?

I. It has a nucleus.

II. It reproduces only in living cells.

III. It contains either DNA or RNA

(a) I only     (b) I and II

(c) II and III     (d) I, II and III.

37. When fungal spores land on a piece of bread left on a table, then after a few days, the bread becomes mouldy. What conditions favour the growth of the fungus?

I. The presence of food.

II. The moist temperature.

III. The absence of water.

(a) I only     (b) I and II

(c) II and III     (d) I, II and III.

38. Which of the following are the uses of IUCN Red Data Book?

(a) Developing awareness about the importance of threatened biodiversity.

(b) Identification and documentation of endangered species.

(c) Providing a global index of the decline of biodiversity.

(d) All of these

39. How does a marine biome differ from a freshwater biome?

(a) Amount of sunlight that strikes the surface of the water.

(b) Amount of salt dissolved in the water.

(c) Amount of algae that is found in the water.

(d) The temperature of the water.

40. Where does the fusion of male and female gametes generally take place?

(a) Fallopian tube

(b) Ovary

(c) Uterus

(d) Zygote

41. The given figure is a type of microscopic cell organelle which is found in all animal cells, but is most numerous in disease-fighting cells, such as white blood cells. This is because white blood cells must digest more material than most other types of cells in their quest to battle bacteria, viruses and other foreign intruders. Identify this cell organelle.

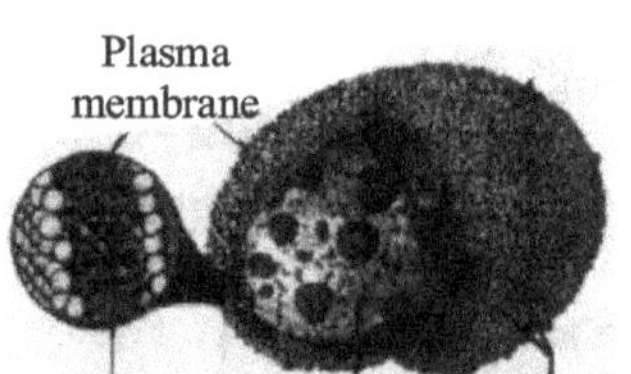

(a) Endoplasmic reticulum

(b) Mitochondria

(c) Lysosome

(d) Nucleus

42. **Statement-I :** Prokaryotes have a cell wall, eukaryotes do not.

   **Statement-II :** Prokaryotes have a true nucleus, eukaryotes have a primitive nucleus.

   (a) Both statement I and statement II are true and statement II is the correct explanation of statement I.

   (b) Both statement I and statement II are true but statement II is not the correct explanation of statement I.

   (c) Statement I is true but statement II is false.

   (d) Both statement I and statement II are false.

43. Which of the given figures represent budding in *Hydra* correctly?

   (a) 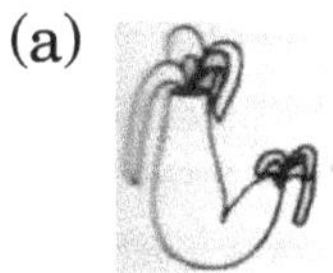       (b) 

   (c) 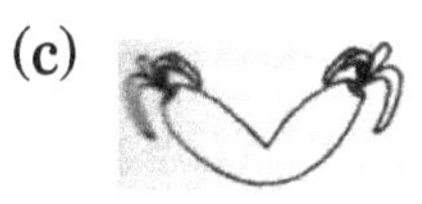       (d) 

44. Silkworm silk is the product of

   (a) salivary gland of the larva.

   (b) cutical of the adult.

   (c) cuticle of the larva.

   (d) salivary gland of the adult.

45. Which of the following is correct about placenta?

   (i) It is an intimate connection between foetal membrane and uterine wall.

   (ii) Foetal blood comes very close to the maternal blood in the placenta.

   (iii) Foetus gets nutrients, oxygen, etc, from the maternal blood and gives off wastes, $CO_2$, etc.

   (a) (ii) only        (b) (i) and (ii)

   (c) (iv) only        (d) (i), (ii) and (iii)

46. In a menstrual cycle, the duration for proliferative phase is

   (a) 1-5 days        (b) 6-13 days

   (c) 15-28 days   (d) 13-15 days

47. **Assertion:** Hormones are similar to enzymes in their action and chemical nature.

   **Reason:** Hormones and enzymes are proteinaceous in nature and act as informational molecules.

   (a) Both Assertion and Reason are true and Reason is the correct explanation of Assertion.

   (b) Both Assertion and Reason are true but Reason is not the correct explanation of Assertion.

   (c) Assertion is true but Reason is false.

   (d) Both Assertion and Reason are false.

48. Which air pollutant is wrongly matched with the effect?
    (a) Dust — reduces photosynth-esis in green plants
    (b) Carbon monoxide — reduces oxygen in the blood
    (c) Chlorofluorocarbon — damages nerves and tissues
    (d) Nicotine — hardens and narrows blood vessels.

49. Monuments of marble can be destroyed by
    (a) sulphur dioxide pollution.
    (b) carbon monoxide pollution.
    (c) pesticide pollution.
    (d) dust particles.

50. Ozone layer in upper atmosphere (stratosphere) is destroyed by –
    (a) hydrochloric acid
    (b) photochemical smog
    (c) chlorofluorocarbon (CFC)
    (d) sulphur dioxide

**Name :** _________

**Max. Marks : 50**

**Number of Questions : 50**

**Time : 2 Hours**

**There is no negative marking in the test.**

## PHYSICS

1. Which activity is not based upon friction?
   (a) Writing      (b) Speaking
   (c) Hearing      (d) Walking

2. If a body is positively changed, then it has
   (a) excess of electrons
   (b) excess of protons
   (c) deficiency of electrons
   (d) deficiency of neutrons

3. Electric current is to be passed from one body to another. For this purpose the two bodies must be joined by
   (a) cotton thread
   (b) plastic string
   (c) copper wire
   (d) rubber band

4. Suppose a new planet is discovered between Uranus and Neptune. Its time period would be
   (a) less than that of Neptune.
   (b) more than that of Neptune.
   (c) equal to that of Neptune or Uranus.
   (d) less than that of Uranus.

5. A small hole P is made in a piece of cardboard. The hole is illuminated by a torch as shown in Fig. The pencil of light coming out of the hole falls on a mirror.

At which point should the eye be placed so that the hole can be seen?
(a) A      (b) B
(c) C      (d) D

6. A dam for water reservoir is built thicker at the bottom than at the top because:
   (a) Pressure of water is very large at the bottom due to its large depth.
   (b) Water is likely to have more density at the bottom due to its large depth.
   (c) Quantity of water at the bottom is large.
   (d) None of these

7. During dry weather, while combing hair, sometimes we experience hair flying apart. The force responsible for this is
   (a) force of gravity
   (b) electrostatic force
   (c) force of friction
   (d) magnetic force

8. Which of the following are correct about different kinds of friction?
   A. When an object is at resists motion and this is due to static friction.
   B. Static friction > Sliding friction > rolling friction
   C. Roller wheels in the shoes provide a better grip and we can easily walk on the ground
   D. Friction can never be entirely eliminated.
   (a) A, B, C
   (b) A & D
   (c) A, B, D
   (d) A & C

9. A object is vibrating at 50 hertz. What is its time period?
   (a) 0.02s
   (b) 2s
   (c) 0.2s
   (d) 20.0s

10. Which of the following statements is correct about rainbow ?
    A. In primary rainbow, red colour is on the outside and violet colour is on the inside.
    B. In primary rainbow, violet colour is on the outside and red colour is on the inside.
    C. Secondary rainbow is brighter than primary rainbow.
    D. In secondary rainbow, light wave suffers one total internal reflection before coming out.
    (a) Only B
    (b) Only A
    (c) B and C
    (d) A and D

11. When an object undergoes acceleration.
    (a) its speed always increases.
    (b) its velocity always increases.
    (c) it always falls towards earth.
    (d) a force always acts on it.

12. Which of the following metals is used in electroplating to make objects appear shining?
    (a) iron
    (b) copper
    (c) chromium
    (d) aluminium

13. Sun appears to move from east to west around the earth. This means that earth rotates from
    (a) east to west
    (b) west to east
    (c) north to south
    (d) west to north

14. A nurse applies a force of 3.8 N to the syringe's piston of radius 0.9 cm. Find the increase in pressure of the fluid in the syringe?
    (a) 14.927 kPa
    (b) 469.13 Pa
    (c) 46.9 mPa
    (d) 422 Pa

15. One metallic sphere $A$ is given positive charge whereas another identical metallic sphere $B$ of exactly same mass as of $A$ is given equal amount of negative charge. Then
    (a) mass of $A$ and mass of $B$ still remain equal
    (b) mass of $A$ increases
    (c) mass of $B$ decreases
    (d) mass of $B$ increases

16. A lightning conductor installed in a building:
    (a) Does not allow the lightning to fall on the building
    (b) Repels the lightning
    (c) Forces the lightning to fall in an area where there are no building
    (d) Conducts electric charge to the ground when lightning strikes the building.

17. A ray of light is incident on a plane mirror at an angle of incidence of 30°. The deviation produced by the mirror is
 (a) 90°          (b) 120°
 (c) 30°          (d) 60°

18. Two objects repel each other. This repulsion could be due to
 (a) frictional force only
 (b) electrostatic force only
 (c) magnetic force only
 (d) either a magnetic or an electrostatic force

19. A constant horizontal force is applied to a body initially at rest on a smooth horizontal table. Which of the following quantities will not change during the application of force?
 (a) The position of the body
 (b) The acceleration of the body
 (c) The velocity of the body
 (d) None of these

## CHEMISTRY

20. Reactivity series gives
 (a) arrangement of metals in the order of decreasing reactivity.
 (b) arrangement of non-metals in the order of decreasing reactivity.
 (c) arrangement of metals in the order of increasing reactivity.
 (d) arrangement of non-metals in the order of increasing reactivity.

21. Which of the following is true for plastics?
 (a) Like synthetic fibres, plastics are also polymers.
 (b) Thermo-plastics are harder and stronger than thermosetting plastics.
 (c) Bakelite is a thermoplastic.
 (d) None of the above is correct.

22. Which of the following is example of spontaneous combustion?
 (a) Burning of matchstick
 (b) Combustion of fuel by motor vehicles.
 (c) Lightning of kerosene lamp.
 (d) Combustion of coal dust in coal mines.

23. Read the following statements and mark the correct ones from the given options.
 (i) Coal, petroleum and natural gas are called fossil fuels.
 (ii) Coal and natural gas are two exhaustible substances.
 (iii) Coke is used in manufacture of steel.
 (iv) Fossil fuels are present in limited quantities.
 (a) (i) and (ii)
 (b) (i) and (iv)
 (c) (i), (ii) and (iii)
 (d) (i), (ii), (iii) and (iv)

24. Fill the boxes with appropriate options

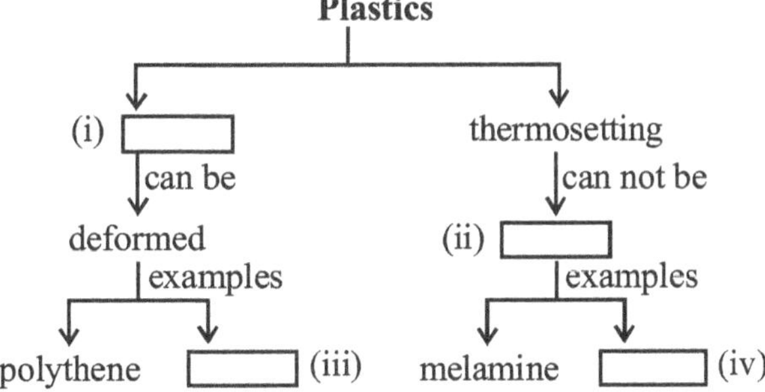

|     | (i) | (ii) | (iii) | (iv) |
|-----|-----|------|-------|------|
| (a) | Non- | Formed | Bakellite | PVC reactive |
| (b) | Thermoplastic | Remoulded | PVC | Bakelite |
| (c) | Cross linked | Manufactured | Polycot | PVC |
| (d) | Thermoplastic | Formed | Silk | Polywood |

25. Match List I (fraction of petroleum) with List II (main uses) and select the correct answer from the given alternatives.

**List I (fraction of petroleum)**  **List II (main uses)**

(i)  Kerosene            (p)  Metalling of roads
(ii) Diesel              (q)  Jet aircraft fuel
(iii)Paraffin wax        (r)  Generation of electricity
(iv)Bitumen             (s)  Lubricants

(a)  (i) - (p), (ii) - (q), (iii) - (r), (iv) - (s)      (b)  (i) - (p), (ii) - (r), (iii) - (s), (iv) - (q)
(c)  (i) - (q), (ii) - (r), (iii) - (s), (iv) - (p)      (d)  (i) - (s), (ii) - (q), (iii) - (r), (iv) - (p)

26. When a candle burns in air, two processes take place. First the change A takes place and then the change B. The following statements correspond to these changes. Choose the correct one.
(a) Process A is chemical change.
(b) Process B is a chemical change.
(c) Both processes A and B are chemical changes.
(d) Process A is a chemical change whereas process B is a physical change.

27. Study the table carefully and select the appropriate options.

| Sample | Conductor of electricity | Malleability | Lustrous |
|--------|--------------------------|--------------|----------|
| W | ✓ | ✓ | ✓ |
| X | ✓ | ✗ | ✓ |
| Y | ✓ | ✗ | ✗ |
| Z | ✓ | ✗ | ✓ |

|     | W | X | Y | Z |
|-----|---|---|---|---|
| (a) | Potassium | Sodium | Graphite | Aluminium |
| (b) | Graphite | Aluminium | Sodium | Potassium |
| (c) | Sodium | Aluminium | Potassium | Graphite |
| (d) | Aluminium | Sodium | Graphite | Potassium |

28. Metals generally react with dilute acids to produce hydrogen gas. Which one of the following metals doesnot react with dilute hydrochloric acid?
(a) Magnesium
(b) Aluminium
(c) Iron
(d) Copper

29. What are X, Y and Z?

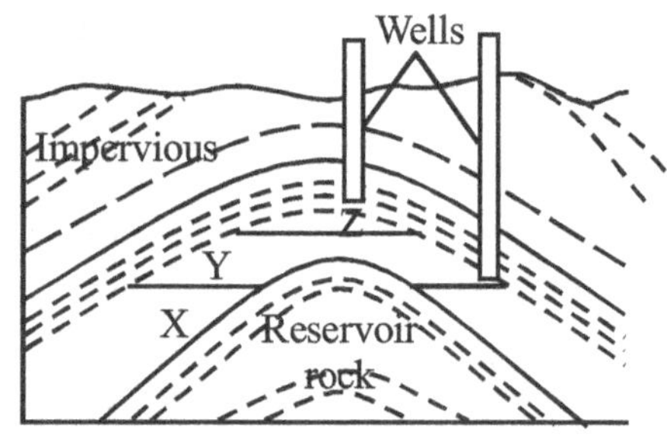


|     | X | Y | Z |
|-----|---|---|---|
| (a) | Water | Oil | Gas |
| (b) | Oil | Water | Gas |
| (c) | Water | Gas | Oil |
| (d) | Gas | Oil | Water |

30. **Assertion :** On combing hair with a nylon comb, it gets charged and starts attracting small pieces of papers.

**Reason :** Synthetic fibres do not generate electric charge.

(a) If both assertion and reason are true and reason is the correct explanation of assertion.

(b) If both assertion and reason are true but reason is not the correct explanation of assertion.

(c) If assertion is true but reason is false.

(d) If assertion is false but reason is true.

31. Which of the following diagrams shows a non-luminous flame?

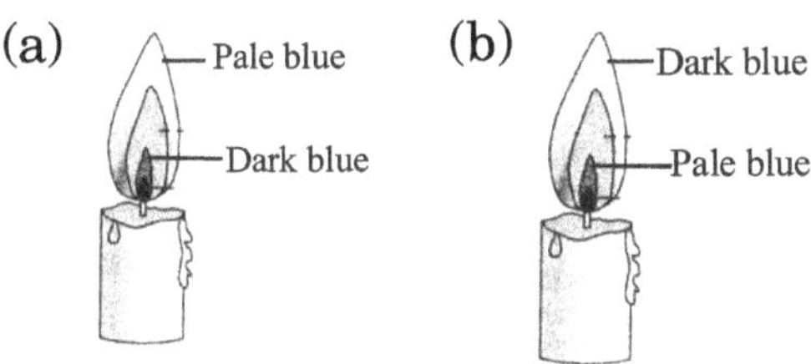


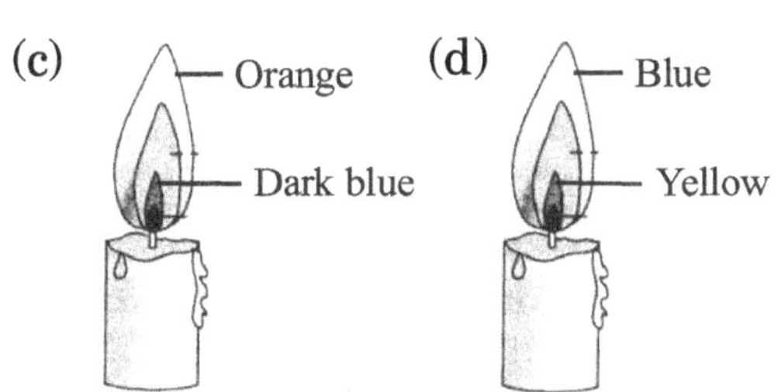


## BIOLOGY

32. Which of the following plants are used as green manure in crop fields and in sandy soils –

(a) *Dicanthium annulatum* and Azolla pinnata

(b) *Crotalaria junecea* and *Alhagi camelorum*

(c) *Calotropis procera* and *Pitylanthus niruri*

(d) *Saccharum munja* and *Lantana camara*

**DIRECTIONS (Qs. 33) :** Read the passage given below and answer the questions that follow.

### PASSAGE

Plough is made of wood and iron. It is drawn by a pair of bulls or other animals. It contains a strong triangular iron strip called ploughshare. The main part of the plough is a long log of wood which is called ploughshaft. The plough is used for tilling the soil, adding fertilisers to the crop, removing the weeds and scraping of soil.

33. The advantage of ploughing is:

(a) It allows penetration of root of plants.

(b) It helps in proparation and eradicates weeds.

(c) It promotes the growth of useful bacteria.

(d) All of these.

34. Read the following pairs of examples of organisms.

The pair that belongs to the group prokaryotes is —————.

(a) Moss and Sponge

(b) Yeast and Amoeba

(c) Bacteria and blue-green alga

(d) Penicillium and Spirogyra

35. How do bacteria help our bodies to function?

(a) They make our muscles and lungs stronger.

(b) They help to digest food in the intestines.

(c) They circulate in our blood and help carry oxygen.

(d) They make our skin flexible and clean.

36. What do black buck, elephant, python and golden cat together represent in a forest?
    (a) fauna
    (b) flora
    (c) ecosystem
    (d) species
37. Species native to a particular habitat is known as:
    (a) Endemic species
    (b) Endangered species
    (c) Threatened species
    (d) Extinct species
38. Which of the following describes the characteristics of tundra?
    (a) Warm climate and high humidity.
    (b) Open landscape and seasonal rainfall.
    (c) Mild climate and warm summers.
    (d) Low temperature and low precipitation.
39. Which of the following statements is correct about plasma membrane?
    (a) It allows all substances to pass into and out of cells.
    (b) It prevents all substances from passing into and out of cell.
    (c) It is composed mainly of a protein bilayer.
    (d) It is composed mainly of a lipid bilayer.
40. The characteristic of a nerve cell that relates directly to its function is its
    (a) long extensions
    (b) flat shape
    (c) ability to change shape
    (d) ability to engulf bacteria
41. The organ that helps in releasing sperms in female body is _____
    (a) vas deference.
    (b) penis.
    (c) testes.
    (d) scrotum.
42. Clone Dolly was produced by the attempts of
    (a) Charles Darwin
    (b) Lederberg
    (c) Ian Wilmut
    (d) Alexander Fleming.
43. Rupturing of follicles and discharge of ova is known as
    (a) copulation
    (b) conjugation
    (c) ovulation
    (d) oviposition
44. An advantage of excreting nitrogenous wastes in the form of uric acid is that –
    (1) Uric acid can be excreted in almost solid form
    (2) The formation of uric acid requires a great deal of energy
    (3) Uric acid is the first metabolic breakdown products of acids
    (4) Uric acid may be excreted through the lungs

45.

| Column I | Column II |
|---|---|
| A. Amla | P. Sodium benzoate |
| B. Vegetables | Q. Drying |
| C. Squashes | R. Cooling |
| D. Spices | S. Oil and vinegar |
| E. Ketchups | T. Sugar |
| | U. Salt |

(a) A → P, B → Q, C → R, D → S, E → T
(b) A → U, B → S, C → T, D → Q, E → P
(c) A → Q, B → P, C → T, D → U, E → S
(d) A → S, B → R, C → P, D → U, E → Q

46. A poisonous gas emitted by Mathura Refinery and other industries in and around Taj which causes acid rain is
    (a) carbon monoxide.
    (b) methane.
    (c) sulphur dioxide.
    (d) oxygen.

47. What is/are the effect(s) of discharging excess heat from electrical power stations into rivers and lakes?
    I.   The biological oxygen demand value of the water decreases.
    II.  Instant death of certain organisms.
    III. The concentration of dissolved oxygen increases.
    (a) I only          (b) II only
    (c) III only        (d) I, II and III.

48. **Assertion :** $CO_2$ controls the earth's heat balance.
    **Reason :** $CO_2$ has caused global warming.
    (a) Both Assertion and Reason are true and Reason is the correct explanation of Assertion
    (b) Both Assertion and Reason are true but Reason is not the correct explanation of Assertion
    (c) Assertion is true but Reason is false
    (d) Both Assertion and Reason are false.

49. Which one out of the following sets of figures correctly depicts reproduction in *Amoeba* and yeast?
    (a)

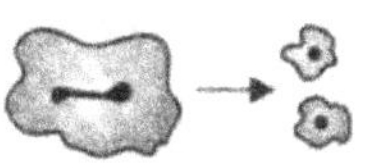

Budding in *Amoeba*

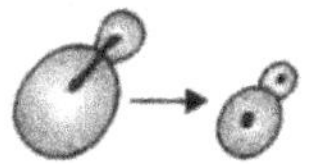

Binary fission in yeast

    (b)

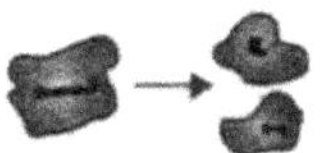

Binary fission in *Amoeba*

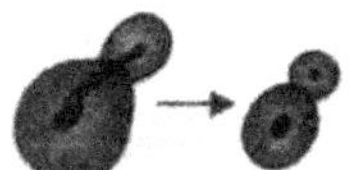

Budding in yeast

    (c)

Binary fission in *Amoeba*

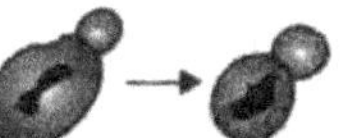

Budding in yeast

    (d)

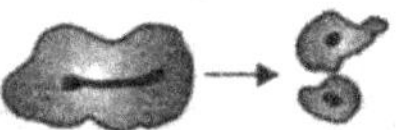

Budding in *Amoeba*

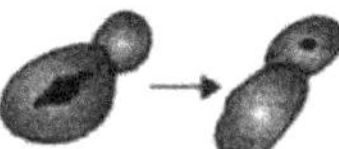

Binary fission in yeast

50. Which of the following pairs are incorrectly matched?
    (i)   Protoplasm – Purkinje
    (ii)  Discovery of cell - Leeuwenhoek
    (iii) Cell theory – Schleiden
    (iv)  *Omnis cellula-e-cellula* – Virchow
    (v)   Discovery of electron microscope – 1930
    (vi)  Black reaction – a Cajal
    (a) (ii), (v) and (vi)
    (b) (i), (v) and (vi)
    (c) (ii) and (iv)
    (d) (ii) and (vi).

# OLYMPIAD
# Mock Test 3

**Name :** __________

**Max. Marks : 50**

**Number of Questions : 50**

**Time : 2 Hours**

**There is no negative marking in the test.**



1. Which one is not a source of electric current?

   A. 

   B. 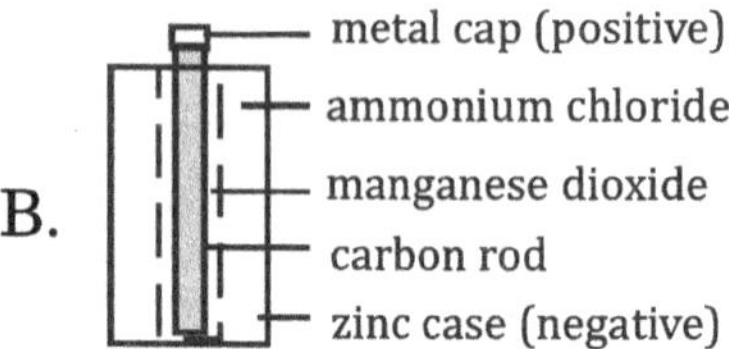
   

   C. 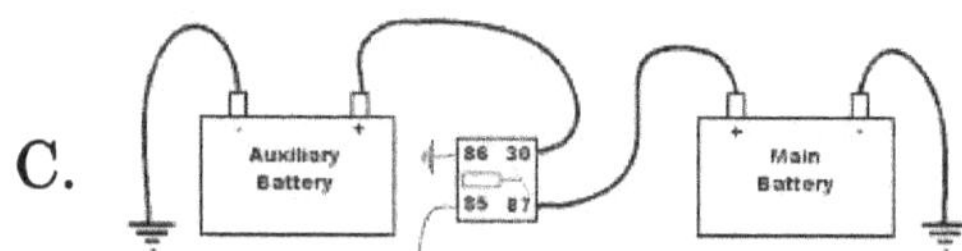
   

   D. 

   (a) A     (b) B

   (c) C     (d) D

2. The given figure is the part of the human ear. The human ear is divided into three parts. Identify the parts of the ear given in the figure below

   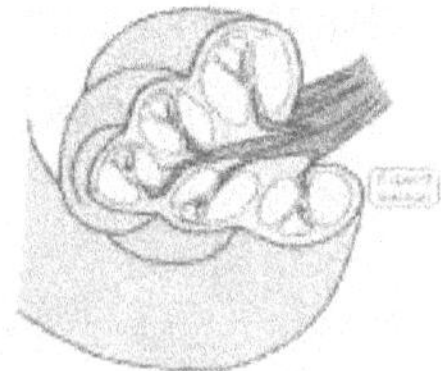

   (a) Tympanum
   (b) Anvil
   (c) Cochlea
   (d) Auditory nerve

3. Which of the following is not likely to cause Tsunami?

   (a) A major nuclear explosion under sea
   (b) Earthquake
   (c) Volcanic eruption
   (d) Lightning

4. The pitch of sound depends on:

   (a) Frequency
   (b) Amplitude
   (c) Both of these
   (d) None of these

5. When electric current is passed through a conducting solution, there is a change of colour of the solution. This indicates
   (a) the chemical effect of current
   (b) the heating effect of current
   (c) the magnetic effect of current
   (d) the lightning effect of current

6. When we say' sound travels in a medium', we mean
   (a) the particles of the medium travel.
   (b) the source travels.
   (c) the disturbance travels.
   (d) the medium travels.

7. 'Asteroids' are found between the orbit of :
   (a) Jupiter and Saturn
   (b) Earth and Mars
   (c) Mars and Jupiter
   (d) Venus and Earth

8. It is difficult to move a cycle with brakes on road because
   (a) Rolling friction opposes motion on road
   (b) Sliding friction opposes motion on road
   (c) Rolling friction is more than sliding friction
   (d) None of these

9. Karan's uncle has set up an electroplating factory near his village. He should dispose off the waste of the factory
   (a) in the nearby river.
   (b) in the nearby pond.
   (c) in the nearby cornfield.
   (d) according to the disposal guidelines of the local authority.

10. Two mirror A and B are placed at right angles to each other as shown in Fig.

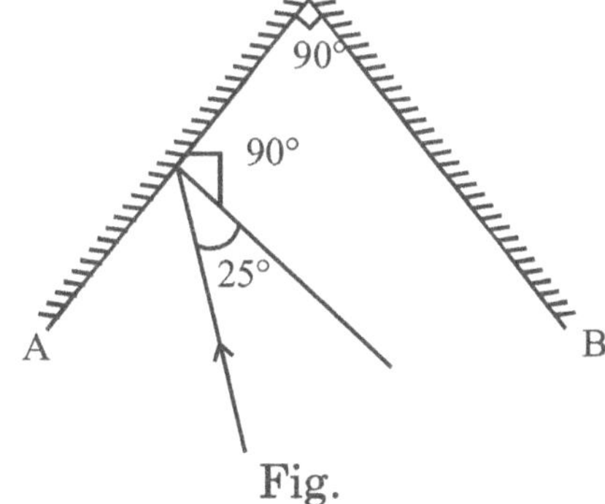

Fig.

A ray of light incident on mirror A at an angle of 25° falls on mirror B after reflection. The angle of reflection for the ray reflected from mirror B would be
   (a) 25°              (b) 50°
   (c) 65°              (d) 115°

11. Figure shown is of a metal blade fixed at one end. B is the mean position, while A and C are the extreme positions of the blade when it is vibrated. If the frequency of the note produced by the blade is 640 Hz and the velocity of sound in air is 320 m/s calculate the wavelength of the sound waves produced.

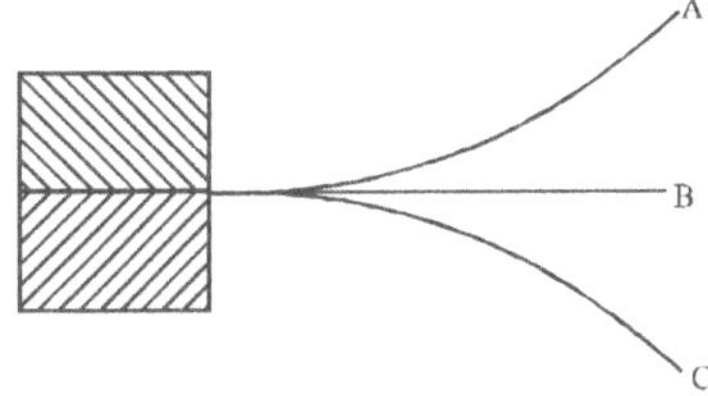


   (a) 0.5m             (b) 2m
   (c) 1m               (d) 4m

12. Which of the following statements describes the best thing to do during heavy lightning?

    (a) Lying on the ground in an open place.

    (b) Going into the nearest water body.

    (c) Staying indoors away from metallic doors or windows.

    (d) Standing under a tall tree.

13. The diagram below shows three neutral metal spheres, $x$, $y$, and $z$, in contact and on insulating stands. Which diagram best represents the charge distribution on the spheres when a positively charged rod is brought near sphere $x$, but does not touch it?

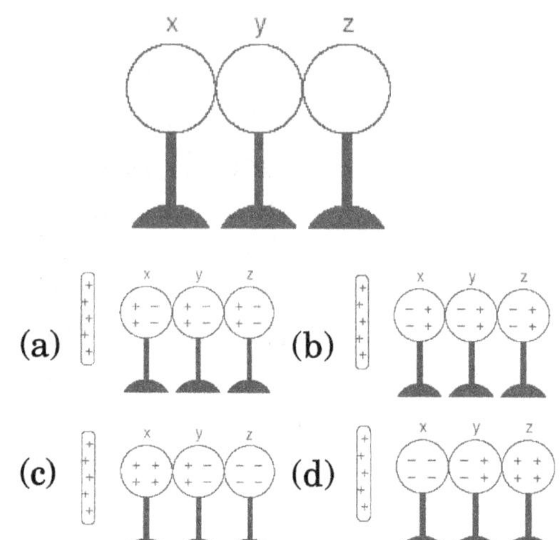

14. Adding common salt to distilled water makes it:

    (a) good conductor

    (b) insulator

    (c) semiconductor

    (d) both (a) and (b)

15. A ray of light is incident on a plane mirror at an angle of incidence 40°. The ray, after reflection, is deviated through

    (a) 30°          (b) 60°

    (c) 90°          (d) 100°

16. An unbalanced force acts on a body. The body

    (a) must remain at rest.

    (b) must move with uniform velocity.

    (c) must be accelerated.

    (d) must move along a circle.

17. We can see a non-luminous object when light

    (a) emitted by the object falls on the eye.

    (b) is reflected from the object towards our eye.

    (c) completely passes through the object.

    (d) gets completely absorbed by the object.

18. By applying a force of one newton, one can hold a body of mass

    (a) 102 grams

    (b) 102 kg

    (c) 102 mg

    (d) None of these

19. When the axle rotates in a sleeve, the friction involved in the process is :

    (a) sliding

    (b) rolling

    (c) static

    (d) None of these

## CHEMISTRY

20. Select the one that could displace copper from a solution of copper sulphate.

    (a) Silver          (b) Mercury

    (c) Tin          (d) Gold

21. Butane gas is used for filling cylinders to be used as LPG because

    (a) it is easily available.

    (b) it is easily compressed into liquid and stored in cylinders.

    (c) it is stored in gaseous state only in the cylinder.

    (d) it is the cheapest gas available.

22. Why is it not advisable to wear synthetic clothes while bursting fire crackers?

    (i) All synthetic fibres are prepared by using raw materials of petroleum origin.

    (ii) Synthetic fibres catch fire easily.

    (iii) On heating, synthetic fibres melt and stick to the body of the person wearing it.

    (a) (i) only              (b) (ii) only

    (c) (i) and (iii)         (d) (ii) and (iii)

23. **Assertion :** Kerosene is not a fossil fuel.

    **Reason:** Kerosene is obtained by fractional distillation of petroleum.

    (a) If both assertion and reason are true and reason is the correct explanation of assertion.

    (b) If both assertion and reason are true but reason is not the correct explanation of assertion.

    (c) If assertion is true but reason is false.

    (d) If assertion is false but reason is true.

24. Shyam was cooking potato curry on a chulha. To his surprise he observed that the copper vessel was getting blackened from outside. It may be due to:

    (a) Proper combustion of fuel.

    (b) Improper cooking of potato curry.

    (c) Improper combustion of the fuel.

    (d) Burning of copper vessel.

25. Rayon is different from synthetic fibres because

    (a) it has a silk like appearance

    (b) it is obtained from wood pulp

    (c) its fibres can also be woven like those of natural fibres

    (d) none of the above

26. Which of the following will take place in the given figure?

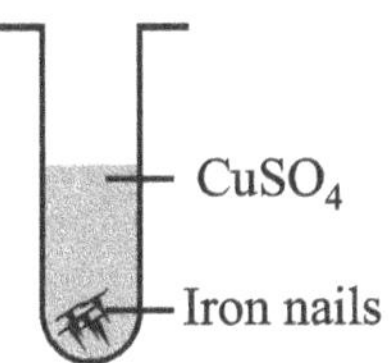


    (a) Iron displaces oxygen from $CuSO_4$.

    (b) Iron displaces Cu from $CuSO_4$.

    (c) Iron displaces S from $CuSO_4$.

    (d) No reaction takes place

27. Y is formed when X is heated in absence of air. Y is tough, porous and black substance. Both X and Y are carbon-rich materials. What could X and Y be?

(a) X = Coal, Y = Coke

(b) X = Petroleum, Y = Petrol

(c) X = Coal, Y = Coal tar

(d) X = Petroleum, Y = Diesel

28. Match the following Column (I and II) and choose the correct option from the codes given below the columns :

| **Column I** | | **Column II** | |
|---|---|---|---|
| 1. | Rapid combustion | (p) | Materials get ignited without any apparent cause |
| 2. | Spontaneous combustion | (q) | Fuel burns rapidly and produces heat and light |
| 3. | Explosion | (r) | Fire extinguisher |
| 4. | Sodium carbonate | (s) | Evolution of large amount of heat, light and sound |

(a) 1 - (q), 2 - (p), 3 - (s), 4 - (r)     (b)    1 - (p), 2 - (q), 3 - (r), 4 - (s)

(c) 1 - (r), 2 - (s), 3 - (q), 4 - (p)     (d)    1 - (s), 2 - (r), 3 - (q), 4 - (p)

29. In the fractional distillation of crude petroleum –

(a) Petrol condenses at the bottom of the column.

(b) The gases condense at the top of the column.

(c) High boiling constituents condense at the bottom of the column.

(d) High boiling constituents condense at the top of the column.

30. An alternative for expensive plastic recycling is

(a) reduce recycling plastic

(b) reduce usage of plastic

(c) developing of biodegradable plastics

(d) All of the above

31. A greenish deposit on the surface of copper vessel is chemically a mixture of ........ .

(a) $Cu(OH)_2$ and $CuO$

(b) $CuO$ and $CuCO_3$

(c) $Cu_2O$ and $CuO$

(d) $Cu(OH)_2$ and $CuCO_3$

### BIOLOGY

32. Organic farming is

(a) a farming with minimal or no use of chemical fertilizers, pesticides etc.

(b) a farming system where organic compounds are used

(c) a farming system in which organic manures, biofertilizers, biopesticides etc, are used

(d) both (a) and (c).

33. Cultivation of *Bt* cotton has been much the news. The prefix *"Bt"* means –

    (a) "Barium-treated" cotton seeds

    (b) "Bigger thread" variety of cotton with better tensile strength

    (c) Production by "biotechnology" using restriction enzymes and ligases

    (d) Carrying an endotoxin gene from *Bacillus thuringiensis*

34. Which of these is the correct sequence of steps to develop a new plant variety?

    P- Evaluation

    Q- Multiplication of improved seeds

    R- Selection

    S- Distribution of improved seeds

    T- Development of gene variation

    (a) T, R, P, Q, S

    (b) R, T, P, Q, S

    (c) S, Q, P, R, T

    (d) P, Q, R, T, S

35. In the list of animals given below, hen is the odd one out.

    Human being , cow , dog , hen The reason for this is

    (a) it undergoes internal fertilization

    (b) it is oviparous

    (c) it is viviparous

    (d) it undergoes external fertilization

36. Match column-I with Column-II and select the correct answer using the code given below the columns.

    **Column-I**       **Column-II**

    (A) Urea           (p) Harvesting and threshing

    (B) Combine        (q) Sowing of seeds

    (C) Seed drills    (r) Sprinklers

    (D) Irrigation     (s) Fertilizers

    (a) A-(q), B-(s), C-(r), D-(p)

    (b) A-(s), B-(r), C-(q), D-(p)

    (c) A-(p), B-(q), C-(r), D-(s)

    (d) A-(s), B-(p), C-(q), D-(r)

37. Which methods are used in the seafood industry to prevent the growth of decomposer bacteria so that the products can be preserved?

    I.   Drying

    II.  Using common salt

    III. Freezing.

    (a) I and II          (b) I and III

    (c) II and III        (d) I, II and III.

38. **Assertion :** Bacterial cell walls are not like the plant cell.

    **Reason :** Bacterial cell wall is not made up of cellulose.

    (a) both Assertion and Reason are true and Reason is the correct explanation of Assertion

    (b) both Assertion and Reason are true but Reason is not the correct explanation of Assertion

    (c) Assertion is true but Reason is false

    (d) both Assertion and Reason are false.

39. A man was infested with germs and was taken to the hospital. On pathological tests, it was found that he had

A. Low number of RBC

B. High number of WBC

C. Low number of WBC

D. High number of platelets

Which of the above statements are correct?

(a) A and B          (b) A and D

(c) C alone          (d) D alone.

40.

Which disease is caused by this agent?

(a) Typhoid          (b) Pneumonia

(c) Diarrhoea        (d) Influenza

41. Given below are some possible reasons for a sharp decline in population of the species given in figure. Which of the following are correct?

(i)   Cleared forests
(ii)  Flooded large areas
(iii) Polluted air and water
(iv)  Scarcity of food

(a) (i) and (ii)

(b) (i) and (iv)

(c) (i), (ii) and (iv)

(d) (i), (ii), (iii) and (iv)

42. A habitat change may result in the decline of the numbers of a given species. Such species slowly become P. This means that the species are on the verge of becoming Q. Some animals whose number has gone down to critically low levels are called R. A species is considered S when no member of the species is still alive.

Which of the following is correct sequence for P, Q, R and S in the above paragraph?

| | P | Q | R | S |
|---|---|---|---|---|
| (a) | Vulnerable | Endemic | Extinct | Endangered |
| (b) | Endangered | Vulnerable | Threatened | Extinct |
| (c) | Vulnerable | Endangered | Critically endangered | Extinct |
| (d) | Endangered | Critically endangered | Extinct | Vulnerable |

43. Which of the following matches is incorrect?

| | Organelle | Function | Presence |
|---|---|---|---|
| (a) | Ribosome | Secretion of enzymes | Plant & animal cell |

    (b) Mitochondria    Site of      Animal cell
                        respiration   only
    (c) Chloroplast     Storage     Plant cell
                        cell sap

    (d) All of the above.

44. Which of the following is incorrect regarding genes?

    (i) They control the tansfer of hereditary characteristics.

    (ii) Nucleolus carry genes.

    (iii) They are part of chromosome.

    (iv) They are found only in the nucleus.

    (a) (iii) & (iv)        (b) (iii) only

    (c) (i) only           (d) (ii) & (iv).

45. **Assertion** : Test tube baby technology is called *in vivo* fertilization.

    **Reason :** It involves fertilization of ova and sperm inside the human body.

    (a) Both Assertion and Reason are true and Reason is the correct explanation of Assertion

    (b) Both Assertion and Reason are true but Reason is not the correct explanation of Assertion

    (c) Assertion is true but Reason is false

    (d) Both Assertion and Reason are false.

46. The number of nymphs that come out from an egg case (ootheca) of a cockroach is generally

    (a) twelve.          (c) ten.

    (c) fourteen.       (d) sixteen.

47. Which of the following describes moulting ?

    (a) The resting stage in the life cycle of a silkworm.

    (b) Change in appearance during the different stages in the life cycle of a silkworm.

    (c) Spinning of cocoon.

    (d) Casting off old skin.

48. Global warming causes

    I. An increase in the sea level.

    II. The melting of ice at mountain peaks.

    III. A decrease in food production by plants.

    (a) I only         (b) I and II

    (c) II and III    (d) I, II and III.

49. Pollution from the burning of fossil fuels can be reduced by:

    I. Using an incinerator

    II. Using renewable energy

    III. Fixing catalytic converters in vehicles.

    (a) I only         (b) II and III

    (c) I and III     (d) I, II and III.

50. A layer of air known as the atmosphere surrounds the earth. The composition of the atmosphere can be changed by air pollution. Which of the following statements about air pollution are correct?

    (i) It affects the weather.

    (ii) It covers the leaves of plants and limits photosynthesis.

    (iii) It may cause breathing difficulties and diseases of the respiratory tract.

    (iv) It is mostly caused by the burning of fossil fuels.

    (a) (iii) and (iv)

    (b) (i), (ii) and (iii)

    (c) (i), (iii) and (iv)

    (d) (i), (ii), (iii) and (iv).

# OLYMPIAD
# Mock Test 4

**Name :** __________          **Max. Marks : 50**

**Number of Questions : 50**          **Time : 2 Hours**

**There is no negative marking in the test.**

## PHYSICS

1. A moving object can come to rest only if it
   (a) has a frictional force acting on it
   (b) has no net force acting on it
   (c) is completely isolated
   (d) applies an impulse to something else

2. If the force on the surface is doubled and area reduced to half, pressure will
   (a) becomes 2 times
   (b) becomes 3 times
   (c) becomes 4 times
   (d) remains unchanged

3. Major earthquakes are less likely to occur in
   (a) North-East India
   (b) Rjasthan
   (c) Rann of Kutch
   (d) Odisha

4. Name the resin which produce spark is:
   (a) Gum
   (b) Amber
   (c) Both (a) and (b)
   (d) None of these

5. The process of bending of seven colours is called:
   (a) Dispersion      (b) Spectrum
   (c) Reflection      (d) Normal

6. Phases of the moon occur because:
   (a) We can see only that part of the moon which reflects light towards us.
   (b) Our distance from the moon keeps changing.
   (c) The shadow of the Earth covers only a part of the moon's surface.
   (d) The thickness of the moon's atmosphere is not constant.

7. A sound wave consists of
   (a) a number of compression pulses one after the other.
   (b) a number of rarefaction pulses one after the other.
   (c) compression and rarefaction pulses one after the other.
   (d) a compression and a rarefaction pulse separated by a distance equal to one wavelength.

8. Fig. shows a container filled with water. Which of the following statements is correct about pressure of water?

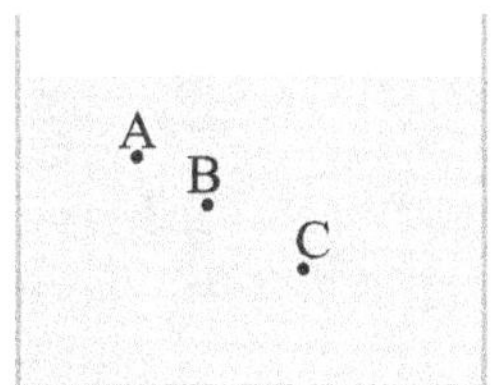

(a) Pressure at A> Pressure at B> Pressure at C

(b) Pressure at A= Pressure at B = Pressure at C

(c) Pressure at A< Pressure at B > Pressure at C

(d) Pressure at A< Pressure at B < Pressure at C

9. Why do we move faster on roller-skates than on shoes, which of the following statements gives proper reasons?

(a) The roller-skates have rollers to reduce friction.

(b) The roller-skates have more surface in contact with the ground.

(c) The roller-skates have no gravitational force.

(d) The roller-skates absorb heat from the ground.

10. If no force acts on a body, it will

(a) get deshaped.

(b) move with increasing speed.

(c) either remain at rest or move in a straight line.

(d) break.

11. A scientist performed an experiment as shown in the figure here.

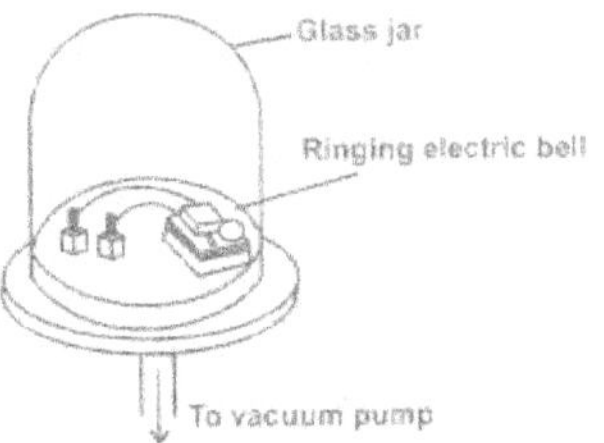


What do you think happened as air was pumped out of the jar and the electric bell rang?

(a) The sound became louder.

(b) The sound became fainter first and then louder once all the air was pumped out.

(c) The sound could not be heard anymore.

(d) The sound was the same as before.

12. The force of friction on a body kept on the surface of a table does not depend upon:

(a) The nature of the surface

(b) The weight of the body

(c) The area of contact

(d) All of these

13. A water tank has four taps fixed at points A, B, C, D as shown in Fig. . The water will flow out at the same pressure from taps at

(a) B and C      (b) A and B
(c) C and D      (d) A and C

14. Match the column :

**Column-I**    **Column-II**

A. Mercury    P. Negatively charged
B. Cathode    Q. Electrical Switches
C. Petrol    R. Conduction
D. Bakelite    S. Poor Conductor

(a) A → R, B → P, C → S; D → Q
(b) A → P, B → R, C → S, D → Q
(c) A → R, B → P, C → Q, D → S
(d) A → P, B → R, C → Q, D → S

15. When a body is stationary
(a) there is no force acting on it.
(b) the force acting on it not in contact with it.
(c) the combination of forces acting on it balances each other.
(d) the body is in vacuum.

16. If we apply oil on door hinges, the friction will
(a) increase
(b) decrease
(c) disappear altogether
(d) will remain unchanged

17. Consider the list of terms given below
(i) Tsunami    (ii) Landslide
(iii) Floods    (iv) Lightning
Earthquakes can cause
(a) (i) & (ii)    (b) (ii) & (iv)
(c) (ii), (iii) & (iv) (d) (iii) & (iv)

18. The force of friction between two bodies is
(a) parallel to the contact surface.
(b) perpendicular to the contact surface.
(c) inclined at 30° to the contact surface.
(d) inclined at 60° to the contact surface.

19. By applying force of 5 N, one can hold a body whose mass is approximately equal to

(a) 100 mg    (b) 500 g
(c) 1 kg    (d) 10 kg

## CHEMISTRY

20. Match the following Column-I and Column-II and choose the correct option

**Column-I**    **Column-II**

(i) Acrylic    (p) Contains repeating ester units
(ii) Cellulose    (q) Used for making sweaters
(iii) Polythene    (r) Made up of large number of glucose units
(iv) Terylene    (s) Used for making electrical switches
   (t) Used for manufacturing toys

(a) (i) - (q), (ii) - (p), (iii) - (s), (iv) - (r)
(b) (i) - (q), (ii) - (r), (iii) - (t), (iv) - (p)
(c) (i) - (s), (ii) - (q), (iii) - (t), (iv) - (p)
(d) (i) - (s), (ii) - (r), (iii) - (q), (iv) - (t)

21. The process of eating away of metals layer by layer due to formation of metal compound on surface is called
(a) Galvanisation
(b) Amalgam formation
(c) Corrosion
(d) Vulcanization

22. Place a piece of burning charcoal on an iron plate and cover it with a jar. The charcoal stop burning because
(a) its ignition temperature is lowered.
(b) supply of oxygen is cut off.
(c) it becomes cold after some time.
(d) none of the above.

23. **Assertion :** Teflon is used to coat non-stick cooking pans.
    **Reason :** Teflon is polytetra-fluoroethene.
    (a) If both assertion and reason are true and reason is the correct explanation of assertion.
    (b) If both assertion and reason are true but reason is not the correct explanation of assertion.
    (c) If assertion is true but reason is false.
    (d) If assertion is false but reason is true.

24. It is said that, the Taj Mahal may be destroyed due to –
    (a) Flood in Yamuna river
    (b) Decomposition of marble as a result of high temperature
    (c) Air pollutants released from oil refinery of Mathura
    (d) All the above

25. Which statement best explains the spontaneous combustion?
    (a) It is the ability of materials to burn with the help of some source of heat like flame or spark.
    (b) It is the ability of certain materials to start burning without any flame, spark, heat or ignition from external source.
    (c) It is the ability of certain materials to remain unburnt.
    (d) It is the ability of certain materials to burn without oxygen.

26. Which of the following is not a constituent of petroleum?
    (a) Paraffin wax      (b) Petrol
    (c) Lubricating oil   (d) Coke

27. Outermost zone of flame is called –
    (a) Luminous zone
    (b) Non-luminious zone
    (c) Dark zone
    (d) None of these

28. Which of the following are incorrectly matched?

| | Material | Natural Source | Artificial Source |
|---|---|---|---|
| (i) | Thermoplastic | √ | × |
| (ii) | Jute | √ | × |
| (iii) | Cellulose | × | √ |
| (iv) | Polythene | √ | × |

    (a) (i) and (ii)
    (b) (i), (ii) and (iii)
    (c) (i), (iii) and (iv)
    (d) All of these

29. Mercury is the ideal liquid for making thermometer because
    (a) it does not stick to glass and is easily visible
    (b) expands on heating
    (c) its boiling point is high
    (d) all of the above

30. Arrange the following liquids in decreasing order of boiling points : coal tar, fuel oil, kerosene, petrol
    (a) coal tar > fuel oil > kerosene > petrol
    (b) fuel oil > kerosene > petrol > coal tar
    (c) kerosene > petrol > coal tar > fuel oil
    (d) petrol > coal tar > fuel oil > kerosene

**DIRECTIONS (Q.31) :** On the basis of following diagram/picture answer the questions given below :

31.
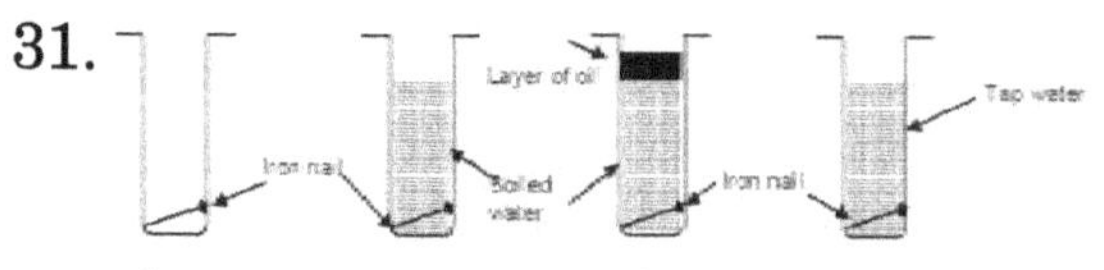


**A      B      C      D**

In which test tubes, the rusting of iron nail will take place?
(a) A and D
(b) A, B and D
(c) B and C
(d) B, C and D

## BIOLOGY

32. Which of the following pollutants are causes as marble cancer?
(i) Sulphur dioxide
(ii) Carbon monoxide
(iii) Nitrogen dioxide
(iv) Chlorofluorocarbons
(v) Mercury
(a) (i), (ii) and (iii)
(b) (i) and (iii)
(c) (ii), (iv) and (v)
(d) All of these
(e) None of these.

33. What form of reproduction is at work when part of the parent plant breaks off to form new plants?
(a) Diversification
(b) Sexual reproduction
(c) Germination
(d) Fragmentation

34. Blood bank of the body is
(a) spleen
(b) heart
(c) liver
(d) bone marrow

35. What happens during menopause?
(i) No menstruation.
(ii) No maturation of new follicles.
(iii) The ovaries stop the secretion of estrogen.
(a) (i) and (ii)
(b) (ii) only
(c) (i), (ii) and (iii)
(d) (iii) only.

36. In the slides showing binary fission in *Amoeba* and budding in yeast, the correct observations are
(a) the daughter cells of *Amoeba* and the bud of yeast are smaller than their respective parent cells.
(b) the daughter cells of *Amoeba* and the bud of yeast are of the same size as their respective parent cells.
(c) the daughter cells of *Amoeba* are bigger than the parent cells but bud of yeast is smaller than the parent.
(d) the daughter cells of *Amoeba* are smaller than the parent but bud of yeast is larger than parent.

37. Gestation does not follow
(a) if the egg is fertilized
(b) if the egg is not fertilized
(c) if the embryo has implanted
(d) none of the above.

38. Match the following and select the correct option from the codes given below.

| Column-I | Column-II | |
|---|---|---|
| (A) Term for component present in the cytoplasm | (p) | Organelle |
| (B) The living substance in the cell | (q) | Protoplasm |
| (C) This is necessary for photosynthesis | (r) | Chlorophyll |
| (D) Empty structure in the cytoplasm | (s) | Tissues |
| (E) A group of cells | (t) | Organs |
| | (u) | Vacuole |

    (a) A-(p), B-(q), C-(r), D-(u), E-(s)
    (b) A-(q), B-(p), C-(r), D-(u), E-(s)
    (c) A-(p), B-(q), C-(r), D-(u), E-(t)
    (d) A-(q), B-(p), C-(r), D-(t), E-(s)

39. Given below are four steps for preparing a temporary mount of human cheek cells.

    (i) Taking scraping from inner side of the cheek and spreading it on a clean slide.
    (ii) Putting a drop of glycerine on the material.
    (iii) Adding two or three drops of methylene blue.
    (iv) Rinsing the mouth with fresh water and disinfectant solution.

What is the correct sequence of the steps?

    (a) (i)-(ii)-(iii)-(iv)
    (b) (iv)-(i)-(iii)-(ii)
    (c) (iv)-(i)-(ii)-(iii)
    (d) (i)-(iii)-(ii)-(iv)

40. Arrange the cell organelles useful for intracellular digestion, intracellular respiration, intracellular movements and cell secretion in a sequence.

    P. Golgi complex  Q. Lysosomes
    R. Mitochondria  S. Microtubules
    (a) Q-R-S-P  (b) R-Q-P-S
    (c) S-P-Q-R  (d) P-S-R-Q

41. Dodo is a/an

    (a) critically endangered species.
    (b) extinct species.
    (c) endangered species.
    (d) vulnerable species.

42. The slogan of Chipko movement is planting five Fs. Which of the following correctly matches the five Fs?

    (a) Food, fodder, fuel, fibre and fertilizer trees
    (b) Food, fodder, fuel, fibre and fertility
    (c) Food, fodder, fibre, fire-wood and furniture
    (d) Food, fire-wood, fibre, fertility and furniture.

43. Which of the following are threatened wild animals?

    (i) Golden cat
    (ii) Pink headed duck
    (iii) Dinosaur
    (iv) Dodo
    (v) Passenger pigeon
    (vi) White tailed mongoose
    (vii) Gharial
    (viii) Marsh crocodile
    (a) (i), (ii), (iv) and (v)
    (b) (v), (vi), (vii) and (viii)
    (c) (ii), (iv), (vi) and (vii)
    (d) (i), (ii), (vii) and (viii)

44. Ram was going through a forest and found many similar plants. What amongst the given below could be the reason for the observed phenomenon. The plants are

    A. of many genera.
    B. of only one species.
    C. capable of interbreeding.
    D. capable of crossbreeding.

Select the correct alternative from the following.

    (a) A and B    (b) B and C
    (c) C and D    (d) A and D.

45. What does P, Q and R respresent in the given figure of nitrogen cycle ?

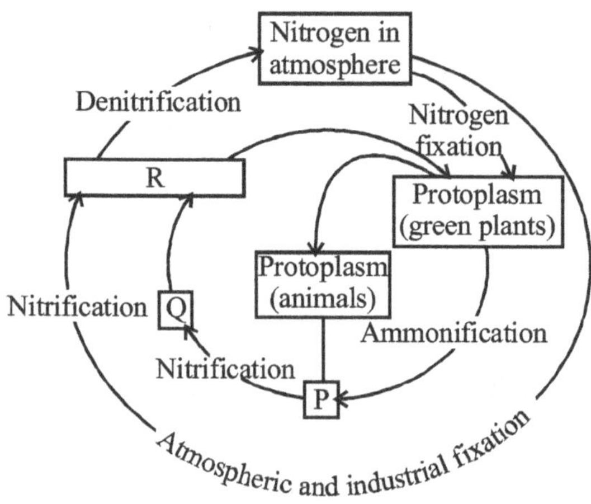


|     | P        | Q        | R        |
|-----|----------|----------|----------|
| (a) | Ammonia  | Nitrates | Nitrites |
| (b) | Ammonia  | Nitrites | Nitrates |
| (c) | Nitrites | Nitrates | Ammonia  |
| (d) | Nitrates | Nitrites | Ammonia. |

46. Match list I and list II and identify the correct match from the following.

**Column-I**             **Column-II**
A. *Rhizopus*     (p) Water moulds
B. *Saprolegnia*  (q) Blue or green moulds
C. *Puccinia*     (r) Cup fungi
D. *Peziza*       (s) Bread mould
E. *Penicillium*  (t) Rust fungi

(a) A - (s), B - (p), C - (t), D - (r), E - (q)
(b) A - (t), B - (p), C - (s), D - (q), E - (r)
(c) A - (p), B - (q), C - (r), D - (s), E - (t)
(d) A - (s), B - (t), C - (r), D - (q), E - (p)

47. Select the correct option which best suits the given descriptions for P, Q, R and S.
   P- A simple tool used for removing weeds.
   Q- A tool which is used for ploughing with the help of tractor.
   R- A tool which is used for sowing with the help of tractor.
   S- A simple tool used for cutting of crops.

|     | P      | Q         | R          | S       |
|-----|--------|-----------|------------|---------|
| (a) | Sickle | Plough    | Cultivator | Khurpi  |
| (b) | Sickle | Cultivator| Hoe        | Cutter  |
| (c) | Khurpi | Plough    | Seed drill | Hoe     |
| (d) | Hoe    | Cultivator| Seed drill | Sickle. |

48. Minimata disease is a pollution-related disease, which results from –
   (a) release of human organic waste into drinking water.
   (b) release of industrial waste mercury into fishing water.
   (c) accumulation of arsenic into atmosphere.
   (d) oil spills into sea.

49. Restoration of ecological equilibrium in mined areas can be achieved through –
   (a) Revegetation of the mined habitats
   (b) Conversion of mined habitats into agricultural ecosystems
   (c) Prevention of soil erosion
   (d) Prevention of grazing

50. Given below are events that lead to pregnancy and development of embryo.
   (i) Fertilization of egg
   (ii) Maturation of egg
   (iii) Release of egg
   (iv) Embedding of embryo in thickened uterine wall
   Which of the following options gives the correct order of sequence in which they occur ?
   (a) (i), (ii), (iii), (iv)
   (b) (ii), (i), (iii), (iv)
   (c) (i), (iv), (ii), (iii)
   (d) (ii), (iii), (i), (iv)

## PHYSICS

1. Mark the correct statement:
   (a) If the incident rays are converging, we have a real object.
   (b) If the final rays are converging, we have a real image.
   (c) The image of the virtual object is called a virtual image.
   (d) If the image is virtual, the corresponding object is called a virtual object.

2. Whenever the surfaces in contact tend to move or move with respect to each other, the force of friction comes into play
   (a) only if the objects are solids
   (b) only if one of the two objects is liquid
   (c) only if one of the two objects is gaseous
   (d) irrespective of whether the objects are solid, liquid or gaseous

3. When a horse pulls a wagon, the force that causes the horse to move forward is the force
   (a) it exerts on the wagon
   (b) the wagon exerts on it
   (c) it exerts on the ground
   (d) the ground exerts on it

4. In the arrangement shown below a block of mass 2700 kg is in equilibrium on applying a force F. The value of force F if $d_{liquid} = 0.75$ g cm$^{-3}$ is

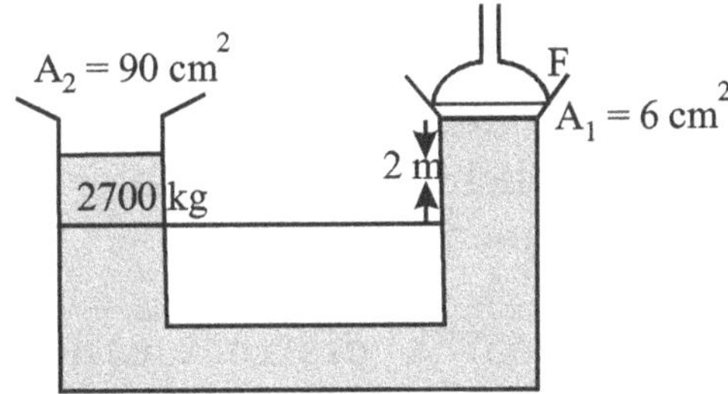


   (a) 147 N        (b) 300 N
   (c) 153 N        (d) 918 N

5. The sun emits ............ radiation to space while the earth radiates ............. or infra-red radiation to space –
   (a) short wave, short wave
   (b) long wave, long wave
   (c) short wave, long wave
   (d) long wave, short wave

6. The image formed by plane mirror is:
   (a) real and inverted
   (b) real and erect
   (c) virtual and inverted
   (d) virtual and erect

7. Which of the following is not a member of the solar system.
   (a) An asteroid     (b) A satellite
   (c) A constellation (d) A comet

8. A boy rolls a rubber ball on a wooden surface. The ball travels a short distance before coming to rest. To make the same ball travel longer distance before coming to rest, he may
   (a) spread a carpet on the wooden surface.
   (b) cover the ball with a piece of cloth.
   (c) sprinkle talcum powder on the wooden surface.
   (d) sprinkle sand on the wooden surface.

9. A toy car released with the same initial speed will travel farthest on
   (a) muddy surface.
   (b) polished marble surface.
   (c) cemented surface.
   (d) brick surface.

10. To hear a distinct echo, the minimum distance of a reflecting surface should be :
    (a) 17 m          (b) 34 m
    (c) 68 m          (d) 94 m

11. A coin flicked across a table stops because
    (a) no force acts on it
    (b) it is very heavy
    (c) the table exerts a frictional force on it
    (d) the earth attract it

12. A force of a given magnitude acts on a body. The acceleration of the body depends on the
    (a) mass of the body
    (b) volume of the body
    (c) density of the body
    (d) shape of the body

13. The change in the focal length of an eye lens is caused by the action of the
    (a) pupil
    (b) retina
    (c) ciliary muscle
    (d) iris

14. A force of 10N is applied on a block, but the block does not move. What is the frictional force on the block?
    (a) 10 N
    (b) Less than 10 N
    (c) More than 10 N
    (d) Depends on the roughness of block and the surface of contact

15. What force is needed to a accelerate a 60 kg wagon from rest to 5.0 meters per second in 2.0 seconds?
    (a) 100 N          (b) 120 N
    (c) 150 N          (d) 130 N

16. Which of the following statements is incorrect?
    (a) Friction acts on a ball rolling along the ground.
    (b) Friction acts on a boat moving on water.
    (c) Friction acts on a bicycle moving on a smooth road.
    (d) Friction does not act on a ball moving through air.

17. The outermost layer of earth is called

   (a) mantle      (b) outer core

   (c) crust      (d) inner core

18. In an electrolyte refining which one of the following is used as an anode?

   (a) Electrode

   (b) Pure metal

   (c) Impure metal

   (d) Reactive metal

19. An object moving at a speed greater than that of sound is said to be moved at

   (a) ultrasonic speed

   (b) sonic speed

   (c) infrasonic speed

   (d) supersonic speed

### CHEMISTRY

20. Which of the following pair of synthetic fibre is used for tyre cords?

   (a) Rayon and nylon

   (b) Nylon and polyester

   (c) Rayon and polyester

   (d) None of these

21. Fossil fuels are obtained from:

   (a) Remains of non-living materials.

   (b) Dead remains of birds only.

   (c) Dead remains of insects only.

   (d) Dead remains of living organisms.

22. The metal which is stored in kerosene is:

   (a) Phosphorus    (b) Magnesium

   (c) Sodium      (d) Zinc

23. Tina set up apparatus for an experiment as shown in the figure. She performed the same experiment by changing threads ($a$, $b$, and $c$). She found that weight required to break the thread is in the order $x > y > z$, where $x$ = weight required to break $a$, $y$ = weight required to break $b$, $z$ = weight required to break $c$. Then $a$, $b$ and $c$ can be

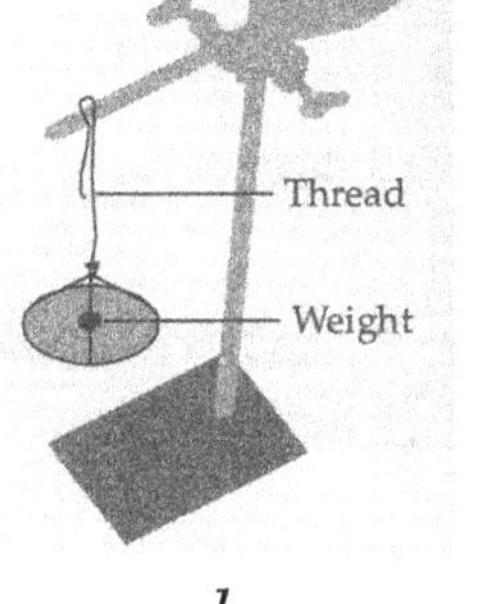


|  | $a$ | $b$ | $c$ |
|---|---|---|---|
| (a) | Nylon | Wool | Cotton |
| (b) | Nylon | Cotton | Wool |
| (c) | Wool | Cotton | Nylon |
| (d) | Cotton | Nylon | Wool |

24. Which of the following metals on reacting with sodium hydroxide solution produce hydrogen gas?

   1. Cu        2. Al

   3. Fe        4. Zn

   (a) 2 and 3      (b) 2 and 4

   (c) 1 and 4      (d) 2 only

25. The substances which have very low ignition temperature and can easily catch fire with a flame are called

   (a) ignition temperature.

   (b) rapid combustion.

   (c) inflammable substances.

   (d) global warming.

26. Coal is mainly carbon, also having some other elements like

    (a) oxygen, hydrogen, nitrogen and sulphur

    (b) chlorine, nitrogen, sulphur and helium

    (c) sulphur, phosphorus, iodine and oxygen

    (d) bromine, nitrogen, phosphorus and hydrogen

27. **Assertion :** On beating with the help of a hammer, coal is converted into small pieces and finally into a powder.

    **Reason :** Coal is made up of carbon which is malleable in nature.

    (a) If both assertion and reason are true and reason is the correct explanation of assertion.

    (b) If both assertion and reason are true but reason is not the correct explanation of assertion.

    (c) If assertion is true but reason is false.

    (d) If assertion is false but reason is true.

28. Match Column I and Column II and choose the correct option.

| Column-I | Column - II |
|---|---|
| (A) Coke | (p) Petroleum, natural gas |
| (B) Lamp black | (q) Global warming |
| (C) Fossil fuels | (r) Smokeless fuel |
| (D) Carbon dioxide | (s) Soot deposited in kerosene lamps |

    (a) A - (q), B - (s), C - (r), D - (p)

    (b) A - (r), B - (s), C - (p), D - (q)

    (c) A - (s), B - (r), C - (q), D - (p)

    (d) A - (r), B - (p), C - (q), D - (s)

29. In presence of water, ignition temperature of paper

    (a) decreases

    (b) increases

    (c) remains constant

    (d) can decrease or increase

30. Which of the following pairs will give displacement reaction?

    (a) NaCl solution and copper metal

    (b) $MgCl_2$ solution and aluminium metal

    (c) $FeSO_4$ solution and silver metal

    (d) $AgNO_3$ solution and copper metal

31. Natural gas is a very important fossil fuel because

    (a) it is easy to transport through pipes.

    (b) it is a mixture of various constituents.

    (c) it is used as a fuel in many industries.

    (d) it is a tough, porous and black substance.

## *BIOLOGY*

**32.** The amount of matter produced that is available for heterotrophs is known as what?

(a) Net primary productivity

(b) Secondary productivity

(c) Gross primary productivity

(d) Primary productivity

**33.** In which of the following agricultural methods, the nutrient needs of one crop are fulfilled by the other crop?

✱ = **Ground nut**       • = **Rice**

♦ = **Wheat**       ❖ = **Soyabeans**

(a)        (b) 

(c)        (d) 

**34.** Match Column I with Column II and select the correct option from the codes given below.

| Column-I | Column-II |
| --- | --- |
| (A) *Rhizobium* | (p) Nitrogen fixation |
| (B) Organic manure | (q) Separation of grain from chaff |
| (C) Threshing | (r) Sowing of seeds |
| (D) Seed drill | (s) Animal excreta, cow dung and plant wastes |
| (E) Leguminous plants | (t) Root nodules |

(a) A-(p), B-(s), C-(q), D-(r), E-(t)

(b) A-(t), B-(s), C-(r), D-(q), E-(p)

(c) A-(s), B-(p), C-(r), D-(q), E-(t)

(d) A-(p), B-(t), C-(q), D-(r), E-(s)

**35.** Which of the following statements is/are incorrect? Pick the correct code to answer this.

(i) *Mycobacteria* phage is a virus.

(ii) Bacteria living in the intestine of a cow, help in digestion of starch.

(iii) Mycoplasmas are resistant to most antibiotics.

(iv) Influenza is a bacterial disease.

(v) Wax is a product of honey.

(vi) Black Minorca is a breed of cattle.

(a) (i), (vi), (iii)

(b) Only (iii)

(c) (ii), (iv), (v), (vi)

(d) (ii), (iii), (v), (vi)

**36.** Match the columns and select the correct option from the codes given below.

| Column-I | Column-II |
| --- | --- |
| (A) Unicellular algae | (i) *Volvox* |
| (B) Filamentous algae | (ii) *Sargassum* |
| (C) Colonial algae | (iii) *Chlamydomonas* |
| (D) Multicellular algae | (iv) *Spirogyra.* |

(a) A-(ii), B-(i), C-(iv), D-(iii)

(b) A-(iii), B-(iv), C-(i), D-(ii)

(c) A-(iv), B-(iii), C-(ii), D-(i)

(d) A-(iii), B-(i), C-(iv), D-(ii)

37. Cyanobacteria have-

    (a) A well-defined nucleus and chloroplast

    (b) A well-defined nucleus but no chloroplast

    (c) Incipient nucleus and vesicles containing chlorophyll.

    (d) Incipient nucleus but no chloroplast or pigment.

38. Which of these national parks is not paired correctly with its state ?

    (a) Gir National Park – Gujarat

    (b) Corbett National Park – Uttaranchal

    (c) Kanha National Park – Madhya Pradesh

    (d) Bhartpur National Park – Karnataka

39. World forest day is

    (a) 21$^{st}$ June      (b) 5$^{th}$ June

    (c) 21$^{st}$ March    (d) 1$^{st}$ December.

40. India contains globally important population of some of the Asia's rarest animals. Which of the following animals belong to that category?

    (i)   Marbled cat

    (ii)  Asiatic lion

    (iii) Indian elephant

    (iv)  Bengal fox

    (v)   Indian rhinoceros

    (vi)  Asiatic wild ass

    (a) (i), (iii) and (vi)

    (b) (i), (ii) and (iii)

    (c) (i), (iv), (v) and (vi)

    (d) (i), (ii), (iii), (iv), (v) and (vi).

41. Match the membranous organelles with their function and select the correct option.

| Membranous organelle | | Functions |
|---|---|---|
| A. | Endoplasmic reticulum | (p) Powerhouse of cells |
| B. | Golgi complex | (q) Storage organelle |
| C. | Mitochondria | (r) Transport of substances |
| D. | Vacuoles | (s) Secretion of chemicals |

    (a) A - (s), B - (q), C - (r), D - (p)

    (b) A - (r), B - (s), C - (p), D - (q)

    (c) A - (s), B - (p), C - (q), D - (r)

    (d) A - (s), B - (r), C - (p), D - (q)

42. Plasma membrane is the outermost covering of the cell that allows them movement of substances through the processes like osmosis and diffusion. Which of the given statements regarding these processes are true?

    (i)   Movement of carbon dioxide occurs by the process of diffusion.

    (ii)  Diffusion is a special case of osmosis that occurs through a selectively permeable membrane.

    (iii) Unicellular fresh water organisms and most plant cells tend to gain water through osmosis.

    (iv)  When a cell is placed in hypertonic solution then endosmosis occurs and when a plasmolysed (flaccid) cell is placed in hypotonic solution then exosmosis occurs.

    (a) (iii) and (iv)   (b) (i) and (iii)

    (c) (i) and (ii)     (d) (ii) and (iii).

43. Refer the given figure of a cell. Which organelle is more in number? Also, identify among P, Q, R and S, the organelle which is responsible for transmission of hereditary information.

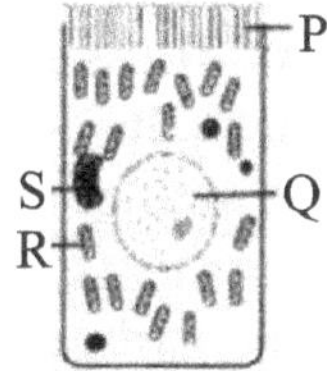


(a) Endoplasmic reticulum; P
(b) Mitochondrion; Q
(c) Ribosome; R
(d) Golgi body; S.

44. The number of nuclei present in a zygote is
(a) none      (b) one
(c) two      (d) four

45. Match each item in Column I with appropriate one in Column II.

| Column-I | Column-II |
|---|---|
| A. Edward Jenner | p. Heredity |
| B. Chromosomes | q. Budding |
| C. *Hydra* | r. Protein biosynthesis |
| | s. Smallpox vaccine |
| | t. Cell membrane |
| | u. Binary fission |
| | v. Antibiotics |

(a) A - (v), B - (p), C - (q)
(b) A - (s), B - (p), C - (q)
(c) A - (v), B - (t), C - (u)
(d) A - (s), B - (q), C - (u)

46. The given figure represents the position of various endocrine glands in human body. Select the correctly labelled parts from the codes given below.

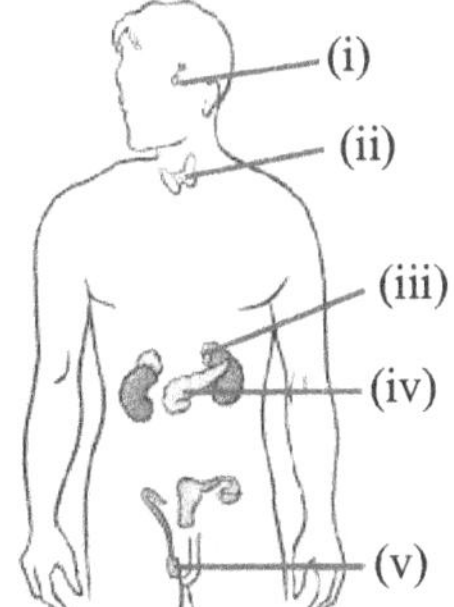


|  | (i) | (ii) | (iii) | (iv) | (v) |
|---|---|---|---|---|---|
| (a) | Thyroid | Pituitary | Adrenal | Pancreas | Testis |
| (b) | Pituitary | Thyroid | Adrenal | Pancreas | Testis |
| (c) | Pituitary | Thyroid | Pancreas | Adrenal | Testis |
| (d) | Thyroid | Pituitary | Testis | Pancreas | Adrenal |

47. Some gases prevent the escape of heat from the earth. An increase in the percentage of such gases in the atmosphere would cause the aquatic temperature to increase world wide which is called green house effect. Some gases causing this effect are methane $CH_4$, $CO_2$, choroflurocarbon (CFC), $N_2O$ etc. In the given figure, the percentage effect of each gas has been shown. Which gas is represented by X ?

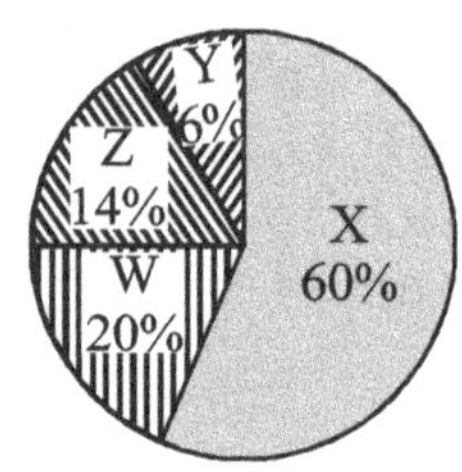



(a) $N_2O$  (b) $CO_2$
(c) $CH_4$  (d) CFC.

48. Match column I with column II and select the correct option from the codes given below.

| | Column-I | | Column-II |
|---|---|---|---|
| A. | Particulate matter | (p) | Chemical water pollutants |
| B. | Oil spills | (q) | Non-degradable soil pollutants |
| C. | Detergents | (r) | Degradable soil pollutants |
| D. | Plastics | (s) | Air pollutants |
| E. | Domestic wastes | (t) | Physical water pollutants |

(a) A-(s), B-(r), C-(p), D-(q), E-(t)

(b) A-(s), B-(t), C-(p), D-(q), E-(r)

(c) A-(p), B-(q), C-(r), D-(s), E-(t)

(d) A-(p), B-(q), C-(r), D-(t), E-(s)

49. **Assertion :** The first menstrual flow begins at puberty and is called menopause.

**Reason :** At 45 to 50 years, the menstrual cycle stops. The stoppage of menstruation is called menarche.

(a) Both Assertion and Reason are true and Reason is the correct explanation of Assertion

(b) Both Assertion and Reason are true but Reason is not the correct explanation of Assertion

(c) Assertion is true but Reason is false

(d) Both Assertion and Reason are false.

50. Which of the following will occur in females at puberty ?

(i) Ovulation

(ii) Enlargement of breasts

(iii) Broadening of hips.

(a) (i) and (ii)

(b) (i) and (iii)

(c) (ii) and (iii)

(d) (i), (ii) and (iii).

# GENERAL KNOWLEDGE

## OLYMPIAD Mock Test 1

Name : __________       Max. Marks : 25

Number of Questions : 25      Time : 1 Hour

**There is no negative marking in the test.**

1. Which of the following is not a correct statement about Buddhist Canonical literature?

   (a) Abhidhamma Pitaka was compiled in third Buddhist Council.

   (b) Digha Nikaya is a part of the Sutta Pitaka.

   (c) Vinaya Pitaka primarily deals with monastic rules for monks and nuns.

   (d) Sutta Pitaka deals with philosophy and psychology and lays down methods for training the mind.

2. Select the correct statements.

   (i) Truffles are a kind of fungi.

   (ii) Autumn skullcap is an edible mushroom.

   (iii) Crosiers are the edible part of some ferns.

   (a) (i) and (ii)

   (b) (ii) and (iii)

   (c) (i) and (iii)

   (d) (i), (ii) and (iii)

3. A year is usually divided into summer, winter, spring and autumn seasons due to the

   (a) rotation of the earth

   (b) changing position of the earth around the sun.

   (c) circle of illumination

   (d) None of these

4. Which of the following statements is true or false? Select the correct alternative:

   (i) All Indians have the same national language.

   (ii) All Indians speak the same language.

   (iii) Caste system is an example of diversity.

   (iv) India is a secular state

(a) False / False / False / True

(b) False / False / False / True

(c) False / False / True / False

(d) False / False / True / True

5. Match the movements associated with the following leaders and select the correct alternative

| Column I | Column II |
| --- | --- |
| (Name of Leader) | (Movement Associated with the Leader) |
| (1) Aung San Suu Kyi | (i) Civil Rights Movement |
| (2) Abraham Lincoln | (ii) National League for Democracy |
| (3) Nelson Mandela | (iii) Abolition of Slavery |
| (4) Martin Luther King | (iv) Movement against Apartheid |

(a) A - (iv), B - (iii), C - (ii), D - (i)

(b) A - (i), B - (iii), C - (iv), D - (ii)

(c) A - (ii), B - (iii), C - (iv), D - (i)

(d) A - (i), B - (iv), C - (ii), D - (iii)

6. The founder of the Arya Samaj was

(a) Raja Ram Mohan Roy

(b) Swami Dayanand Saraswati

(c) Swami Vivekananda

(d) Jyotiba Phule

7. The first process of photography produced a highly detailed permanent photograph on a silver-plated sheet of copper. It was developed by a Frenchman after whom it was named in 1839. What was this called?

(a) Calotype

(b) Heliograph

(c) Daguerreotype

(d) Pantograph

8. In which of the following cases, VD Savarkar was sentenced to transportation for life to the infamous Cellular Jail in the Andaman and Nicobar Islands (Kala Pani) in 1911?

(a) Alipore Bomb Case

(b) Nasik Conspiracy Case

(c) Delhi Conspiracy case

(d) Lahore Conspiracy Case

9. With which of the following sports is Ankit Sharma who qualified for 2016 Rio Olympics associated?

(a) Swimming   (b) Boxing

(c) Long jump   (d) Archery

10. Which of the following Rock Edicts of Ashoka speaks of religious synthesis?

    (a) Rock Edict II

    (b) Rock Edict X

    (c) Rock Edict XII

    (d) Rock Edict XIII

11. In which Constitutional Amendment Act, seats of Lok Sabha were increased from 525 to 545?

    (a) 21st Constitutional Amendment Act, 1967

    (b) 24th Constitutional Amendment Act, 1971

    (c) 25th Constitutional Amendment Act, 1971

    (d) 31st Constitutional Amendment Act, 1973

12. Who among the following actresses has won the maximum number of Filmfare Awards for the best actress?

(a) 

Kajol

(b) 

Madhuri Dixit

(c) 

Jaya Bachchan

(d) 

Shabana Azmi

13. He was a South Africa anti-apartheid revolutionary politician who also served as President of South Africa. During the struggle against the apartheid movement, he was imprisoned for 27 years. Who was he?

(a) 

Jacob Zuma

(b) 

Desmond Tutu

(c) 

Jomo Kenyatta

(d) 

Nelson Mandela

14. He is an Indian American actor best known for his performances in the 'Harold and Kumar' comedy films. In 2009, he joined Obama Administration as an Associated Director of the White House Office of Public Engagement. Name him.

    (a) Kunal Nayyar

    (b) Kal Penn

    (c) Jimi Mistry

    (d) Naveen Andrews

15. What is common between Oktoberfest, Mainz and Frankfurters?

   (a) They all are dog breeds.

   (b) They all are related to Germany.

   (c) They all are famous sight seeings.

   (d) They all are type of German dishes.

16. What is the full form of 4G?

   (a) 4$^{th}$ Generation

   (b) 3 Gigabytes

   (c) 3 gms

   (d) None of these

17. Which among the following is known as the Great Andaman Trunk Road that connects Port Blair and Mayabunder in the Andaman and Nicobar Islands?

   (a) National Highway 221

   (b) National Highway 222

   (c) National Highway 223

   (d) National Highway 224

18. Identify the name of the Indian female athlete of 21$^{th}$ century, who won India's first ever gold medal in wrestling at the Commonwealth Games in 2010?

(a) 

(b) 

Kavita Dalal          Geeta Phogat

(c) 

(d) 

Pooja Dhanda          Alka Tomar

19. Chishti Order is a Sufi order which arose from Chisht, a small town in which among the following countries?

   (a) Afghanistan

   (b) Turkmenistan

   (c) Kazakhstan

   (d) Uzbekistan

20 . National Panchayat Day is celebrated on

   (a) 20$^{th}$ April

   (b) 24$^{th}$ April

   (c) 26$^{th}$ April

   (d) 30$^{th}$ April

21. Yisrael Kristal, the world's oldest man who died in 2017, hailed from which country?

(a) Israel  (b) Japan
(c) France  (d) Germany

22. On July 27 -28, 2018, a rare celestial event of the longest lunar eclipse called the _____ was seen?

(a) Rare Moon

(b) Red Moon

(c) Blood Moon

(d) Black Moon

23. The Bhadra Wildlife Sanctuary is located in which state?
(a) Assam
(b) Bihar
(c) Karnataka
(d) Uttar Pradesh

24. Which state government has launched "Apni Gaddi Apna Rojgar" scheme for jobless youth?
(a) Punjab
(b) Assam
(c) Haryana
(d) Maharashtra

25. Who among the following Indians have won the 2018 Ramon Magsaysay Award?
(a) Thodur Madabusi Krishna and Sanjiv Chaturvedi

(b) Bharat Vatwani and Sonam Wangchuk

(c) Devdutt Pattanaik and Ramachandra Guha

(d) Medha Patkar and Kailash Satyarthi

# OLYMPIAD
# Mock Test 2

**Name :** _________

**Number of Questions : 25**

**Max. Marks : 25**

**Time : 1 Hour**

**There is no negative marking in the test.**

1. Which of the following mountain ranges form the longest mountain chain in the world?
   (a) The Rockies of North America
   (b) The Andes of South America
   (c) The Alaska Range
   (d) The Great Dividing Range of Australia

2. Which of the following statements is incorrect?
   (a) A male ostrich can roar like a lion
   (b) Potatoes are good source of vitamin $B_6$, Potassium and carbohydrates.
   (c) Jasmine is the national flower of Sudan.
   (d) A group of porcupines is called a prickle.

3. This fruit is a staple diet in the Pacific Islands. It is eaten baked or boiled, or sliced and fried. It is rich in starch. Name the fruit.
   (a) Dates
   (b) Breadfruit
   (c) Jackfruit
   (d) peaches

4. Match column-I with Column-II and select the correct answer using the code given below the columns.

   | Column-I | Column-II |
   | --- | --- |
   | (A) Transparent substances | (p) Iron nails |
   | (B) Translucent substances | (q) Wood |
   | (C) Opaque substance | (r) Clean glass |
   | (D) Magnetic substances | (s) Oily paper |

   (a) A – (p); B – (s); C – (q); D – (r)
   (b) A – (r); B – (s); C – (q); D – (p)
   (c) A – (p); B – (q); C – (s); D – (r)
   (d) A – (r); B – (q); C – (s); D – (p)

5. Which of the following animals are /is endemic to Pachmarhi Biosphere Reserve area?
   (a) Indian giant squirrel

   (b) Flying squirrel

   (c) Bison

   (d) All the these

6. Who observed and coined the word cells for the first time?

   (a) Robert Cook

   (b) Robert Brown

   (c) Robert Hooke

   (d) LeeuwenHock

7. Name the type of root shown in the figure?

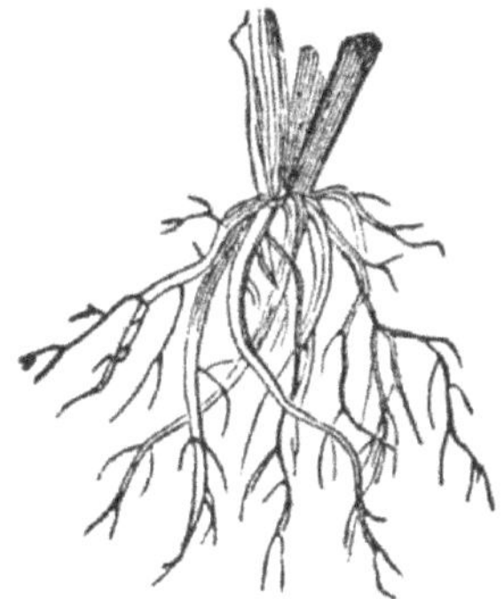

   (a) Lateral root    (b) Tap root

   (c) Fibrous root    (d) None of these

8. From where was India's multipurpose telecommunication satellite INSAT-2E launched?

   (a) Thumba      (b) Baikanour

   (c) Kourou      (d) Sriharikota

9. He was a great Hindu Saint born on 12 Jan. 1863. His original name was Narendranath Datta. He founded the Ramakrishna Mission. Who was he?

(a) Krishnadevaraya    (b) Swami Vivekananda

(c) Swami Dayananda Saraswati    (d) Swami Shraddhanad

10. What is Archives?
   (a) A place where documents and manuscripts are kept
   (b) A place where paintings are kept
   (c) Both (a) and (b)
   (d) None of these

11. The Earth is the only planet in our Solar System that is not named after a God or Goddess of the Roman pantheon. The name of the Earth is derived from:
   (a) Greek      (b) Persian
   (c) Germanic      (d) Babylonian

12. Which state government will observe 2018 Independence Day eve as Shahid Samman Divas to honour martyrs?

   (a) Madhya Pradesh

   (b) Andhra Pradesh

   (c) Himachal Pradesh

   (d) Arunachal Pradesh

13. From which animal is Shahtoosh wool is obtained?
 (a) Polar Bear
 (b) Yak
 (c) Tibetan antelope
 (d) None of these

14. Rukmini Devi Arundale is considered the most important revivalist of this Indian classical dance form from its original 'sadhir' style, prevalent amongst the temple dancers, the devadasis. Which dance form did Ms Arundale promote?
 (a) Kuchipudi
 (b) Bharatanatyam
 (c) Mohiniattam
 (d) Odissi

15. What is the main variety of coffee produced in the world?
 (a) Arabica      (b) Robusta
 (c) Persian      (d) Hindutva

16. Indian space agency ISRO is setting up the country's first space park at which location?
 (a) Hyderabad
 (b) Chennai
 (c) Bengaluru
 (d) Madurai

17. The President is elected by
 (a) the direct election by the citizens who have attained 18 years
 (b) an indirect election by the electoral college
 (c) the Prime Minister and his council of ministers
 (d) None of these

18. National Bank for Agriculture and Rural Development (NABARD) was established in _______?
 (a) 1980
 (b) 1981
 (c) 1982
 (d) 1983

19. Identify the Indian scientist who is acknowledged as the 'Father of Indian nuclear power'?

(a) 
Homi J. Bhabha

(b) 
C.V. Raman

(c) 
C.N.R. Rao

(d) 
M.S. Swaminathan

20. What is the generally accepted period of Indus Valley Civilization?
 (a) 2500-2100 B.C.
 (b) 2600-1700 B.C.
 (c) 2300-1750 B.C.
 (d) 2000-1500 B.C.

21. Which one of the following should not be consumed if one cannot digest lactose?
 (a) Alcohol      (b) Honey
 (c) Sugar        (d) Milk

22. The delightful movie 'Angry Birds' is a 2016 3D computer-animated comedy film. Who gave the voice of the bird named 'Red'?
    (a) Jason Sudeikis
    (b) Josh Gad
    (c) Danny McBride
    (d) Maya Rudolph

23. Antim Yadav has won bronze at the 2017 Commonwealth Youth Games (CYG). He hails from which Indian state?
    (a) Jharkhand
    (b) Madhya Pradesh
    (c) Uttar Pradesh
    (d) Manipur

24. The Desert National Park (DNP) is located in which state?
    (a) Gujarat          (b) Haryana
    (c) Rajasthan     (d) Assam

25. Which of the following is the official mascot for the 2020 Tokyo Paralympic Games?
    (a) Someity
    (b) Keito
    (c) Zabivaka
    (d) Miraitowa

**Name :** _________

**Max. Marks : 25**

**Number of Questions : 25**

**Time : 1 Hour**

**There is no negative marking in the test.**

1. I am a primate that lives in the forests of Sumatra and Borneo in Southeast Asia. I have an ability to reason and think. My fur is orange reddish-brown. My name means 'Person of the forest' in Malay. Who am I?

   (a) Chimpanzee (b) Orangutan

   (c) Gorilla (d) Bonobos

2. Where is the Duncan Pass located?

   (a) South and Little Andaman

   (b) North and South Andaman

   (c) North and Middle Andaman

   (d) Andaman and Nicobar

3. A wooden spoon is dipped in a cup of ice-cream. Its other end becomes cold

   (a) due to the process of conduction.

   (b) due to the process of convection.

   (c) due to the process of radiation.

   (d) It does not become cold.

4. Which of the following statements is true?

   (a) Digestion of food is a chemical change.

   (b) Photosynthesis by plants is a physical change.

   (c) Melting of ice is a chemical change.

   (d) Change of smell of food is an indication of physical change.

5. Permafrost, a permanently frozen soil, found in high altitudes is melting due to global warming. Which of the following gases are released from its melting?

   (a) Ozone and methane

   (b) Hydrogen and ozone

   (c) Nitrogen oxide and hydrogen

   (d) Carbon dioxide and methane

6. Shri Devendra Jhajharia who was Arjun award recipient of 2017 belongs to which game?

   (a) Football (b) Cricket

   (c) Athletics (d) Javelin

7. Heating of water and gases takes place due to

   (a) convection (b) conduction

   (c) radiation (d) None of these

8. The data of estimation of India's National Income is issued by ?

   (a) Planning Commission

   (b) National Data Center

   (c) Central Statistical Organsation

   (d) None of above

9. The symptom of the disease are the presence of blood in sputum during cough, pain in the chest, breathlessness on excretion and sweating. Identify the disease.

   (a) Diptheria

   (b) Food poisoning

   (c) Malaria

   (d) Tuberculosis

10. Which of the following Vedas was the earliest composition?

    (a) Atharvaveda

    (b) Yajurveda

    (c) Samaveda

    (d) Rigveda

11. Which of the following dynasties belonged to Kanishka?

    (a) Vardhana dynasty

    (b) Maurya dynasty

    (c) Kushana dynasty

    (d) Gupta dynasty

12. The legendary American author Ernest Hemingway won the Nobel Prize in Literature in 1954. Which of these is a famous novel by this eminent writer?

    (a) The Old Man and the Sea

    (b) The Grapes of Wrath

    (c) The Great Gatsby

    (d) Gone With the Wind

13. The English East India Company's first presidency in India was at ________.

    (a) Hooghly    (b) Surat

    (c) Madras    (d) Masulipatnam

14. Match column I with column II and select the correct answer using the code given below the columns.

| Column I | Column II |
| --- | --- |
| A. B R Ambedkar | I. Deputy prime minister |
| B. Vallabhbhai Patel | II. Different state-Andhra Pradesh-for Telgu speaking people |
| C. Potti Siriamulu | III. Father of Indian constitution |
| D. Krishna Menon | IV. Led the Indian delegation to UN |

    (a) A - III; B - I; C - IV; D - II

    (b) A -III; B -I; C - II; D - IV

    (c) A - IV; B -III; C - I; D - II

    (d) A - IV; B - III; C - II; D - I

15. Which acclaimed personality has been selected for 2018 Rajiv Gandhi Sadbhavana Award for promoting communal harmony and peace?

    (a) Raghuram Rajan

    (b) Muzaffar Ali

(c) Amitabh Bachchan

(d) Gopalkrishna Gandhi

16. Match column I with column II and select the correct answer using the code given below the columns:

| Column I | Column II |
|---|---|
| (Water falls) | (Countries) |
| (A) Angel falls | (i) Africa |
| (B) Niagara falls | (ii) India |
| (C) Victoria falls | (iii) South America |
| (D) Jog falls | (iv) North America |

**Codes:**

(a) A – iii, B – iv, C – i, D – ii

(b) A – iii, B – ii, C – iv, D – i

(c) A – iii, B – ii, C – i, D – iv

(d) A – iv B – ii, C – i, D – iii

17. He is one of the most popular Mexican players of the 1990s. This goalkeeper was known for eccentric behaviour and risky plays. His outfit during the 1994 World Cup also made him an unforgettable image. Who is he?

(a) Jorge Campos

(b) Fabien Barthez

(c) Gianluigi Buffon

(d) Lev Ivanovich Yashin

18. What was the theme of Indian Science Congress 2015?

(a) Science and Technology for Inclusive Development

(b) Science and Technology for India's Development

(c) Science and Technology for Rural Development

(d) Science and Technology for Human Development

19. Which of the following is correct?

(a) India is a secular, sovereign, democratic, socialist republic

(b) India is a sovereign, socialist, secular, democratic, republic

(c) India is a secular, democratic, republic, socialist, sovereign

(d) None of these

20. Which of the following is India's first nuclear reactor:

(a) Apsara

(b) Dhruva

(c) Rawatbhatta

(d) Kudankulam

21. Which of the following statements is/are true about Mangalyaan?

(a) It has been called "The Super Smart Spacecraft".

(b) It was launched on 5 November 2013 by the Indian Space Research Organisation (ISRO).

(c) Both (a) and (b) are true

(d) None of these

22. When a bank statement says ₹ 500 debited to your account, it means _______.

(a) 500 is deposited in your account

(b) 500 is withdrawn from your account

(c) 500 is fined on your account

(d) None of these

23. Who among the following coined the term "cosmic rays" ?

(a) Henri Becquerel

(b) Theodor Wulf

(c) Robert Millikan

(d) Bruno Rossi

24. The Murlen National Park is located in which state?

(a) Nagaland

(b) Himachal Pradesh

(c) Mizoram

(d) Karnataka

25. Which of these dances is performed on the edge of brass plates ?

(a) Bharatnatyam

(b) Kuchipudi

(c) Kathakali

(d) Manipuri

# OLYMPIAD
# Mock Test 

**4**



1. Resperine is used to
   (a) cure Arthritis
   (b) Alleviate pain
   (c) reduce high blood pressure
   (d) increase blood pressure when it is low

2. Which statement is true about the cat family?

   (a) All cats can both purr and roar.
   (b) Only domestic cats can purr.
   (c) Lion and tiger can purr.
   (d) None of these

3. It looks like a giant guinea pig, but it is not a pig. It is the world's largest rodent native to South America. Its partly-webbed feet make it a good swimmer. It spends much of its time around water or wallowing in mud. Which animal is this?
   (a) Dormouse  (b) Kangaroo rat
   (c) Capybara  (d) Slow loris

4. Which of the following non-metals have shining lustrous surfaces?
   (a) Graphite and phosphorus
   (b) Graphite and iodine
   (c) Iodine and phosphorus
   (d) Phosphorus and chlorine

5. Which one of the following is not correctly matched?
   (a) Haemoglobin: Skin
   (b) Vitamin C: Scurvy
   (c) Carbohydrate: Potato
   (d) Fat: Butter

6. Lakshadweep Islands are _________ Islands located in the Arabian Sea
   (a) Coral
   (b) Maldives
   (c) Both 'a' and 'b'
   (d) None of these

7. In order to reduce land pollution from industrial operations, some methods have been developed to reduce the volume of waste. Name the method in which waste is burned in the absence of oxygen. This method also produces stable end products.

   (a) Shredding

   (b) Pyrolysis

   (c) Scrubbing

   (d) Electrostatic induction

8. Why is earth called a 'Blue planet'?

   (a) Colour of earth is blue

   (b) Earth is covered with the layer of blue air

   (c) 71% of earth is covered with oceans, which appear blue from above

   (d) None of them

9. In nature, this simple organic acid is found in the sting of many insects, particularly ants after which it is named. What is it called?

   (a) Benzoic acid

   (b) Formic acid

   (c) Hyaluronic acid

   (d) Sulphuric acid

10. Which of the following carries impure blood?

   (a) Pulmonary artery

   (b) Pulmonary vein

   (c) Alveoli

   (d) Aorta

11. The entire body of Sikhs used to meet at Amritsar at the time of Baisakhi and Diwali to take collective decisions known as "________________ of the Guru"

   (a) Decisions     (b) Resolutions

   (c) Head          (d) Meeting

12. Which state government has launched a 360 degree nation-wide publicity campaign publicity campaign for 2018 men's hockey World Cup?

   (a) Maharashtra

   (b) Goa

   (c) Odisha

   (d) West Bengal

13. Observe the figure given below and identify the features shown in the figures.

   (a) Uranus and Venus

   (b) Earth and Mars

   (c) Natural satellite and Saturn

   (d) Natural satellite and artificial satellite

14. The Swaran Singh Committee recommended :

(a) The Constitution of State-Level Election Commissions.

(b) Panchayati-Raj reforms.

(c) Inclusion of Fundamental Duties in the Indian Constitution.

(d) Interlinking of Himalayan and peninsular rivers.

15. Which one of the following planets has the largest number of natural satellites or moons?

(a) Jupiter    (b) Mars

(c) Saturn    (d) Venus

16. This folk dance from Tamil Nadu can be performed individually or in pairs, by both the genders. Some of the steps are acrobatic. The dancers balance pots decorated with attractive flower arrangements, topped by a moving paper parrot on their head. Music from drums and pipes add vigour to the dance. What is this dance form called?

(a) Yakshagana (b) Karagam

(c) Chhau    (d) Garadi

17. Araku Valley is a hill station in Visakhapatnam district in the state of Andhra Pradesh in India. It has rich biodiversity. It is famous for its plantation of:

(a) Tea    (b) Tobacco

(c) Coffee    (d) Rubber

18. This tribe is chiefly found in Tamil Nadu and Palakkad district of Kerala. In recent times, they helped in catching snakes and collected the snake venom. These tribes also work as fishermen, and as labourers in the rice fields at the time of sowing and harvesting or in the rice mills. Who are they?

(a) Gond    (b) Bhil

(c) Irula    (d) Bhutia

19. Who is the author of book 'We Indians'?

(a) Nirad C. Choudry

(b) Subramaniya Swamy

(c) Khushwant Singh

(d) Muluk Raj Anand

20. When was the prestigious award Pulitzer Prize established?

(a) 1901    (b) 1889

(c) 1911    (d) 1917

21 Konkani writer Mahabaleshwar Sail has been honoured with which

award for his novel Hawthan?

(a) Saraswati Samman

(b) National Literary Award

(c) Pulitzer

(d) None of the above

22. Match column I with column II and select the correct answer using the code given below the columns:

**Column I**          **Column II**

A. South West      (i)   Winter
   Monsoon                Season

B. Cold Weather    (ii)  Rainy
                          Season

C. Hot Weather     (iii) Summer
                          Season

D. Season of       (iv)  Autumn
   Retreating
   Monsoons

(a) A-(i); B-(ii); C-(iii); D-(iv)

(b) A-(ii); B-(i); C-(iii); D-(iv)

(c) A-(iii); B-(ii); C-(iv); D-(i)

(d) A-(iv); B-(iii); C-(ii); D- (i)

23. The museum for all former Prime Ministers of India will be constructed in which city?

(a) New Delhi

(b) Gandhinagar

(c) Lucknow

(d) Kolkata

24. It provides us forests, grasslands for grazing, land for agriculture and human settlements. It is also a source of mineral wealth. Which of the following is discussed in the above passage?

(a) Atmosphere   (b) Hydrosphere

(c) Biosphere    (d) Lithosphere

25. Taj Mahal is made from which type of rock?

(a) Sedimentary  (b) Igneous

(c) Metamorphic  (d) None of these

26. What is the theme of 2018 World Youth Skills Day (WYSD)?
(a) Skills for All
(b) Improving the image of TVET
(c) Skills Development to Improve Youth Employment
(d) World Skills for peace and prosperity

27. What is geothermal energy?

(a) It is muscular energy

(b) It is energy produced by human beings

(c) It is the natural heat found in the interiors of the earth

(d) None of these

28. Which Indian personality has won the Woman of the Year award at the 2016 International Indian Film Academy Awards?

(a)                 (b) 

(c)                 (d) 

29. Which of the following is a correct statement about Indus Valley

Civilization?

(a) Both Harappa and Mohejodero are located on the banks of Indus River.

(b) Both Chanhudaro and Kalibangan were located within the boundaries of present day Rajasthan.

(c) Both Surkotada and Dholavira are located in Kutch of Gujarat.

(d) Lothal site was located on bank of Narmada river.

30. A pedestrian crosswalk consists of black and white stripes each 0.4 m wide. The crosswalk begins and ends with a white stripe, and there are 8 white stripes in all. How wide is the crosswalk?

(a) 6 m            (b) 6.6 m

(c) 5.4 m          (d) 5 m

31. The function(s) of Governor is/are

(a) He is executive head of state

(b) He ensures that the state government works within rules and regulation of the constitution

(c) Both (a) and (b) are correct

(d) None of these

32. What is 'Sedentary Agriculture'?

(a) Farming of land at different sites

(b) Farming of land at a fixed location instead of moving from one site to another

(c) Farming of cereals and pulses

(d) None of these

33. The members of Rajya Sabha are:

(a) elected directly

(b) elected indirectly

(c) nominated

(d) partly directly and partly indirectly elected

34. 'Rozgar Badhao' is the slogan launched by which Prime Minister?

(a) Dr. Manmohan Singh

(b) Rajiv Gandhi

(c) Indira Gandhi

(d) V.P. Singh

35. Which among the following is the driest desert on Earth?

(a) Kalahari

(b) Atacama

(c) Mojave Desert

(d) Tabernas Desert

36. The National Gandhi Museum (NGM) is located in which city?

(a) Mumbai

(b) Ahmedabad

(c) New Delhi

(d) Gandhinagar

37. Liu Xiaobo, the Nobel Peace Prize

laureate has passed away. He hailed from which country?

(a) Indonesia      (b) China

(c) Taiwan         (d) Japan

38. Who is the author of the book "Narendra Modi: The Making of a Legend"?

(a) Sanjay Mathur

(b) Bindeshwar Pathak

(c) Aditya Sen

(d) Mohan Chauhan

39. Which Indian-origin personality was appointed as the UNICEF's Global Goodwill Ambassador?

(a) Ishani Duttagupta

(b) Jasleen Laghari

(c) Shand Panesar

(d) Lilly Singh

40. What was the theme for the 2017 International Day of UN Peacekeeper?

(a) Investing in peace around the world

(b) Investing in security across the globe

(c) Investing in peace across the globe

(d) Investing in security around the world

**Name :** ________

**Max. Marks : 40**

**Number of Questions : 40**

**Time : 2 Hours**

**There is no negative marking in the test.**

1. This breed of dog shown in the picture is most commonly kept as a companion dog. In China, it is referred to as Songshi Quan which means puffy-lion dog. Identify it.

   (a) Shih Tzu  (b) Chow-Chow
   (c) Lhasa Apso  (d) Pekingese

2. Which of the following National parks has become the largest habitat of the endangered estuarine crocodiles in India?

   (a) Jim Corbett National Park

   (b) Bhitarkanika National Park

   (c) Ranthambore National Park

   (d) Nagarhole National Park

3. The term 'ecosystem' represents a group of living organisms, non-living things such as air, water and soil, and their interaction in the habitat in which they live and thrive. Who first coined the term ecosystem?

(a) 
Carl Linnaeus

(b) 
Arthur Tansley

(c) 
J B S Haldane

(d) 
E P Odum

4. Soap and detergents are the source of organic pollutants like:

   (a) Glycerol

   (b) Polyphosphates

   (c) Sulphonated hydrocarbons

   (d) All of these

5. Earthquake occurs
   (a) When magma inside earth comes out
   (b) When high pressure wind blows
   (c) When lithosphere plates move, causing the earth's surface to vibrate.
   (c) None of these

6. Which resource fulfils 95% of our food requirement?
   (a) Land          (b) Water
   (c) Solar         (d) Wind

7. The liquid used in a simple barometer is:
   (a) mercury       (b) water
   (c) alcohol       (d) kerosene

8. The India Indian Space Research Organisation (ISRO) is set to launch first solar mission in 2019. What is it called?
   (a) Aditya-L
   (b) SuryaNamaskar-L1
   (c) Aditya-L1
   (d) Surya-L1

9. Which of the following planets is the brightest?
   (a) Mercury       (b) Venus
   (c) Mars          (d) Jupiter

10. Rahul mixes small stone particles in water. Then shake the mixture and allow to stand, after few times, the stone particles settles at the bottom of the container of water. This represents the phenomena of:
   (a) decantation
   (b) sedimentation
   (c) filtration
   (d) None of these

11. Which of the following is used to measure the magnitude of the earthquake?
   (a) Barometer
   (b) Richter scale or Moment magnitude scale.
   (c) Barograph
   (d) Windvane

12. Which of the following parts/provisions of the Indian Constitution cannot be amended :
   (a) Preamble to the Constitution
   (b) Directive Principles of State Policy
   (c) Fundamental Rights
   (d) Judicial Review

13. The technique of mural painting executed upon freshly laid lime plaster is known as -
   (a) Fresco
   (b) Gouache
   (c) Tempera
   (d) Cubism

14. Who finally approves the draft of the five year plans?

(a) President of India

(b) Planning Commission

(c) National Development Council

(d) Parliament and State Legislature

15. The stomach contains an enzyme called pepsin that helps in the breakdown of what macromolecule?

(a) lipids

(b) carbohydrates

(c) water

(d) proteins

16. The book 'Cricket my Lifestyle' is written by:

(a) Sunil Gavaskar

(b) Sachin Tendulkar

(c) Mohinder Amarnath

(d) Kapil Dev

17. Which one of the following gives the correct chronological order of the vedas?

(a) Rigveda, Samaveda, Atharvaveda, Yajurveda

(b) Rigveda, Samaveda, Yajurveda, Atharvaveda

(c) Atharvaveda, Yajurveda, Samaveda, Rigveda

(d) Rigveda, Yajurveda, Samaveda, Atharvaveda

18. What is the modern name of Patliputra?

(a) Patna      (b) Allahabad

(c) Bhagalpur  (d) Munger

19. Which state government has launched the Ganga Hariteema Yojana ( or Ganga Greenery scheme)?

(a) Bihar

(b) West Bengal

(c) Uttar Pradesh

(d) Jharkhand

20. Arrange the increasing order of these planets based on their distance from the sun

1. Mars        2. Jupiter

3. Earth       4. Saturn

(a) 1, 2, 3, 4      (b) 3, 2, 1, 4

(c) 3, 1, 2, 4      (d) 3, 2, 4, 1

21. Which of the following statements is not correct?

(a) The earth rotates on its axis

(b) The earth is inclined at $96\frac{1}{2}°$ with its orbital plane.

(c) Day and night are caused due to the rotation of the earth.

(d) The earth receives light from the sun.

22. Which of the following are the non-Indian neighboring islands across the sea to the south of India?

(i) Andaman and Nicobar Islands

(ii) Sri Lanka

(iii) Lakshadweep Islands

(iv) Maldives

(a) (i) and (ii)      (b) (ii) and (iii)

(c) (ii) and (iv)     (d) (iii) and (iv)

23. Match column I with column II and select the correct answer using the code given below the columns:

| Column I | Column II |
| --- | --- |
| A. Tiger | (i) Assam |
| B. Peacock | (ii) National Animal |
| C. Asiatic lion | (iii) Gir forest |
| D. One horned rhinoceroses | (iv) National bird |

(a) A - (iii), B - (i), C - (iv), D - (ii)

(b) A - (ii), B - (iv), C - (iii), D - (i)

(c) A - (iii), B - (i), C - (iv), D - (ii)

(d) A - (iv), B - (i), C - (ii), D - (iii)

24. Consider the following pairs

I. Savannah   – East Africa

II. Prairies   – North America

III. Veld   – Europe

IV. Down   – Australia

Which of the above pairs are correct?

(a) I, II, III and IV

(b) I, II and IV

(c) I and II

(d) III and IV

25. Soil and water are contaminated with hydrocarbons by —.

(a) oil spills

(b) leaking of petrol

(c) both (a) and (b)

(d) None of them

26. The boat race is an important part of which festival?

(a) Diwali          (b) Onam

(c) Holi          (d) Bhai Dooj

27. Which state government has rolled out 'Rupashree Scheme' for marriage of poor girls?

(a) Tamil Nadu

(b) Odisha

(c) West Bengal

(d) Assam

28. Poll Monitoring System was implemented in which among the following states of India for the first time?

(a) Goa

(b) Manipur

(c) Assam

(d) Tripura

29. This painless medical process makes use of computer-processed combinations of many X-ray images taken from different angles to produce cross-sectional (virtual "slices") of specific areas of a scanned object, allowing the user to see inside the object without cutting. What is it called?

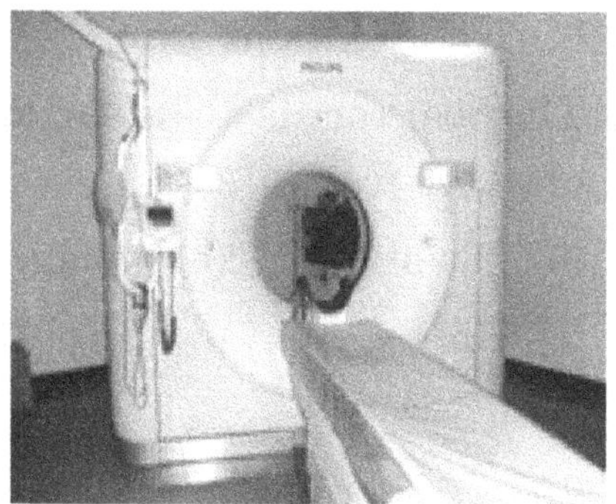

(a) X-ray imaging

(b) Electroencephalography

(c) Electrocardiography

(d) Computer Aided Tomography

30. Prince William, the second in line to the throne of Great Britain, and his brother, Henry, are the sons of a famous and beautiful mother who promoted many humane causes. What was her name?

(a) Lady Elizabeth Bowes-Lyon

(b) Lady Diana Spencer

(c) Lady Camilla Parker Bowles

(d) Lady Sarah Ferguson

31. Who was the last Mughal emperor deposed by the British and exiled to Burma after the Indian Rebellion of 1857?

(a) Shah Alam II

(b) Akbar Shah II

(c) Bahadur Shah II

(d) Aurangzeb

32. Which country hosted the 15th Asia Media Summit (AMS-2018)?

(a) Philippines  (b) Singapore

(c) Malaysia  (d) India

33. He was an English comic actor, filmmaker and composer who rose to fame in the silent era. The famous quote, 'A day without laughter is a day wasted' was quoted by him. Identify him.

(a) 

Bob Marley

(b) 

Charlie Chaplin

(c) 

Ben Turpin

(d) 

Harold Llyod

34. Who among the following was the owner of Jaipur Pink Panthers team, one of the Pro Kabaddi League 2016 teams?

(a)

(b)

(c)

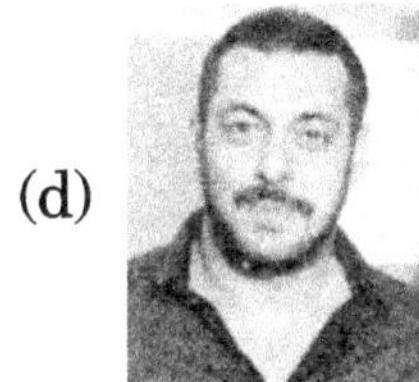

(d)

35. Identify the yogasana shown in the given picture.

(a) Halasana

(b) Sarvangasana

(c) Savasana

(d) Parsvottanasana

36. Who planted the 'Tree of Liberty' at Srirangapatnam?
   (a) Hyder Ali

   (b) Tipu Sultan

   (c) Chin Quilich Khan

   (d) Murshid Quli Khan

37. The Grizzled Squirrel Wildlife Sanctuary (GSWS) is located in which state?

   (a) Uttrakhand

   (b) Tamil Nadu

   (c) Gujarat

   (d) Chhattisgarh

38. ISRO has successfully launched navigation satellite IRNSS-1I into the orbit from which launch vehicle?
   (a) PSLV-C41

   (b) PSLV-C43

   (c) PSLV-C42

   (d) PSLV-C44

39. The Mughalsarai junction has recently renamed as Deen Dayal been Upadhyaya railway station. It is located in which state?

(a) Bihar

(b) Uttar Pradesh

(c) Uttarakhand

(d) Delhi

40. Who has become the first Indian Women Wrestler to bag gold at the 18th Asian Games 2018 ?

(a) Pooja Dhanda

(b) Sakshi malik

(c) Vinesh Phogat

(d) Priyanka Phogat

**Name :** _____________

**Number of Questions : 25**

**There is no negative marking in the test.**

**Max. Marks : 25**

**Time : 1 Hour**

---

1. Complete the series : 13, 24, 46, 90, 178, .........

   (a) 354       (b) 266

   (c) 364       (d) 344

**DIRECTION (Q. 2):** In the following question, choose the missing term out of the given alternatives. Reference : A B C D E F G H I J K L M N O P Q R S T U V W X Y Z

AZ, CX, FU, .......

   (a) IR       (b) IV

   (c) JQ       (d) KP

3. If the first three letters of the word COMPREHENSION are reversed, then the last three letters are added and then the remaining letters are reversed and added, then which letter will be exactly in the middle?

   (a) H       (b) N

   (c) R       (d) S

**DIRECTION (Qs. 4) :** In the following questions, a group of letters is given which are numbered 1, 2, 3, 4, 5 and 6. Below are given four alternatives containing combinations of these numbers. Select that combination of numbers so that letters arranged accordingly form a meaningful word.

4.   I   P   E   L   O   C

      1   2   3   4   5   6

   (a) 1, 4, 3, 5, 2, 6

   (b) 2, 5, 4, 1, 6, 3

   (c) 3, 4, 5, 1, 2, 6

   (d) 4, 5, 1, 2, 3, 6

**DIRECTION (Q.5) :** In the following question, four pairs of words are given out of which the words in three pairs bear a certain common relationship. Choose the pair in which the words are differently related.

5. (a) Bottle : Wine

   (b) Cup : Tea

   (c) Pitcher : Water

   (d) Ball : Bat

**DIRECTION (Q.6)** : In the following number series, one term is wrong. The wrong term is given as one of the four alternatives. Find the wrong term in each case.

6.  2, 12, 32, 63, 102

(a) 12       (b) 32

(c) 63       (d) 102

**DIRECTIONS (Qs. 7 & 8)** : In each question, there are four terms in each question. The terms right to symbol :: have same relationship as the term of the left to symbol ::. Out of the four, one term is missing which is one of the four alternatives given below. Find out the correct alternatives.

7.  UVST : WTUR :: ? : RILO

(a) P K J Q

(b) T S U V

(c) U V T S

(d) T S V U

8.  Race : Fatigue : : Fast : ?

(a) Food

(b) Appetite

(c) Hunger

(d) Weakness

**DIRECTION (Qs. 9)** : Words are coded in a particular way in terms of numbers. Find the code of the word given in the following equation.

9.  If DRIVER = 7 and CAR = 4, then BOOK = ?

(a) 5       (b) 8

(c) 12       (d) 14

10. In a certain code language, 'ne ri so' means 'good rainy day' 'si ne po' means 'day is wonderful' and 'ri jo' means 'good boy'. Which of the following means 'rainy' in the code?

(a) ne       (b) si

(c) ri       (d) so

11. In a class of 43 students. Sarita is at 27th position from the top What is her rank from the other side?

(a) $16^{th}$       (b) $17^{th}$

(c) $15^{th}$       (d) $21^{th}$

**DIRECTIONS (Qs. 12 & 13)** : These series are based on mixed operations in which various figures change their directions/positions, increase or decrease in number as well as change qualitatively. The problem is that the figure contains several separate figures and a blank space. The answer choices are several numbered figures marked 1, 2, 3, 4, 5. You have to choose one of the answer figures which should replace the question mark or appropriately fit in the blank space given in the problem figure.

12. **Question figures:**

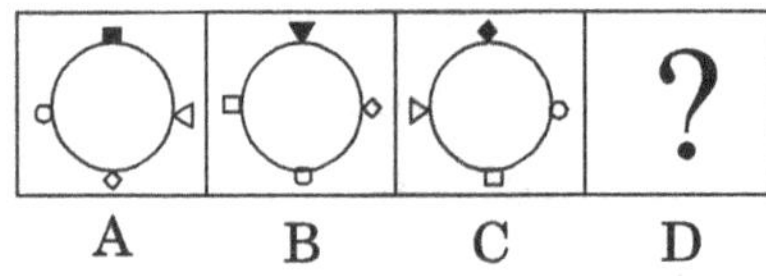

A     B     C     D

**Answer figures:**

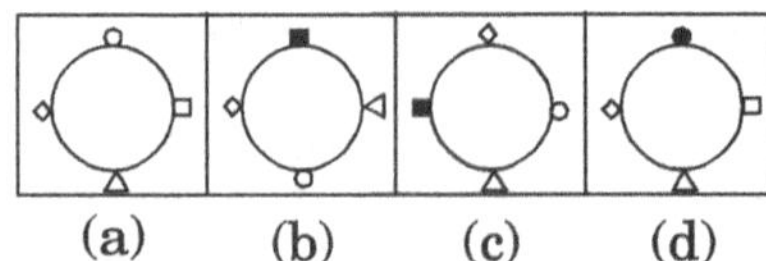

(a)     (b)     (c)     (d)

13.

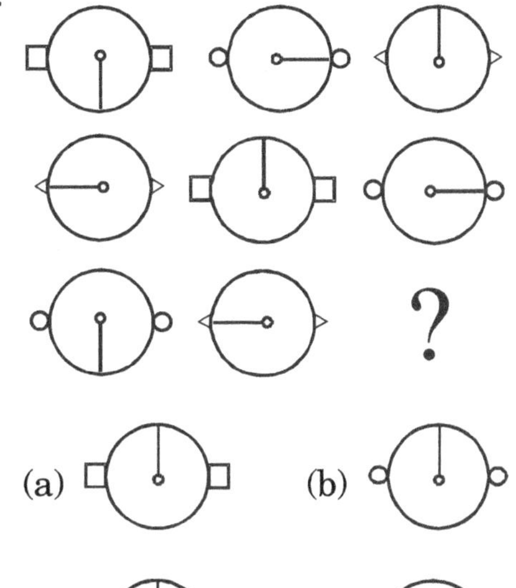

(a) 425

(b) 1625

(c) 4125

(d) 2541

---

**DIRECTIONS (Qs. 14 & 15) :** S and R are brothers. T is daughter of S. U is the spouse of R and mother of Q. P is the daughter of V, who is the spouse of T.

---

14. Who is the grandfather of P ?

    (a) U         (b) S

    (c) R         (d) V

15. Who is the cousin of Q ?

    (a) T         (b) V

    (c) R         (d) P

---

**DIRECTION (Qs. 16):** In the following question, three statements of numbers following same rules are given. Find the rule and accordingly find the value of the number.

---

16. If 213 = 419; 322 = 924; 415 = 16125, then 215 = ?

17. Six persons are sitting in a circle. 'J' is between 'N' and 'O'; 'N' is opposite 'M'; and 'L' is not in either of the neighbouring seats of 'N'. Who is opposite to 'K'?

    (a) M         (b) O

    (c) J         (d) L

18. Which one of the following diagrams best depicts the relationship among Mammals, Cows and Crows?

    (a) 

    (b) 

    (c) 

    (d) 

19. The figure represents three classes of youth in a village. How many educated youth is poor?

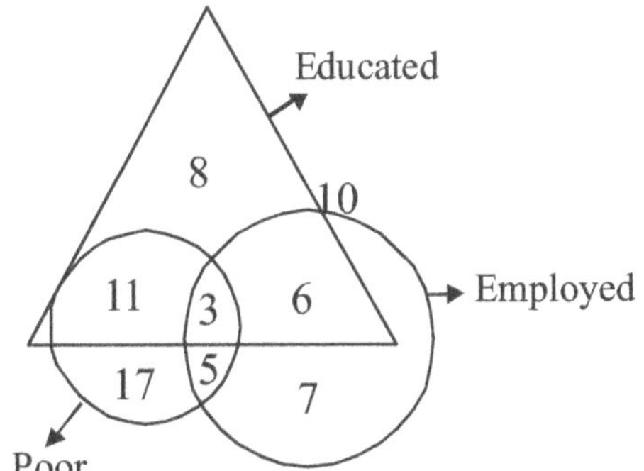

(a) 14      (b) 9

(c) 6      (d) 19

**DIRECTION (Qs. 20) :** Which answer figure completes the pattern given in the question figure?

20. **Question Figure :**

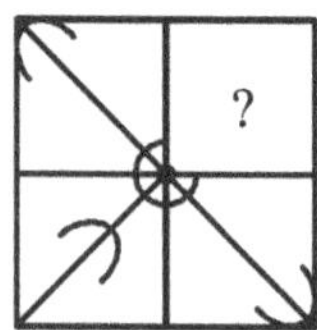

**Answer Figures :**

(a) 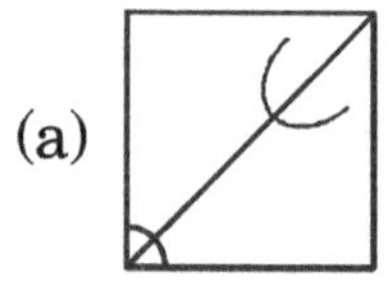    (b) 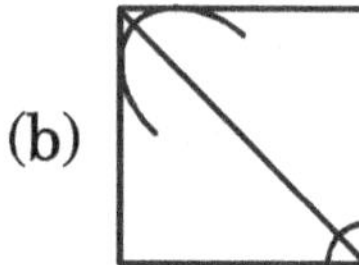

(c) 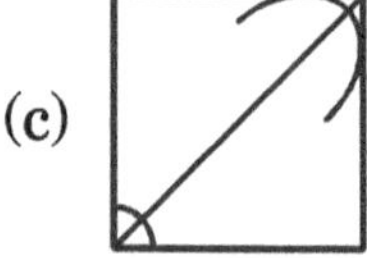    (d) 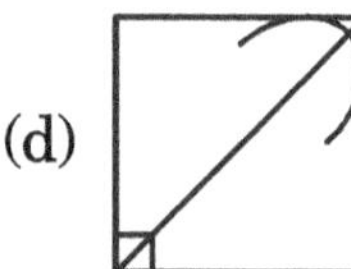

**DIRECTION (Q. 21) :** In each of the following question, select the answer figure in which the question figure is hidden/embedded.

21. **Question Figure:**

**Answer Figures :**

(a) 

(b) 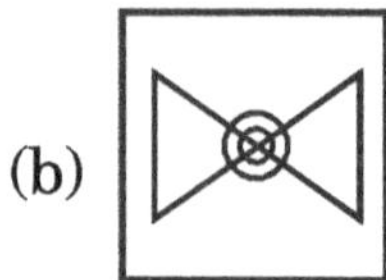

(c) 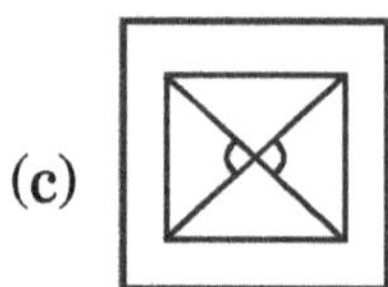

(d) 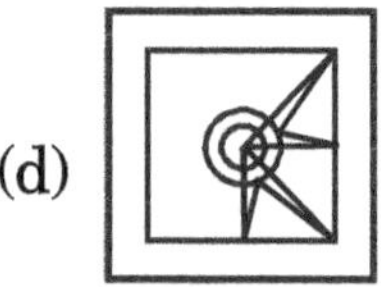

**DIRECTION (Qs. 22):** In the following question, select the missing number front the given responses.

22. 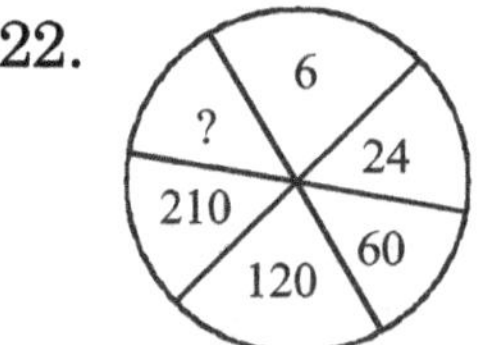

(a) 330      (b) 336

(c) 428      (d) 420

23. A boy running towards South, turns to his right and runs. Then he turns to his right and finally turns to his left. Towards which direction is he running now?

(a) East

(b) West

(c) South

(d) North

24. If '+' means 'x', '−' means '÷', '×' means '−' and '÷' means '+', then what will be the value of $16 \div 64 - 8 \times 4 + 2$ ?

    (a) 12      (b) 24

    (c) 16      (d) 18

25. If the mirror is placed on the line LM, then which of the answer figures is the right image of the given question figure?

**Question Figure :**

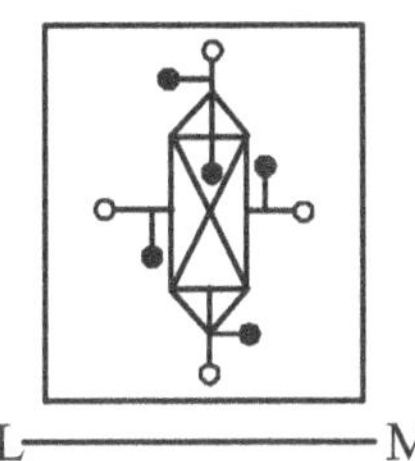

L————————M

**Answer Figures :**

(a) 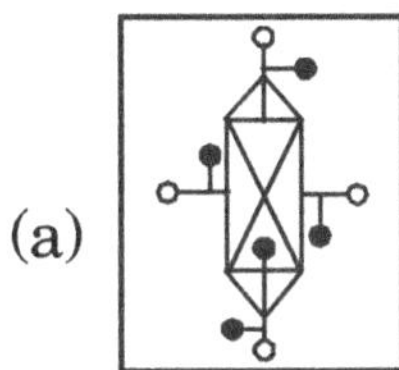      (b) 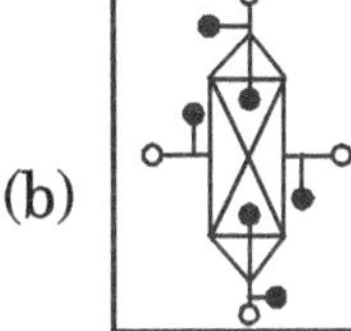

(c) 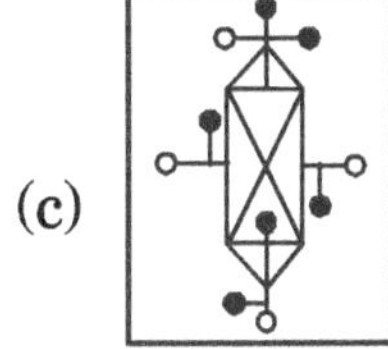      (d) 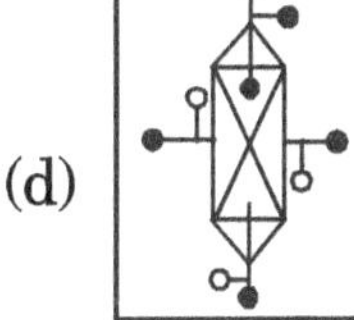

# OLYMPIAD
# Mock Test  2

**Name :** _____________

**Number of Questions : 25**

**There is no negative marking in the test.**

**Max. Marks : 25**

**Time : 1 Hour**

1. Two positions of a dice are given. Which number would be at the top when bottom is 2?

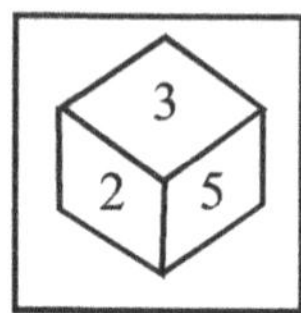 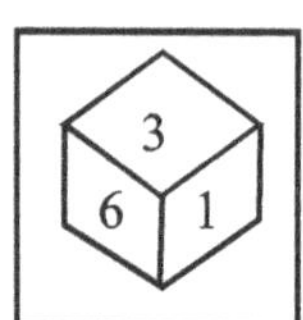

   (a) 4       (b) 1
   (c) 5       (d) 6

2. In the following figure, the boys who are cricketer and sober are indicated by which number ?

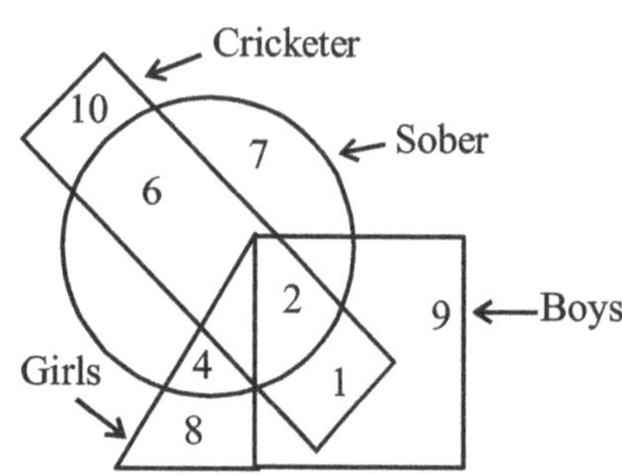


   (a) 6       (b) 5
   (c) 4       (d) 2

3. If the day before yesterday was Sunday, what day will it be three days after the day after tomorrow?
   (a) Sunday     (b) Monday
   (c) Wednesday  (d) Saturday

4. If a mirror is placed on the line MN, then which of the answer figures is the right image of the given figure?

**Question figure:**

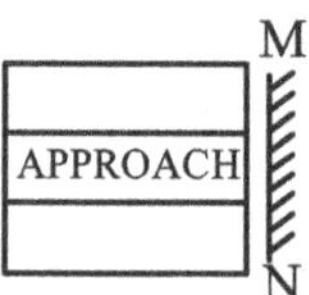


**Answer figures:**

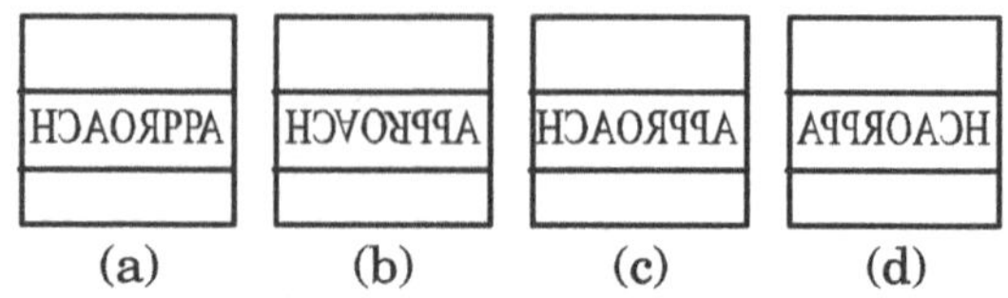


---

**DIRECTIONS (Qs. 5 & 6) :** In the following question a series is given with one term missing. Choose the correct alternative from the given ones that will complete the series.

---

5. 2, 3, 6, 7, 14, 15, ?
   (a) 16       (b) 30
   (c) 31       (d) 32

6. STU, WXY, ABC, ____?
   (a) DEF       (b) EFG
   (c) FCG       (d) EGF

**DIRECTIONS (Qs. 7 & 8) :** In the following questions, select the missing number from the given responses.

7.  | 5 | 25 | 5 |
    | 7 | 49 | 7 |
    | 6 | ? | 6 |

   (a) 38            (b) 40
   (c) 36            (d) 35

8. Select the missing number from the given responses.

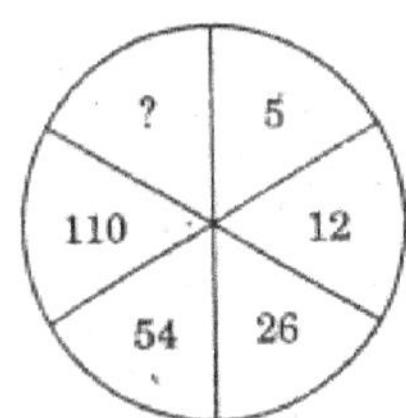

   (a) 132          (b) 122
   (c) 222          (d) 212

9. Select the venn diagram that correctly shows the relationship.
   Continent, City, Country

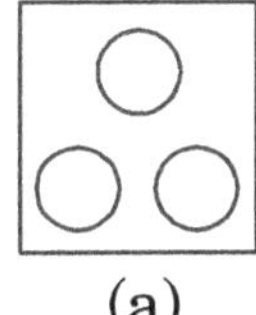 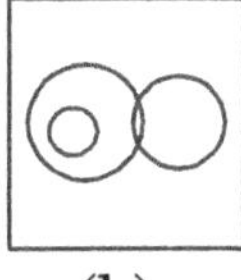 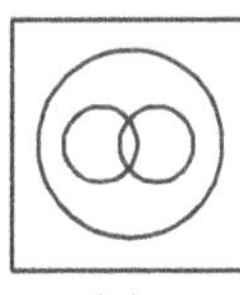 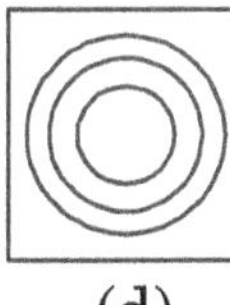

   (a)       (b)       (c)       (d)

10. A triangular piece of paper is folded and cut as shown below. Find out from the answer figures how it will appear when opened.

**Question Figures :**

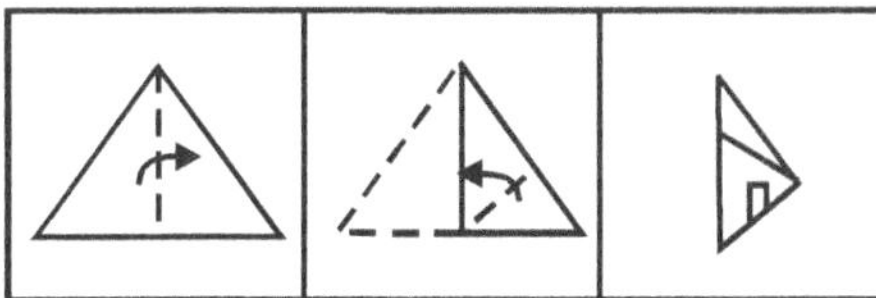

**Answer Figures :**

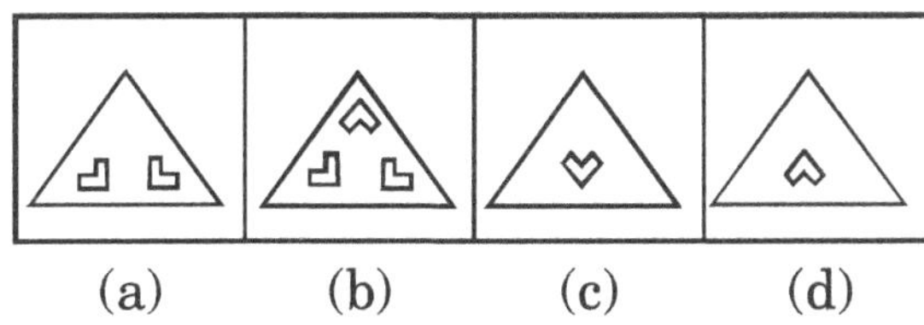

   (a)       (b)       (c)       (d)

11. If '–' stands '÷'; '+' stands for '×'; '÷' stands for '–' and '×' stands for '+', which one of the following is correct?
    (a) $10 + 5 - 5 \div 5 \times 5 = 10$
    (b) $10 - 5 + 5 \div 5 \times 5 = 25$
    (c) $10 \times 5 \div 5 + 5 - 5 = 0$
    (d) $10 \div 5 \times 5 - 5 + 5 = 15$

12. Veni is a year older than Smith. Smith is two years older than Salim. Raju is a year older than Salim. Who is the youngest of all ?
    (a) Raju       (b) Salim
    (c) Veni       (d) Smith

13. A cyclist goes 30 km to North and then turning East he goes 40 km. Again he turns to his right and goes 20 km. After this, he turns to his right and goes 40 km. How far is he from his starting point ?
    (a) 25 km      (b) 40 km
    (c) 6 km       (d) 10 km

14. A family consists of a man, his wife, his three sons, their wives and three children in each son's family. How many members are there in the family ?
    (a) 12       (b) 13
    (c) 15       (d) 17

**DIRECTIONS (15 & 16):** In each of the following questions, find the odd word/number/letters/word/number pair from the given alternatives.

15. (a) VWY      (b) QRT
    (c) LMO      (d) JKL

16. (a) 12–16     (b) 60–80
    (c) 30–50     (d) 36–48

17. Five policemen are standing in a row facing south. Shekhar is to the immediate right of Dhanush. Bala

is between Basha and Dhanush. David is at the extreme right end of the row. Who is standing in the middle of the row?
(a) Bala            (b) Basha
(c) Shekhar         (d) Dhanush

18. Which of the answer figures include the separate components found in the question figure?

**Question figure:**

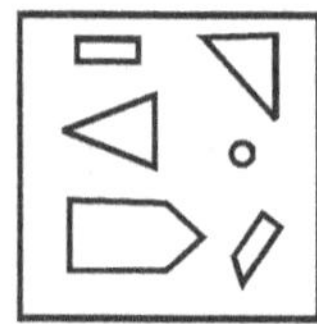

**Answer figures:**

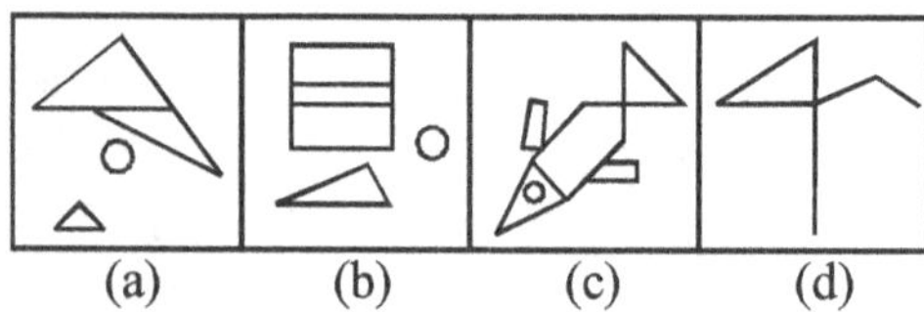

(a)         (b)         (c)         (d)

19. From the given answer figures, select the one in which the question figure is hidden/ embedded.

**Question Figure:**

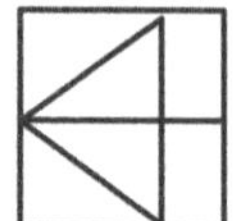

**Answer Figures:**

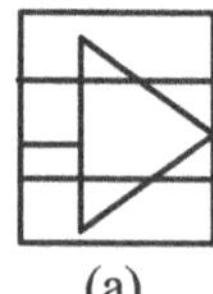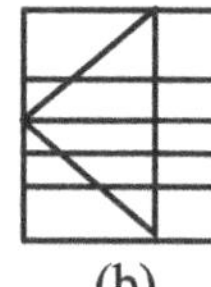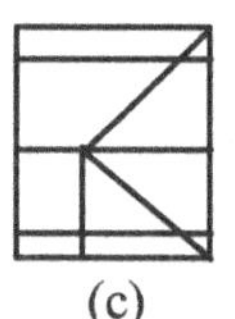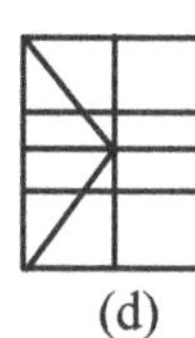

(a)         (b)         (c)         (d)

20. Which answer figure will complete the pattern in the question figure?

**Question Figure**

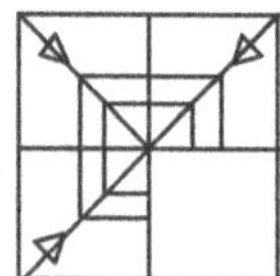

**Answer Figures:**

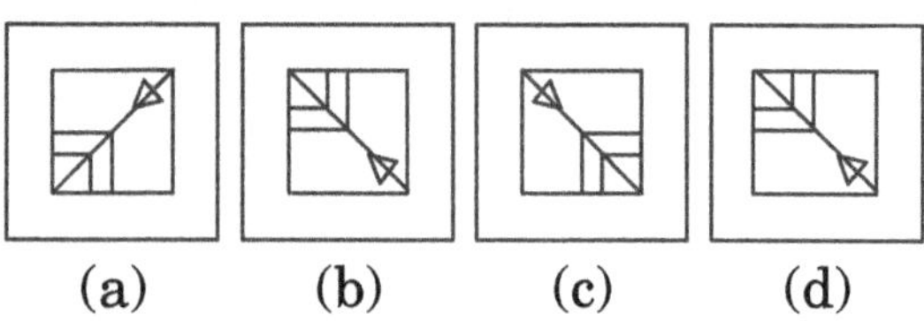

(a)         (b)         (c)         (d)

21. If SEASONAL is written as ESSANOLA, how can SEPARATE be written in that code?
(a) SEAPARET    (b) ESPARATE
(c) ESPAARTE    (d) ESAPARET

22. If FLATTER is coded as 7238859 and MOTHER is coded as 468159, then how is MAMMOTH coded?
(a) 4344681        (b) 4344651
(c) 4146481        (d) 4346481

23. Arrange the following words according to the dictionary order.
1.  Banquet      2.  Bangle
3.  Bandage      4.  Bantam
5.  Bank
(a) 3, 2, 4, 5, 1    (b) 3, 5, 2, 1, 4
(c) 3, 2, 1, 5, 4    (d) 3, 2, 5, 1, 4

**DIRECTION (Qs. 24) :** From the given alternatives select the word which cannot be formed using the letters of the given word.

24. REASONABLE
(a) NOBLE          (b) BONES
(c) BRAIN          (d) ARSON

**DIRECTION (Qs. 25) :** Select the related letter / word / number from the given alternatives.

25. Square : Cube :: Circle : ?
(a) Ellipse          (b) Parabola
(c) Cone             (d) Sphere

# OLYMPIAD Mock Test 3

Name : _____________

Number of Questions : 25

There is no negative marking in the test.

Max. Marks : 25

Time : 1 Hour

---

**DIRECTIONS (Qs. 1-2)** : In each of the following questions, choose the missing term out of the given alternatives. Reference : A B C D E F G H I J K L M N O P Q R S T U V W X Y Z

1. AZ, CX, FU, .......
   - (a) IR
   - (b) IV
   - (c) JQ
   - (d) KP

2. 3F, 6G, 11I, 18L, ....
   - (a) 21O
   - (b) 25N
   - (c) 27P
   - (d) 27Q

3. If the first and second letters in the word DEPRESSION were interchanged, also the third and the fourth letters, the fifth and the sixth letters and so on, which of the following would be the seventh letter from the right ?
   - (a) R
   - (b) O
   - (c) S
   - (d) None of these

4. Arrange the given words in alphabetical order and choose the one that comes in the 2nd position.
   - (a) Restrict
   - (b) Rocket
   - (c) Robber
   - (d) Radom

5. In a row of students, Deepak is seventh from the left and Madhu is twelfth from the right. If they interchange their positions, Deepak becomes twenty-second from the left. How many students are there in the row?
   - (a) 19
   - (b) 31
   - (c) 33
   - (d) Can't be found

6. Ajay is the brother of Vijay. Mili is the sister of Ajay. Sanjay is the brother of Rahul and Mehul is the daughter of Vijay. Who is Sanjay's Uncle ?
   - (a) Rahul
   - (b) Ajay
   - (c) Mehul
   - (d) Data inadequate

7. Pointing out to a photograph, a man tells his friend, " she is the daughter of the only son of my father's wife. How is the girl in the photograph related to the man?
   - (a) Daughter
   - (b) Cousin
   - (c) Mother
   - (d) Sister

8. Jatin leaves his house and walks 12 km towards North. He turns right and walks another 12 km. He turns right again, walks 12 km more and turns left to walk 5 km. How far is he from his home and in which direction ?

(a) 7 km East

(b) 10 km East

(c) 17 km East

(d) 24 km East

9. Which of the following diagrams correctly represents the relationship among Tennis fans, Cricket players and students.

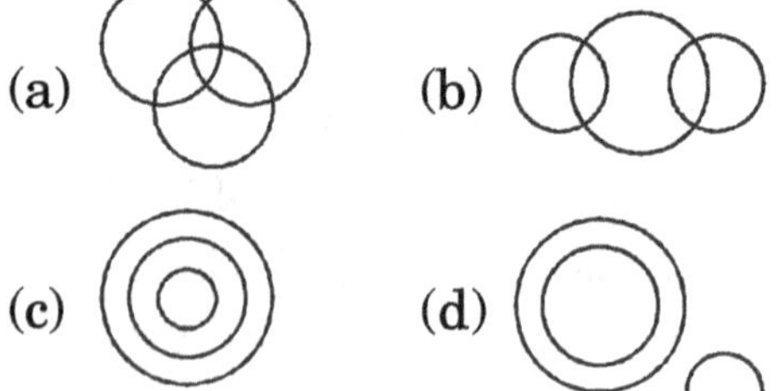

DIRECTIONS (Qs. 10 & 11) : Find the missing number in the following sets of number around the circle from the choice given below :

10.

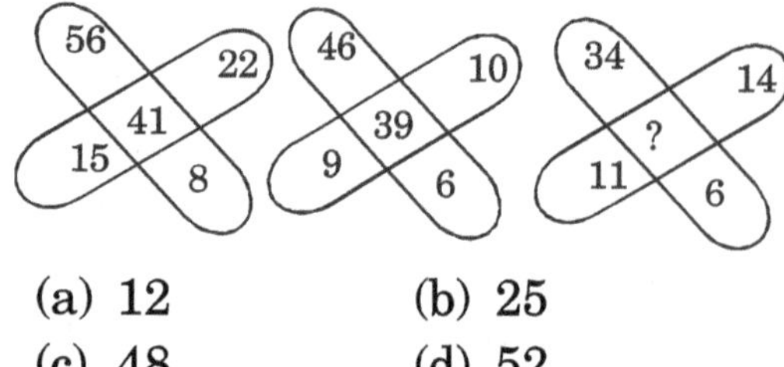

(a) 12              (b) 25
(c) 48              (d) 52

Find the missing term.

11.

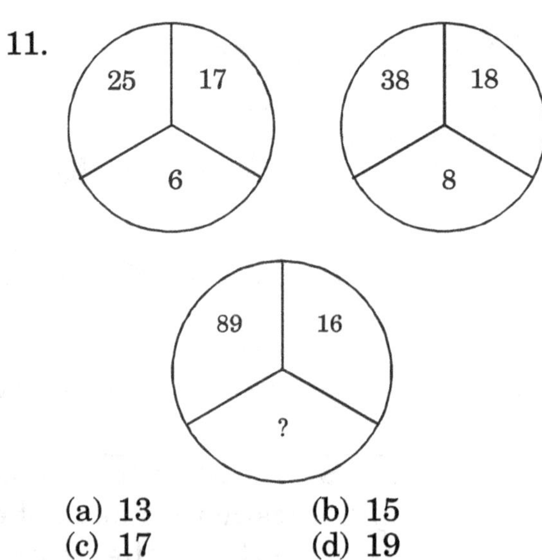

(a) 13              (b) 15
(c) 17              (d) 19

DIRECTION (Q.12) : In each of the following questions, a figure series is given out of which the last figure is missing. Find which one would complete the series.

12.

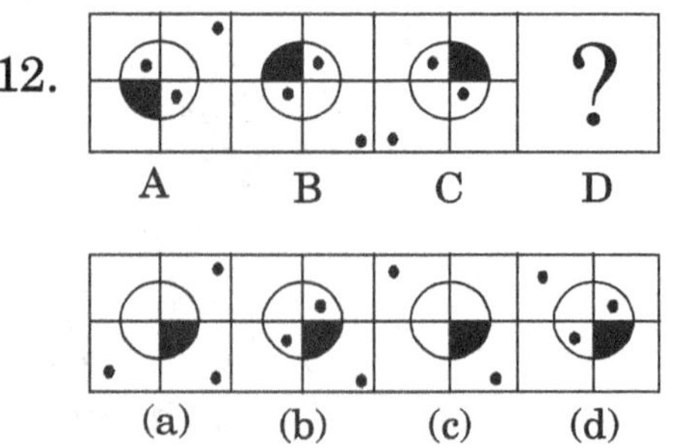

13. Group the following figures into three classes on the basic of identical properties.

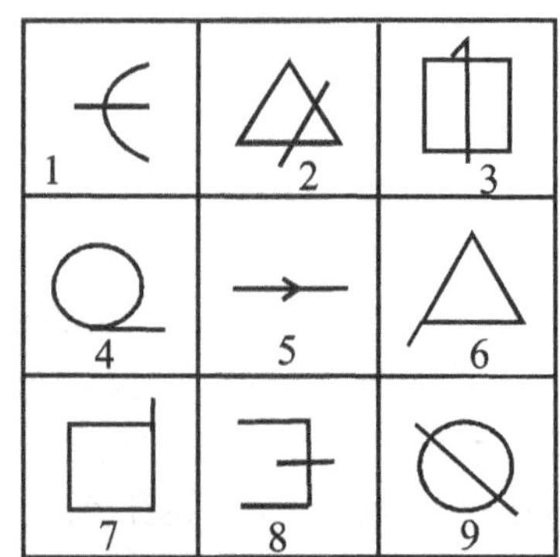

   (a) 1, 3, 9 ; 2, 5, 8 ; 4, 6, 7

   (b) 4, 8, 9 ; 1, 2, 5 ; 3, 6, 7

   (c) 2, 5, 9 ; 1, 3, 8 ; 2, 6, 7

   (d) 1, 8, 9 ; 4, 6, 7 ; 2, 3, 5

14. When the following figure is folded to form a cube, how many dots would lie opposite the face bearing five dots ?

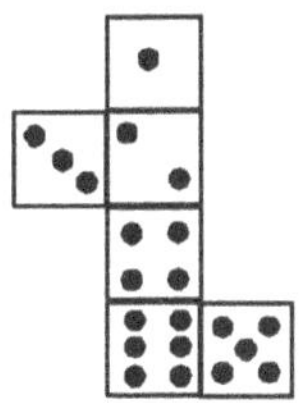

   (a) 1           (b) 2

   (c) 3           (d) 4

15. What is the number of squares in fig ?

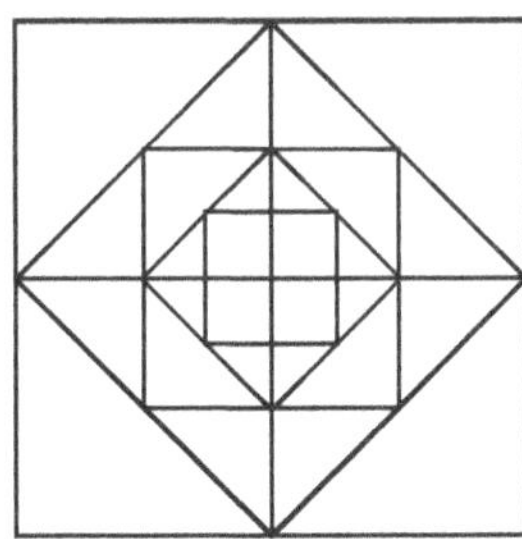

   (a) 12         (b) 13

   (c) 15         (d) 17

16. If the word LEADER is coded as 20-13-9-12-13-26, how would you write LIGHT?

   (a) 20-15-16-18-23

   (b) 20-17-15-16-28

   (c) 20-16-15-17-22

   (d) 20-16-17-15-27

17. In a line, Naresh is $17^{th}$ from the left & $22^{nd}$ from the right. How many students are there in the line?

   (a) 40         (b) 38

   (c) 39         (d) 37

18. If '−' denotes '+'
   '+' denotes '×'
   '+' denotes '×'
   '×' denotes '÷'
   then $27 \times 3 + 6 + 9 - 8 = ?$

   (a) 35         (b) 17

   (c) 15         (d) 14.5

19. A group of friends are sitting in an arrangement one each at the corner of an octagon. All are facing the centre. Mahima is sitting diagonally opposite Rama, who is on Sushma's right. Ravi is next to Sushma and opposite Girdhar, who is on Chandra's left. Savitri is not on mahima's right but opposite Shalini. Who is on Shalini's right?

   (a) Ravi       (b) Mahima

   (c) Girdhar    (d) Rama

**DIRECTIONS (Qs. 20 & 21) :** Select the related letter / word / number from the given alternatives.

20. Length : Metre :: Power : ?
   (a) Calories    (b) Degree
   (c) Watt       (d) Kilogram

21. 7 : 56 :: 9 : ?
   (a) 63         (b) 81
   (c) 90         (d) 99

22. Find the answer figure which completes the question figure.

**Question Figure:**

**Answer Figures:**

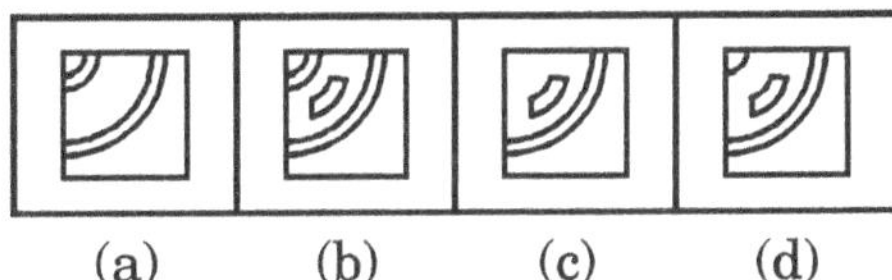

   (a)      (b)      (c)      (d)

23. In the following question, a piece of paper is folded and cut as shown below in the question figures. From the given answer figures, indicate how it will appear when opened.

**Question Figures:**

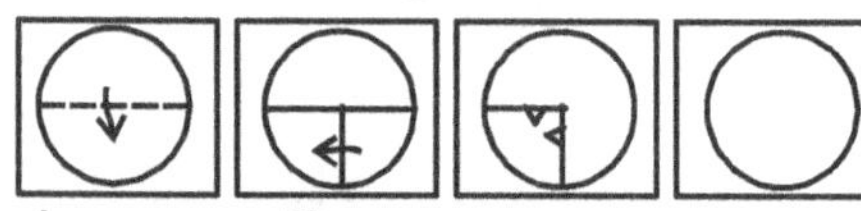

**Answer figures:**

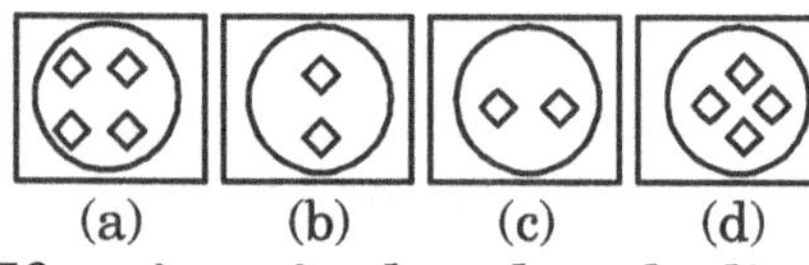

   (a)        (b)        (c)        (d)

24. If a mirror is placed on the line MN, then which of the answer figures is the right image of the given figure?

**Question Figure :**

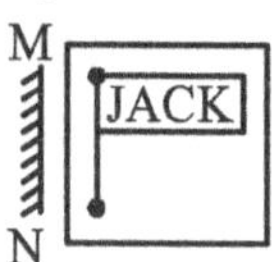

**Answer Figures :**

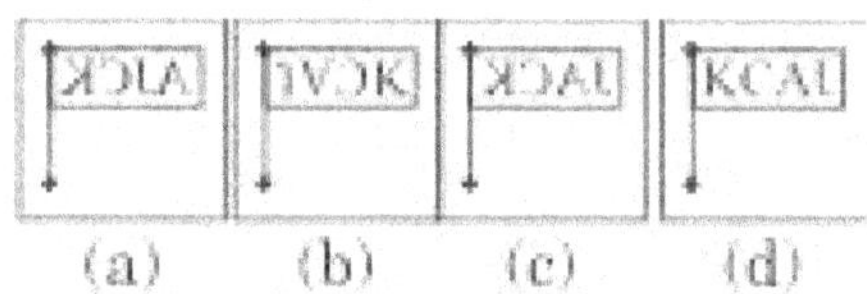

   (a)        (b)        (c)        (d)

25. In certain code, RAGHAVAN is written as GARVAHNA. In that code which word will be written as MATHAVAN?
    (a) TAMVAHNA
    (b) TAMVAHAN
    (c) TAMHAVNA
    (d) MATVAHNA

# OLYMPIAD
# Mock Test 4

Name : _____________

Number of Questions : 40

There is no negative marking in the test.

Max. Marks : 40

Time : 2 Hours

1. Find the missing term.
   7, 13, 27, 53, ?, 213
   (a) 106          (b) 107
   (c) 105          (d) 108

**DIRECTION (Q. 2)** : Which of the following would come in place of the question mark? in the following letter number series ?

2. P 3 C    R 5 F    T 8 I    V 12 L ?
   (a) Y 17 O        (b) X 17 M
   (c) X 17 O        (d) X 16 O

3. If the positions of the third and tenth letters of the word DOCUMENTATION are interchanged, and likewise the positions of the fourth and seventh letters, the second and sixth letters is interchanged, which of the following will be eleventh from the right end ?
   (a) C            (b) I
   (c) T            (d) U

4. Select the combination of numbers so that letters arranged accordingly will form a meaningful word.
   ```
   R  A  C  E  T
   1  2  3  4  5
   ```
   (a) 1, 2, 3, 4, 5    (b) 3, 2, 1, 4, 5
   (c) 5, 2, 3, 4, 1    (d) 5, 1, 2, 3, 4

**DIRECTION (Q. 5)** : Arrange the given words in the sequence in which they occur in the dictionary and then choose the correct sequence.

5. I. Page    II. Pagan    III. Palisade
   IV. Pageant V. Palate
   (a) I, IV, II, III, V
   (b) II, IV, I, III, V
   (c) II, I, IV, V, III
   (d) I, IV, II, V, III

**DIRECTION (Q. 6)** : Find which one word cannot be made from the letters of the given word.

6. CREDENTIAL
   (a) DENTAL       (b) CREATE
   (c) TRAIN        (d) CREAM

**DIRECTIONS (Qs. 7 to 9):** In each of the following questions, four alternatives are given, out of which three are alike in a certain way while one is different. Choose the odd one.

7. (a) Judge        (b) Scant
   (c) Crowd        (d) Flush

8. (a) Rose         (b) Lotus
   (c) Marigold     (d) Lily

9. (a) 9611         (b) 7324
   (c) 2690         (d) 1754

**DIRECTIONS (Q. 10 & 11) :** Choose the correct answer.

10. TSR : FED :: WVU ?
    (a) CAB    (b) MLK
    (c) PQS    (d) GFH
11. Neck is related to Tie in the same way as Waist is related to–
    (a) Watch    (b) Belt
    (c) Ribbon   (d) Shirt
12. 583 : 293 :: 488 : ?
    (a) 291    (b) 378
    (c) 487    (d) 581
13. In a certain language, if 1 is coded as a, 2 as B, 3 as C, and so on, how is flower coded in that code?
    (a) 6121523518  (b) 6121823515
    (c) 6211523518  (d) 6218123515
14. In the following question, select the word which cannot be formed using the letters of the given word.
    CARBONATE
    (a) CARBON   (b) BORN
    (c) EARN     (d) BOSE
15. In a certain code, "RATIONAL' is written as 'RTANIOLA'. How would 'TRIBAL' be written in that code ?
    (a) TRIALB   (b) TIRALB
    (c) TIRLBA   (d) TIRABL
16. In a certain code language, 'low nas hsi ploy' means 'she is bringing coffee'; 'wis sat, low ploy' means 'he is bringing milk'; and 'sat lim nas' means 'milk and coffee'. Which word in that language means 'he' ?
    (a) Sat    (b) Wis
    (c) Ploy   (d) Lew
17. If the cook is called butler, butler is called manager, manager is called teacher, teacher is called clerk and clerk is called principal, who will teach in the class?
    (a) Cook     (b) Butler
    (c) Manager  (d) Clerk
18. Anmol finds that he is twelfth from the right in a line of boys and fourth from the left, how many boys should be added to the line such that there are 35 boys in the line?
    (a) 19    (b) 13
    (c) 14    (d) 20
19. If the day before yesterday was Thursday, when will be Sunday?
    (a) Today
    (b) Two days after today
    (c) Tomorrow
    (d) Day after tomorrow

**DIRECTIONS (Qs. 20 to 22) :** Five persons are sitting in a row. One of the persons at the extreme ends is intelligent and other one is fair. A fat person is sitting to the right of a weak person. A tall person is to the left of the fair person and the weak person is sitting between the intelligent and the fat person.

20. Tall person is at which place counting from right ?
    (a) First    (b) Second
    (c) Third    (d) Fourth
21. Person to the left of weak person possesses which of the following characteristics?
    (a) Intelligent  (b) Fat
    (c) Fair         (d) Tall
22. Which of the following persons is sitting at the centre?
    (a) Intelligent  (b) Fat
    (c) Fair         (d) Weak

**DIRECTIONS (Qs. 23 & 24) :** Read the following information carefully to answer the questions.
(i)   'A $ B' means 'A' is mother of B'
(ii)  A' # B' means "A" is father of B'
(iii) 'A @ B' Means 'A' is husband of B'
(iv)  'A % B' means A is daughter of B'

23. P @ Q $ M # T indicates what relationship of P with T
    (a) Paternal grandmother
    (b) Maternal grandmother
    (c) Paternal grandfather
    (d) Maternal grandfather

24. Which of the following expressions indicates 'R is the sister of H'?
    (a) H $ D @ F # R
    (b) R % D @ F $ H
    (c) R $ D @ F # H
    (d) H % D @ F $ R

25. E is the son of A. D is the son of B. E is married to C. C is B's daughter. How is D related to E?
    (a) Brother
    (b) Uncle
    (c) Father-in-law
    (d) Brother-in-law

26. If ' + ' means ' divided by', '–' means 'added to', '×' means ' subtracted from' and ÷ means ' multiplied by', then what is the value of 24 ÷ 12 – 18 + 9 ?
    (a) – 25            (b) 0.72
    (c) 15.30           (d) 290

27. I am facing south. I turn right and walk 20 m. Then I turn right again and walk 10 m. Then I turn left and walk 10 m and then turning right walk 20 m. Then I turn right again and walk 60 m. In which direction am I from the starting point?
    (a) North           (b) North-west
    (c) East            (d) North-east

28. One day, Ravi left home and cycled 10 km southwards, turned right and cycled 5 km and turned right and cycled 10 km and turned left and cycled 10 km. How many kilometres will he have to cycle to reach his home straight?
    (a) 10 km           (b) 15 km
    (c) 20 km           (d) 25 km

29. Which of the following diagrams correctly represents the relationship among smokers, bidi smokers, cancer patients.

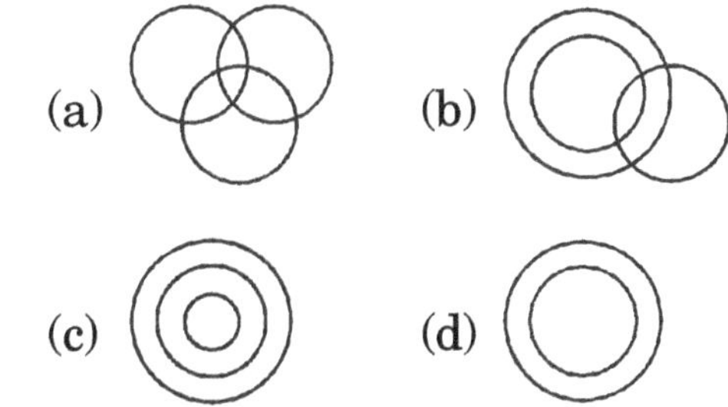

**Directions (Qs. 30 & 31) :** Find the missing character in each of the following questions.

30.
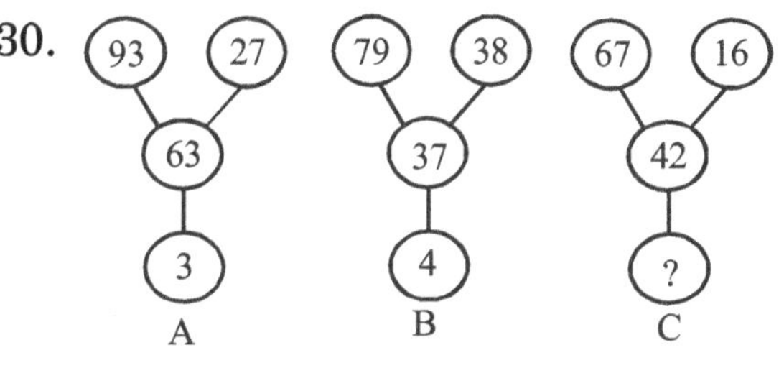

    (a) 5              (b) 6
    (c) 8              (d) 9

**31.** 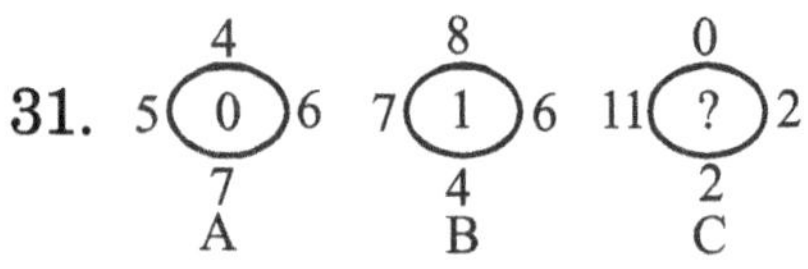

(a) 0        (b) 2

(c) 11       (d) 12

**32.** Which square should replace the question mark ?

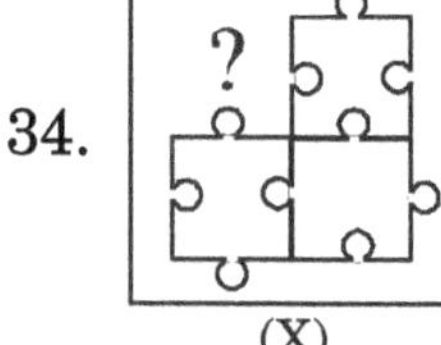

(a) 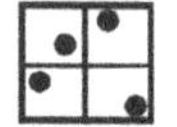        (b) 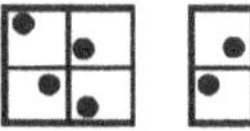

(c) 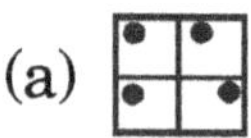        (d) 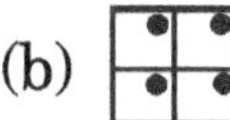

**33.** What comes in the sequence ?

(a)         (b) 

(c) 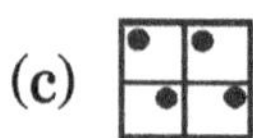        (d) 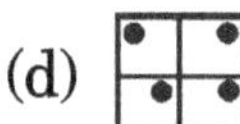

**34.**

(X)

(a) 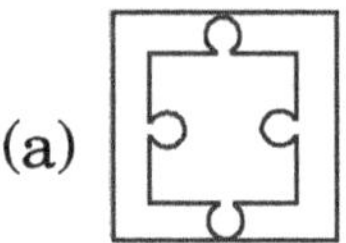        (b) 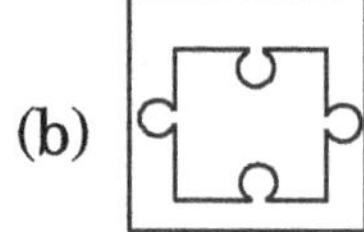

(c) 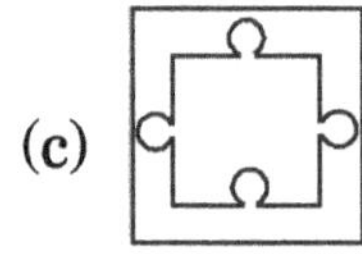        (d) 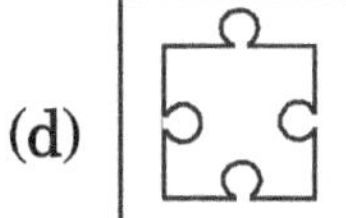

**DIRECTION (Q. 35) :** In the following question, you are given a combination of alphabets followed by four alternatives (a), (b), (c) and (d). Choose the alternative which most closely resembles the mirror-image of the given combination.

**35.** NATIONAL

(a) ＪＶИОＩＴＡИ        (b) ＪＶИОＩＴＡИ

(c) ＪＶИОＩＴＡИ        (d) ＬＡИОＩＴＡИ

**DIRECTION (Q. 36) :** In the following question, choose the correct water image of the figure (X) from amongst the four alternatives (1), (2), (3) and (4) given alongwith it.

**36.** 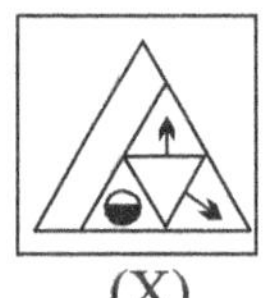

(X)

(a) 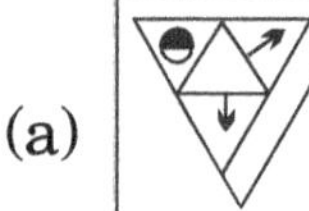        (b) 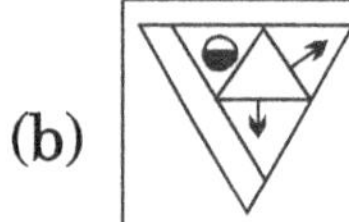

(c) 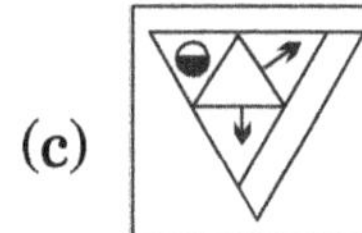        (d) 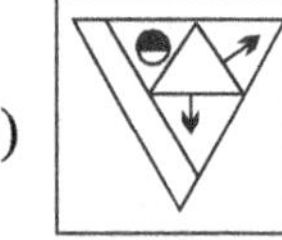

**DIRECTION (Q. 37):** In the question, a piece of paper is folded and cut as shown below in the question figures. From the given answer figures, indicate how it will appear when opened.

**Question Figures:**

37. 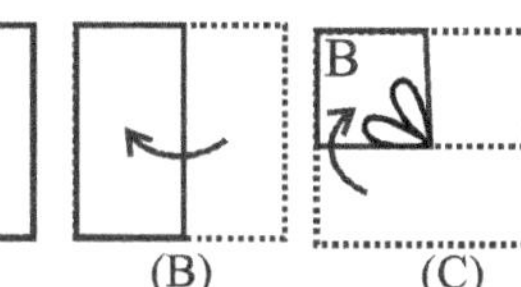

    (A)        (B)        (C)

**Answer Figures:**

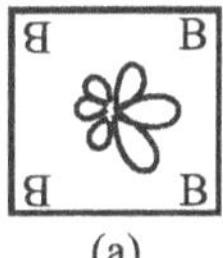 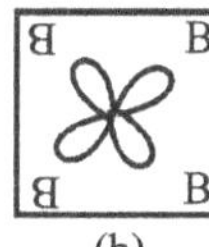 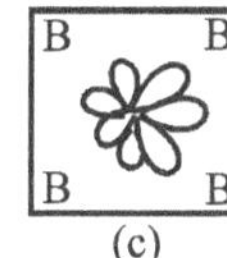 

    (a)        (b)        (c)        (d)

**DIRECTION (Qs. 38) :** In the following questions, you are given a figure (X) followed by four alternative figures (1), (2), (3) and (4) such that fig (X) is embeded in one of them. Trace out the alternative figure which contains fig (X) as its part.

38. 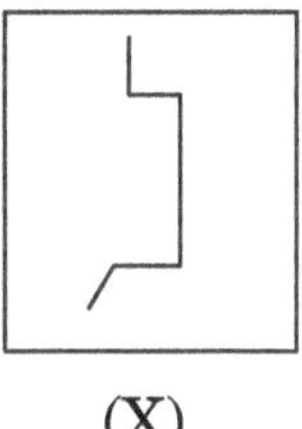

    (X)

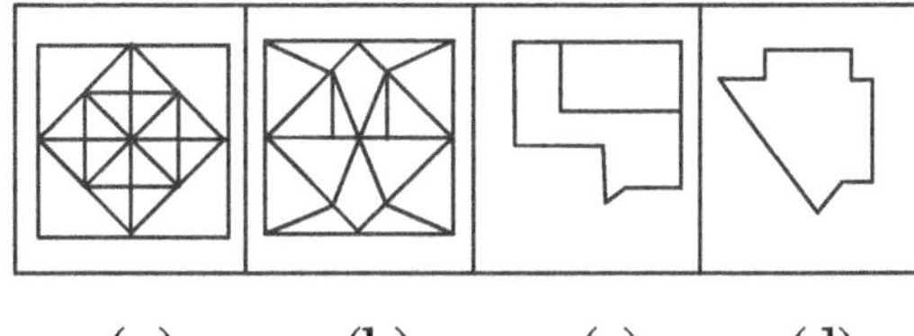

    (a)        (b)        (c)        (d)

39. Ashish is heavier than Govind. Mohit is lighter than Jack. Pawan is heavier than Jack but lighter than Govind. Who among them is the heaviest ?

    (a) Ashish          (b) Govind
    (c) Mohit           (d) Pawan

40. How many parallelograms are there in the figure ?

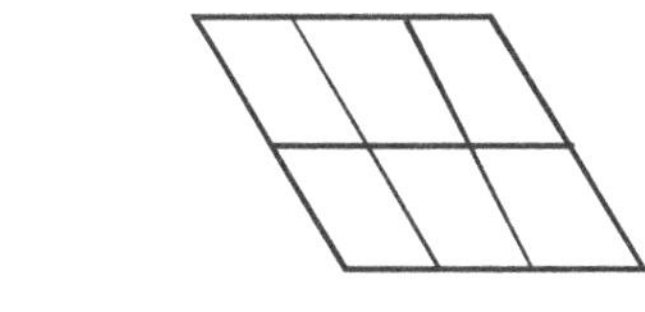

    (a) 14              (b) 15
    (c) 16              (d) 18

**Name :** _______________

**Max. Marks : 40**

**Number of Questions : 40**

**Time : 2 Hours**

**There is no negative marking in the test.**

1. Two positions of a dice are shown below. If 1 is at the bottom, which number will be on top?

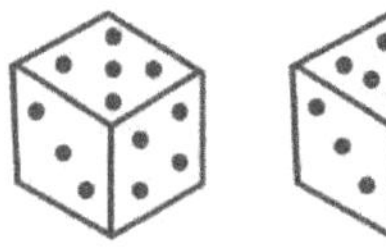

  (a) 4        (b) 3
  (c) 8        (d) 5

2. If a mirror is placed on the line MN, then which of the answer figures is the right image of the given figure.

**Question Figure :**

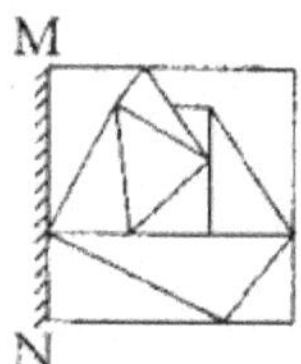

**Answer figures:**

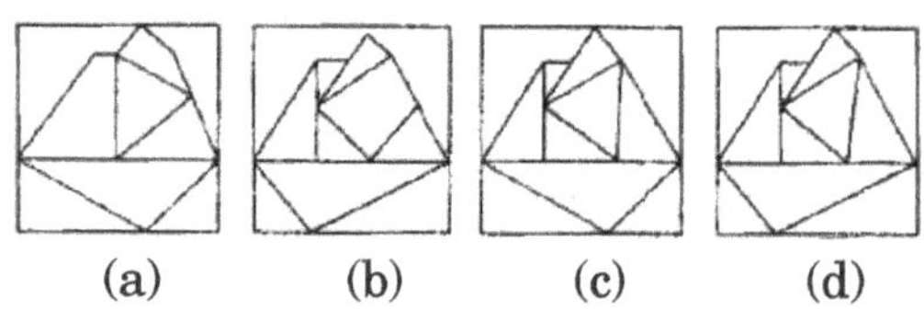

   (a)      (b)      (c)      (d)

3. From the given alternatives select the word which can be formed using the letters of the given word.

**DICTIONARY**

  (a) BINARY        (b) DAIRY
  (c) NATION        (d) ADDITION

4. Which figure best represents the relationship between Editor, Newspaper and Journalist?

  (a)            (b)
  (c)            (d)

5. Shiela and Belah start from their office and walk in opposite direction each travelling 10 kms. Shiela then turns left and walks 10 kms. Belah turns right and walks 10 km. How far are they now from each other ?

  (a) 20 km        (b) 10 km
  (c) 5 km         (d) 8 km

6. Name a single letter, which can be prefixed to the following words in order to obtain entirely new words?

TILL TABLE PILE TAB PRING

  (a) S        (b) B
  (c) H        (d) C

7. Arrange the following words as per order in the dictionary.
   1. Command    2. Commit
   3. Connect    4. Conceive
   5. Conduct    6. Commerce
   (a) 6 2 1 5 4 3    (b) 6 1 2 4 5 3
   (c) 1 6 2 4 5 3    (d) 1 2 6 5 3 4

**DIRECTIONS (Qs. 8):** In each of the following questions, select the related word/ letter/ number from the given alternatives.

8. Body: Stomach :: Library: ?
   (a) Cash           (b) Book
   (c) Headmaster (d) School

9. HAND : JBPE :: PALM: ?
   (a) RBNM          (b) RBMN
   (c) QBNN          (d) RBNN

10. 76: 42:: 66: ?
    (a) 36            (b) 63
    (c) 12            (d) 35

11. A piece of paper is folded and punched as shown below in the question figures. From the given answer figures, indicate how it will appear when opened.

**Question figures :**

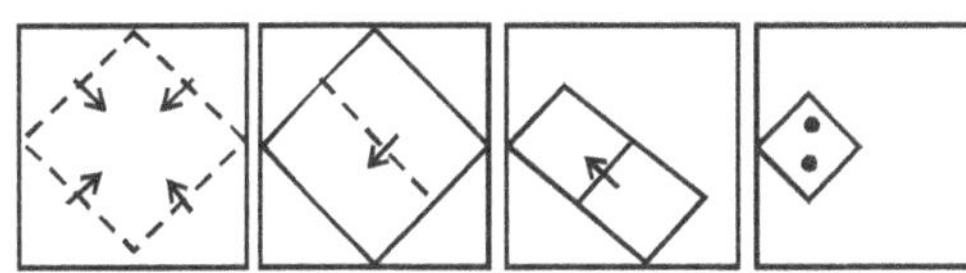

**Answer Figures**

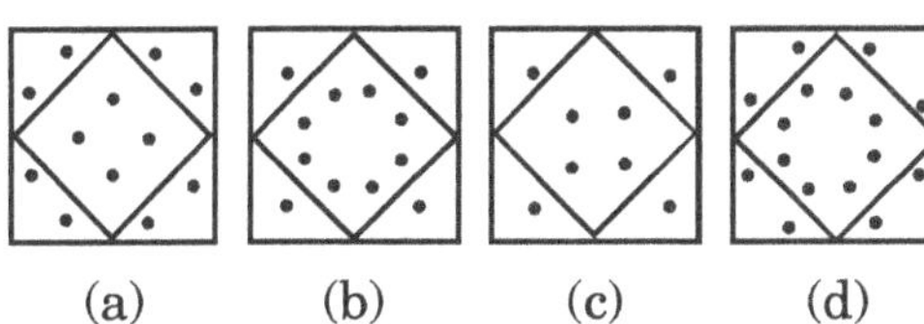

   (a)     (b)     (c)     (d)

12. If Blue means Pink, Pink means Green, Green means Yellow, Yellow means Red and Red means White, then what is the colour of turmeric?
    (a) Pink           (b) Yellow
    (c) Red            (d) Green

13. How many triangles can be found out from the following figure?

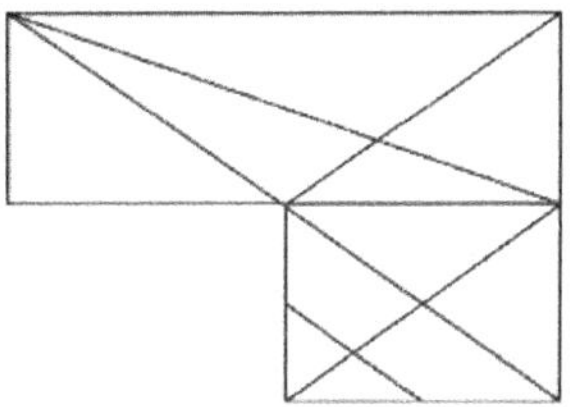

    (a) 17             (b) 21
    (c) 24             (d) 25

**DIRECTIONS (Qs. 14 to 16) :** Select the one which is different from the other three responses.

14. (a) Steering wheel
    (b) Engine
    (c) Car
    (d) Tyre

15. (a) 325           (b) 360
    (c) 230           (d) 256

16. (a) NLM           (b) YXZ
    (c) NMO           (d) RQS

17. Arrange the following words in their descending order.
    1. Weekly         2. Bi-annual
    3. Fortnightly  4. Monthly
    5. Annual
    (a) 1, 3, 4, 2, 5    (b) 2, 5, 4, 1, 3
    (c) 4, 1, 2, 3, 5    (d) 5, 2, 4, 3, 1

18. Which one of the following is water image of "COMMISSION"?
    (a) ИOISSIWWOϽ  (b) COMMIƧƧIOИ
    (c) ϹOWWIƧƧIOИ (d) ИOISSIWWOϽ

19. Study the diagram given below and answer question.

    The qualified and experienced doctors working in villages are represented by.

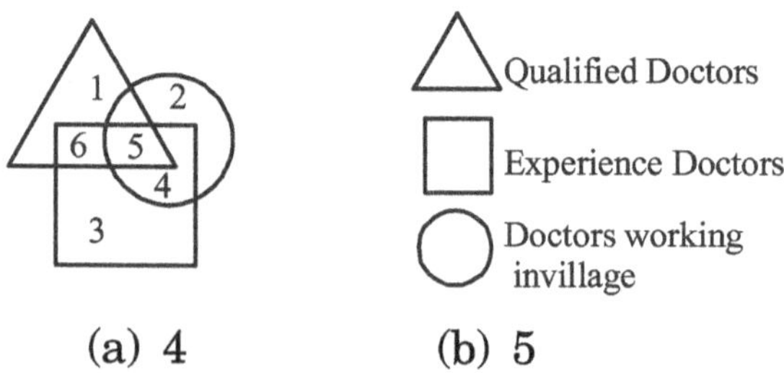

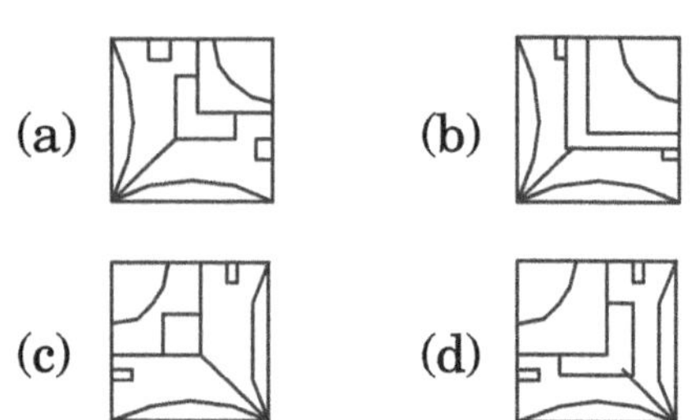

    (a) 4            (b) 5
    (c) 2            (d) 6

20. Rani and Sarita started from a place X. Rani went West and Sarita went North, both travelling with the same speed. After sometime, both turned their left and walked a few steps. If they again turned to their left, in which directions the faces of Rani and Sarita will be with respect to X ?

    (a) North and East
    (b) North and West
    (c) West and North
    (d) East and South

**DIRECTION (Q. 21):** In the following question, which answer figure will complete the pattern in the question figure?

21. **Question Figure:**

    **Answer Figures:**

**DIRECTION (Q. 22):** In the following question, from the given answer figures, select the one in which the question figure is hidden/embedded.

22. **Question Figure**

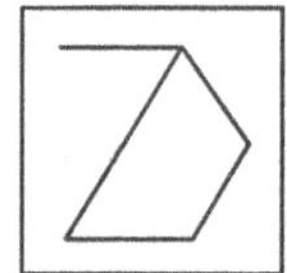

    **Answer Figures:**

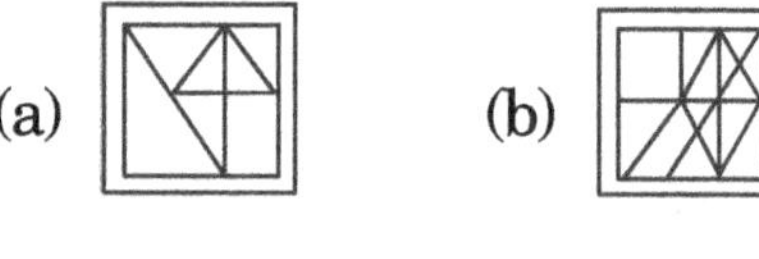

23. If '–' stands for addition, '+' for multiplication, '÷' for subtraction and '×' for division, which one of the following equations is correct?

    (a) $5 + 2 - 12 \times 6 \div 2 = 10$
    (b) $5 \div 2 + 12 \times 6 - 2 = 4$
    (c) $5 - 2 + 12 \times 6 \div 2 = 27$
    (d) $5 + 2 - 12 \div 6 \times 2 = 13$

24. If P denotes ÷ Q denotes ×, R denotes + and S denotes –, then 16Q12P6R5S4?

    (a) 32            (b) 33
    (c) 30            (d) 31

25. 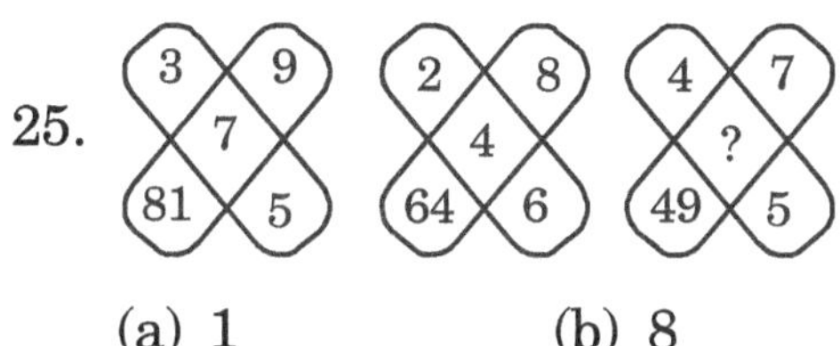

(a) 1      (b) 8

(c) 6      (d) 16

**DIRECTION (Q. 26):** Select the missing number from the given responses.

26. 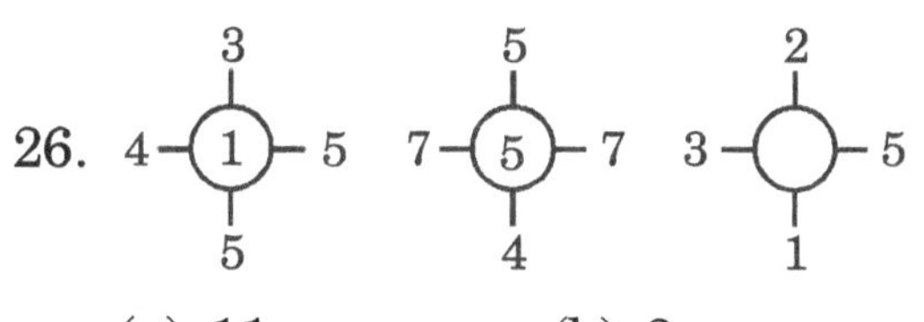

(a) 11      (b) 3

(c) 1      (d) 5

27. The digits are given as follows:

562, 871, 438, 753

If the position of the first and the third digits of each of the numbers are interchanged, which of the following will be the sum of the first and the second digits of the third highest number?

(a) 9      (b) 7

(c) 6      (d) 8

28. In a class of 45, Neha's rank is 15th from first, what is her rank from the last ?

(a) 30      (b) 32

(c) 33      (d) 31

29. Kathir is senior of Ganesh. Ganesh is senior of Apparu. Apparu is junior of Raju. Raju is junior of Ganesh. Who is the most senior?

(a) Ganesh      (b) Raju

(c) Kathir      (d) Apparu

**DIRECTIONS (Qs. 30 & 31) :** In the following questions, a series is given, with one term missing. Choose the correct alternative from the given ones that will complete the series.

30. 7, 14, 23, 34, ?

(a) 46      (b) 47

(c) 44      (d) 45

31. AE, FJ, KO, ? UY

(a) QN      (b) TQ

(c) NP      (d) PT

**DIRECTIONS (Qs. 32 to 34) :** Read the following information carefully and answer the questions given below.

Ravi and Kunal are good in Hockey and Volleyball. Sachin and Ravi are good in Hockey and Baseball. Gaurav and Kunal are good in Cricket and Volleyball. Sachin, Gaurav and Micheal are good in Football and Baseball.

32. Who is good in Hockey, Cricket and Volleyball ?

(a) Sachin      (b) Kunal

(c) Ravi      (d) Gaurav

33. Who is good in Baseball, Cricket, Volleyball and Football ?

(a) Sachin      (b) Kunal

(c) Gaurav      (d) Ravi

34. Who is good in Baseball, Volleyball and Hockey ?

(a) Sachin      (b) Kunal

(c) Ravi      (d) Gaurav

**DIRECTIONS (Qs. 35 & 36) :**

A + B means 'A is father of B'

A − B means 'A is wife of B'

A × B means 'A is brother of B'

A ÷ B means ' A is daughter of B'

35. P ÷ R + S + Q, which of the following is true ?
    (a) P is daughter of Q
    (b) Q is aunt of P
    (c) P is aunt of Q
    (d) P is mother of Q
36. If P – R + Q, which of the following is true
    (a) P is mother of Q
    (b) Q is daughter of P
    (c) P is aunt of Q
    (d) P is sister of Q

**DIRECTIONS (Qs. 37 & 38)** : Read the following information carefully and answer the questions that follow.

A, B, C, D, E and F are seated in a circle facing the centre. D is between F and B. A is second to the left of D and second to the right of E.

37. Who is facing A?
    (a) B      (b) D
    (c) F      (d) Either F or B
38. Who among the following is facing D?
    (a) A
    (b) C
    (c) E
    (d) Cannot be determined
39. If the first and second digits in the sequence 5 9 8 1 3 2 7 4 3 8 are interchanged. Also the third and fourth digits, the fifth and sixth digits and so on, which digit would be the seventh counting to your left?
    (a) 1      (b) 4
    (c) 7      (d) 8
40. In a certain code language '526' means 'sky' is blue'; '24' means 'blue colour' and '436' means 'colour is fun'. Which of the following digit stands for 'fun'?
    (a) 5      (b) 4
    (c) 3      (d) 2

# CYBER

## OLYMPIAD
# Mock Test 1

Name : __________                    Max. Marks : 25
Number of Questions : 25             Time : 1 Hour
**There is no negative marking in the test.**

1. Which of the following is NOT related to power supply of computer?
   (a) USB
   (b) Surge Projector
   (c) UPS
   (d) SMPS

2. Identify the following:
   – It is a type of memory on which data has been pre-recorded. Once data has been written into it, it cannot be removed and can only be read.
   – It is extensively used in Calculators.
   (a) RAM      (b) ROM
   (c) Hard Disk      (d) Flash drive

3. Select the INCORRECT match.
   (A) Start and End an HTML file    (a) <HTML>...</HTML>
   (B) Make paragraphs    (b) <P>...</P>
   (C) Putting a horizontal line    (c) <Line>
   (D) Adding an image    (d) <img src ="image filename">

4. Which of the following statements is true for flash CS6?
   (a) Flash is a multimedia platform.
   (b) It is used for creating digital animation, rich web applications, websites, movies, etc.
   (c) It is used for making games such as Pac Man, Minesweeper, Tetris, etc.
   (d) All of these

5. Which of the following will you use to convert the selected text into a hyperlink?

   (a)       (b) 

   (c)       (d) 

6. Which of the following statements hold (s) true?

   **Statement 1 :** You can play the slide show without narration (even when narrations is inserted in your presentation).

**Statement 2:** You can play the slide show without animation (even when animation is inserted in your presentation).

(a) Only Statement 1
(b) Only Statement 2
(c) Neither Statement 1 nor Statement 2
(d) Both Statement 1 and Statement 2

7. Which of the following is CORRECT with respect to MS - Excel?

(a) SORT function is used to find the square root of a number.
(b) A formula always begins with a + (plus) sign.
(c) Mixed referencing can be used only when both row and column are fixed.
(d) The formula given in one sheet of a workbook can be linked to other worksheet.

8. What is the maximum number of characters that can be used to define a table name?

(a) 64 characters including letters, number and spaces.
(b) 64 characters excluding letters, numbers and spaces.
(c) 128 characters including letters, numbers and spaces.
(d) 128 characters excluding letters, numbers and spaces.

9. Identify the type of virus from the given symptoms :

– It attempts to attack both the boot sector and the executable or program files at the same time.
– This virus may also take different actions on an infected computer.
– This type of virus spreads in multiple ways.
– It may also depend on the existence of certain files on the PC.

(a) Multipartite virus
(b) Sabotage virus
(c) Web scripting virus
(d) Direct action virus

10. Which of the following statements hold (s) true regarding the Bus topology?

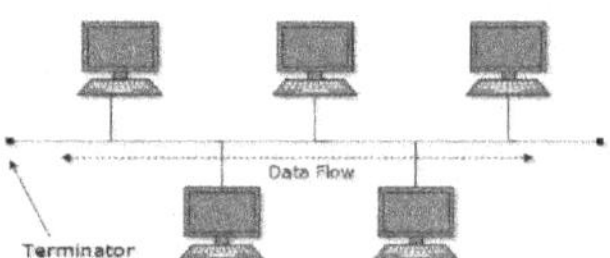


**Statement 1 :** It is a network setup in which each computer and network device are connected to a single cable or backbone.

**Statement 2 :** It requires less cable length than star topology.

(a) Only Statement 1
(b) Only statement 2
(c) Both Statement 1 and Statement 2
(d) Neither Statement 1 nor Statement 2

11. What is Google keep?

(a) Google's new operating system for Mobile devices.
(b) A digital scratchpad note taking application for the Android mobile OS.
(c) Google's new application for the cloud service.
(d) Google's new web browser with advanced browsing features.

12. Which of the following statements is INCORRECT about iPad Mini 4?
    (a) It is a fourth generation ipad Mini tablet computer by Apple Inc.
    (b) It comes with iOS 9 operating system.
    (c) It is a smartphone developed by Microsoft.
    (d) It supports Apple Pay online service.

13. The term _________ refers to any computer component that is required to perform work.
    (a) bootstrap      (b) kernel
    (c) resource      (d) source code

14. Which of the following is not a function of the control unit?
    (a) Read instructions
    (b) Execute instructions
    (c) Interpret instructions
    (d) Direct operations

15. Which of the following memory chip is faster?
    (a) There is no certainty
    (b) DRAM
    (c) SRAM
    (d) DRAM is faster for larger chips

16. The most common type of storage devices are
    (a) persistent      (b) optical
    (c) magnetic      (d) flash

17. Oracle is an example of _________ application software.
    (a) database
    (b) word processing
    (c) project management
    (d) presentation graphics

18. What is the process of copying software programs from secondary storage media to the hard disk called?
    (a) Configuration
    (b) Download
    (c) Storage
    (d) Installation

19. Peripheral devices such as printers and monitors are considered to be _________.
    (a) data      (b) software
    (c) hardware      (d) information

20. Meaningful filename helps in easy file ______.
    (a) Storing
    (b) Accessing
    (c) Identification
    (d) Printing

21. Files are organised by storing them in _________ .
    (a) tables      (b) databases
    (c) folders      (d) graphs

22. A modem is connected to
    (a) a telephone line
    (b) a keyboard
    (c) a printer
    (d) a monitor

23. To reload a Web page, press the ________ button.
    (a) Redo      (b) Reload
    (c) Restore      (d) Refresh

24. Window is a ________ and Window 95, Window 98 are _________.
    (a) Graphical User Interface, Operating Systems.
    (b) Graphics Useful Interface, Executing Systems
    (c) Graph User Interval, Expert Systems
    (d) None of these

25. For opening and closing of the file in Excel, you can use which bar ?
    (a) Formatting
    (b) Standard
    (c) Title
    (d) Formatting or Title

# OLYMPIAD Mock Test 2

**Name :** _________

**Number of Questions : 25**

**Max. Marks : 25**

**Time : 1 Hour**

**There is no negative marking in the test.**

1. The digital data is converted to analog format by the modem at _________.
   (a) The source computer
   (b) The destination computer
   (c) Both the source and the destination computers
   (d) Neither the source nor destination computers

2. Which of the following statements holds true about SD cards?
   **Statement 1 :** It is a non - volatile memory card used in portable devices, such as tablet computers, mobile phones, etc.
   **Statement 2 :** SD stands for Static Dynamic.
   (a) Only Statement 1
   (b) Only Statement 2
   (c) Neither Statement 1 nor Statement 2
   (d) Both Statement 1 and Statement 2

3. Match the following HTML tags with their functions.

| Column – I | Column – II |
|---|---|
| (A) <\|>... </\|> | (i) To strike a line through the middle of the text. |
| (B) <STRIKE> ...</STRIKE> | (ii) To italicize text. |
| (C) <SUP> ... </SUP> | (iii) To make text appear appear slightly below the normal line of text. |
| (D) <SUB> ...</SUB> | (iv) To define the start and end of a paragraph. |
| (E) <P>....</P> | (v) To make text appear slightly above the normal line of text. |

  (a) (A)-(ii),(B)-(i),(C)-(v), (D)-(iii),(E)-(iv)

  (b) (A)-(ii),(B)-(iv),(C)-(iii), (D)-(i), (E)- (v)

  (c) (A)-(ii),(B)-(i),(C)-(iii), (D)-(iv),(E)-(v)

  (d) (A)-(ii),(B)-(iii),(C)-(i), (D)-(v), (E)- (iv)

4.   _____ tool is used to _________.

  (a) Select an object in free form

  (b) Draw an oval

  (c) Zoom in and zoom out the view of the movie.

  (d) Give color to the outline of an object

5. Which of the following statements is CORRECT?

  (a) You cannot add a comment, if you have not selected any word.

  (b) You cannot track the formatting changes.

  (c) You cannot combine the revisions from multiple documents.

  (d) You can edit a document, once you have marked it as final, by clicking "Edit Anyway" command, displayed at the top of the window.

6. Bluetooth is an example of

  (a) Personal area network

  (b) Local area network

  (c) Virtual private network

  (d) None of the above

7. _____ is NOT a function in MS-Excel.

  (a) SUM     (b) ADD

  (c) MAX     (d) SQRT

8. Which of the following statements is CORRECT?

  (a) Reports can be used to retrieve data from tables.

  (b) Queries can be printed and presented as the information.

  (c) Queries can include calculated fields that may not exist in table.

  (d) Reports and forms are more or less similar. Only differences being, forms are printed, reports are viewed online.

9. _____ is considered to be the first computer virus for MS-DOS. It was a boot-sector virus.

  (a) Creeper    (b) Brain

  (c) Ghostball   (d) Cascade

10. Which of the following statements hold(s) true regarding the similarity between FTP and HTTP?

**Statement 1 :** FTP works in the same way as HTTP for transferring web pages from a server to a user's browser.

**Statement 2 :** Both FTP and HTTP uses client server architecture.

  (a) Only Statement 1

  (b) Only Statement 2

(c) Both Statement 1 and Statement 2

(d) Neither Statement 1 nor Statement 2

11. Which of the following networking topology is displayed in this diagram?

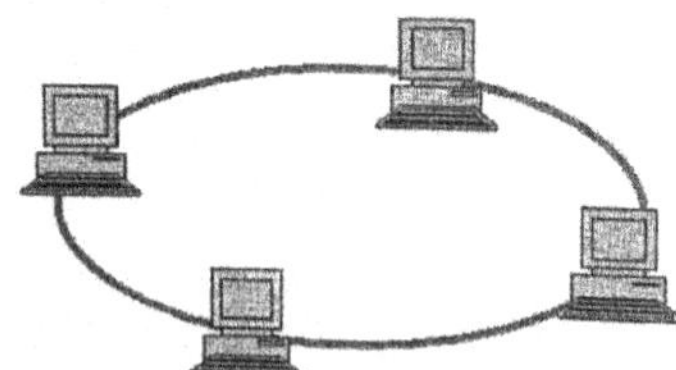

(a) Star          (b) Bus

(c) Mesh          (d) Ring

12. Which of the following statements is INCORRECT about Kinect?

(a) It is a motion sensing input device for Xbox One video game consoles.

(b) Its predecessor is Xbox Live Vision.

(c) It connects via bluetooth.

(d) It enables the user to control and interact with their console through a natural user interface.

13. ___________ is a technology, using which machines can mimic the behaviour of human nose, tongue or eye.

(a) Immersive Reality

(b) E-sensing

(c) E-Immersion

(d) Augmented Reality

14. The first computer mouse was built by

(a) Douglas Engelbart

(b) William English

(c) Oaniel Coogher

(d) Robert Zawacki

15. Different types of modern digital computers come under which generation.

(a) Forth          (b) Third

(c) Second          (d) Fifth

16. Which of the following is needed for sound recording?

(a) Speaker          (b) Microphone

(c) Talker          (d) Mouse

17. What is usually used for displaying information at public places?

(a) Monitor

(b) Overhead Projections

(c) Monitors and Overhead Projections

(d) Touch Screen Kiosks

18. All of the following statements concerning files are true EXCEPT:

(a) Files should be organized in folders

(b) Files are stored in RAM.

(c) Files can be generated from an application.

(d) A file is a collection of related pieces of information stored together for easy reference.

19. _____ is the process of dividing the disk into tracks and sectors.

(a) Tracking     (b) Formatting

(c) Crashing     (d) Allotting

20. Android is a mobile operating system designed primarily for touch screen mobile devices such as smartphones and tablets. Which among the following was the first Android Operating System?

    (a) Cupcake     (b) Alpha

    (c) Gingerbread (d) Doughnut

21. If a new device is attached to a computer, such as a printer or scanner, its __________ must be installed before the device can be used.

    (a) buffer     (b) driver

    (c) pager     (d) server

22. The name of the location of a particular piece of data is its _____.

    (a) Memory name

    (b) Address

(c) Storage site

(d) data location

23. Bluetooth is an example of

    (a) Personal area network

    (b) Local area network

    (c) Virtual private network

    (d) None of the above

24. What is e-commerce?

    (a) Buying and selling of international goods

    (b) Buying and selling of products and services over the Internet

    (c) Buying and selling of products and services not found in stores

    (d) Buying and selling of products having to do with computers

25. Help menu is available at which button?

    (a) End     (b) Start

    (c) Turnoff     (d) Restart

# OLYMPIAD
# Mock Test 3

Name : __________          Max. Marks : 25

Number of Questions : 25          Time : 1 Hour

**There is no negative marking in the test.**

1. Which of the following statements is NOT true for a software package?
   (a) It consists of one of more programs.
   (b) It is created to perform a particular type of work.
   (c) It is a set of human readable instructions that directs a CPU to perform specific operations.
   (d) it is a computer application.

2. The BIOS (Basic Input/Output System) is a type of firmware used during the booting process on computers. It is the first software, which runs, when powered on. It is usually stored in __________.
   (a) ROM          (b) RAM
   (c) Cache          (d) Hard Disk

3. Hspace attribute of <img> tag adds __________ side of an image.
   (a) Space to the left and right
   (b) Space to the top and bottom

   (c) Height to all sides
   (d) None of these

4. Which of the following statements will let the image placed against the right margin?
   (a) < img src = " my image. gif" align = "wrap">
   (b) <img src = " myImage. gif" align = " right">
   (c) <img src = "myImage. gif" wrap = " right">
   (d) <img src = "myImage.gif" – right">

5. Match the following.

   | Column – I | Column – II |
   | --- | --- |
   | (A) 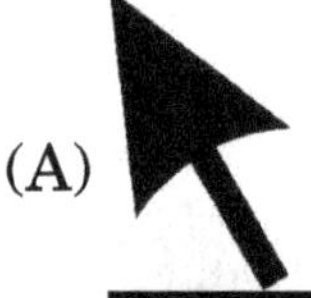 | (i) Lasso Tool |
   | (B) 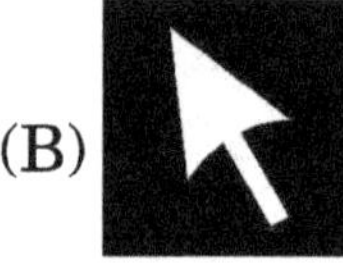 | (ii) Free Transform Tool |
   | (C) 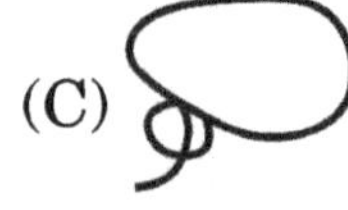 | (iii) Subselection Tool |

(D)           (iv) Selection Tool

(a) (A) – (iv), (B) – (iii), (C) – (ii), (D) – (i)

(b) (A) – (iii), (B) – (iv), (C) – (i), (D) – (ii)

(c) (A) – (ii), (B) – (i), (C) – (iii), (D) – (iv)

(d) (A) – (iv), (B) – (iii), (C) – (i), (D) – (ii)

6. While using tables, how would you forbid table rows to be split across pages in an MS – Word document when you have already selected the current table?

(a) Right Click, then click Table Properties. Click on Table tab and uncheck "Allow row to break across pages"

(b) Right Click, then click Table Properties. Click on Table tab, click Options and uncheck "Allow row to break across pages"

(c) Right Click, then click Table Properties. Click on Row tab and uncheck "Allow row to break across pages"

(d) Right Click, then click Split Cells

7. Which of the following statements is INCORRECT?

(a) You can add a comment about the selection.

(b) You can change the screen resolution for the full-screen slide show.

(c) You can send the copy of the presentation via email.

(d) Publish Slides option will allow you to only track the changes.

8. The result of a formula in a cell is called

(a) label

(b) value

(c) range

(d) displayed value

9. Identify the given icon.

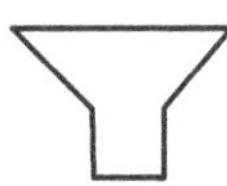

(a) Sort          (b) Filter

(c) Selection     (d) View

10. Which of the following terms is used for an unskilled hacker who breaks into computer system by using automated tools written by others?

(a) Script kiddie

(b) Elite cracker

(c) Grey hat

(d) Phenophyte Diddlr

11. Which of the following statements hold(s) true about repeaters?

**Statement 1 :** It connects two segments of the same LAN.

**Statement 2 :** It does not forward every frame because it has frame filtering capability.

(a) Only statement 1

(b) Only Statement 2

(c) Neither Statement 1 nor Statement 2

(d) Both Statement 1 and Statement 2

12. What is iWork?

(a) It is an office suite of applications for OS X and iOS operating systems.

(b) It is an internet platform for users to download the new games on iOS devices.

(c) It is a website which allows the user to download the songs, pictures, videos, movies, etc. on OSX compatible systems.

(d) Both (b) and (c)

13. _________ is the latest version of the game in 'Angry Birds' services by 'Rovio Entertainment' released on July 2015.

(a) Angry Birds GO!

(b) Angry Birds Epic

(c) Angry Birds 2

(d) Angry Birds Star Wars II

14. Information on a computer is stored as

(a) analog data   (b) digital data

(c) modern data   (d) watts data

15. Faster Supercomputer in the world as of June 2016,

(a) Sunway Taihulight

(b) IBM HS20

(c) Cray xc40

(d) SAGA

16. Back up of the data files will help to prevent ______

(a) loss of confidentiality

(b) duplication of data

(c) virus infection

(d) loss of data

17. Printed information, called ______, exists physically and is a more permanent form of output than that presented on a display device.

(a) soft copy     (b) carbon copy

(c) hard copy    (d) desk copy

18. Rearranging and allocating space in memory to provide for multiple computing tasks is called

(a) Multiprogramming

(b) Multitasking

(c) Memory Management

(d) Networking

19. Which of the following is used to access a file from the computer store?

(a) Insert        (b) Retrieve

(c) File          (d) Find

20. On August 25, 2016 Linux celebrated its 25 years of its existence, Features of LINUX are:

(a) Portability

(b) Open source

(c) Multi-user & Multi Programming

(d) All of the above

21. A device that is connected to the motherboard is _________.

    (a) called an external device

    (b) called an adjunct device

    (c) called a peripheral device

    (d) must connect using ribbon cable

22. A collection of unprocessed items is _________.

    (a) information  (b) data

    (c) memory       (d) reports

23. Computers connected to a LAN can

    (a) run faster

    (b) go on line

    (c) share information and/or share peripheral equipment

    (d) E-mail

24. What is Windows Explorer?

    (a) A drive

    (b) A personal computer

    (c) A File manager

    (d) A network

25. Window 7, the latest operating system from Microsoft Corporation has .............. Indian languages fonts.

    (a) 14              (b) 26

    (c) 37              (d) 49

# OLYMPIAD
# Mock Test 4

**Name :** _________

**Number of Questions : 40**

**There is no negative marking in the test.**

**Max. Marks : 40**

**Time : 2 Hours**

1. Which of the following statements hold(s) true regarding the given device.

**Statement 1 :** It us used to read credit/debit cards.

**Statement 2:** It is known as Optical Mark Reader.

(a) Only Statement 1

(b) Only Statement 2

(c) Both Statement 1 and Statement 2

(d) Neither Statement 1 nor Statement 2

2. Identify the following:

The basic purpose of it, is to store program instructions that are frequently referenced by software during operation. Fast access to these instructions increases the overall speed of the software program.

(a) Cache memory

(b) Hard Disk

(c) Zip Disk

(d) Compact Disc

3. Optical discs are ideal storage medium. They are most useful for reading large block of sequential data.

Such data can be both audio or video data. They can do this due to ____________.

(a) Compact size and light weight

(b) Absence of mechanical read/write head

(c) Presence of single spiral track,

when reading or writing data there is no need to stop the flow of data to switch tracks.

(d) Less loss per bit of storage.

4. CPRM technology is associated with SD card standards. What does CPRM stand for?

(a) Copy Protection for Rewritable Media

(b) Copy right Protection for Recordable Media

(c) Content Protection for Recordable Media

(d) Copy Protection for Recording Mechanism

5. A vlink is a _________ link.

(a) Active       (b) Virtual

(c) Visited       (d) Verified

6. Which of the following HTML codes is CORRECT in context of tags and their attributes?

(a) <Body alink = "red">

Hello

<para> good IQ ! </para>

</Body>

(b) <font width = 8 bgcolor = yellow> </font>

(c) <image source = "Fish.JPG" < image>

(d) <ul>

<li> one

<li> two

</ul>

7. Identify the given tool.

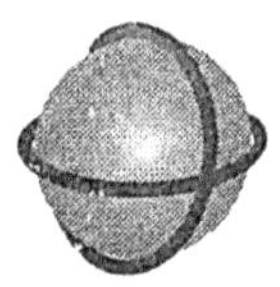

(a) Circle Tool

(b) 3D Rotation Tool

(c) Lasso Tool

(d) Bone Tool

8. Match the Adobe Flash term names with their description.

| Column – I | Column – II |
| --- | --- |
| (A) Movie | (i) Transparent sheets containing various objects, can be placed on top of each other. |
| (B) Scene | (ii) The first file that opens when you open a flash document. |
| (C) Timeline | (iii) Area where |

you add every piece of content to be added in a movie.

(D) Layer       (iv) It consists of animated objects.

(E) Stage       (v) The area on screen to work with layers and frames.

(a) (A) – (v), (B) – (iv), (C) – (i), (D) – (ii), (E) – (iii)

(b) (A) – (ii), (B) – (iv), (C) – (i), (D) – (iii), (E) – (v)

(c) (A) – (ii), (B) – (iv), (C) – (v), (D) – (i), (E) – (iii)

(d) (A) – (ii), (B) – (v), (C) – (iii), (D) – (iv), (E) – (i)

9. Which of the following statements is INCORRECT?

(a) You can show the revisions of track changes in a separate window.

(b) You cannot change tracking options.

(c) You can accept all the changes at once in the document.

(d) All of these

10. Which of the following statements hold(s) true regarding the given feature?

**Statement 1 :** Compare two versions of a document

**Statement 2 :** Combine revisions from multiple authors into a single document.

(a) Only Statement 1

(b) Only Statement 2

(c) Both Statement 1 and Statement 2

(d) Neither Statement 1 nor Statement 2

11. If your computer keeps rebooting itself, then it is likely that ________

(a) It has a virus

(b) It does not have enough memory

(c) There is no printer

(d) There has been a power surge

12. What is a modem connected to?

(a) processor       (b) motherboard

(c) printer        (d) phone line

13. Match the following MS – Excel functions given in Column – I with their uses in Column – II.

| **Column – I** | | **Column – II** |
| --- | --- | --- |
| (A) AVERAGE (range) | (i) | Returns the number rounded to the nearest odd integer. |
| (B) ODD (number) | (ii) | Current date is displayed in the Cell. |
| (C) MOD (number 1, number 2) | (iii) | Rounds the number 1 to the digits specified in number 2. |
| (D) ROUND (number 1, number 2) | (iv) | Returns the remainder when number 1 is divided by the number 2. |
| (E) TODAY ( ) | (v) | Finds the average of the given range of numbers. |

(a) (A) – (v), (B) – (i), (C) – (iii), (D) – (iv), (E) – (ii)

(b) (A) – (i), (B) – (v), (C) – (iii), (D) – (iv), (E) – (ii)

(c) (A) – (i), (B) – (v), (C) – (iv), (D) – (iii), (E) – (ii)

(d) (A) – (v), (B) – (i), (C) – (iv), (D) – (iii), (E) – (ii)

14. Which of the following should be used to find the minimum score among different subjects?

|   | A | B | C | D | E | F | G |
| --- | --- | --- | --- | --- | --- | --- | --- |
| 1 | Subject | Mathematics | Physics | Chemistry | Biology | Computer | |
| 2 | Marks | 44 | 32 | 48 | 47 | 45 | |

(a) =MIN (B2 : F2)

(b) = MIN (B2, F2)

(c) = MIN (B1 : F1)

(d) = MIN (B1, F1)

15. [scroll icon] is used to __________.

(a) Show the report wizard which helps you create simple and customized reports

(b) Show the form wizard which helps you create simple and customizable forms

(c) Add logic to your database to automate repetitive tasks

(d) Show the query wizard

16. A device that connects to a network without the use of cables is said to be

(a) distributed

(b) centralised

(c) open source

(d) wireless

17. Social networking can be harmful or confusing if _______________ .

    (a) You accidentally post sensitive information that will be seen by many different people

    (b) you need to set numerous options to protect your privacy

    (c) It becomes addictive and you tend to spend more than required time on social networks and make them an alternative for "real-life" communication

    (d) All of these

18. What is Flaming?

    (a) An act of posting and sending offensive messages over the Internet.

    (b) A program that contacts a remote server for instructions and then steals files or captures screen shots of the infected computer system.

    (c) A program that secretly and maliciously integrates itself into program or data files. It spreads by integrating itself into more files each time the host program is run.

    (d) All of these

19. Identify the following.

    – It is responsible for full - fledged data connectivity and transmitting the data end–to–end by providing other functions, including addressing, mapping and acknowledgement.

    – It is a language, a computer uses to access the internet.

    (a) TCP/IP          (b) SMTP

    (c) FTP             (d) NNTP

20. When a computer network is built on the top of another network such peer–to–peer networks and client–server applications, it is called __________ .

    (a) Bottom – top network

    (b) Overlay network

    (c) Rooted network

    (d) One-to-One network

21. Which of the following is the most recent version of Windows Media player released along with Windows 7?

(a) Windows Media Player 10

(b) Windows Media Player 11

(c) Windows Media Player 12

(d) Windows Media Player 14

22. _________ feature of Windows 8 Enterprise edition allows you to boot and run from mass storage devices such as USB flash drives and external hard disk drives.

(a) Wingo

(b) Windows To Go

(c) WinBoot

(d) WinGo Loader

23. The basic goal of computer process is to convert data into _________.

(a) information    (b) tables

(c) files              (d) graphs

24. The first computers were programmed using

(a) assembly language

(b) machine language

(c) spaghetti code

(d) source code

25. Which of the following could be digital input devices for computers?

(a) Digital camcorder

(b) Microphone

(c) Scanner

(d) All of the above

26. Most of the commonly used personal computers/ laptops do not have a command key known as _________.

(a) Turnover     (b) Shift

(c) Alter             (d) Delete

27. SAN, Google Docs, and Network drive are all examples of _________ Storage.

(a) Primary      (b) RAM

(c) Remote        (d) Volatile

28. EPROM can be used for.

(a) erasing the contents of ROM

(b) reconstructing the contents of ROM

(c) erasing and reconstructing the contents of ROM

(d) duplicating the ROM

29. The errors that can be found out by a compiler are

(a) Logical errors

(b) Internal errors

(c) Semantic errors

(d) Syntax errors

30. Which of the following is not an operating system?

    (a) Android        (b) Vista

    (c) iOS            (d) Opera

31. Which of the following will you require to hear music on your computer?

    (a) Video Card

    (b) Tape Recorder

    (c) Mouse

    (d) Sound Card

32. A device that connects to a network without the use of cables is said to be

    (a) distributed    (b) centralised

    (c) open source    (d) wireless

33. Sending an e-mail is same as

    (a) writing a letter

    (b) drawing a picture

    (c) talking on phone

    (d) sending a package

34. What menu is selected to change font and style?

    (a) Tools          (b) File

    (c) Format         (d) Edit

35. This is not a function category in Excel

    (a) Logical        (b) Data Series

    (c) Financial      (d) Text

36. Which of the following is NOT available as a category in Control Panel of Windows 7?

    (a) Bluetooth settings

    (b) Ease of Access

    (c) System and Security

    (d) Programs

37. The function of given icon in MS-Word 2010 is __________.

    (a) Merge document to PDF files

    (b) Insert Flash video 8.

    (c) To add caption to a picture or other image

    (d) To insert an index into the document

38. Which of the following is CORRECT in HTML?

    (a) <HR>

    (b) <hr>

    (c) <B>Bold Text</B>

    (d) All of these

39. Computers use the seven digit code called ASCII. What does ASCII stand for?

    (a) American Scientists Convention for Information Interchange

    (b) Association of Software Coding and Information Institute

    (c) American Standard Code for Information Interchange

    (d) American Standard Computing and Information Institute

40. How many sheets are there in MS-Excel 2010 workbook by default?

    (a) 3            (b) 4

    (c) 5            (d) 6

**Name :** __________

**Number of Questions : 40**

**There is no negative marking in the test.**

**Max. Marks : 40**

**Time : 2 Hours**

1.  Which of the following software/ programs manages computer hardware and software resources and provides common services for computer application?

    (a) Application drivers

    (b) Utility software

    (c) Operating system

    (d) Cloud software

2.  Identify the following.

    – It is a software.

    – Products like remote control, digital watches, microwave ovens uses this software.

    – It is stored in the ROM chips.

    (a) Firmware

    (b) Middleware

    (c) Net software

    (d) Application software

3.  Inside its chip, each memory holds one bit of information and is made up of two parts - a transistor and a capacitor. It is used as main memory in personal computers.

    (a) Dynamic RAM

    (b) Static RAM

    (c) Video RAM

    (d) Audio RAM

4.  What does PCMCIA stand for?

    (a) Portable Card Memory for Computers International Association

    (b) Personal Computer Multimedia Card International Association

    (c) Personal Computer Memory Card International Association

    (d) Personal Card Memory of computers International Association

5. Which of the given options can give the following output?

$4_a7_b$

(a)  <html>

  <body>

  4<SUP>a</SUP>7<SUP>b</SUP>

  <body>

  </html>

(b)  <html>

  <body>

  4<SUB>a</SUB>7<SUB>b</SUB>

  <body>

  </html>

(c)  <html>

  <body>

  <SUB>4a7b<SUB>

  <body>

  </html>

(d)  <html>

  <body>

  <SUP>4a7b<SUP>

  <body>

  </html>

6. If you use _________,by default the items will be displayed in bulleted form.

(a) <ol> and </ol>

(b) <b> and </b>

(c) <li> and </li>

(d) <th> and </th>

7. What is the use of  tool?

(a) It selects a part of the object

(b) It adds text to a flash document.

(c) It fills an object with color.

(d) It copies a color from one object to another.

8. Which of the following is not a Lasso Tool option?

(a) 3D Translation

(b) Polygon Mode

(c) Magic Wand settings

(d) Magic Wand

9. You have to edit an existing letter in MS-Word. You want to review the modifications to the letter while editing. Which of the following features of MS – Word should you use?

(a) Auto Summarize

(b) Compare and Merge documents

(c) Track Changes

(d) Mail Merge Wizard

10. A communication network which is used by large organizations over regional, national or global area is called:
    (a) LAN          (b) WAN
    (c) MAN          (d) VAN

11. Which of the following Check for Issues options (which appears when you go to File tab and click on Info option) will help you to check the presentation for content that people with disabilities might find difficult to read?
    (a) Inspect Document
    (b) Check Compatibility
    (c) Check Accessibility
    (d) Add a Digital Signature

12. In Open window (which appears when you click on Open option of file tab), to open a copy of the file, leaving the original untouched, you need to select _____________ option from the drop-down list of Open button in Open dialog box.
    (a) Open
    (b) Open and Repair
    (c) Open in Browser
    (d) Open as Copy

13. The first step while creating a formula for a cell is to _________.
    (a) Select the cell you want to place the formula into
    (b) type the equals sign (=) to tell Excel that you're about to enter a formula
    (c) Enter the formula using any input values and the appropriate mathematical operators that make up your formula
    (d) Choose the new command from the file tab

14. The error value #NULL! appears in a cell because _________.
    (a) The formula is trying to multiple a value
    (b) The formula refers to a cell that is not valid
    (c) The formula uses an intersection of two ranges that do not intersect
    (d) The formula is trying to divide by zero

15. Match the MS – Excel shortcut sequences given in Column – I with their decriptions in Column – II.

Column – I    Column – II

(A) [Ctrl] + [⇧ Shift] + [=]   (i) Enters the current time into the active cell

(B) [Ctrl] + [⇧ Shift] + [:]   (ii) Copies the value from the cell above the active cell into the cell

(C) [Ctrl] + [⇧ Shift] + [;]   (iii) Displays the insert dialog box

(a) (A) – (iii), (B) – (ii), (C) – (i)

(b) (A) – (i), (B) – (iii), (C) – (ii)

(c) (A) – (ii), (B) – (iii), (C) – (i)

(d) (A) – (i), (B) – (ii), (C) – (iii)

16. What is the other name of LAN card?

(a) Modem

(b) Network connector

(c) Internet card

(d) NIC

17. Which of the following is a type of relationship that can be applied in Access database?

(a) One – to – One

(b) One – to – Many

(c) Many – to – Many

(d) All of these

18. Which of the following is a use of telnet service?

(a) For using computing power of a remote computer

(b) For accessing information from a database or archive on a remote computer

(c) For logging into one's own computer from another computer

(d) All of these

19. To erase cookies, you should delete the _________ on your PC.

(a) Temporary internet Files

(b) Web Activity folder

(c) Drivers folder

(d) All of these

20. Why are wireless networks flexible?

(a) You cannot connect any number of computers to one router.

(b) You do not need hardware to set up a wireless network

(c) You do not need an internet connection to connect to the internet.

(d) You don't need wires to connect your computer to the router.

21. Which of the following statements is/are CORRECT about FTP?

    (1) It uses the internet's TCP/IP protocols to enable data transfer.

    (2) It promotes sharing of files via remote computers with reliable and efficient data transfer.

    (3) It uses client server architecture.

    (a) (1) only
    (b) (2) only
    (c) (3) only
    (d) (1), (2) and (3)

22. Which of the following is the successor to the Xbox 360, a home video game console developed by Microsoft?

    (a) Xbox One
    (b) Xbox Two
    (c) Xbox 460
    (d) Xbox 360 Duo

23. Smart Covers in tablet computers are used to ________.

    (a) Protect the touchscreen and save energy
    (b) Fix the device to a wall
    (c) Type and input text
    (d) Provide internet connectivity

24. A computer used at supermarkets, departmental stores and restaurant etc is called ______ terminal

    (a) P-O-S (Point of scale)
    (b) Dumb
    (c) Intelligent
    (d) Smart

25. Which of the following refers to the fastest, biggest and most expensive computers?

    (a) Notebooks
    (b) Personal Computers
    (c) Laptops
    (d) Supercomputers

26. The part of the CPU that accesses and decodes program instructions and coordinates the flow of data among various system components is the

    (a) ALU
    (b) control unit
    (c) megahertz
    (d) motherboard

27. Which of the following functions is not performed by the CPU?

    (a) Graphical display of data
    (b) Arithmetic calculations
    (c) Managing memory
    (d) Play cricket on the ground.

28. The BOOT sector files of the system are stored in _____.

    (a) Hard disk

    (b) ROM

    (c) RAM

    (d) Fast solid state chips in the motherboard

29. Storage media such as a CD read and write information using __________.

    (a) a laser beam of red light

    (b) magnetic dots

    (c) magnetic strips

    (d) All of these

30. Which of the following software could assist someone who cannot use their hands for computer input?

    (a) Synthesizer

    (b) Speech Recognition

    (c) Audio Digitizer

    (d) Video Conferencing

31. When a computer is switched on, the booting process performs

    (a) Integrity Test

    (b) Power-On-Self-Test

    (c) Correct Functioning Test

    (d) Reliability Test

32. Bluetooth is an example of __________.

    (a) Personal area network

    (b) Local area network

    (c) Virtual private network

    (d) Wide area network

33. Which of the following softwares allows the user to move from page to page on the Web by clicking on or selecting a hyperlink or by typing in the address of the destination page?

    (a) Web browser

    (b) Web home page

    (c) Web home page

    (d) Web service

34. In Excel, the contents of the active cell are displayed in the __________.

    (a) footer bar

    (b) tool bar

    (c) task bar

    (d) formula bar

35. Data is organized in a work sheet as __________.

    (a) charts and diagrams

    (b) rows and columns

    (c) tables and boxes

    (d) graphs

36. What is the use of Format Painter in MS-PowerPoint 2010?
    (a) Reset the position, size and formatting of the slide
    (b) Format text to the left
    (c) Copy formatting from one place and apply it to another
    (d) Increase the indent level
37. Which of the following statements is INCORRECT about memory and storage devices?
    (a) ROM loses its data when you turn off the computer.
    (b) A storage device is a hardware component that writes data to and reads data from a storage medium.
    (c) Cache memory makes memory transfer rates higher and thus raises the speed of the processor.
    (d) Hard disks can be divided into one or more logical disks called partitions.
38. Which of the following statements is CORRECT about 'Sneaker-net'?
    (a) The process of converting data in a form so that an unauthorized person cannot understand it.
    (b) Un-authorized access of information from a wireless device.
    (c) Transferring computer files between computers by physically moving removable media such as CDs, flash drives.
    (d) A private computer network in which multiple PCs are connected to each other.
39. In Flash CS6, is called ____ tool.
    (a) Paint bucket
    (b) Fill color
    (c) Ink bottle
    (d) Lasso
40. Rearrange the steps given below to insert a motion tween in Flash CS6, first and last steps are given for you. First : Draw a shape at Frame 1
    (i) Go to Insert tab → Motion tween Last: Press Ctrl + to play the tween.
    (ii) Select the shape and convert it to a symbol
    (iii) Drag the play-head to a new frame and reposition your object
    (a) (ii) → (i) → (iii)
    (b) (i) → (iii) → (ii)
    (c) (iii) → (i) → (ii)
    (d) (iii) → (ii) → (i)

# HINTS AND EXPLANATIONS

## ENGLISH

**MOCK TEST 1**

| | | | | | | | | | |
|---|---|---|---|---|---|---|---|---|---|
| **ANSWER KEY** | | | | | | | | | |
| 1 | (b) | 11 | (c) | 21 | (b) | 31 | (a) | 41 | (d) |
| 2 | (d) | 12 | (a) | 22 | (b) | 32 | (c) | 42 | (b) |
| 3 | (b) | 13 | (a) | 23 | (b) | 33 | (d) | 43 | (a) |
| 4 | (b) | 14 | (b) | 24 | (d) | 34 | (c) | 44 | (c) |
| 5 | (c) | 15 | (c) | 25 | (b) | 35 | (b) | 45 | (a) |
| 6 | (b) | 16 | (b) | 26 | (b) | 36 | (a) | 46 | (a) |
| 7 | (b) | 17 | (b) | 27 | (a) | 37 | (d) | 47 | (b) |
| 8 | (b) | 18 | (c) | 28 | (a) | 38 | (a) | 48 | (b) |
| 9 | (b) | 19 | (c) | 29 | (c) | 39 | (a) | 49 | (c) |
| 10 | (a) | 20 | (a) | 30 | (d) | 40 | (d) | 50 | (c) |

1. **(b)** The excerpt that I want to read from the book includes a description of the fall of the Roman Empire.

2. **(d)** He was caught pilfering book from the shop.

3. **(b)** After the wrestling match, the wrestler had run out of steam. He was completely out of energy.

4. **(b)** It proved to be a great learning experience for Brian.

5. **(c)** The reporter provided a detailed account of the whole incident.

6. **(b)** The exact origin of this civilisation is not known.

7. **(b)** Mr. Abrol's character was quite stolid. He didn't seem to succumb to any challenge.

8. **(b)** That lady is very elusive. She is as slippery as an eel.

9. **(b)** She was not well yet she went for the party.

10. **(a)** Ten kilometres is a long distance to walk.

11. **(c)** He has the habit of jumping to conclusions.

12. **(a)** I want to meet the actress.

13. **(a)** "You may go back home now", said the teacher.

14. **(b)** Besides

15. **(c)** It was terrible earthquake, but the lady was miraculously unhurt.

16. **(b)** Carefully

**17. (b)** I must leave now because I have to be at my workplace by 11 o' clock.

**18. (c)** Not many people came for the show.

**19. (c)** The ozone layer will continue to deplete, if we don't find a way to stop its depletion.

**20. (a)** The Façade Stadium that has been in existence for more than fifty years, is now in shambles.

**21. (b)** Endeavour

**22. (b)** Poverty and illiteracy are two of the greatest social evils.

**23. (b)** He is quite dull.

**24. (d)** He was very polite to me.

**25. (b)** A government run by a dictator is known as autocracy.

**26. (b)** A person in charge of a museum is a curator.

**27. (a)** The parcel will be delivered today by the delivery man.

**28. (a)** The building was destroyed by the earthquake.

**29. (c)** Mats are made by him.

**30. (d)** She has been given a notice by her manager.

**31. (a)** An experiment was done by the teacher.

**32. (c)** Stupas were built to house the relics of Buddha and later saints.

**33. (d)** Dynamite, anti-tank mines and anti-aircraft guns were used to destroy the statues.

**34. (c)** Artillery means heavy weaponry.

**35. (b)** The archaeologists discovered empty caverns and debris at Bamiyan.

**36. (a)** Caverns mean a tunnel or a large cave.

**37. (d)** Urbanisation, Pollution of wetlands, Illegal trapping and hunting are causing destruction of habitat for birds.

**38. (a)** 116 bird sanctuaries are there in India.

**39. (a)** Six states have less than 12 bird sanctuaries.

**40. (d)** The source of the information given here is from the Ministry Of Environment Forest & Climate Change.

**41.(d)** We need to have bird sanctuaries to protect bird population, to provide habitat to them and help them against the onslaught by hunters and trappers.

**42. (b)** Oh! That I could paint.

**43. (a)** Alas! She has left the world.

**44. (c)** Terrific news! We won the world cup.

**45. (a)** Harris: Have you ever heard her singing? How well she sings!

**46. (a)** Ginni: I wish I hadn't spent all my pocket money.

**47. (b)** Devi: Sure! You can take it tomorrow.

**48. (b)** Hema: Don't worry; I'll help you find it.

**49. (c)** Samson: Fine, which one would you like to see?

**50. (c)** Amita: Okay, let's go to the mall.

$$\boxed{\textbf{MOCK TEST 2}}$$

| ANSWER KEY | | | | | | | | | |
|---|---|---|---|---|---|---|---|---|---|
| **1** | (b) | **11** | (c) | **21** | (a) | **31** | (a) | **41** | (a) |
| **2** | (b) | **12** | (a) | **22** | (c) | **32** | (c) | **42** | (a) |
| **3** | (c) | **13** | (b) | **23** | (a) | **33** | (a) | **43** | (a) |
| **4** | (b) | **14** | (c) | **24** | (d) | **34** | (b) | **44** | (c) |
| **5** | (a) | **15** | (b) | **25** | (b) | **35** | (a) | **45** | (b) |
| **6** | (b) | **16** | (a) | **26** | (d) | **36** | (c) | **46** | (d) |
| **7** | (c) | **17** | (b) | **27** | (c) | **37** | (d) | **47** | (a) |
| **8** | (a) | **18** | (a) | **28** | (d) | **38** | (c) | **48** | (b) |
| **9** | (b) | **19** | (b) | **29** | (a) | **39** | (d) | **49** | (c) |
| **10** | (a) | **20** | (a) | **30** | (a) | **40** | (b) | **50** | (a) |

**1. (b)** That university is an autonomous university. It does not have to follow the government policies.

**2. (b)** He has won accolades for creating an inexpensive water treatment plant for his school science project.

**3. (c)** He knew how to exalt someone to the height of a mountain.

**4. (b)** This organisation comprises of all the major countries of the world.

**5. (a)** The foreign tourist was appalled at the state of poor people in India.

**6. (b)** He is not going to tolerate any restrictions in his office.

**7. (c)** He has usurped power from the king.

**8. (a)** The secret agent unveiled his country's plans of invading our country.

**9. (b)** Don't be near-sighted; look to the future.

**10. (a)** The destruction caused by floods is going to push the area back by a decade or more.

**11. (c)** It was widely perceived that the rural population of the country was neglected.

**12. (a)** Where is the silver cutlery which was kept here?

**13. (b)** Planning for future is very important.

**14. (c)** I ought to tell the car owner about the crash.

**15. (b)** You forgot to tell me why you went to the hospital.

**16. (a)** They sincerely wished me good luck in my exams.

**17. (b)** Dennis fell from his bicycle and broke his right arm.

**18. (a)** You can't rest until you have met her and resolved the matter with her.

**19. (b)** Verb + Basics means to return, especially to a former position or activity.

**20. (a)** He saw an animal that looked like a goat.

**21. (a)** One of the students whom I approached to ask for the way to principal's office was on duty outside his office.

**22. (c)** He was calm.

**23. (a)** The opposition party was not able to renounce power from the ruling party.

**24. (d)** He gave me a very unnecessary offer.

**25. (b)** A man who has no money is called a pauper.

**26. (d)** A sleep enjoyed in the afternoon is siesta.

**27. (c)** All the fruits are kept in the fridge.

**28. (d)** A new editorial has been written by them.

**29. (a)** The notebooks were given back to the students by the teacher.

**30. (a)** She was selected as the captain of the team.

**31. (a)** Can my computer be repaired?

**32. (c)** Bolster means to strengthen .

**33. (a)** 'Beefed up the process' means to strengthen the process.

**34. (b)** NASA's Jet Propulsion Laboratory (JPL) is going to handle the new traffic system.

**35. (a)** The name of the orbiter sent in 1997 was Mars Global Surveyor.

**36. (c)** The traffic is supposed to get managed around Mars.

**37. (d)** The word lauded means appreciated.

**38. (c)** Japan leads in active mobile broadband subscribers is false. It is the United Kingdom that leads in active broadband subscription.

**39. (d)** 'India has lot of catching up to do' means that India has to work hard to reach the same standard as other countries.

**40. (b)** This data is based on a survey done in 2013.

**41. (a)** This data is indicative of digital penetration.

**42. (a)** This data has been done per hundred of population.

**43. (a)** Who broke the world record?

**44. (c)** How disappointing! I could not win the race.

**45 (b)** What a fantastic view we have of the city from here!

**46. (d)** Thanks Ma'am.

**47. (a)** Yes, but it's only a trial test.

**48. (b)** I feel sick.

**49. (c)** I have a race tomorrow.

**50. (a)** Gautam should end the email With regards.

## MOCK TEST 3

### ANSWER KEY

| | | | | | | | | | |
|---|---|---|---|---|---|---|---|---|---|
| **1** | (a) | **11** | (b) | **21** | (b) | **31** | (b) | **41** | (a) |
| **2** | (d) | **12** | (a) | **22** | (a) | **32** | (c) | **42** | (d) |
| **3** | (b) | **13** | (b) | **23** | (d) | **33** | (b) | **43** | (b) |
| **4** | (b) | **14** | (a) | **24** | (a) | **34** | (c) | **44** | (d) |
| **5** | (b) | **15** | (b) | **25** | (a) | **35** | (b) | **45** | (a) |
| **6** | (b) | **16** | (a) | **26** | (a) | **36** | (d) | **46** | (c) |
| **7** | (c) | **17** | (a) | **27** | (a) | **37** | (d) | **47** | (d) |
| **8** | (c) | **18** | (a) | **28** | (a) | **38** | (c) | **48** | (b) |
| **9** | (a) | **19** | (d) | **29** | (a) | **39** | (c) | **49** | (d) |
| **10** | (b) | **20** | (c) | **30** | (b) | **40** | (c) | **50** | (b) |

1. **(a)** A lot of reading improves one's vocabulary.
2. **(d)** I ought to tell you the truth, but I am scared.
3. **(b)** Mint
4. **(b)** The thief stood silently in the police station.
5. **(b)** He was trying hard to put the baggage on the trolley.
6. **(b)** We spotted Sam and chatted with him during the rehearsal.
7. **(c)** There is so much to tell that I don't know where to begin from.
8. **(c)** Agreement Collates with adjectives like-formal, written, legal, binding.
9. **(a)** This is the highway on which the accident happened.
10. **(b)** You always leave late for work even though I tell you to leave early.
11. **(b)** He drove very fast so that he could reach the airport on time.
12. **(a)** It is futile suggesting anything to him because he always does what he thinks is right.
13. **(b)** The reports of widespread infection are not accurate.
14. **(a)** He had to change our plan at the eleventh hour because of sudden onset of fever.
15. **(b)** His fickle-mindedness bewildered the entire class.
16. **(a)** He was a brave, honest man and we all honoured him.
17. **(a)** My car crashed into a stationary jeep.
Stationary means not moving or still. Stationery means office supplies.
18. **(a)** Hitin is a restless child. He doesn't remain attentive in class.
19. **(d)** I haven't seen Ram since last Friday.
20. **(c)** 'Red letter day' means an important day.

**21. (b)** I heard a faint sound and realised that there was someone listening to the whole conversation.

**22. (a)** It was a fertile place.

**23. (d)** He is quite immune to falling.

**24. (a)** It is insignificant that you restrict everything that can make you sick.

**25. (a)** Your strong points are known to me.

**26. (a)** Harry's schedule was kept busy.

**27. (a)** A gift was given to her.

**28. (a)** A parcel was sent to me.

**29. (a)** A lot of people have been bitten by this dog.

**30. (b)** Dry ice is silver iodide aerosols.

**31. (b)** The first cloud seeding experiment was conducted in 1946. It was conducted at Langmuir Laboratories, New York.

**32. (c)** Only a small amount of silver iodide is added to clouds to avoid risk of pollution.

**33. (b)** This notice seems to be issued by a beach authority.

**34. (c)** We should not swim after a heavy rainfall because bacteria levels are higher after a heavy rainfall.

**35. (b)** We should never swallow beach water.

**36. (d)** Protocol means an agreement, a treaty and a settlement.

**37. (d)** The acidifying of air leads to the loss of nutrients from soils, release of toxic elements into soil and water and acidification of lakes and streams.

**38. (c)** EEA stands for European Environmental Agency.

**39. (c)** An ecosystem is a system formed by the interaction of the organisms with their physical environment.

**40. (c)** Ever since the dawn of civilisation, man has been fighting with man.

**41. (a)** The history of mankind is full of such fightings between communities, nations and people.

**42. (d)** A modern war is scientific in character, but the effect is the same, wiping human existence out of this earth.

**43. (b)** From the primitive weapon of warfare, man has advanced to the modern nuclear weapons.

**44. (d)** The only difference now seem to be in the efficiency of the instruments used for killing each other.

**45. (a)** It is a terrible tragedy.

**46. (c)** Walk carefully! The floor is slippery.

**47. (d)** Unless you work harder you will fail, means if you do not put more efforts, then you will fail.

**48. (b)** "You are thinking very highly about Ravi but he is not so" means you have a good opinion about Ravi but he is not as good as you think.

**49. (d)** Owing to the acute power shortage, the people of our locality have decided to resort to use of electricity only when it is inevitable.

**50. (b)** "The food in this hotel is no match to what were forced at late hours in Hotel Kohinoor "Hotel Kohinoor means served us good quality food than what we get here.

**MOCK TEST 4**

| ANSWER KEY | | | | | | | | | |
|---|---|---|---|---|---|---|---|---|---|
| **1** | (a) | **11** | (b) | **21** | (c) | **31** | (a) | **41** | (c) |
| **2** | (b) | **12** | (c) | **22** | (a) | **32** | (b) | **42** | (a) |
| **3** | (b) | **13** | (a) | **23** | (d) | **33** | (c) | **43** | (b) |
| **4** | (b) | **14** | (d) | **24** | (a) | **34** | (a) | **44** | (d) |
| **5** | (c) | **15** | (b) | **25** | (b) | **35** | (b) | **45** | (b) |
| **6** | (d) | **16** | (b) | **26** | (a) | **36** | (b) | **46** | (c) |
| **7** | (c) | **17** | (c) | **27** | (d) | **37** | (a) | **47** | (b) |
| **8** | (a) | **18** | (d) | **28** | (a) | **38** | (b) | **48** | (d) |
| **9** | (c) | **19** | (b) | **29** | (a) | **39** | (a) | **49** | (a) |
| **10** | (b) | **20** | (b) | **30** | (b) | **40** | (a) | **50** | (a) |

1. **(a)** Sleeping for more than 8 hours is not good for health.

2. **(b)** You must not yell at me like that ever again.

3. **(b)** pure

4. **(b)** The mischievous kids deliberately threw the wrappers out of the window .

5. **(c)** It is quite hot today; the temperature seems to be above forty five degrees.

6. **(d)** He got up twice while we were having breakfast.

7. **(c)** Our principal is going away for a few weeks.

8. **(a)** This is a story about a king who used to disguise himself.

9. **(c)** It is not difficult to find a person who has suffered in the similar manner.

10. **(b)** His brainstorming methods explained in his easily read book are being employed in colleges and business offices.

11. **(b)** A collection of poems is called an anthology.

12. **(c)** I found neither of the movies interesting.

13 **(a)** Keep the keys under the doormat after locking the door carefully.

14. **(d)** Two wrongs do not make a right.

15. **(b)** My car brakes failed on the highway.

16. **(b)** After the landslide the tourists were left in a pitiable condition.

17. **(c)** Let's go to the seashore and collect some sea shells. Sea shells can be found only at the seashores.

18. **(d)** I think iodine is best for wounds. The doctor advised that any wound or cut should be thoroughly cleaned.

19. **(b)** My father has undergone a surgery for the removal of his gallbladder.

**20. (b)** Her presentation at the seminar was so good that she received many compliments. Compliment means appreciation, whereas complement means to add extra features to something else.

**21. (c)** The singer was mobbed by a herd of fans.

**22. (a)** The soldiers were condemned going for war every now and then.

**23. (d)** The king could not judge that there was disappointment among the people.

**24. (a)** It is a transmittable disease.

**25. (b)** You are requested to remain standing and not to start running.

**26. (a)** An interesting novel was given by his sister to him to read.

**27. (d)** A pair of binoculars was bought by my father for me.

**28. (a)** Maths is taught by Mr Rahim to us.

**29. (a)** Is the newspaper read by them every day?

**30. (b)** The last time that the dollar's cost was ₹66 was in the year 2013.

**31. (a)** The word that has the same meaning as working together at the same time is sync. Sync means working together at the same time, speed and same way.

**32. (b)** Rupee is among the top five currencies of the world.

**33. (c)** The fall of rupee is less than four per cent.

**34. (a)** A word from the above passage that is the opposite of dying is emerging. Emerging means to rise.

**35. (b)** India lost more soldiers in war with Pakistan than in war with China.

**36. (b)** India Gate was constructed in memory of Indian soldiers who were killed defending the British Empire.

**37. (a)** A glacier is a moving river of ice.

**38. (b)** Insurgency means revolt against the government.

**39. (a)** Moot is the opposite of definite. Moot means debatable or problematic.

**40. (a)** In which year were the first Asian Games held.

**41. (c)** Because we need to change the machine.

**42. (a)** The market was closed today. I will buy one tomorrow.

**43. (b)** Mother: I have made your favourite dish.

**44. (d)** The driver: It met with a small accident.

**45. (b)** Gauri: I like to watch football; I don't miss any match.

**46. (c)** James: I want to buy a microwave for them.

**47. (b)** Friend: Sure, let me first finish reading it.

**48. (d)** Seeta: Which way are you going?

**49. (a)** The meaning of ambiguity is the quality of being open to more than one interpretation; inexactness. Hence, option (a) is the correct choice.

**50. (a)** The meaning of affluence is the state of having a great deal of money; wealth. Hence, the option (a) is the correct choice.

**MOCK TEST 5**

| | | | | | | | | | |
|---|---|---|---|---|---|---|---|---|---|
| **1** | **(b)** | **11** | **(c)** | **21** | **(a)** | **31** | **(c)** | **41** | **(c)** |
| **2** | **(a)** | **12** | **(b)** | **22** | **(a)** | **32** | **(b)** | **42** | **(a)** |
| **3** | **(a)** | **13** | **(a)** | **23** | **(d)** | **33** | **(b)** | **43** | **(a)** |
| **4** | **(a)** | **14** | **(c)** | **24** | **(a)** | **34** | **(d)** | **44** | **(b)** |
| **5** | **(c)** | **15** | **(b)** | **25** | **(b)** | **35** | **(b)** | **45** | **(a)** |
| **6** | **(b)** | **16** | **(a)** | **26** | **(a)** | **36** | **(d)** | **46** | **(b)** |
| **7** | **(b)** | **17** | **(b)** | **27** | **(a)** | **37** | **(b)** | **47** | **(c)** |
| **8** | **(c)** | **18** | **(a)** | **28** | **(b)** | **38** | **(b)** | **48** | **(a)** |
| **9** | **(a)** | **19** | **(b)** | **29** | **(a)** | **39** | **(d)** | **49** | **(c)** |
| **10** | **(b)** | **20** | **(b)** | **30** | **(b)** | **40** | **(d)** | **50** | **(a)** |

1. **(b)** Listening is also an art, which many people do not have.

2. **(a)** Ma'am, Can I ask a question?

3. **(a)** Bite

4. **(a)** It was surprisingly very cold today in the afternoon.

5. **(c)** Chronic

6. **(b)** Hitler wrote Mein Kampf during his stay in the prison.

7. **(b)** Mr. Smith's office is the first one from the right.

8. **(c)** There was a programme on TV about dangers to the environment.

9. **(a)** Lexicographer

10. **(b)** India is projected to surpass China's population by 2022.

11. **(c)** He was convicted and sent to lifetime imprisonment.

12. **(b)** He was conferred the award for his efforts for promoting world peace.

13. **(a)** Thomas Edison tried more than thousand experiments before he developed a successful incandescent lamp.

14. **(c)** But

15. **(b)** Our class teacher is the ideal of many students. Idel means a statue.

16. **(a)** It's an absolutely ridiculous idea! It is not going to work.

17. **(b)** The number of participants who are participating in this event is quite impressive.

18. **(a)** We were supposed to write the central idea of this poem.

19. **(b)** Sameer could not understand the basic principles of physics.

20. **(b)** He can't decide right now, give him a little more time to think.

21. **(a)** You have not done the right thing; now you face the music.

**22. (a)** He <u>favoured</u> the whole incident.

**23. (d)** He was full of <u>respect</u> for all the poor people.

**24. (a)** He came out as a content man.

**25. (b)** Some money was given to him as loan by the bank.

**26. (a)** Was this picture drawn by Kamal?

**27. (a)** Let all the books be put away.

**28. (b)** Meals should be eaten by you at regular times.

**29. (a)** The mail may kindly be sent to us as soon as possible.

**30. (b)** The above advertisement requires teachers.

**31. (c)** The eligibility for design faculty is graduate and post Graduate from NID/NIFT/IIT, etc.

**32. (b)** One can send their resume for any requirement via e-mail.

**33. (b)** If one has to send a resume to a company for employment, one will write regards at the end.

**34. (d)** Post graduation means a degree obtained after graduation.

**35. (c)** Ridhima was trying very hard to entertain her cousins.

**36. (a)** Things will simply occur.

**37. (a)** Ended her relationships.

**38. (d)** At the end

**39. (b)** Help me

**40. (c)** Closely observed

**41. (c)** Francis: The one which was flying from Indonesia to Delhi.

**42. (a)** Francis: They want to get the terrorists released.

**43. (a)** Ela: I think I have met him once before

**44. (b)** Ram: Yes, we did. We went to the beach and enjoyed.

**45. (a)** Cacographer

**46. (b)** Arbitrator

**47. (c)** Cannibal

**48. (a)** Debonair

**49. (c)** Fatalist

**50. (a)** Emigrant

# MATHEMATICS

MOCK TEST-1

ANSWER KEY

| 1 | (c) | 11 | (b) | 21 | (d) | 31 | (a) | 41 | (b) |
|---|-----|----|-----|----|-----|----|-----|----|-----|
| 2 | (a) | 12 | (c) | 22 | (c) | 32 | (b) | 42 | (b) |
| 3 | (b) | 13 | (a) | 23 | (b) | 33 | (b) | 43 | (b) |
| 4 | (b) | 14 | (b) | 24 | (b) | 34 | (a) | 44 | (c) |
| 5 | (b) | 15 | (b) | 25 | (c) | 35 | (d) | 45 | (b) |
| 6 | (b) | 16 | (c) | 26 | (d) | 36 | (b) | 46 | (b) |
| 7 | (a) | 17 | (b) | 27 | (b) | 37 | (c) | 47 | (c) |
| 8 | (a) | 18 | (c) | 28 | (d) | 38 | (b) | 48 | (c) |
| 9 | (c) | 19 | (c) | 29 | (d) | 39 | (c) | 49 | (d) |
| 10 | (a) | 20 | (c) | 30 | (b) | 40 | (a) | 50 | (d) |

**1.** (c) $\dfrac{a}{2} + b = 0.8$ and $\dfrac{7}{a + \dfrac{b}{2}} = 10$

$$7 = 10\left(a + \dfrac{b}{2}\right)$$

$$\dfrac{7}{10} = a + \dfrac{b}{2}$$

$$a = \dfrac{7}{10} - \dfrac{b}{2} \quad ...(i)$$

Now, substitute value of 'a' from

(i) in eqⁿ $\dfrac{a}{2} + b = 0.8$

$$\dfrac{1}{2}\left(\dfrac{7}{10} - \dfrac{b}{2}\right) + b = 0.8$$

$$\dfrac{7}{20} - \dfrac{b}{4} + b = 0.8$$

$$\dfrac{7}{20} + \dfrac{3}{4}b = 0.8$$

$$\dfrac{3}{4}b = \dfrac{8}{10} - \dfrac{7}{20}$$

$$\dfrac{3}{4}b = \dfrac{16 - 7}{20}$$

$$\dfrac{3}{4}b = \dfrac{9}{20}$$

$$b = \dfrac{9}{20} \times \dfrac{4}{3}$$

$$b = \dfrac{3}{5}$$

$$b = 0.6$$

From eqⁿ $\dfrac{a}{2} + b = 0.8$

$$\dfrac{a}{2} + 0.6 = 0.8$$

$$\dfrac{a}{2} = 0.8 - 0.6$$

$$\dfrac{a}{2} = 0.2$$

$$a = 0.4$$

**2.** **(a)** It is given that the remainder is 25 in each case when we divide 1305, 4665 and 6905 by K.

So, subtracting 25 from each of the numbers, we get 1280, 4640 and 6880.

HCF (1280, 4640 and 6880) = 160

So the greatest number is 160.

$\therefore$ K = 160

Sum of its digits = 1 + 6 + 0 = 7

So, the answer is 7.

**3.** **(b)** Let the desired angle be $x°$

Its complement = $(90 - x)$

Its supplement = $(180 - x)$

Now, according to question

$$6(90 - x) = 2(180 - x) - 12$$

$$\Rightarrow \quad 3(90 - x) = 180 - x - 6$$

$$\Rightarrow \quad 270 - 3x = 174 - x$$

$$\Rightarrow \quad 3x - x = 270 - 174$$

$$\Rightarrow \quad 2x = 96$$

$$\Rightarrow \quad x = 48°$$

**4.** **(b)**

$$\begin{array}{cccccc} 240 & \boxed{240} & 120 & 40 & 10 & 2 \\ & \times 1 & \times 2 & \times 3 & \times 4 & \times 5 \end{array}$$

**5.** **(b)** Let the required number be x.

We have,

$$\frac{3x}{4} - \frac{3x}{14} = 150$$

$$\frac{21x - 6x}{28} = 150$$

$$x = \frac{150 \times 28}{15} = 280.$$

**6.** **(b)** $\sqrt{0.04 \times 0.4 \times a}$

$$= 0.4 \times 0.04 \times \sqrt{b}$$

Squaring both sides,

$$0.04 \times 0.4 \times a = (0.4)^2 \times (0.04)^2 \times b$$

$$\frac{b}{a} = \frac{0.04 \times 0.4}{0.04 \times 0.04 \times 0.4 \times 0.4}$$

$$\frac{b}{a} = \frac{1}{0.04 \times 0.4}$$

$$\frac{b}{a} = \frac{1000}{16}$$

$$\frac{b}{a} = \frac{125}{2}$$

**7.** **(a)** Let the ratio be $k$

$\therefore$  $a + b = 6k, b + c = 7k, c + a = 8k$

$$\Rightarrow \quad (a + b) + (b + c) + (c + a)$$

$$= 6k + 7k + 8k$$

$$\Rightarrow \quad 2(a + b + c) = 21k$$

$$\Rightarrow \quad k = \frac{2 \times 14}{21} = \frac{4}{3}$$

$\therefore$  $(a + b) = 6k$

$$= 6 \times \frac{4}{3} = 8$$

**8.** **(a)**

Given  ab = 120 cm$^2$

bc = 72 cm$^2$

ca = 60 cm$^2$

ab × bc × ca = 120 × 72 × 60

$$abc = \sqrt{5184000} = 720 \text{ cm}^3$$

Now, volume of cuboid

$$= a \times b \times c = 720 \text{ cm}^3$$

**9.  (c)** Let $f(x) = x^2 + \dfrac{4}{x^2} = (x)^2 + \left(\dfrac{2}{x}\right)^2$

$$\Rightarrow \ f(x) = (x)^2 + 2.x.\dfrac{2}{x} + \left(\dfrac{2}{x}\right)^2 - 2.x.\dfrac{2}{x}$$

$$\Rightarrow \ f(x) = \left(x + \dfrac{2}{x}\right)^2 - (2)^2$$

$$f(x) = \left(x + \dfrac{2}{x} + 2\right)\left(x + \dfrac{2}{x} - 2\right)$$

**10. (a)** Loss $= 0.005 \times 7 \times 24$ hrs.

$$= 0.84 \text{ hrs.}$$

Gain $= 0.42$ hrs.

Overall loss $= 0.42$ hrs.

$$= 25 \text{ min. } 12 \text{ sec.}$$

$\therefore$  Time shown at end of 2nd week
$= 11{:}34$ a.m.

**11. (b)**

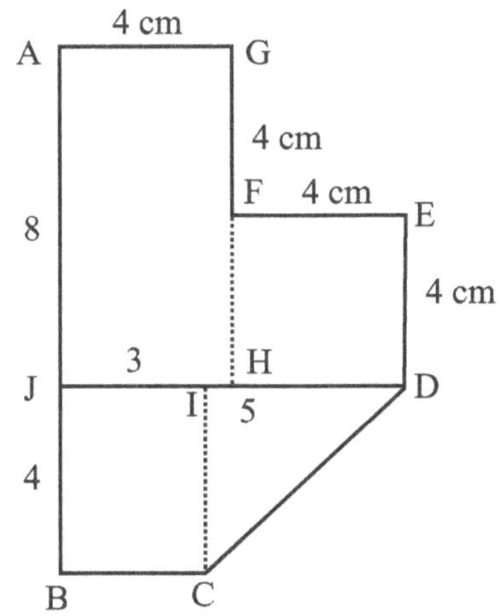


Area ABCDEFG

= Area AJHG + Area HFED + Area
JICB + Area ICD

$$= (8 \times 4) + (4 \times 4) + (4 \times 3) + \dfrac{1}{2}$$
$$\times (5 \times 4)$$
$$= 32 + 16 + 12 + 10$$
$$= 70 \text{ cm}^2$$

**12. (c)** Let the marked price $= ₹x$

After a discount of 20% price $=$

$$x - \dfrac{20}{100}x = \dfrac{4x}{5}$$

After a 10% discount on new price

$$= \dfrac{4x}{5} - \dfrac{10}{100} \times \dfrac{4x}{5}$$

$$= \dfrac{4x}{5} - \dfrac{2x}{25}$$

$$= \dfrac{18x}{25}$$

As given $\dfrac{18x}{25} = 108$

$$\Rightarrow \ x = \dfrac{108 \times 25}{18} = ₹150$$

**13. (a)** Add all the four numbers and then take its square root.

**14. (b)** Here, Ravi starts from home at A, moves 10 km southwards up to B, turns right and moves 5 km up to C, turns right again and moves 10 km up to D and finally turns left and moves 10 km up to E.

Thus, his distance from initial position A = AE

= AD + DE

$$= BC + DE = (5 + 10) \text{ km}$$
$$= 15 \text{ km.}$$

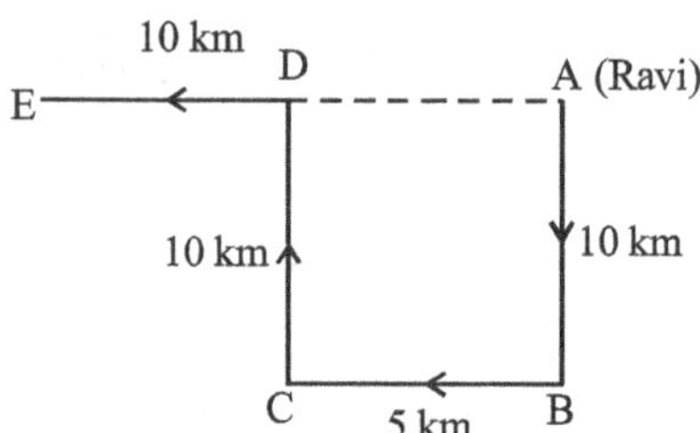



**15. (b)** Let one number = a

$\therefore$ Second number = 4a

$\Rightarrow \quad 4a \times a = 1936$

$\Rightarrow \quad a^2 = \dfrac{1936}{4} = 484$

$\Rightarrow \quad a^2 = 484$

$\Rightarrow \quad a^2 = (2 \times 2) \times (11 \times 11)$

$\Rightarrow \quad a = 2 \times 11 = 22$

$\qquad$ and $\quad 4a = 4 \times 22 = 88$

$\therefore$ Numbers are 22 and 88.

**16. (c)** x + 8% of x = 135

$$\dfrac{108x}{100} = 135$$

$$x = 135 \times \dfrac{100}{108} = 125.$$

**17. (b)** a + b + c = 0

$\qquad a^3 + b^3 + c^3 - 3abc = (a + b + c)$
$\qquad\qquad \{a^2 + b^2 + c^2 - (ab + bc + ca)\}$

$\Rightarrow a^3 + b^3 + c^3 = 3abc \qquad ....(\text{i})$

$$\dfrac{(b+c)^2}{3bc} + \dfrac{(c+a)^2}{3ca} + \dfrac{(a+b)^2}{3ab}$$

$$= \dfrac{a^2}{3bc} + \dfrac{b^2}{3ca} + \dfrac{c^2}{3ab}$$

$$\left[ \begin{array}{l} \because a+b+c=0 \\ \Rightarrow a+b=-c \\ \Rightarrow b+c=-a \\ \Rightarrow a+c=-b \end{array} \right]$$

$$= \dfrac{a^3}{3abc} + \dfrac{b^3}{3abc} + \dfrac{c^3}{3abc}$$

$$= \dfrac{a^3 + b^3 + c^3}{3abc} = \dfrac{3abc}{3abc} = 1$$

**18. (c)** There are 2 series :

$$\left(+3\frac{1}{4}\right): 27, 30\frac{1}{4}, 33\frac{1}{2}, 36\frac{3}{4}, 40$$

$$\left(-3\frac{1}{4}\right): 27, 23\frac{3}{4}, 20\frac{1}{2}, 17\frac{1}{4}, 14$$

**19. (c)** The movements of Lokesh are as shown in figure. (A to B, B to C, C to D to E). Clearly, his final position is E which is to the North of his house A.

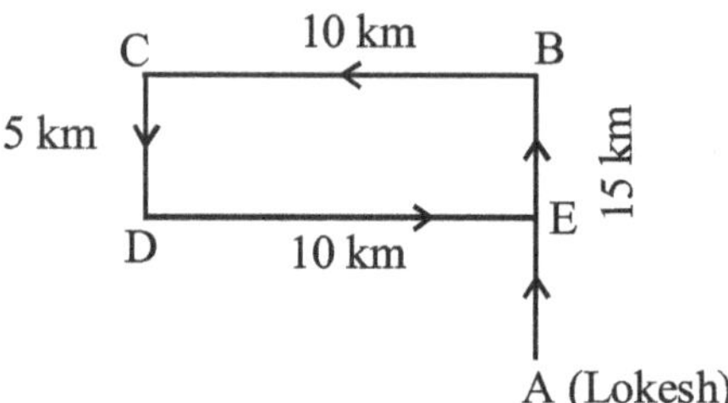



**20. (c)** Surface area of sphere of radius $r = 4\pi r^2$

After increase of P%, the radius becomes $= r + \dfrac{Pr}{100}$

Hence new surface area

$$= 4\pi\left(r + \frac{Pr}{100}\right)^2$$

$$= 4\pi r^2\left(1 + \frac{P}{100}\right)^2$$

Percentage increase

$$= \frac{\text{New surface area} - \text{initial surface area}}{\text{initial surface area}} \times 100$$

$$= \left[\frac{4\pi r^2\left(1 + \frac{P}{100}\right)^2 - 4\pi r^2}{4\pi r^2}\right] \times 100$$

$$= \left[1 + \frac{P^2}{100^2} + \frac{2P}{100} - 1\right] \times 100$$

$$= \left(\frac{P^2}{100} + 2P\right)\%$$

**21. (d)** The required number must be a multiple of 7 and also of L.C.M. of 6, 9, 15, 18 when 4 is subtracted from it.

L.C.M. of 6, 9, 15, 18 is 90.

90 + 4 = 94,

but it is not divisible by 7

180 + 4 = 184

it is not divisible by 7

Also 270 + 4 = 274

is not divisible by 7

But, 360 + 4 = 364

is divisible by 7

Hence, the required number is 364.

**22. (c)** $\dfrac{a(x-b)}{a-b} + \dfrac{b(x-a)}{b-a} = 1$

$$\frac{a(x-b)}{a-b} = 1 - \frac{b(x-a)}{b-a}$$

or $\dfrac{a(x-b)}{a-b} = \dfrac{a-b+b(x-a)}{a-b}$

or $ax - bx = a - b - ab + ab$

or $x(a-b) = a-b$

or $x = \dfrac{a-b}{a-b} = 1$

**23. (b)** Volume of cube $= a^3$

Now, $\dfrac{V_a}{V_b} = \dfrac{343}{1331}$

$$\frac{a^3}{b^3} = \left(\frac{7}{11}\right)^3, \ a : b = 7 : 11$$

**24. (b)** Let the two parts are $x$ and $(78-x)$

$$\therefore \quad \frac{5x}{4(78-x)} = \frac{15}{14}$$

$$\Rightarrow \quad \frac{x}{2(78-x)} = \frac{3}{7}$$

$$\Rightarrow \quad 7x = 468 - 6x$$

$$\Rightarrow \quad 13x = 468$$

$$\Rightarrow \quad x = 36$$

**25. (c)** Area of each square on chessboard $= 6.25 \text{ cm}^2$

Area of 64 squares on chessboard $= 6.25 \times 64 \text{ cm}^2$

$\therefore$ Side of chessboard

$$= \sqrt{6.25 \times 64} + 4 = 2.5 \times 8 + 4$$

Side of chessboard = 20 + 4

= 24 cm

[Side includes the border also]

**26. (d)** Clearly, HCF is 1

**27. (b)**

$$\because \left(x - \frac{1}{x}\right)^2 = x^2 + \frac{1}{x^2} - 2x\left(\frac{1}{x}\right)$$

$$\therefore x^2 + \frac{1}{x^2} = \left(x - \frac{1}{x}\right)^2 + 2 \geq 2$$

[For any natural number x]

**28. (d)** From figures (i) and (iv) we conclude that 6, 5, 2 and 3 lie adjacent to 4. It follows that 1 lies opposite 4.

**29. (d)**

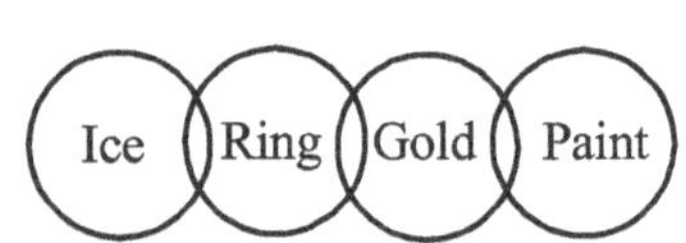


*or*



*or*



**30. (b)** The total of 32 observations

= 32 × their mean

= 32 × 28 = 896

The total of remaining 18 observations = 540

Hence, the total of 50 observation = 896 + 540 = 1436

Now, the required mean

$$= \frac{1436}{50} = 28.72$$

**31. (a)**

$\because \quad \angle A + \angle B + \angle C + \angle D = 360°$

(By angle sum property)

$x + 2x + 3x + 4x = 360°$

$\Rightarrow 10x = 360°$

$\angle x = 36°$

**32. (b)** Total number of observations = 10 (an even number)

$\therefore$ median = average of $\left(\frac{n}{2}\right)^{th}$ and

$$\left(\frac{n}{2} + 1\right)^{th}$$

observation i.e average of $5^{th}$ and $6^{th}$ observation.

$$\therefore \quad \text{median} = \frac{x + 2 + x + 4}{2} = 25$$

(Given)

$\Rightarrow 2x + 6 = 50$

$\Rightarrow 2x = 44$

$\Rightarrow x = 22$

**33. (b)** Let CP = ₹$x$

First SP = 115% of $x = \frac{23}{20}x$

second CP = 90% of x = $\frac{9x}{10}$

second SP = 120% of $\frac{9x}{10}$

$$= \frac{120}{100} \times \frac{9x}{10}$$

$$= \frac{27x}{25}$$

It is given that,

$$\frac{23x}{20} - \frac{27x}{25} = 28$$

$$\Rightarrow \frac{115x - 108x}{100} = 28$$

$$\Rightarrow x = \frac{28 \times 100}{7} = ₹400$$

**34. (a)** Let $r_1$ be the radius of hemisphere and $r_2$ be the radius of the cone.

Given that volume of hemisphere = volume of cone.

$$\frac{2}{3}\pi r_1^3 = \frac{1}{3}\pi r_2^2 h$$

$$\Rightarrow \frac{2}{3}\pi 6^3 = \frac{1}{3}\pi r_2^2 \times 75$$

$$\Rightarrow r_2^2 = \frac{2 \times 6 \times 6 \times 6}{75}$$

$$r_2 = \frac{12}{5} = 2.4 \text{ cm}$$

**35. (d)** Let the numerator of rational number = x

Then, the denominator of rational number = x + 8

$$\therefore \text{ rational number} = \frac{x}{x+8}$$

Now, according to question

$$\frac{x+17}{x+8-1} = \frac{3}{2}$$

$$\Rightarrow \frac{x+17}{x+7} = \frac{3}{2}$$

$$\Rightarrow 2x + 34 = 3x + 21$$

$$\Rightarrow 3x - 2x = 34 - 21$$

$$\Rightarrow x = 13$$

$\therefore$ The required rational number

$$= \frac{x}{x+8} = \frac{13}{13+8} = \frac{13}{21}$$

**36. (b)** Let edge of new cube be x. So according to question,

$$x^3 = 6^3 + 8^3 + 10^3$$

$$\Rightarrow x = 12 \text{ cm}$$

**37. (c)** The rule is $a + b = \left(\dfrac{a+b}{2}\right)^2$

$$3 + 5 = \left(\frac{3+5}{2}\right)^2 \text{ etc.}$$

$$\therefore 11 + 3 = \left(\frac{11+3}{2}\right)^2 = 49$$

**38. (b)** $\because$ Distance travelled in the first one hour = 35 km/hr

So, speed of car in the first one hour = 35 km/hr

As, the speed of car increases by 2 km after every one hour.

Therefore, the total distance travelled in 12 hours

$$= 35 + 37 + 39 + 41 + 43 + 45 + 47 + 49 + 51 + 53 + 55 + 57$$
$$= (35 + 57) + (37 + 55) + (39 + 53) + (41 + 51) + (43 + 49) + (45 + 47)$$
$$= 92 + 92 + 92 + 92 + 92 + 92$$
$$= 92 \times 6 = 552 \text{ km}$$

**39. (c)** $\dfrac{3^x}{1+3^x} = \dfrac{1}{9}$

$$\Rightarrow 3^x \cdot 9 = 1 + 3^x$$

$$\Rightarrow 3^x (9 - 1) = 1$$

$$\Rightarrow \quad 3^x = \frac{1}{8}$$

$$\Rightarrow \quad \left(3^x\right)^2 = \left(\frac{1}{8}\right)^2 \Rightarrow 9^x = \frac{1}{64}$$

$$\therefore \quad \frac{9^x}{1+9^x} = \frac{\dfrac{1}{64}}{1+\dfrac{1}{64}}$$

$$= \frac{1/64}{65/64} = \frac{1}{65}$$

**40. (a)**

**41. (b)** $(7 \times 8) - (5 \times 4) = 36$

$(9 \times 3) - (5 \times 2) = 17$

$(8 \times 5) - (6 \times 3) = 22$

**42. (b)** Let the original radius = r

$\therefore$ Driginal area $A = \pi r^2$

increased area $A' = \pi(r + 1)^2$

Now, $A' = A + 22$

$\pi(r + 1)^2 = \pi r^2 + 22$

$\Rightarrow \pi[(r + 1)^2 - r^2] = 22$

$\Rightarrow \pi[(r + 1 + r)(r + 1 - r)] = 22$

$\Rightarrow \pi(2r + 1) = 22$

$$2r + 1 = \frac{22 \times 7}{22} \qquad \left[\because \pi = \frac{22}{7}\right]$$

$\Rightarrow 2r + 1 = 7$

$\Rightarrow 2r = 6$

$\Rightarrow r = 3$ cm

**43. (b)** $\left[\left(\sqrt[n]{x^2}\right)^{n/2}\right]^2 = \left[\left\{\left(x^2\right)^{\frac{1}{n}}\right\}^{\frac{n}{2}}\right]^2$

$$= x^{2 \times \frac{1}{n} \times \frac{n}{2} \times 2} = x^2$$

**44. (c)** Let actual sides of rectangle are '$l$' and '$b$' respectively.

Actually measured sides are $(l + 0.05l)$ and $(b + 0.03b)$ i.e. $1.05l$ and $1.03b$

Measured area $= (1.05l)(1.03b)$ $= 1.0815lb$

Actual Area $= lb$

Error in area $= 1.0815lb - lb$

$$\therefore \quad \% \text{ error} = \left(\frac{0.0815lb}{lb} \times 100\right)\%$$

$$= 8.15\%$$

**45. (b)**

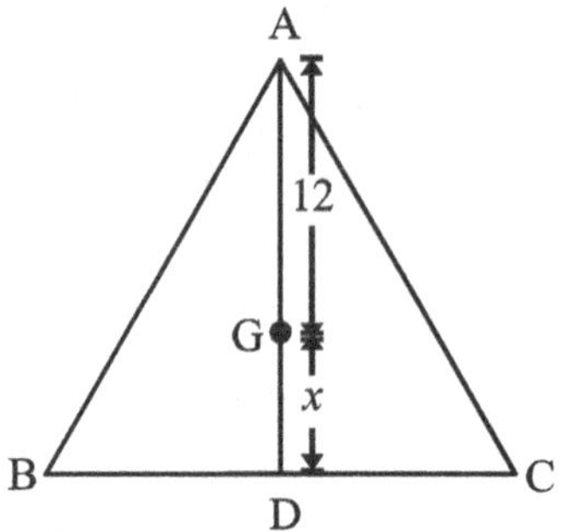


Here AD be the median of $\Delta$ABC.

$\therefore$ GD = x unit

$\therefore$ length of median = 12 + x.

Since, G divides median in 2 : 1 ratio.

$\therefore$ 12 : x = 2 : 1

$$\Rightarrow \frac{12}{x} = \frac{2}{1}$$

$\Rightarrow$ x = 6

Hence, length of median $= 12 + 6 = 18$ units

**46. (b)**

| Class Interval | Midpoint $(x_i)$ | Frequency $f_i$ | $f_i x_i$ |
|---|---|---|---|
| 90 – 100 | 95 | 10 | 950 |
| 80 – 90 | 85 | 15 | 1275 |
| 70 – 80 | 75 | 14 | 1050 |
| 60 – 70 | 65 | 12 | 780 |
| 50 – 60 | 55 | 9 | 495 |
| | | $\sum f_i = 60$ | $\sum f_i x_i = 4550$ |

$$\therefore \quad \text{mean, } \overline{x} = \frac{\sum f_i x_i}{\sum f_i} = \frac{4550}{60}$$

$$= 75.83$$

**47. (c)**
$$\frac{P(1+r)^3}{P(1+r)^2} = \frac{714}{672}$$

$$\Rightarrow (1+r) = \frac{714}{672}$$

$$\Rightarrow r = \frac{42}{672} = \frac{1}{16}$$

$$\Rightarrow r = 6.25\% = 6\frac{1}{4}\%.$$

**48. (c)** Total rose producation
$$= (15 + 12.5 + 12.45 + 20 + 12.4$$
$$+ 22.5 + 22.4 + 25) \times 1000$$
$$= 142250$$

Now, 10% of total production

$$= \frac{142250 \times 10}{100} = 14,225.$$

Obviously, Haryana, Karnataka and Rajasthan contribute less than 10% in the total production.

**49. (d)** Total production of rose by all the states = 142250

$$\therefore \quad \text{Average} = \frac{142250}{8}$$

$$= 18 \text{ thousand (approx).}$$

**50. (d)** Total production of states having production below 20,000 = 15000 + 12500 + 12450 + 12400 = 52,350

$$\therefore \quad \text{Required \%} = \frac{52,000}{142250} \times 100$$

$$= 36.6\%$$

It is 36.6% approximately.

## MOCK TEST-2

### ANSWER KEY

| 1 | (c) | 11 | (a) | 21 | (d) | 31 | (a) | 41 | (b) |
|---|-----|----|-----|----|-----|----|-----|----|-----|
| 2 | (b) | 12 | (a) | 22 | (b) | 32 | (c) | 42 | (b) |
| 3 | (a) | 13 | (b) | 23 | (d) | 33 | (d) | 43 | (d) |
| 4 | (b) | 14 | (b) | 24 | (c) | 34 | (d) | 44 | (c) |
| 5 | (c) | 15 | (b) | 25 | (b) | 35 | (d) | 45 | (a) |
| 6 | (b) | 16 | (c) | 26 | (b) | 36 | (c) | 46 | (a) |
| 7 | (b) | 17 | (c) | 27 | (b) | 37 | (c) | 47 | (b) |
| 8 | (a) | 18 | (d) | 28 | (d) | 38 | (c) | 48 | (d) |
| 9 | (c) | 19 | (b) | 29 | (a) | 39 | (a) | 49 | (c) |
| 10 | (c) | 20 | (a) | 30 | (c) | 40 | (a) | 50 | (b) |

**1.** (c) $\left(x+\dfrac{1}{x}\right)^2 = \left(x^2+\dfrac{1}{x^2}\right)+2$

$\left(x+\dfrac{1}{x}\right)^2 = 27+2$

$x+\dfrac{1}{x} = \sqrt{29}$

**2.** (b) $L.C.M.(a,b) = \dfrac{a \times b}{HCF(a,\ b)}$

$= \dfrac{1800}{12} = 150$

**3.** (a) $\angle PSR = \angle PQR = 68°$

(opp. $\angle$s of a || gm are equal)

$\angle PTS = 180° - 139° = 41°$

(PTQ is a straight line)

$\therefore$ $\angle RST = \angle PTS = 41°$

(SR || PQ alt. $\angle$s are equal)

$\therefore$ $y = \angle PSR - \angle RST = 68° - 41°$

$= 27°.$

**4.** (b) 210

$7 \times 6 \times 1 \times 5 = 210$

**5.** (c) Mean of 121 observations

given n = 121, $\bar{x} = 59$

Sum of 121 observation = mean × no. of observations

$= 121 \times 59 = 7139$

If each observation is multiplied by 4, then new sum

$= 4 \times$ (old total)

$= 4 \times 7139 = 28556$

$\therefore$ New mean $= \dfrac{28556}{121} = 236$

**6.** (b) $18432 = 2 \times 2 \times 2 \times 2 \times 2 \times 2 \times 2$
$\times 2 \times 2 \times 2 \times 2 \times 3 \times 3$

18432 must be divided by 36, so that the quotient is a perfect cube

$18432 \div 36 = 512$

So, 512 is a cube of 8.

**7.** **(b)** There is a gap of four letters between first and second, second and third letter of each term. Also there is a gap of 4 letters between the last letter of a term and the first letter of the next term.

**8.** **(a)** Total number of events = 52.

There are 26 red cards including 2 red kings and there are 2 more black kings. Hence there are 28 cards which are either red or king. Out of this, 1 card can be drawn.

$\therefore$ Required probability $= \dfrac{28}{52}$

$$= \dfrac{7}{13}$$

**9.** **(c)**

| Prime No. | Composite No. | LCM |
|---|---|---|
| 3 | 28 | 3×8 ≠ 220 |
| 5 | 26 | 5×26 ≠ 220 |
| 7 | 24 | 7×24 ≠ 220 |
| 11 | 20 | 11×20 = 220 |
| 13 | 18 | 13×18 ≠ 220 |
| 17 | 14 | 17×14 ≠ 220 |
| 19 | 12 | 19×12 ≠ 220 |

**10.** **(c)** Let the denominator be x and the numerator be $(x - 4)$

According to the question

$8\,(x - 4 - 2) = (x + 1)$

$\Rightarrow 8\,(x - 6) = (x + 1)$

$\Rightarrow 8x - 48 = x + 1$

$\Rightarrow 8x - x = 1 + 48$

$\Rightarrow 7x = 49$

$\Rightarrow x = 7$

$\therefore$ Required fraction $= \dfrac{x - 4}{x}$

$$= \dfrac{7 - 4}{7} = \dfrac{3}{7}$$

**11.** **(a)**

$\therefore$ The cost of levelling and turfing a lawn at ₹ 4.00 per m² = ₹6400

$\therefore$ Area of lawn $= \dfrac{6400}{4} = 1600 \text{ m}^2$

$\Rightarrow$ side of lawn = 40 m

So, the cost of fencing at ₹10 per metre = 4 × 40 × 10 = ₹1600

**12.** **(a)** Sides are in the ratio $\dfrac{1}{2} : \dfrac{1}{3} : \dfrac{1}{4}$

i.e. $6 : 4 : 3$

Let the ratio be x

$\therefore$ Sides are 6x, 4x and 3x

Given that 6x + 4x + 3x = 104

$\Rightarrow 13x = 104$

$\Rightarrow x = 8$

$\therefore$ Longest side = 6x = 6 × 8

$$= 48 \text{ cm}$$

**13.** **(b)** The year 1979 being an ordinary year, it has 1 odd day.

So, the day on 12th January 1980 is one day beyond on the day of 12th January, 1979.

But, January 12, 1980 being Saturday.

$\therefore$ January 12, 1979 was Friday.

**14. (b)** $1\frac{1}{4} = \frac{5}{4}, \quad 1\frac{2}{3} = \frac{5}{3}, \quad 2\frac{1}{2} = \frac{5}{2}$

LCM of $\left(\frac{5}{4}, \frac{5}{3} \text{ and } \frac{5}{2}\right)$

$$= \frac{\text{LCM of } (5, 5 \text{ and } 5)}{\text{HCF of } (4, 3, 2)}$$

$$= \frac{5}{1} = 5$$

**15. (b)** Let the required number be 'x'

Now, as per question

$$x \times \frac{1}{3}x + 18 = 2901$$

$$\Rightarrow \quad \frac{x^2}{3} = 2901 - 18 = 2883$$

$$\Rightarrow \quad x^2 = 8649$$

$$x^2 = (3 \times 3) \times (31 \times 31)$$

$$\Rightarrow \quad x = 3 \times 31 = 93$$

**16. (c)** Let cost of two watches are ₹x and ₹y respectively

∴ Total cost price = ₹(x + y)

Selling price with 10% profit

$$= x + \frac{10}{100}x = \frac{11}{10}x$$

∴ Selling price of watch = ₹5000

∵ $\frac{11}{10}x = 500$

$$\Rightarrow \quad x = \frac{5000}{11}$$

Selling price with 10% loss

$$= y - \frac{10}{100}y = \frac{9y}{10}$$

$$\frac{9y}{10} = 500$$

$$\Rightarrow \quad y = \frac{5000}{9}$$

∴ Total cost price = x + y

$$= \frac{5000}{11} + \frac{5000}{9}$$

$$= ₹\,\frac{5000 \times 20}{99} > 1000$$

∴ x + y > 1000

[total selling price]

So, there is a loss

$$\therefore \quad \text{Loss} = \frac{5000 \times 20}{99} - 1000$$

$$= ₹\,1000 \times \frac{1}{99}$$

$$\% \text{ Loss} = \left(\frac{1000 \times \dfrac{1}{99}}{5000 \times \dfrac{20}{99}} \times 100\right)\%$$

$$= \left(\frac{1000 \times 99}{5000 \times 20 \times 99} \times 100\right)\%$$

% Loss = 1%

**17. (c)** $A = P\left(1 + \dfrac{TR}{100}\right)$

$$81 = 72\left(1 + \frac{T \times \dfrac{25}{4}}{100}\right)$$

$$\frac{16+T}{16}=\frac{81}{72}$$

$$16 + T = 18$$

$$T = 2 \text{ years.}$$

**18. (d)** Let principal = ₹ 1, then amount = ₹ 16

$$\left(1+\frac{r}{100}\right)^{4}=\frac{16}{1}$$

$$1+\frac{r}{100}=2$$

$$r = 100\%$$

**19. (b)** Since $(x - 1)$ is the HCF of $(x^2 - 1)$ and $px^2 - q(x + 1)$

∴ $(x - 1)$ will divide both $(x^2 - 1)$ and $px^2 - q(x + 1)$

So, $x = 1$ will make each of them equal to zero. Then,

$$p(1)^2 - q(1+ 1) = 0$$

$$p - 2q = 0$$

$$p = 2q$$

**20. (a)** Let $f(x) = 2x^2 - 3x - 2$ and

$$q(x) = x^3 - 4x^2 + 4x$$

$$f(x) = 2x^2 - 4x + x - 2$$

$$f(x) = 2x (x - 2) + 1(x - 2)$$

$$= (x - 2) (2x + 1)$$

$$q(x) = x(x^2 - 4x + 4)$$

$$q(x) = x(x - 2)^2$$

∴ LCM of f (x) and q(x)

$$= x(x - 2)^2 (2x + 1)$$

**21. (d)** Interchanging $(+$ and $\div)$ and $(2$ and $4)$, we get :

(a) $4 \div 2 + 3 = 3$ or

5 = 3, which is false

(b) $2 \div 4 + 6 = 1.5$ or

6.5 = 1.5, which is false.

(c) $2 + 4 \div 3 = 4$ or

$$\frac{10}{3}= 4, \text{ which is false.}$$

(d) $4 \div 2 + 6 = 8$ or

8 = 8, which is true.

**22. (b)** Let costs of 1 chair and 1 table are x and y respectively.

∵ Cost of 3 chairs and 2 tables

$$= ₹700$$

⇒ $3x + 2y = 700$ ...(1)

And, cost of 5 chairs and 3 tables

$$= ₹1100$$

⇒ $5x + 3y = 1100$ ...(2)

From equation (1) and (2), we get

x = ₹100, y = ₹200

Then, the cost of 2 chairs and 2 tables is

$$= 2x + 2y = 2 \times 100 + 2 \times 200 = 600$$

**23. (d)**

**24. (c)**

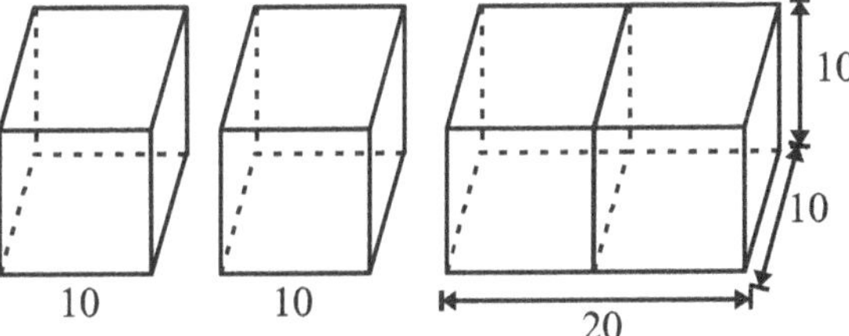


Length of cuboid = (10 + 10)

$$= 20 \text{ cm}$$

Breadth = 10 cm, Height = 10 cm

Surface area of cuboid

$$= 2 \, (l \times b + b \times h + h \times l)$$

$= 2(20 \times 10 + 10 \times 10 + 10 \times 20)$

$= 2(200 + 100 + 200)$

$= 1000$ sq. cm

**25. (b)** Let slower speed $= u$ km/hr

As the distance is fixed

$$u \times 8 = (u + 5) \times \frac{20}{3}$$

$$\left[\because 6 \text{ hr } 40 \text{ min } = 6\text{hr} + \frac{40}{60}\text{hr}\right.$$

$$\left. = 6\,\frac{2}{3} = \frac{20}{3}\text{ hrs}\right]$$

$\Rightarrow \quad 24\,u = 20\,u + 100$

$\Rightarrow \quad 4\,u = 100$

$\Rightarrow \quad u = 25$ km/hr

**26. (b)** The number inside the circle is the difference of the numbers on its right and left.

**27. (b)**

$\therefore \quad$ Radius of wheel $= 1.4$ decimeter

$\qquad\qquad\qquad = 0.14$ meter

$\therefore \quad$ Circumference of wheel

$$= 2 \times \frac{22}{7} \times 0.14 = 0.88 \text{ meter}$$

So, number of revolutions for 0.66

$$\text{km} = \frac{0.66}{0.88} \times 1000 = 750$$

**28. (d)** 10 mason 8 hrs 50 m long wall 25 days

1 mason 8 hrs 50 m long wall $25 \times 10$ days

1 mason 1 hr 50 m long wall 25

$\times 10 \times 8$ days

1 mason 1 hr 1 m long wall

$$\frac{25 \times 10 \times 8}{50} \text{ days}$$

1 mason 1 hr 36 m long wall

$$\frac{25 \times 10 \times 8 \times 36}{50} \text{ days}$$

1 mason 6 hr 36 m long wall

$$\frac{25 \times 10 \times 8 \times 36}{50 \times 6} \text{ days}$$

15 mason 6 hr 36 m long wall

$$\frac{25 \times 10 \times 8 \times 36}{50 \times 6 \times 15} \text{ days}$$

$= 16$ days

**29. (a)** The sequired expression that must be subtracted

$= 3a^2 - 6ab - 3b^2 - 1 - 4a^2$

$+ 7ab + 4b^2 - 1$

$= 3a^2 - 4a^2 - 6ab + 7ab - 3b^2$

$+ 4b^2 - 1 - 1$

$= -a^2 + ab + b^2 - 2$

**30. (c)** (A) - (p, r), (B) - (p, r),

(C) - (q, s, r), (D) - (q, r)

**31. (a)** Let the numbers be a and b, where $b > a$.

According Euclid's Division Lemma,

$b = a \times 2 + r_1$, where $0 < r_1 < a$

$a = r_1 \times 4 + r_2$, where $0 < r_2 < r_1$

$r_1 = r_2 \times 6 + 0$

H.C.F. $= r_2 = 7$

$\therefore \quad r_1 = 7 \times 6 = 42$

$$a = 42 \times 4 + 7 = 175$$

$$b = 175 \times 2 + 42 = 392$$

**32. (c)** $\angle ADC = 180º - 100º = 80º$

$$\angle CAD = \angle ACD = \frac{180° - 80°}{2}$$

$$= 50° = \angle DAB$$

$$\angle ABD = 180º - 100º - 50º = 30º$$

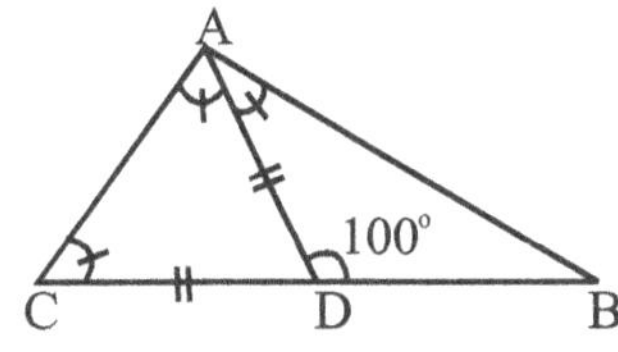

**33. (d)** Let $A = 2x$, $B = 3x$, $C = 4x$

$$\therefore \frac{A}{B} = \frac{2}{3}, \frac{B}{C} = \frac{3}{4}, \frac{C}{A} = \frac{4}{2} = \frac{2}{1}$$

Now, $\dfrac{A}{B} : \dfrac{B}{C} : \dfrac{C}{A} = \dfrac{2}{3} : \dfrac{3}{4} : \dfrac{2}{1}$

$$= \frac{2}{3} \times 12 : \frac{3}{4} \times 12 : \frac{2}{1} \times 12$$

$$= 8 : 9 : 24$$

**34. (d)** Error in measurement
$= 100 - 80 = 20$ cm

$\therefore$ % gain

$$= \left( \frac{\text{Error}}{\text{True value} - \text{Error}} \times 100 \right) \%$$

$$\text{% gain} = \left( \frac{20}{100 - 20} \right) \times 100 \%$$

$$= \frac{20 \times 100}{80} \%$$

$$= 25\%$$

**35. (d)** Clearly comparing the direction of A w.r.t C in the second diagram with that in the first diagram, A will be south-west of C.

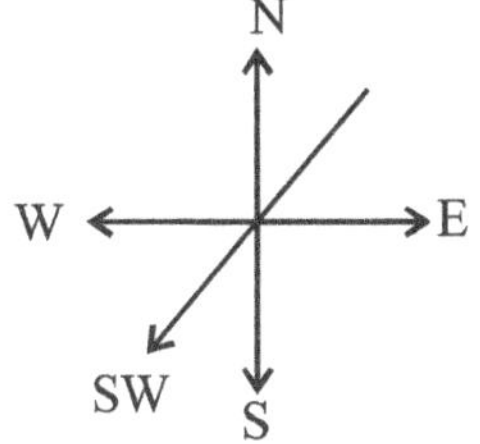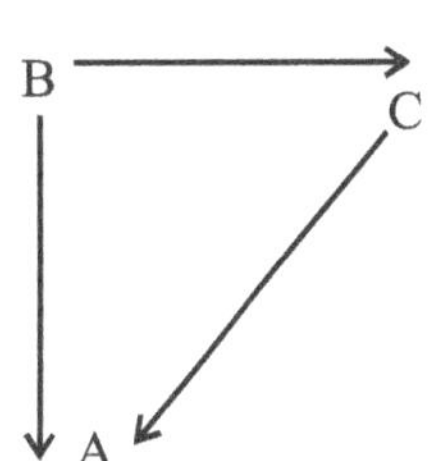

**36. (c)** When this figure is folded to form a cube then the face bearing three dots will lie opposite to the face bearing five dots.

**37. (c)** In $\triangle ADG$, E is the mid-point of AD and EF $\parallel$ DG .

So, EF must bisect AG.

$\therefore$ F is the midpoint of AG.

So AF = FG

In $\triangle BCF$, D is the mid-point of BC and DG $\parallel$ BF.

So DG must bisect FC.

$\therefore$ G is the mid-point of FC

So FG = GC

Thus, AF = FG = GC

$$AF = \frac{1}{3} \times AC = \frac{1}{3} \times 5.4$$

$$= 1.8 \text{ cm}$$

**38. (c)** $(12 \text{ km} + 5 \text{ km} = 17 \text{ km})$

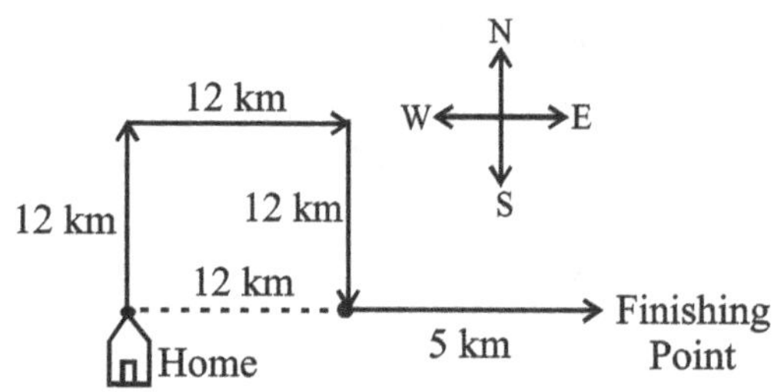


**39. (a)**

**40. (a)** Let the required number be x.

$$\frac{20}{100} \times \frac{60}{100} \times x = 144$$

$$x = 1200.$$

**41. (b)** $(3x - 4)(5x + 7) = 15x^2 - ax - 28$

$15x^2 + x - 28 = 15^2 - ax - 28,$
then $a = -1$

**42. (b)** $P = ₹1800; R = 7.3\%; SI = ?$

No. of days $= 7 + 31 + 12 = 50$ days.

$$T = \frac{50}{365} \text{ years.}$$

$$S.I = \frac{P \times T \times R}{100}$$

$$= \frac{1800 \times \dfrac{50}{365} \times 7.3}{100} = ₹18$$

**43. (d)** Every trapezium is not a parallelogram.

(In ∥ gm each pair of opposite sides should be parallel.)

**44. (c)** Let the radii of first and second cylinder be 2x and 3x; and let their heights be 5y and 3y, respectively.

$$\frac{\text{Volume of first cylinder}}{\text{Volume of second cylinder}}$$

$$= \frac{\pi \times (2x)^2 \times 5y}{\pi \times (3x)^2 \times 3y} \qquad [\because V = \pi r^2 h]$$

$$= \frac{20}{27}.$$

**45. (a)** Curved surface area $= \pi r l.$

New curved surface area

$$= \pi r\left(\ell + \frac{P\ell}{100}\right)$$

Percentage increase

$$= \frac{\pi r\left(\ell + \dfrac{P\ell}{100}\right) - \pi r \ell}{\pi r \ell} \times 100 = P\%$$

**46. (a)** Let the side of square field $= $ 'a' m

$\therefore$ Area of square field $= a^2$ sq. m

$\Rightarrow a^2 = 22500 \text{ m}^2$

$\Rightarrow a = 150 \text{ m}$

Speed of cycling $= 15 \text{ km / hr}$

$$= \frac{15 \times 1000}{60 \times 60} = \frac{25}{6} \text{ m/s.}$$

Now, total distance to be covered along the boundary

$$= 4 \times 150 = 600 \text{ m}$$

$\because \dfrac{25}{6}$ m is covered in 1 sec.

$\therefore$ 600 m is covered in

$$= \frac{600}{25} \times 6 = 144 \text{ sec}$$

$$= 2 \text{ min } 24 \text{ sec.}$$

**47. (b)** Total amount spent on football
$= 15\%$

Total amount spent on hockey
$= 15\%$

Ratio $= 15 : 15 = 1 : 1$

**48. (d)** Total amount spent $= ₹1,20,000$

Amount spent on basketball

$= 12\dfrac{1}{2}\% = \dfrac{25}{2}\%$

of total amount spent

$= \dfrac{1,20,000 \times \dfrac{25}{2}}{100}$

$= ₹\,15000$

**49. (c)** Most popular game is cricket $(25\%)$.

**50. (b)** The country spent the same amount on golf and basket ball $(12½\%)$.

## MOCK TEST-3

### ANSWER KEY

| | | | | | | | | | |
|---|---|---|---|---|---|---|---|---|---|
| 1 | (a) | 11 | (b) | 21 | (b) | 31 | (c) | 41 | (d) |
| 2 | (d) | 12 | (c) | 22 | (b) | 32 | (d) | 42 | (c) |
| 3 | (d) | 13 | (a) | 23 | (d) | 33 | (a) | 43 | (d) |
| 4 | (b) | 14 | (a) | 24 | (c) | 34 | (b) | 44 | (a) |
| 5 | (c) | 15 | (b) | 25 | (c) | 35 | (b) | 45 | (c) |
| 6 | (c) | 16 | (b) | 26 | (a) | 36 | (a) | 46 | (d) |
| 7 | (a) | 17 | (a) | 27 | (d) | 37 | (d) | 47 | (d) |
| 8 | (c) | 18 | (b) | 28 | (a) | 38 | (b) | 48 | (b) |
| 9 | (c) | 19 | (c) | 29 | (b) | 39 | (d) | 49 | (b) |
| 10 | (d) | 20 | (d) | 30 | (d) | 40 | (c) | 50 | (b) |

1. **(a)** It is a perfect cube.

2. **(d)** $\sqrt{3^n} = 81$

   $\Rightarrow 3^{n/2} = 3^4$

   $\Rightarrow \dfrac{n}{2} = 4$

   $\Rightarrow n = 8.$

3. **(d)** $\dfrac{2}{3} \times \dfrac{3}{\dfrac{5}{6} \div \dfrac{2}{3} \text{ of } 1\dfrac{1}{4}}$

   $= \dfrac{2}{3} \times \dfrac{3}{\dfrac{5}{6} \div \dfrac{2}{3} \times \dfrac{5}{4}} = \dfrac{2}{3} \times \dfrac{3}{\dfrac{5}{6} \div \dfrac{5}{6}}$

   $= \dfrac{2}{3} \times \dfrac{3}{1} = 2.$

4. **(b)** 63

   Start at 1 and jump clockwise to alternate segments while adding 2, 4, 8, 16, 32, 64 in turn.

5. **(c)** Given, AD = EC

   $\Rightarrow$ AD + DE = DE + EC

   $\Rightarrow$ AE = DC

   Also, AB = BC

   $\Rightarrow \angle$BCA = $\angle$BAC

   (isos. $\Delta$ property)

   $\Rightarrow \angle$BCD = $\angle$BAE

   $\therefore$ In $\Delta$ABE and $\Delta$CBD,

   AB = CB    (Given)

   AE = DC    (Proved above)

   $\angle$BAE = $\angle$BCD

   (Proved above)

   $\therefore \Delta$ABE $\cong \Delta$CBD   (by SAS)

6. **(c)** Let the angles of the quadrilateral be 3x, 7x, 6x and 4x.

   Then, 3x + 7x + 6x + 4x = 360°

   $\Rightarrow$ 20x = 360°

   $\Rightarrow$ x = 18°

   $\therefore$ The angles A, B, C and D are respectively 3 × 18°, 7 × 18°, 6 × 18° and 4 × 18°, i.e. 54°, 126°, 108° and 72°

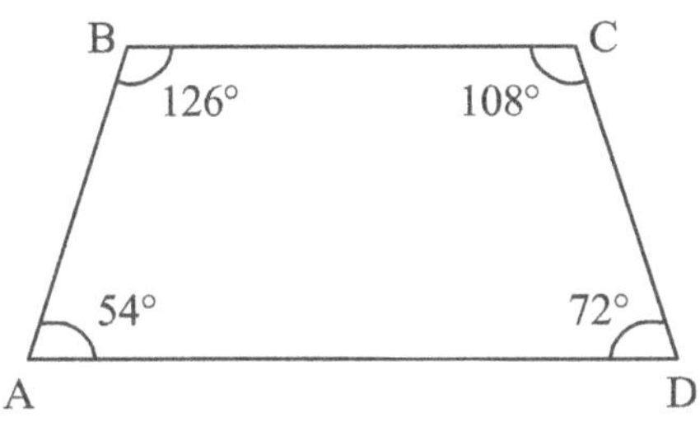

which shows that

$\angle A + \angle B = 180°$ and $\angle C + \angle D = 180°$

$\Rightarrow$ AD ∥ BC

Hence, ABCD is a trapezium.

**7. (a)** Each side of the rhombus

$$= \sqrt{\left(\frac{24}{2}\right)^2 + \left(\frac{10}{2}\right)^2}$$

$$= \sqrt{12^2 + 5^2} = \sqrt{144 + 25}$$

$$= \sqrt{169}$$

$$= 13 \text{ cm}$$

$\therefore$ Perimeter = 4 × 13 cm = 52 cm.

Area of the rhombus

$$= \frac{1}{2} \times 24 \text{ cm} \times 10 \text{ cm}$$

$$= 120 \text{ cm}^2$$

**8. (c)** Volume of the bigger cube
= $(10)^3$ cm$^3$ = 1000 cm$^3$

Volume of the smaller cube
= 500 cm$^3$

Required ratio

$$= \frac{\text{Edge smaller cube}}{\text{Edge of bigger cube}}$$

$$= \frac{(500)^{1/3}}{(1000)^{1/3}} = \left(\frac{500}{1000}\right)^{1/3} = \left(\frac{1}{2}\right)^{1/3}$$

**9. (c)** Add the number to the reverse of its digits

For example : 163 + 361 = 524,

In the some way,

1898 + 8981 = 10879

**10. (d)** L.C.M. = 28 × H.C.F.

Also, L.C.M. + H.C.F. = 1740

$\Rightarrow$ 28H.C.F. + H.C.F. = 1740

$\Rightarrow$ 29H.C.F. = 1740

$\Rightarrow$ H.C.F. = $\dfrac{1740}{29}$ = 60

$\Rightarrow$ L.C.M. = 28 × 60 = 1680

Since, one number = 240

$\therefore$ Other number

$$= \frac{\text{H.C.F.} \times \text{L.C.M.}}{\text{One number}}$$

$$= \frac{60 \times 1680}{240} = 420.$$

**11. (b)**

```
            1   2   6
       1 | 1  58  76
          -1    ↓
      22 |    58    
          -44      ↓
     246 |    14 76
          -14 76
       |      0
```

$\therefore$  $\sqrt{15876}$ = 126

$\Rightarrow$ Digit in units' place in $\sqrt{15876}$ = 6.

**12. (c)** x$^4$ + 4

$$= x^4 + 4 + 4x^2 - 4x^2$$

(Note the step)

$$= (x^2 + 2)^2 - (2x)^2$$

$$= (x^2 + 2x + 2)(x^2 - 2x + 2)$$

**13. (a)** C's share $= \dfrac{5}{12} \times ₹6000$

$= ₹2500$

B's share $= \dfrac{4}{12} \times ₹6000$

$= ₹2000$

∴ C gets ₹500 more than B.

**14. (a)** Let the original price of the book be ₹100

Decreased price of the book $= ₹75$

Increased price of the book after 20% increase

$= \dfrac{120}{100} \times ₹75 = ₹90$

∴ Net change in price $= ₹10$ decrease

∴ % change $= \dfrac{10}{100} \times 100$

$= 10\%$ decrease

**15. (b)** Let the principal $= ₹x$ and rate of interest $= R\%$ p.a.

Then, S.I. $= 30\%$ of $₹x = \dfrac{30}{100} \times x$

∴ $\dfrac{x \times R \times 6}{100} = \dfrac{30}{100} \times x$

$\Rightarrow R = \dfrac{30}{6} = 5\%$ p.a.

Let the time in which the principal is equal to simple interest be t years, then

$\dfrac{x \times 5 \times t}{100} = x$

$\Rightarrow t = \dfrac{100}{5}$ years $= 20$ years

**16. (b)** The pattern in the series is $-5$ i. e.

$$\begin{array}{ccccccccc} X & & S & & N & & I & & \boxed{D} & & Y \\ \end{array}$$
$$\underbrace{\phantom{XX}}_{-5}\ \underbrace{\phantom{XX}}_{-5}\ \underbrace{\phantom{XX}}_{-5}\ \underbrace{\phantom{XX}}_{-5}\ \underbrace{\phantom{XX}}_{-5}$$

D should be in place of C.

**17. (a)** Let the numbers be a, b, c, d. Then,

$abc = 385$ and $bcd = 1001$

$\Rightarrow \dfrac{abc}{bcd} = \dfrac{385}{1001}$

$\Rightarrow \dfrac{a}{d} = \dfrac{5}{13}$

$\Rightarrow a = 5, d = 13.$

**18. (b)** Let the total number of students in the school be x.

Then, number of girls $= \dfrac{3x}{7}$

Number of boys

$= \left( x - \dfrac{3x}{7} \right) = \dfrac{4x}{7}$

Number of boys below ten years of age $= \dfrac{1}{4} \times \dfrac{4x}{7} = \dfrac{x}{7}$

Number of girls below ten years of age $= \dfrac{5}{6} \times \dfrac{3x}{7} = \dfrac{5x}{14}$

∴ Total number of students below 10 years of age $= \dfrac{x}{7} + \dfrac{5x}{14} = \dfrac{7x}{14} = \dfrac{x}{2}$

∴ Total number of students above 10 years of age

$$= x - \frac{x}{2} = \frac{x}{2}$$

Given, $\dfrac{x}{2} = 500$

$\Rightarrow\ x = 1000.$

**19. (c)** $(a + b + c)^2 = a^2 + b^2 + c^2 + 2(ab + bc + ca)$

$\Rightarrow\ a^2 + b^2 + c^2 = 11^2 - 2 \times 20$

$\qquad\qquad = 121 - 40 = 81$

Also, we know that

$a^3 + b^3 + c^3 - 3abc$

$= (a + b + c)\,(a^2 + b^2 + c^2 - ab - bc - ca)$

$\Rightarrow\ a^3 + b^3 + c^3 - 3abc$

$\qquad = 11 \times (81 - 20)$

$\Rightarrow\ a^3 + b^3 + c^3 - 3abc$

$\qquad = 11 \times 61$

$\qquad = 671.$

**20. (d)** $x^4 + 5x^2 + 9$

$\qquad = x^4 + 6x^2 + 9 - x^2$

$\qquad = (x^2 + 3)^2 - x^2$

$\qquad = (x^2 - x + 3)\,(x^2 + x + 3)$

**21. (b)** Differences of the first set of differences are increasing by 1 viz.

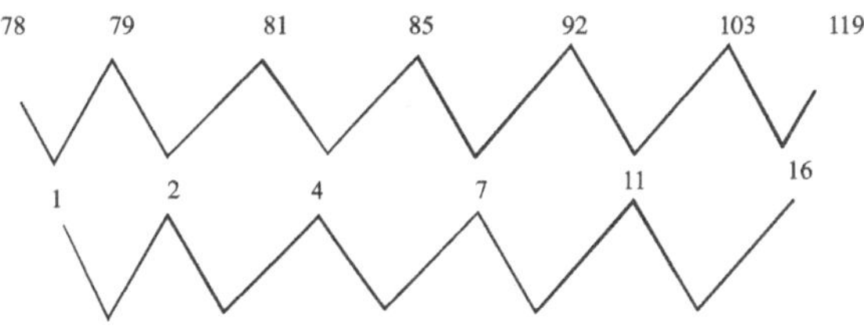


**22. (b)**

$$\sqrt{(0.798)^2 + 0.404 \times 0.798 + (0.202)^2}\ + 1$$

$$= \sqrt{(0.798)^2 + 2 \times 0.202 \times 0.798 + (0.202)^2}\ + 1$$

$$= \sqrt{(0.798 + 0.202)^2}\ + 1 = \sqrt{1}\ + 1$$

$= 1 + 1 = 2.$

**23. (d)** Common difference between divisors and respective remainders

$= (4 - 1) = (6 - 3) = (14 - 11)$

$= (20 - 17) = 3$

L.C.M. of $(4, 6, 14, 20)$

$= 2 \times 2 \times 3 \times 7 \times 5 = 420$

| 2 | 4, 6, 14, 20 |
|---|---|
| 2 | 2, 3, 7, 10 |
|   | 1, 3, 7, 5 |

Greatest number of five digits $= 99999$

Dividing 99999 by 420 and subtracting the remainder 39 from 99999, we get

$99999 - 39 = 99960$

```
              238
       ___________
420 )   99999
       -840
       ___________
        1599
       -1260
       ___________
        3399
       -3360
       ___________
          39
```

$\therefore\ $ The required number

$= 99960 - 3 = 99957.$

**24. (c)** $\sqrt{4a^2 - 4a + 1} + 3a$

$$= \sqrt{(1)^2 - 2 \times 2a \times 1 + (2a)^2} + 3a$$

$$= \sqrt{(1 - 2a)^2} + 3a$$

$$= (1 - 2a) + 3a = 1 + a$$

$$= 1 + 0.1039 = 1.1039$$

**25. (c)** $(4)^{0.5} \times (0.5)^4 = (2^2)^{0.5} \times \left(\dfrac{1}{2}\right)^4$

$$= 2^1 \times 2^{-4} = 2^{-3} = \dfrac{1}{2^3} = \dfrac{1}{8}.$$

**26. (a)** S.P. of 100 pencils – C.P. of 100 pencils

= S.P. of 20 pencils

$\Rightarrow$ S.P. of 80 pencils = C.P. of 100 pencils

Let C.P. of 1 pencil = ₹ 1.

Then,

S.P. of 80 pencils = ₹ 100

C.P. of 80 pencils = ₹ 80

$\therefore$ Profit % $= \dfrac{100 - 80}{80} \times 100$

$$= \dfrac{20}{80} \times 100 = 25\%.$$

**27. (d)** Let the required number be y.

$a : b :: x : y$

$a \times y = b \times x$

$$y = \dfrac{bx}{a}$$

**28. (a)** Using the correct symbols, we have

Given expression

$$= \dfrac{(36 - 4) \div 8 - 4}{4 \times 8 - 2 \times 16 + 1}$$

$$= \dfrac{32 \div 8 - 4}{32 - 32 + 1}$$

$$= \dfrac{4 - 4}{0 + 1} = 0.$$

**29. (b)** Let the numerator be x.

Then,

denominator = 11 – x

Given, $\dfrac{x + 1}{11 - x - 2} = \dfrac{2}{3}$

$\Rightarrow$ $3x + 3 = 2(9 - x)$

$\Rightarrow$ $3x + 3 = 18 - 2x$

$\Rightarrow$ $5x = 15$

$\Rightarrow$ $x = 3$

$\therefore$ Numerator = 3,

Denominator = 11 – 3 = 8

$\therefore$ Fraction $= \dfrac{3}{8}.$

**30. (d)** C.P. = ₹80,

M.P. = ₹120,

Discount = 40%

$\therefore$ S.P. = 60% of ₹120

$$= \dfrac{60}{100} \times ₹120 = ₹72$$

$\therefore$ Loss = ₹80 – ₹72 = ₹8

Loss % $= \dfrac{8}{80} \times 100 = 10\%.$

**31. (c)** P = ₹4800, r = 6% p.a., n = 2

$\therefore$ C.I. $= A - P = P\left(1 + \dfrac{r}{100}\right)^n - P$

$$= 4800 \left(1 + \frac{6}{100}\right)^2 - 4800$$

$$= 4800 \times \frac{53 \times 53}{50 \times 50} - 4800$$

$$= 5393.28 - 4800 = ₹\ 593.28.$$

**32. (d)** 5 spiders in 5 minutes catch

= 5 flies

5 spiders in 1 minute catch

$$= \frac{5}{5} \text{ flies}$$

1 spider in 1 minute catches

$$= \frac{5}{5 \times 5} \text{ flies}$$

1 spider in 100 minutes catches

$$= \frac{5}{5 \times 5} \times 100 \text{ flies}$$

100 spiders in 100 minutes

$$\text{catch} = \frac{5}{5 \times 5} \times 100 \times 100 \text{ flies}$$

$$= 2000 \text{ flies.}$$

**33. (a)** $a + b + c = 9$

Squaring on both sides

$(a + b + c)^2 = 81$

$a^2 + b^2 + c^2 + 2ab + 2bc + 2ca = 81$

$a^2 + b^2 + c^2 + 2(ab + bc + ca) = 81$

$a^2 + b^2 + c^2 + 2(26) = 81$

$a^2 + b^2 + c^2 = 81 - 52 = 29$

Now, $a^3 + b^3 + c^3 - 3abc$

$= (a + b + c)(a^2 + b^2 + c^2 - ab - bc - ca)$

$= (a + b + c)[(a^2 + b^2 + c^2) - (ab + bc + ca)]$

$$= (9)(29 - 26)$$

$$= 9 \times 3 = 27$$

**34. (b)** As per the data, D faces North. A faces towards west. So, its partner B will face towards A and hence towards East. So, C who will face D will face towards south.

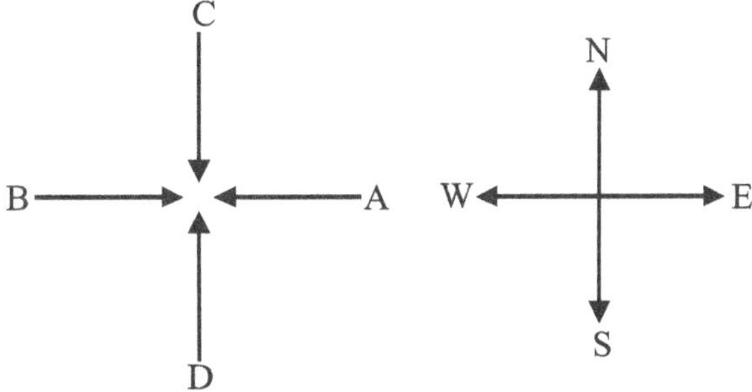


**35. (b)** By Pythagoras theorem, we find that the given triangle is a right-angled triangle with 12 as height and 5 as base.

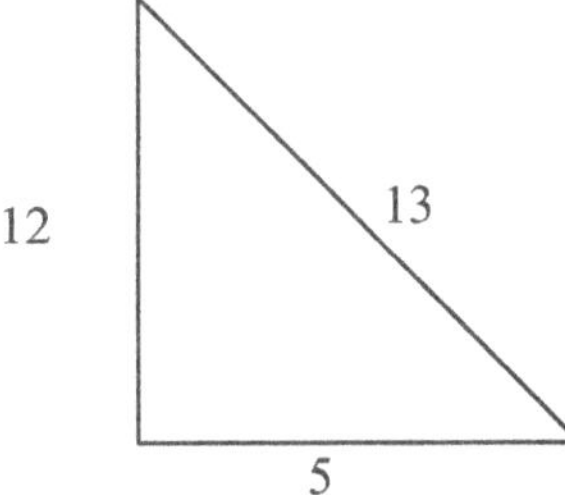


∴ Area of the triangle

$$= \frac{1}{2} \times 12 \times 5 \text{ sq. units} = 30 \text{ sq. units}$$

∴ Area of the rectangle

= length × breadth = 30

$$\Rightarrow \text{ Length} = \frac{30}{\text{breadth}} = \frac{30}{10}$$

$$= 3 \text{ units}$$

∴ Perimeter of the rectangle

$$= 2 \times (10 + 3)$$

$$= 26 \text{ units.}$$

**36. (a)** When the sheet shown in fig. (X) is folded to from a cube, then the face bearing the dot lies opposite to the shaded face, the face bearing a circle (With '+' sign inside it) lies opposite to a blank face and the remaining two blank faces lie opposite to each other. Clearly, the cubes shown in figures (B) and (D) cannot be formed since they have the shaded face adjacent to the face bearing a dot and the cube shown in fig. (C) cannot be formed since it shown all the three blank face adjacent to each other. Hence, only the cube shown in fig.(A) can be formed.

**37. (d)**

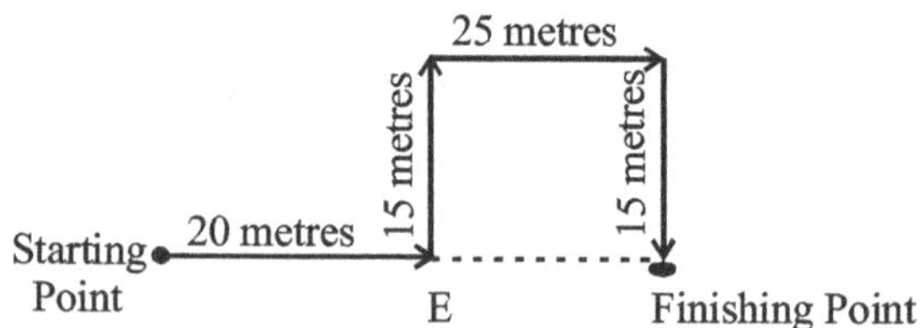


Shobha turns left after walking 20 metres towards East. Now she walks 15 metres towards North. She turns right towards East again and walks 25 metres further. Finally turning right towards South, she walks 15 metres. The distance moved towards North and towards South is same, i.e., 15 metres. So, Shobha is 20 + 25 metres = 45 metres away from her starting point.

**38. (b)** Area of rectangle CEFH + Area of trapezium FHAG

$$= (4 \times 6)\ m^2 + \left(\frac{1}{2} \times (6+4) \times 6\right) m^2$$

$= 24\ m^2 + 30\ m^2 = 54\ m^2$

∴ Area of parallelogram ABCH

$= 84\ m^2 - 54\ m^2$

$= 30\ m^2$

$\Rightarrow 6 \times BD = 30$

$\Rightarrow BD = 5\ m.$

**39. (d)** Height of the water in the tank

$$= \frac{4.5 \times 1000}{25 \times 20}\ cm$$

$= 9\ cm\ (\because 1\ litres = 1000\ cm^3)$

∴ Rise in height $= 11\ cm - 9\ cm$
$$= 2\ cm$$

∴ Volume of cube = Volume of water displaced

$= 25\ cm \times 20\ cm \times 2\ cm$

$= 1000\ cm^3$

$\Rightarrow$ Each edge of the cube

$= \sqrt[3]{1000}\ cm = 10\ cm.$

**40. (c)** Using the correct symbols, we have,

$= (10 \times 4) + (4 \times 4) - 6$

$= 40 + 16 - 6$

$= 56 - 6 = 50.$

**41. (d)** $64^a = \dfrac{1}{256^b} \Rightarrow (2^6)^a = \dfrac{1}{\left(2^8\right)^b}$

$\Rightarrow 2^{6a} \times 2^{8b} = 1$

$\Rightarrow 2^{6a + 8b} = 2^0$

$\Rightarrow 6a + 8b = 0$

$\Rightarrow 3a + 4b = 0$

**42. (c)** $64a^3 + 48a^2 b + 12ab^2 + b^3$

$= (4a + b)^3$

$[\because (a + b)^3 = a^3 + b^3 + 3a^2 b + 3ab^2]$

∴ Required value $= (4 - 1)^3$
$$= 3^3 = 27.$$

**43. (d)** Let Keith's age now be x year
Then,

Dennis's age now = $\dfrac{x}{3}$ years

Keith's age 5 years ago = $(x-5)$ years

Dennis's age 5 years ago = $\left(\dfrac{x}{3}-5\right)$ years

Given, $\left(\dfrac{x}{3}-5\right)=\dfrac{1}{4}(x-5)$

$\Rightarrow \dfrac{x-15}{3}=\dfrac{x-5}{4}$

$\Rightarrow 4x-60=3x-15$

$\Rightarrow x=45$

$\therefore$ Keith's age 5 years from now
= $(45+5)$ years = 50 years

**44. (a)** $2x^2-11x+15=0$

$\Rightarrow 2x^2-6x-5x+15=0$

$\Rightarrow 2x(x-3)-5(x-3)=0$

$\Rightarrow (x-3)(2x-5)=0$

$\Rightarrow x-3=0$ or $2x-5=0$

$\Rightarrow x=3,\ \dfrac{5}{2}$

**45. (c)** $\angle DAB=180°-\angle ADC$

$=180°-64°=116°$

$(AB\,||\,DC$, co-int. $\angle$s are supp.)
In $\triangle DAB$,
$DA=AB$

$\Rightarrow \angle ABD=\angle ADB$  (isos. $\triangle$ prop.)

$\therefore \angle ADB=\dfrac{180°-116°}{2}=\dfrac{64°}{2}$

$=32°$

$\therefore \angle BDC=64°-32°=32°$
Hence, in $\triangle DBC$,
$\angle DBC=180°-(\angle BDC+\angle BCD)$

$=180°-(32°+54°)$

$=180°-86°=94°$.

**46. (d)** Let the height (h) and radius (r)
of the cylinder = x cm

Then, $\pi r^2 h=25\dfrac{1}{7}$

$\dfrac{22}{7}x^2 \cdot x=25\dfrac{1}{7}$

$\Rightarrow \dfrac{22x^3}{7}=\dfrac{176}{7}$

$\Rightarrow x^3=\dfrac{176}{22}=8$

$\Rightarrow x=2$ cm

**47. (d)** Sector angle corresponding to
recreation
$=360°-(72°+90°+54°)$
$=360°-216°=144°$

$\therefore$ % age expenses incurred on
account of recreation

$=\left(\dfrac{144°}{360°}\times 100\right)\%=40\%.$

**48. (b)** Total number of exhaustive
cases $=6\times6=36$
A total of 11 may be obtained
in 2 ways as $(5,6),(6,5)$

$\therefore$ P(total of 11) $=\dfrac{2}{36}=\dfrac{1}{18}.$

**49. (b)**

**50. (b)** As we know,
sum of angles of pentagon
$=540°$

$\therefore x°+(x+20)°+(x+40)°+(x+60)°+(x+80°)=540°$

$5x°+200°=540°$

$\Rightarrow x=68°$

$\therefore$ Largest angle $=(x+80)°$
$=68°+80°=148°.$

## MOCK TEST-4

### ANSWER KEY

| | | | | | | | | | |
|---|---|---|---|---|---|---|---|---|---|
| 1 | (a) | 11 | (b) | 21 | (c) | 31 | (c) | 41 | (b) |
| 2 | (d) | 12 | (d) | 22 | (a) | 32 | (c) | 42 | (c) |
| 3 | (a) | 13 | (d) | 23 | (c) | 33 | (a) | 43 | (a) |
| 4 | (a) | 14 | (d) | 24 | (d) | 34 | (d) | 44 | (d) |
| 5 | (d) | 15 | (d) | 25 | (d) | 35 | (b) | 45 | (c) |
| 6 | (c) | 16 | (d) | 26 | (c) | 36 | (a) | 46 | (a) |
| 7 | (a) | 17 | (b) | 27 | (a) | 37 | (b) | 47 | (c) |
| 8 | (d) | 18 | (b) | 28 | (a) | 38 | (a) | 48 | (d) |
| 9 | (b) | 19 | (c) | 29 | (b) | 39 | (c) | 49 | (b) |
| 10 | (c) | 20 | (a) | 30 | (c) | 40 | (c) | 50 | (d) |

**1.** **(a)** $N = 4Q + 3$, where Q is the quotient

$$\therefore \quad 2N = 8Q + 6 = 4 \times 2Q + 4 + 2$$
$$= 4(2Q + 1) + 2$$

$\Rightarrow$ Required remainder = 2.

**2.** **(d)**

$$\frac{1\frac{1}{7} - \frac{2}{3} + \dfrac{\frac{2}{5}}{1 - \frac{1}{25}}}{1 - \frac{1}{7}\left(\frac{1}{3} + \dfrac{\frac{2}{5}}{1 - \frac{2}{5}}\right)} = \frac{\frac{8}{7} - \frac{2}{3} + \dfrac{\frac{2}{5}}{\frac{24}{25}}}{1 - \frac{1}{7}\left(\frac{1}{3} + \dfrac{\frac{2}{5}}{\frac{3}{5}}\right)}$$

$$= \frac{\frac{8}{7} - \frac{2}{3} + \frac{2}{5} \times \frac{25}{24}}{1 - \frac{1}{7}\left(\frac{1}{3} + \frac{2}{3}\right)}$$

$$= \frac{\frac{8}{7} - \frac{2}{3} + \frac{5}{12}}{1 - \frac{1}{7}} = \frac{\dfrac{96 - 56 + 35}{84}}{\dfrac{6}{7}}$$

$$= \frac{75}{84} \times \frac{7}{6} = \frac{25}{24} = 1\frac{1}{24}.$$

**3.** **(a)** In each row, out of the letters A, B and C, each of these must appear once. Also, in each column. The product of first and third numbers is equal to the second numbers, so the missing number will be $(2 \times 4)$ i.e., 8 and the missing letter will be C. Thus, the answer is 8C.

**4.** **(a)**

```
              8   2   4
        8 | 68  06  21
          | -64  ↓
      162 |     4  06
          |   - 3  24 ↓
     1644 |        82  21
          |      - 65  76
          |        16  45
```

∴ Least number to be added to 680621 to make the sum a perfect square

$$= (825)^2 - 680621$$

$$= 680625 - 680621 = 4.$$

**5.** **(d)** $x + \dfrac{1}{x} = 3$

$$\Rightarrow \left(x + \dfrac{1}{x}\right)^3 = 3^3$$

$$\Rightarrow x^3 + \dfrac{1}{x^3} + 3\left(x + \dfrac{1}{x}\right) = 27$$

$$\Rightarrow x^3 + \dfrac{1}{x^3} + 3 \times 3 = 27$$

$$\Rightarrow x^3 + \dfrac{1}{x^3} = 18$$

Now squaring both the sides,

$$\left(x^3 + \dfrac{1}{x^3}\right)^2 = 18^2$$

$$\Rightarrow x^6 + 2 + \dfrac{1}{x^6} = 324$$

$$\Rightarrow x^6 + \dfrac{1}{x^6} = 322.$$

**6.** **(c)** Let the two rates of simple interests p.a. be x% and y%. Then,

$$\dfrac{1500 \times x \times 3}{100} - \dfrac{1500 \times y \times 3}{100} = 13.50$$

$$\Rightarrow 45x - 45y = 13.50$$

$$\Rightarrow 45(x - y) = 13.50$$

$$\Rightarrow x - y = \dfrac{13.50}{45} = 0.3\%.$$

**7.** **(a)** Since the diagonals of a rhombus bisect each other at right angle.

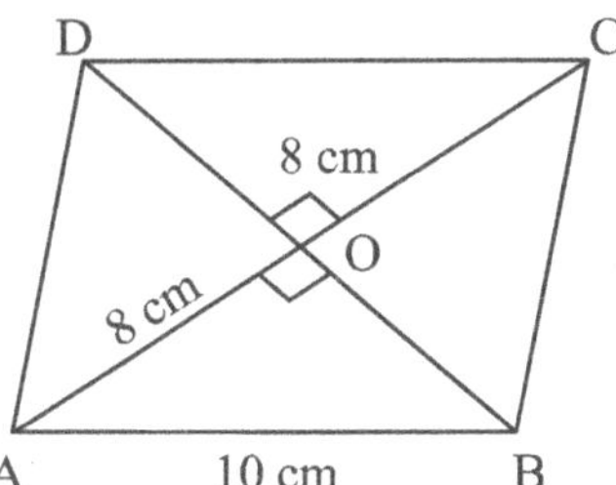


In $\triangle AOB$,

$$BO^2 = \sqrt{AB^2 - AO^2}$$

$$= \sqrt{100 - 64} \text{ cm}$$

$$= \sqrt{36} \text{ cm} = 6 \text{ cm}$$

∴ The other diagonal $= 2 \times 6$ cm $= 12$ cm

∴ Area of the rhombus

$$= \dfrac{1}{2} \times 16 \text{ cm} \times 12 \text{ cm} = 96 \text{ cm}^2.$$

**8.** **(d)** The movements of the person are from A to F, as shown in fig.

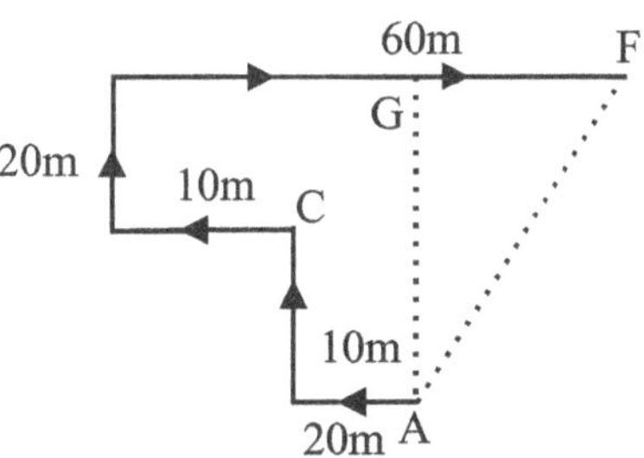


Clearly, the final position is F which is to the north east of the starting point A.

**9.** **(b)** 10

**10.** **(c)** $(64)^{\frac{-2}{3}} \times \left(\dfrac{1}{4}\right)^{-3}$

$$= \left(4^3\right)^{\frac{-2}{3}} \times \left(4^{-1}\right)^{-3}$$

$$= 4^{-2} \times 4^3 = 4^{-2+3} = 4^1 = 4$$

**11.** **(b)** Let the total money with the person be ₹x

Then, money spent on clothes

$$= ₹\dfrac{x}{3}$$

Remaining money

$$= ₹\left(x - \dfrac{x}{3}\right) = ₹\dfrac{2x}{3}$$

∴ Money spent on food

$$= \dfrac{1}{5} \times ₹\dfrac{2x}{3} = ₹\dfrac{2x}{15}$$

Now, remaining money

$$= \dfrac{2x}{3} - \dfrac{2x}{15} = ₹\dfrac{8x}{15}$$

∴ Money spent on travel

$$= \dfrac{1}{4} \times ₹\dfrac{8x}{15} = ₹\dfrac{2x}{15}$$

Given, $\dfrac{x}{3} + \dfrac{2x}{15} + \dfrac{2x}{15} + 100 = x$

$$\Rightarrow \dfrac{5x + 2x + 2x + 1500}{15} = x$$

$$\Rightarrow 9x + 1500 = 15x$$

$$\Rightarrow 6x = 1500$$

$$\Rightarrow x = \dfrac{1500}{6} = ₹250.$$

**12.** **(d)** A : B = 5 : 12

B : C = 4 : 5.5 = 12 : 16.5

$\Rightarrow$ A : B : C = 5 : 12 : 16.5

∴ The share of C will exceed that of B by

$$\dfrac{(16.5 - 12)}{5 + 12 + 16.5} \times ₹2010$$

$$= \dfrac{4.5 \times 2010}{33.5} = ₹270$$

**13.** **(d)** Diagonals of a rectangle are equal and bisect each other.

∴ In $\triangle$AOB, $\angle$AOB = 162° − 3x

(vert. opp. $\angle$s)

$\angle$OBA = $\angle$OAB = 2x

($\because$ OA = OB)

∴ $\angle$AOB + $\angle$OBA + $\angle$OAB = 180°

$\Rightarrow$ 162° − 3x + 2x + 2x = 180°

$\Rightarrow$ x = 18°.

**14.** **(d)** Given, $2\pi r = 66$

$$\Rightarrow r = \dfrac{66 \times 7}{2 \times 22} = \dfrac{21}{2} \text{ cm}$$

$$\therefore V = \pi r^2 h = \dfrac{22}{7} \times \dfrac{21}{2} \times \dfrac{21}{2} \times 40$$

$$= 13860 \text{ cm}^3.$$

**15.** **(d)** We have: $(3 \times 4 \times 2 \times 5) \div 10 = 12$;

$(6 \times 2 \times 3 \times 5) \div 10 = 18$.

So, missing number

$= (2 \times 2 \times 9 \times 5) \div 10 = 18$

**16. (d)** Let the lesser number be x. Then,

Greater number = x + 45

Given, $\dfrac{x + 45}{x} = 4$

$\Rightarrow$  x + 45 = 4x

$\Rightarrow$  3x = 45 $\Rightarrow$ x = 15

Then, required sum

= x + x + 45 = 30 + 45 = 75

**17. (b)** Let the original stock of rice be x kg.

Parts of the stock sold first time

$= \left(\dfrac{2x}{3} + 100\right)$ kg

$\therefore$  Remaining stock

$= \left[x - \left(\dfrac{2x}{3} + 100\right)\right]$ kg

$= \left(\dfrac{x}{3} - 100\right)$ kg

Part of the stock sold second time

$= \left[\dfrac{1}{2}\left(\dfrac{x}{3} - 100\right) + 100\right]$

$= \left(\dfrac{x}{6} - 50 + 100\right)$ kg

$= \left(\dfrac{x}{6} + 50\right)$ kg

$\therefore$  Remaining stock

$= \left(\dfrac{x}{3} - 100\right) - \left(\dfrac{x}{6} + 50\right)$

$= \left(\dfrac{x}{3} - \dfrac{x}{6} - 100 - 50\right)$ kg

$= \left(\dfrac{x}{6} - 150\right)$ kg

Given, $\dfrac{x}{6} - 150 = 150$

$\Rightarrow$  $\dfrac{x}{6} = 300$

$\Rightarrow$  x = 1800 kg.

**18. (b)** LCM of (10, 12, 15 and 18)

= 2 × 3 × 5 × 2 × 3 = 180

| 2 | 10, 12, 15, 18 |
|---|---|
| 3 | 5, 6, 15, 9 |
| 5 | 5, 2, 5, 3 |
|  | 1, 2, 1, 3 |

The greatest five digit number = 99999

Dividing (99999 + 3769) = 103768 by 180, we get:

```
            576
   180) 103768
        - 900
        ------
         1376
        -1260
        ------
         1168
        -1080
        ------
           88
```

Remainder = 88

$\therefore$  Required number = 99999 − 88

= 99911.

**19. (c)** $3a = 4b = 6c$

$\Rightarrow 4b = 6c$

$\Rightarrow b = \dfrac{3}{2}c$ and

$3a = 6b$

$\Rightarrow a = 2c$

$\therefore a + b + c = 27\sqrt{29}$

$\Rightarrow 2c + \dfrac{3}{2}c + c = 27\sqrt{29}$

$\Rightarrow \dfrac{9}{2}c = 27\sqrt{29}$

$\Rightarrow c = 6\sqrt{29}$

Now, $\sqrt{a^2 + b^2 + c^2}$

$= \sqrt{(a + b + c)^2 - 2(ab + bc + ca)}$

$= \sqrt{\left(27\sqrt{29}\right)^2 - 2\left(2c \times \dfrac{3}{2}c + \dfrac{3}{2}c \times c + c \times 2c\right)}$

$= \sqrt{729 \times 29 - 2\left(3c^2 + \dfrac{3}{2}c^2 + 2c^2\right)}$

$= \sqrt{729 \times 29 - 2 \times \dfrac{13c^2}{2}}$

$= \sqrt{729 \times 29 - 13 \times \left(6\sqrt{29}\right)^2}$

$= \sqrt{29(729 - 468)} = \sqrt{29 \times 261}$

$= \sqrt{29 \times 29 \times 9}$

$= 29 \times 3 = 87.$

**20. (a)** There are two alternate sequences that increase by 2 and 5, respectively, i.e., 1, 3, 5, 7 and 1, 6, 11, 16.

**21. (c)** Given expression:

$= 1 + \left(8^2\right)^{-\frac{1}{2}} + \left(2^5\right)^{\frac{4}{5}} - \left(2^5\right)^{-\frac{4}{5}}$

$= 1 + 8^{-1} + 2^4 - 2^{-4}$

$= 1 + \dfrac{1}{8} + 16 - \dfrac{1}{16}$

$= \dfrac{16 + 2 + 256 - 1}{16}$

$= \dfrac{273}{16} = 17\dfrac{1}{16}.$

**22. (a)** $625a^{12} - 81b^{12}$

$= (25a^6)^2 - (9b^6)^2$

$= (25a^6 - 9b^6)(25a^6 + 9b^6)$

$= [(5a^3)^2 - (3b^3)^2](25a^6 + 9b^6)$

$= (5a^3 - 3b^3)(5a^3 + 3b^3)(25a^6 + 9b^6)$

**23. (c)** C.P. of 11 articles = ₹10

C.P. of 1 article = ₹$\dfrac{10}{11}$

S.P. of 10 articles = ₹11

$\Rightarrow$ S.P. of 1 article = ₹$\dfrac{11}{10}$

$\therefore$ Profit % = $\dfrac{\dfrac{11}{10} - \dfrac{10}{11}}{\dfrac{10}{11}} \times 100$

$$= \frac{\dfrac{121-100}{110}}{\dfrac{10}{11}} \times 100$$

$$= \frac{21 \times 11}{110 \times 10} \times 100 = 21\%.$$

**24. (d)** Let the breadth of the rectangular field be a m.

Then, its length = 2a m

Given, $2(2a + a) = x$

$\Rightarrow 6a = x$

$\Rightarrow a = \dfrac{x}{6}$ m

$\therefore$ Length $= 2a = 2 \times \dfrac{x}{6} = \dfrac{x}{3}$ m

$\therefore$ Area of the rectangular field

$$= \frac{x}{3} \times \frac{x}{6} = \frac{x^2}{18} \text{ m}^2.$$

**25. (d)** Area of cross-section $= 720 \text{ m}^2$

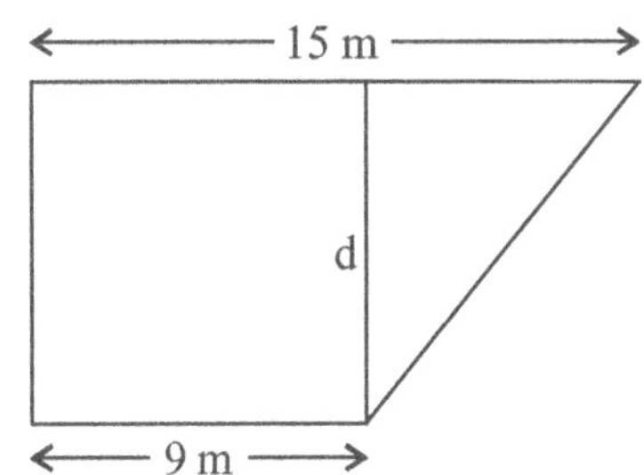


$$\Rightarrow \frac{1}{2} \times (9 + 15) \times d = 720$$

$$\Rightarrow d = \frac{720 \times 2}{24} \text{ m} = 60 \text{ m}.$$

**26. (c)** $\dfrac{\left(x^{2^{n-1}}\right)^2 - \left(y^{2^{n-1}}\right)^2}{x^{2^n} - y^{2^n}}$

$$\Rightarrow \frac{\left[x^{(2^{n-1} \times 2)}\right] - \left[y^{(2^{n-1} \times 2)}\right]}{x^{2^n} - y^{2^n}}$$

$$\Rightarrow \frac{x^{2^{n-1+1}} - y^{2^{n-1+1}}}{x^{2^n} - y^{2^n}}$$

$$\Rightarrow \frac{x^{2^n} - y^{2^n}}{x^{2^n} - y^{2^n}}$$

$\Rightarrow 1$

**27. (a)** Given that: $20 - 10 = 200$.

But, actually $20 \times 10 = 200$, so $-$ means $\times$.

Given that $8 \div 4 = 12$, but actually $8 + 4 = 12$.

So, $\div$ means $+$.

Given that : $6 \times 2 = 4$ but actually $6 - 2 = 4$.

So, $\times$ means $-$

Given that $10 + 2 = 5$, but actually $10 + 2 = 12$

So, $+$ means $\div$

Thus, in the given mathematical language $-$ means $\times$, $\div$ means $+$, and $\times$ means $-$, $+$ means $\div$

So, given expression

$$= 100 \times 10 - 1000 + 1000 \div 100 - 10$$

$$= 1000 - 1000 + 10 - 10 = 0.$$

**28. (a)** Total surface area of the cube

$$= 6a^2 = 6 \times 1^2$$

$$= 6 \text{ sq. units}$$

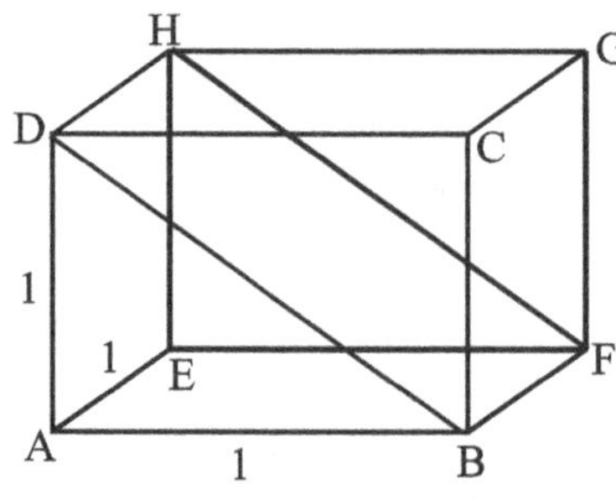


$$DB = \sqrt{AD^2 + AB^2}$$

$$= \sqrt{1+1} = \sqrt{2}$$

Surface area of the section DBFH

$$= DB \times BF = \sqrt{2} \times 1 \text{ sq. units}$$

$$= \sqrt{2} \text{ sq. units}$$

$\therefore$ Total surface area of one part

$$= \frac{6}{2} + \sqrt{2}$$

$$= \left(3 + \sqrt{2}\right) \text{ sq. units}$$

**29. (b)** In order to strike 12, there are 11 intervals of equal time

$$= \frac{33}{11} = 3 \text{ seconds each}$$

Therefore, to strike 6 it has 5 equal intervals, it requires

$$5 \times 3 = 15 \text{ sec.}$$

**30. (c)** $(0.5)^2 = 0.25;$

$$\sqrt{0.49} = 0.7;$$

$$\sqrt[3]{0.008} = 0.2; \quad 0.23$$

Arranging in ascending order the numbers are:

0.2, 0.23, 0.25, 0.7

$\therefore$ $\sqrt[3]{0.008} = 0.2$ is the least.

**31. (c)** L.C.M. of 12, 24, 36 and 40

$$= 360$$

Any number which when divided by 12, 24, 36 and 40 leaving a remainder 1 is of the form 360k + 1. Now, we have to find the least value of k for which 360k + 1 is divisible by 7.

$$
\begin{array}{r}
51k \\
7\overline{)\,360k + 1} \\
-357k \\
\hline
3k + 1
\end{array}
$$

By inspection, we find that for k = 2,

$$3 \times 2 + 1 = 7$$

$\therefore$ Required number $= 360 \times 2 + 1$
$$= 721.$$

**32. (c)**

$$
\require{enclose}
\begin{array}{r}
3x^3 - x^2 - x - 4 \\[2pt]
x-1\enclose{longdiv}{3x^4 - 4x^3 - 3x - 1} \\[2pt]
\underline{3x^4 - 3x^3} \phantom{} \\
-\ \ \ \ \ + \\
\underline{\phantom{3x^4 - 3x^3}} \\
-x^3 \\
-x^3 + x^2 \\
+\ \ \ \ \ - \\
\underline{\phantom{-x^3 + x^2}} \\
-x^2 - 3x \\
-x^2 + x \\
+\ \ \ \ \ - \\
\underline{\phantom{-x^2 + x}} \\
-4x - 1 \\
-4x + 4 \\
+\ \ \ \ \ - \\
\underline{\phantom{-4x + 4}} \\
-5
\end{array}
$$

**33.** **(a)** $a^4 - 20a^2 + 64$

$= a^4 - 16a^2 - 4a^2 + 64$

$= a^2(a^2 - 16) - 4(a^2 - 16)$

$= (a^2 - 16)(a^2 - 4)$

$= (a + 4)(a - 4)(a + 2)(a - 2)$

**34.** **(d)** Let my age 16 years ago be x years

Then, my grandfather's age 16 years ago = 8x years

At present,

My age = (x + 16) years

Grandfather's age = (8x + 16) years

8 years from now,

My age = (x + 16 + 8) years

= (x + 24) years

Grandfather's age

= (8x + 16 + 8) years

= (8x + 24) years

Given, $8x + 24 = 3(x + 24)$

$\Rightarrow 8x + 24 = 3x + 72$

$\Rightarrow 5x = 48$

$\Rightarrow x = \dfrac{48}{5} = 9.6$ years

$\therefore$ My age 16 years ago = 9.6 years

Grandfather's age 16 years ago

= 8 × 9.6 years

= 76.8 years

Required ratio

$= \dfrac{9.6 + 8}{76.8 + 8} = \dfrac{17.6}{84.8} = \dfrac{11}{53}$

= 11 : 53.

**35.** **(b)** $a - 3 = \dfrac{10}{a} \Rightarrow a^2 - 3a = 10$

$\Rightarrow a^2 - 3a - 10 = 0$

$\Rightarrow a^2 - 5a + 2a - 10 = 0$

$\Rightarrow a(a - 5) + 2(a - 5) = 0$

$\Rightarrow (a - 5)(a + 2) = 0$

$\Rightarrow a - 5 = 0$ or $a + 2 = 0$

$\Rightarrow a = 5, -2.$

**36.** **(a)** Let the price of the article be ₹ x and daily sale be y units.

Then, daily sale receipts = ₹ xy

Reduced price of the article

= x − 25% of x

$= x - \dfrac{25}{100}x = x - \dfrac{1}{4}x =$

$= ₹\dfrac{3}{4}x$

Increased daily sale

$= y + \dfrac{30}{100}y = \dfrac{13}{10}y$

$\therefore$ Daily sale receipts

$= ₹\dfrac{3}{4}x \times \dfrac{13}{10}y = ₹\dfrac{39}{40}xy$

$\therefore$ % reduction

$= \dfrac{xy - \dfrac{39}{40}xy}{xy} \times 100\%$

$= \dfrac{100}{40}\% = 2\dfrac{1}{2}\%.$

**37.** **(b)**

$\sqrt{12.96} + \sqrt{0.1296} + \sqrt{0.001296} + \sqrt{0.00001296}$

$= \sqrt{\dfrac{1296}{100}} + \sqrt{\dfrac{1296}{10000}} + \sqrt{\dfrac{1296}{1000000}} + \sqrt{\dfrac{1296}{100000000}}$

$= \dfrac{36}{10} + \dfrac{36}{100} + \dfrac{36}{1000} + \dfrac{36}{10000}$

$= 3.6 + 0.36 + 0.036 + 0.0036 = 3.9996$

**38.** **(a)** A = ₹4913, n = 3,

$$r = 6\frac{1}{4}\% = \frac{25}{4}\%,\ P = ?$$

$$\therefore\ 4913 = P\left(1 + \frac{25}{400}\right)^3$$

$$\Rightarrow\ 4913 = P\left(1 + \frac{1}{16}\right)^3$$

$$\Rightarrow\ 4913 = P\left(\frac{17}{16}\right)^3$$

$$\Rightarrow\ 4913 = P \times \frac{4913}{4096}$$

$$\Rightarrow\ P = ₹4096.$$

**39.** **(c)** In Δ's AOC and BOD

   OA = OB     (Given)
   OC = OD     (Given)
   ∠AOB = ∠COD
$\Rightarrow$ ∠AOB − ∠COB

           = ∠COD − ∠COB,
   i.e. ∠AOC = ∠BOD
$\therefore$ ΔAOC ≅ ΔBOD    (SAS)
$\Rightarrow$ AC = BD     (cpct)

**40.** **(c)** $\therefore$ Opp. ∠s of a rhombus are equal

   $2x + 15° = 3x − 30°$
$\Rightarrow$ $x = 45°$
   In ΔBCD, CD = CB
$\Rightarrow$ ∠CBD = ∠BDC
   Also,
   ∠DCB = 3 × 45° − 30°
         = 105°

$$\therefore\ \angle BDC = \frac{180° − 105°}{2} = \frac{75°}{2}$$

         = 37.5°.

**41.** **(b)** It is clear that all cubes about the edges have either two or three sides painted. Only one central either two or three sides painted. Only one central cube in each face as shown in figure will have one face painted, since all it other faces are hidden inside the large cube.

So, there are total 6 cubes with only one side painted red.

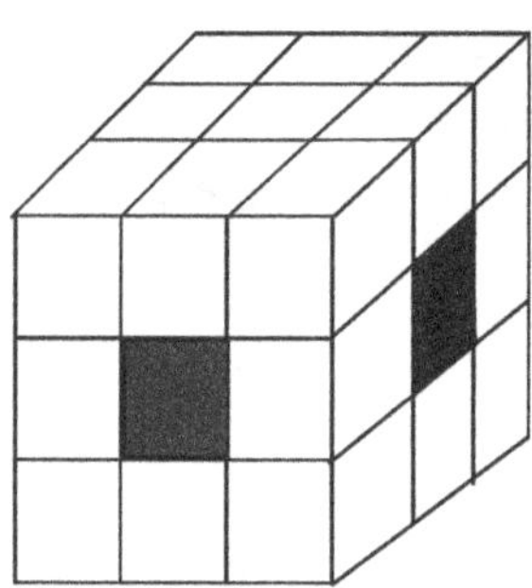

**42.** **(c)** Let $l$, b, h be the length, breadth and height of the cuboid.

$\therefore$ $l + b + h = 19$ and

$$\sqrt{l^2 + b^2 + h^2} = 5\sqrt{5}$$

$$\Rightarrow l^2 + b^2 + h^2 = \left(5\sqrt{5}\right)^2 = 125$$

   Surface area of the cuboid
   = 2($l$b + bh + $l$h)
   = ($l$ + b + h)² − ($l^2$ + b² + h²)
   = 19² − 125 = 361 − 125
   = 236 cm².

**43.** **(a)** The movements of Radhika are as shown in fig (A to B, B to C, C to D and D to A)

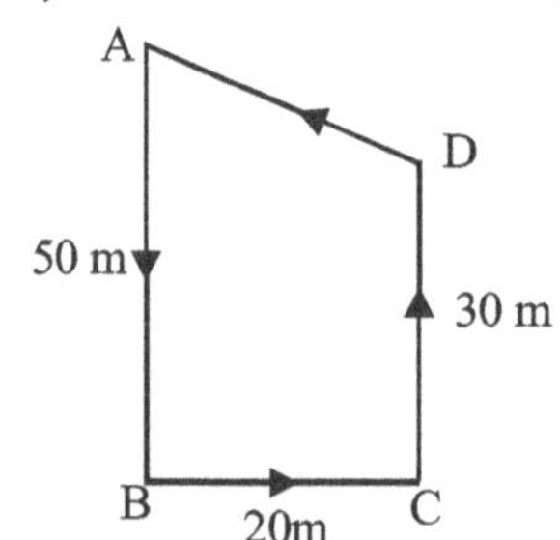

Clearly she is finally moving in the direction DA i.e, north west.

**44. (d)** The persons who know all the three language are represented by the region which is common to all the three circles.

So, number of such persons = 100

The persons who do not know Sanskrit are represented by the region outside circle S.

So, number of such persons = $(200 + 120 + 220) = 540$.

$\therefore$ Required ratio = $100 : 540 = 5 : 27$

**45. (c)** Volume of the bigger cube = $(10)^3$ cm$^3$ = 1000 cm$^3$

Volume of the smaller cube = 500 cm$^3$

Required ratio

$$= \frac{\text{Edge of smaller cube}}{\text{Edge of bigger cube}}$$

$$= \frac{(500)^{\frac{1}{3}}}{(1000)^{\frac{1}{3}}} = \left(\frac{500}{1000}\right)^{\frac{1}{3}} = \left(\frac{1}{2}\right)^{\frac{1}{3}}.$$

**46. (a)** Curved surface area of a cone = $\pi r l$.

$\sqrt{\text{Also,}}$ as shown in diagram, $l^2$ = $r^2 + h^2 = 4^2 + 3^2$

or $l = 5$ cm.

$$\therefore \quad \text{CSA} = \frac{22}{7} \times 4 \times 5 = \frac{440}{7}$$

$$= 62\frac{6}{7} \text{ sq. cm.}$$

**47. (c)** $\dfrac{A}{6} = \dfrac{B}{4} = \dfrac{C}{3}$

$A : B : C = 6 : 4 : 3$

**48. (d)**

| Wages (in ₹) | Class mark ($x$) | Frequency (No. of workers) ($f$) | $fx$ |
|---|---|---|---|
| 30-40 | 35 | 10 | 350 |
| 40-50 | 45 | 20 | 900 |
| 50-60 | 55 | 40 | 2200 |
| 60-70 | 65 | 16 | 1040 |
| 70-80 | 75 | 8 | 600 |
| 80-90 | 85 | 6 | 510 |
|  |  | $\Sigma f$ = 100 | $\Sigma fx$ =5600 |

$$\therefore \quad \text{Mean} = \frac{\Sigma fx}{\Sigma f} = \frac{5600}{100} = 56$$

**49. (b)** Number of students getting marks equal to or more than 40 = 9(44, 45, 46, 42, 48, 40, 43, 47, 44)

$\therefore$ P(pass)

$$= \frac{\text{Number of students who passed}}{\text{Total number of students}}$$

$$= \frac{9}{15} = \frac{3}{5}.$$

**50. (d)** Required numbers = $(13 - 9)\%$ of 95400 = 4% of 95400 = 3816

## MOCK TEST-5

### ANSWER KEY

| | | | | | | | | | |
|---|---|---|---|---|---|---|---|---|---|
| 1 | (b) | 11 | (b) | 21 | (d) | 31 | (a) | 41 | (b) |
| 2 | (d) | 12 | (a) | 22 | (b) | 32 | (b) | 42 | (a) |
| 3 | (d) | 13 | (d) | 23 | (b) | 33 | (c) | 43 | (b) |
| 4 | (a) | 14 | (c) | 24 | (b) | 34 | (d) | 44 | (d) |
| 5 | (b) | 15 | (b) | 25 | (d) | 35 | (d) | 45 | (b) |
| 6 | (c) | 16 | (c) | 26 | (a) | 36 | (b) | 46 | (c) |
| 7 | (a) | 17 | (d) | 27 | (d) | 37 | (c) | 47 | (a) |
| 8 | (d) | 18 | (c) | 28 | (b) | 38 | (c) | 48 | (b) |
| 9 | (b) | 19 | (a) | 29 | (a) | 39 | (d) | 49 | (d) |
| 10 | (c) | 20 | (c) | 30 | (c) | 40 | (d) | 50 | (b) |

**1.** **(b)** $\sqrt{9a^4 b^8}$

$$= \sqrt{3 \times 3 \times a^2 \times a^2 \times b^4 \times b^4}$$

$$= \sqrt{3a^2 b^4 \times 3a^2 b^4} = 3a^2 b^4.$$

**2.** **(d)** The sum of the numbers in each row and each column is 30.

**3.** **(d)** The total number of students in the square = 1156

The number of students on each side = $\sqrt{1156}$ = 34

$$\begin{array}{r} 34 \\ 3\overline{)\,11\ 56} \\ 9 \\ 64\ \overline{)\,2\ 56} \\ 2\ 56 \\ \hline 0 \end{array}$$

There are 34 students on each side of the square.

**4.** **(a)** $\dfrac{38a^3 b^3 c^2 - 19a^4 b^2 c}{19a^2 bc}$

$$= \frac{38a^3 b^3 c^2}{19a^2 bc} - \frac{19a^4 b^2 c}{19a^2 bc}$$

$$= 2ab^2 c - a^2 b.$$

**5.** **(b)** $10xy - 5y + 8 - 16x$

$$= \underline{10xy - 5y} - \underline{16x + 8}$$

$$= 5y(2x - 1) - 8(2x - 1)$$
$$= (2x - 1)(5y - 8)$$

**6.** **(c)** $4^{\sqrt{x}^{\sqrt{x}}} = 256 = 4^4$

$$\Rightarrow \sqrt{x}^{\sqrt{x}} = 4 = 2^2$$

$$\Rightarrow \sqrt{x} = 2 \Rightarrow x = 4$$

**7.** **(a)**

$$\begin{array}{r|l} 2 & 21952 \\ \hline 2 & 10976 \\ \hline 2 & 5488 \\ \hline 2 & 2744 \\ \hline 2 & 1372 \\ \hline 2 & 686 \\ \hline 7 & 343 \\ \hline 7 & 49 \\ \hline & 7 \end{array}$$

$\therefore$ $21952 = 2 \times 2 \times 2 \times 2 \times 2 \times 2 \times 7$
$\times 7 \times 7$
$= 2^3 \times 2^3 \times 7^3$

$\therefore$ $\sqrt[3]{21952} = \sqrt[3]{2^3 \times 2^3 \times 7^3}$
$= 2 \times 2 \times 7 = 28$

$\therefore$ Digit in the units' place of
$\sqrt[3]{21952}$ = 8.

8. **(d)** $x^2 - 7x + 10 = 0$
$\Rightarrow$ $(x - 5)(x - 2) = 0$
$\Rightarrow$ $x = 5, 2$
$x^2 - 10x + 16 = 0$
$\Rightarrow$ $(x - 8)(x - 2) = 0$
$\Rightarrow$ $x = 8, 2$
$\therefore$ Common root = 2.

9. **(b)** S.I. for 10 years
$= ₹\left(1000 \times \dfrac{5}{100} \times 10\right) = ₹500$

Principal after 10 years
becomes = ₹(1000 + 500)
= ₹1500

Amount on that principal after
t years = ₹2000

$\therefore$ S.I. on it = ₹(2000 − 1500)
= ₹500

$\therefore$ $t = \left(\dfrac{500 \times 100}{1500 \times 5}\right)$ years
$= 6\dfrac{2}{3}$ years

$\therefore$ Total time = $\left(10 + 6\dfrac{2}{3}\right)$ years
$= 16\dfrac{2}{3}$ years

10. **(c)** P = ₹16000, r = 10% p.a.
= 5% per half year
n = 2 years = 4 half years

$\therefore$ Amount = $16000\left(1 + \dfrac{5}{100}\right)^4$
$= 16000 \times \left(\dfrac{21}{20}\right)^4$
$= \dfrac{16000 \times 194481}{160000}$
$= 19448.10 = ₹19448$ (approx.)

11. **(b)** 12 men can complete in 12
days, 1 work

1 man can complete in 1 day
$\dfrac{1}{12 \times 12}$ part of the work

$\therefore$ 6 men can complete in 6 days
$\dfrac{6 \times 6}{12 \times 12}$ part of the work

$= \dfrac{1}{4}$th part of the work

Number of remaining men = 6,

Remaining work = $\dfrac{3}{4}$

$\because$ 12 men can complete 1 work in
12 days

6 men can complete $\dfrac{3}{4}$ work in

$$\dfrac{12 \times 12 \times 3}{6 \times 4} = 18 \text{ days}$$

∴   Number of extra days

$$= 18 - 6$$

$$= 12 \text{ days.}$$

**12. (a)** The given series when written in the reverse order becomes.

13, 11, 5, 0, 1, 2, 6, 4, 8, 3, 0, 7, 9, 3, 7

The 7th number from the left is 6. The 4th number to the right of 6 is 0.

**13. (d)** Remaining part

$$= 1 - \left(\dfrac{1}{3} + \dfrac{1}{6}\right) = \dfrac{1}{2}$$

Average rate % per annum (R)

$$= \left(\dfrac{1}{3} \times 3\right) + \left(\dfrac{1}{6} \times 6\right) + \left(\dfrac{1}{2} \times 8\right) = 6\%$$

SI = ₹ 600

T = 2 years, P = ?

$$\text{SI} = \dfrac{\text{PTR}}{100}$$

$$\text{P} = \dfrac{100 \times \text{SI}}{\text{TR}} = \dfrac{100 \times 600}{2 \times 6}$$

$$= ₹5000.$$

**14. (c)** Each side of the rhombus

$$= \dfrac{40 \text{ cm}}{4} = 10 \text{ cm}$$

Length of the other diagonal

$$= 2 \times \sqrt{10^2 - \left(\dfrac{12}{2}\right)^2}$$

$$= 2 \times \sqrt{100 - 36}$$

$$= 2 \times \sqrt{64} \text{ cm} = 16 \text{ cm.}$$

**15. (b)** Amount, A = ₹5324

P = ₹4000

Rate = 10%

$$A = P\left(1 + \dfrac{r}{100}\right)^t$$

$$5324 = 4000\left(1 + \dfrac{10}{100}\right)^t$$

$$= 4000\left(\dfrac{110}{100}\right)^t$$

$$= 4000 \times \left(\dfrac{11}{10}\right)^t$$

$$\dfrac{5324}{4000} = \left(\dfrac{11}{10}\right)^t$$

$$\dfrac{1331}{1000} = \left(\dfrac{11}{10}\right)^t$$

$$\left(\dfrac{11}{10}\right)^3 = \left(\dfrac{11}{10}\right)^t$$

∴   t = 3 years

**16. (c)** Sindhu's age = 40 years

Smita's age = 20 years

Let us suppose x years ago, Sindhu's age was thrice Smita's age.

Hence,

x years ago, Sindhu's age

$= 40 - x$

x years ago, Smita's age

$= 20 - x$

x years ago, Sindhu's age

$= 3$ times Smita's age

$\Rightarrow\ 40 - x = 3(20 - x)$

$40 - x = 60 - 3x$

$40 - x + 3x = 60 - 3x + 3x$

(adding 3x on both sides)

$40 + 2x = 60$

$40 + 2x - 40 = 60 - 40$

(subtracting 40 from both sides)

$2x = 20$

$x = 10$ years

Thus, 10 years ago, Sindhu was three times as old as Smita.

**17. (d)** Let the cost price be ₹100.

So, when C.P. = 100, loss of 20% means

S.P. $= 100 - 20 = 80$

Profit of 5% means S.P.

$= 100 + 5 = 105$

The difference of two S.P.

$= 105 - 80 = 25$

If the difference is 25, C.P. $=$ ₹100

If the difference is ₹800, C.P.

$= \dfrac{100}{25} \times 800$

$=$ ₹3200.

**18. (c)** Amount = ₹9125

Interest = ₹625

Principal = Amount − Interest

$=$ ₹9125 − ₹625

$=$ ₹8500

**19. (a)** Using the proper signs in the given expression , we get

$175 \div 25 + 5 \times 20 - 3 \times 10$

$= 7 + 5 \times 20 - 3 \times 10$

$= 7 + 100 - 30 = 107 - 30 = 77.$

**20. (c)**

$$\sqrt[3]{\sqrt[3]{a^3}} = \left(\left(a^3\right)^{\frac{1}{3}}\right)^{\frac{1}{3}} = a^{3 \times \frac{1}{9}} = a^{\frac{1}{3}}.$$

**21. (d)** $8^{x-2} \times \left(\dfrac{1}{2}\right)^{4-3x} = (0.0625)^x$

$\Rightarrow\ (2^3)^{x-2} \times (2^{-1})^{4-3x} = \left(\dfrac{625}{10000}\right)^x$

$\Rightarrow\ 2^{3x-6} \times 2^{-4+3x} = \left(\dfrac{1}{16}\right)^x$

$= (2^{-4})^x = 2^{-4x}$

$\Rightarrow\ 2^{3x-6-4+3x} = 2^{-4x}$

$\Rightarrow\ 2^{6x-10} = 2^{-4x}$

$\Rightarrow\ 6x - 10 = -4x$

$\Rightarrow\ 10x = 10$

$\Rightarrow\ x = 1.$

**22. (b)** Given, $A + B + C = 53$ ... (i)

Also, $A = B + 7$ and $B = C + 8$

$\therefore$ From (i), we get

$(B + 7) + B + (B - 8) = 53$

$\Rightarrow \ 3B = 54 \Rightarrow B = 18$

$\Rightarrow \ A = 25$ and $C = 10$

$\therefore \ A : B : C = 25 : 18 : 10.$

**23. (b)** Actual height = 5 feet 5 inches

$= 5 \times 12$ inches $+ 5$ inches

$= 65$ inches

Height given by mistake

$= \dfrac{125}{100} \times 65$ inches $= 81.25$ inches

$\therefore$ Required percentage error

$= \dfrac{(81.25 - 65)}{81.25} \times 100\%$

$= \left(\dfrac{16.25}{81.25} \times 100\right)\% = 20\%.$

**24. (b)** Area of the quadrilateral

$= \dfrac{1}{2} \times$ diagonal $\times$ sum of the off-sets

$= \dfrac{1}{2} \times 230 \times (60 + 70)$ sq. m.

$= 115 \times 130$ sq. m.

$= 14950$ sq. m.

**25. (d)** Volume of the godown $= 7 \times 4.5 \times 2 \ m^3$

$= 700 \times 450 \times 200 \ cm^3$

Volume of the carton

$= 70 \times 22.5 \times 40 \ cm^3$

Number of cartons

$= \dfrac{\text{Volume of godown}}{\text{Volume of carton}}$

$\therefore$ Number of cartons

$= \dfrac{700 \times 450 \times 200}{70 \times 22.5 \times 40} = 1000$

**26. (a)** Let the height be x, given length $= 8$ cm and breadth $= 6$ cm

Total Surface Area = 208

$= 2(lb + lh + bh) =$

$2(8 \times 6 + 8 \times x + 6 \times x) = 208$

$2(48 + 14x) = 208$

$96 + 28x = 208$

$28x = 112$

$x = \dfrac{112}{28} = 4$ cm.

**27. (d)** Area of an equilateral triangle

$= \dfrac{\sqrt{3}a^2}{4}$

$36\sqrt{3} = \dfrac{\sqrt{3}}{4}a^2$

$a^2 = \dfrac{36\sqrt{3} \times 4}{\sqrt{3}} = 144$

$\therefore \ a = \sqrt{144} = 12$

$\therefore$ Each side of the equilateral triangle $= 12$ m.

**28. (b)** The numbers in the right half form the series : 2, 3, 4, 5.

The numbers in the left half form the series : 5, 7, 9, 11.

**29. (a)** Let B's salary be ₹ 100, so A's salary is ₹ 150.

So % of B's salary less than A

$$= \frac{50}{150} \times 100 = \frac{100}{3} = 33\frac{1}{3}\%$$

**30. (c)** Let the breadth of the wall = h metres

∴ Height of the wall = 5h metres

Length of the wall = 40h metres

∴ 40h × 5h × h = 18225

⇒ $h^3 = 91.125$

⇒ h = 4.5 m

**31. (a)** Given 2x – 5y = 3

cubing both sides, we get

$(2x - 5y)^3 = (3)^3$

⇒ $(2x)^3 - (5y)^3 - 3\,(2x)\,(5y)$
$$(2x - 5y) = 27$$

⇒ $8x^3 - 125y^3 - 30xy\,(3) = 27$

⇒ $8x^3 - 125y^3 - 90\,(4) = 27$

⇒ $8x^3 - 125y^3 = 27 + 360 = 387$

**32. (b)** We know

$3x^2 - 6x - 105 = 3(x^2 - 2x - 35)$
$$= 3(x - 7)\,(x + 5)$$

$5x^2 - 125 = 5(x^2 - 25)$
$$= 5\,(x + 5)\,(x - 5)$$

$x^2 - 12x + 35 = (x - 7)\,(x - 5)$

$x^2 - 5x = x\,(x - 5).$

Consider

$$\frac{3x^2 - 6x - 105}{5x^2 - 125} \div \frac{x^2 - 12x + 35}{x^2 - 5x}$$

$$= \frac{3x^2 - 6x - 105}{5x^2 - 125} \times \frac{x^2 - 5x}{x^2 - 12x + 35}$$

$$= \frac{3(x - 7)(x + 5)}{5(x + 5)(x - 5)} \times \frac{x(x - 5)}{(x - 7)(x - 5)}$$

$$= \frac{3x}{5(x - 5)}.$$

**33. (c)** Given $\dfrac{1}{3}(4x + 5) - \dfrac{1}{2}(5a - 3) = \dfrac{1}{6}$

Where, x = 2a – 1

On substituting, we get

$$\frac{1}{3}[4(2a - 1) + 5] - \frac{1}{2}[5a - 3] = \frac{1}{6}$$

Multiplying both sides by 6 (L.C.M of 3, 2 and 6),

we get

$2[8a - 4 + 5] - 3\,[5a - 3] = 1$

⇒ 16a + 2 – 15a + 9 = 1

⇒ 16a – 15a = 1 – 11

⇒ a = – 10

**34. (d)**

| 10 | 1 |
|----|---|
| 2x | x |

The number is = 21x

If the digits are interchanged

| 10 | 1 |
|----|---|
| x | 2x |

Then, the number = 12x

So, 12x = 21x – 36

$9x = 36$

$x = 4$

$\therefore$ The number $= 21 \times 4 = 84$.

**35. (d)** Sum of interior angles of a pentagon $= (2 \times 5 - 4)$ right angles.

$\Rightarrow \angle A + \angle ABC + \angle C + \angle D + \angle E$
$$= 540°$$

$\Rightarrow 110° + \angle ABC + 80° + 135°$
$$+ 105° = 540°$$

$\Rightarrow \angle ABC = 540° - 430°$

$\Rightarrow \angle ABC = 110°$

Now $\angle ABC + x = 180°$

{An ext. angle + adjacent int. angle $= 180°$}

$\Rightarrow 110° + x = 180°$

$\Rightarrow x = 180° - 110°$

$\Rightarrow x = 70°$.

**36. (b)** Time taken by the tap to fill the tank $= p$ hours

Time taken by the tap to empty the tank $= q$ hours

$\therefore$ In one hour the tap fills $\dfrac{1}{p}$th part of the tank.

In one hour the tap empties $\dfrac{1}{q}$th part of the tank.

Thus, in one hour $\left(\dfrac{1}{p} - \dfrac{1}{q}\right)$th part is filled.

But given tank is filled in r hours when both the taps are opened.

$\therefore$ In 1 hour $\dfrac{1}{r}$th part of tank is filled.

$\therefore \quad \dfrac{1}{r} = \dfrac{1}{p} - \dfrac{1}{q}$.

**37. (c)** LCM of 58/57 and 609/608 is 1218/19 Sec.

In 1 hour, they will tick together $= 3600 \times 19/1218$

$= 56.1$

Times after the first stroke

$\Rightarrow$ 57 times per hour.

**38. (c)** S.P. $= ₹178$, Loss $= 11\%$

$\therefore$ C.P. $= \dfrac{178 \times 100}{(100 - 11)} = \dfrac{178 \times 100}{89}$

$= 200$

Now, C.P. $= ₹200$, Profit $= 11\%$

$\therefore$ S.P. $= \dfrac{200 \times 111}{100} = ₹222$.

**39. (d)** P $= ₹800$, r $= 10\%$ p.a. $= 5\%$ per half year,

A $= ₹926.10$, Time $= 2n$

$\therefore \quad 926.10 = 800\left(1 + \dfrac{5}{100}\right)^{2n}$

$\Rightarrow \quad \dfrac{9261}{8000} = \left(1 + \dfrac{1}{20}\right)^{2n}$

$$\Rightarrow \left(\frac{21}{20}\right)^3 = \left(\frac{21}{20}\right)^{2n}$$

$$\Rightarrow 2n = 3$$

$$\Rightarrow n = \frac{3}{2} = 1\frac{1}{2} \text{ years.}$$

**40. (d)** In $\Delta$s ADB and ACB,

AD = BC　　(Given)

AC = BD

AB = BA　　(Common)

$\therefore \quad \Delta\text{ADB} \cong \Delta\text{BCA}$　(SSS)

$\Rightarrow \angle\text{ABD} = \angle\text{CAB}$　(cpct)

$\Rightarrow \angle\text{ABP} = \angle\text{PAB}$

$\Rightarrow$ PA = PB (Sides opp. equal angles are equal)

$\Rightarrow \Delta$PAB is isosceles.

**41. (b)** Total area = Area of $\Delta$AFC + Area of $\Delta$AGD + Area of trapezium FCEH + Area of $\Delta$BHE + Area of $\Delta$DGB

$$= \frac{1}{2} \times AF \times FC + \frac{1}{2} \times AG \times DG$$

$$+ \frac{1}{2} \times (CF + EH) \times HF + \frac{1}{2} \times$$

$$BH \times HE + \frac{1}{2} \times BG \times DG$$

$$\Rightarrow \frac{1}{2} \times 25 \times 20 + \frac{1}{2} \times 50 \times 40$$

$$+ \frac{1}{2} \times (20 + x) \times 50 + \frac{1}{2} \times 25 \times x$$

$$+ \frac{1}{2} \times 50 \times 40 = 3500$$

$$\Rightarrow 250 + 1000 + (20 + x)25 + 12.5x + 1000 = 3500$$

$$\Rightarrow 2250 + 500 + 25x + 12.5x = 3500$$

$$\Rightarrow 37.5x = 3500 - 2750 = 750$$

$$\Rightarrow x = \frac{750}{37.5} = 20 \text{ m}$$

**42. (a)** Surface area of the open tank

$$= [2 \times (20 \times 12 + 30 \times 12) + 30 \times 20] \text{ m}^2$$

$$= [2 \times (240 + 360) + 600] \text{ m}^2$$

$$= 1800 \text{ m}^2$$

$\therefore$　Length of the iron sheet

$$= \frac{1800}{3} = 600 \text{ m}$$

Cost of the iron sheet = ₹(600 × 10) = ₹6000.

**43. (b)** $\dfrac{\text{Volume}}{\text{Curved Surface Area}}$

$$= \frac{\pi r^2 h}{2\pi rh} = \frac{924}{264}$$

$$\Rightarrow \frac{r}{2} = \frac{7}{2}$$

$$\Rightarrow r = 7 \text{ m and } 2\pi rh = 264$$

$$\Rightarrow h = 264 \times \frac{7}{22} \times \frac{1}{2} \times \frac{1}{7} = 6 \text{ m}$$

$\therefore$　Required ratio $= \dfrac{2r}{h} = \dfrac{14}{6}$

$$= 7 : 3.$$

**44. (d)** First we cannot assume that PS and RU as diametres.

$\angle PXR = \angle UXS$. But X is not the centre of the circle.

**45. (b)**

**46. (c)** Mean of x and $\frac{1}{x}$, $M = \dfrac{x + \dfrac{1}{x}}{2}$

$$\Rightarrow \quad x + \frac{1}{x} = 2M$$

We have,

$$\Rightarrow \quad x^2 + \frac{1}{x^2} = \left(x + \frac{1}{x}\right)^2 - 2x\left(\frac{1}{x}\right)$$

$$= (2M)^2 - 2 = 4M^2 - 2$$

$$= 2(2M^2 - 1)$$

Now, the mean of $x^2$ and $\dfrac{1}{x^2}$

$$= \dfrac{x^2 + \dfrac{1}{x^2}}{2} = \frac{2(2M^2 - 1)}{2}$$

$$= 2M^2 - 1$$

**47. (a)** No. of children likes Green colour = 8

No. of children likes Blue colour = 10

No. of children likes Red colour = 1

Similarly, no. of childrens like yellow and others are 6 and 5 respectively.

Hence, total no. of childrens

$$= 8 + 10 + 1 + 6 + 5 = 30$$

**48. (b)** From the graph it is clear that the mode = Blue colour

**49. (d)** Required angle

$$= \frac{6}{30} \times 360° = \frac{360°}{5} = 72°$$

**50. (b)** Number of face cards (Jack, Queen, King and Ace) in a deck of cards = 4×4 = 16

Total no. of cards = 52.

$\therefore$ total number of possible outcomes = 52

Let $E_1$ represents event of drawing a face card.

$\therefore$ no. of favourable outcomes = 16

$\therefore$ $P(E_1)$

$$= \frac{\text{Number of favourable outcomes}}{\text{Total number of outcomes}}$$

$$= \frac{16}{52} = \frac{4}{13}.$$

# SCIENCE

MOCK TEST-1

| ANSWER KEY | | | | | | | | | |
|---|---|---|---|---|---|---|---|---|---|
| 1 | (a) | 11 | (c) | 21 | (d) | 31 | (a) | 41 | (a) |
| 2 | (b) | 12 | (a) | 22 | (c) | 32 | (d) | 42 | (d) |
| 3 | (c) | 13 | (b) | 23 | (c) | 33 | (a) | 43 | (d) |
| 4 | (d) | 14 | (d) | 24 | (c) | 34 | (a) | 44 | (a) |
| 5 | (c) | 15 | (c) | 25 | (a) | 35 | (a) | 45 | (d) |
| 6 | (a) | 16 | (a) | 26 | (d) | 36 | (c) | 46 | (b) |
| 7 | (a) | 17 | (a) | 27 | (c) | 37 | (b) | 47 | (d) |
| 8 | (d) | 18 | (d) | 28 | (d) | 38 | (d) | 48 | (c) |
| 9 | (a) | 19 | (c) | 29 | (b) | 39 | (b) | 49 | (a) |
| 10 | (b) | 20 | (a) | 30 | (b) | 40 | (a) | 50 | (c) |

## PHYSICS

1. **(a)** $F = m \times a, F \propto a$

2. **(b)** Mars's surface gravity is only 38 percent of the gravity of Earth.

4. **(d)** The best conductor of electricity is sea water.

6. **(a)** We can never see the back side of the moon from the earth because the moon completes one rotation on its axis as it completes one revolution around the earth.

7. **(a)** Baby girl will have minimum frequency.

8. **(d)** A convex mirror always forms a virtual erect and diminished image.

9. **(a)** When an object tends to come in motion from the rest, the frictional force acting on the object is called static friction.

10. **(b)** A vehicle slows down after applying brakes because of frictional force.

12. **(a)** Electroscope is used to find charge.

14. **(d)** Sugar solution does not break into ions.

15. **(c)** Ear drum is one of the part of hearing organ.

17. **(a)** Pressure is measured in unit called pascal.

18. **(d)** Light does not require any medium to travel.

19. **(c)** Sand is used to increase the friction.

## CHEMISTRY

20. **(a)** As cotton can absorb a large amount of water, inferior grade cotton fabrics are used as "mops" in the household cleaning. There is too much air

space within the cotton fibre which stores air too. These are the causes due to which cotton cloth absorbs water efficiently and burns at a moderate speed.

**21. (d)** Material for food container should have all these properties.

**22. (c)** A more active metal displaces less active metal from its salt solution. Mg and Al are more reaction than Cu and Fe respectively.

**23. (c)**



**24. (c)** Formation of coal is a slow process which requires high pressure and high temperature which is not possible in laboratory.

**25. (a)** Sodium and magnesium react with cold and warm water but zinc reacts only after boiling and copper does not react at all.

**26. (d)** The minimum temperature required for a combustible substance to catch fire is known as ignition temperature. The temperature of flame is high enough to overcome ignition temperature of alcohol and the substances which can easily set on fire are known as inflammable substances.

**27. (c)** Aluminium and iron are metals and metals are good conductors of electricity thus the bulb will light up. Coal and graphite are non-metals and non-metals do not conduct electricity but graphite is an exception and it conducts electricity.

**29. (b)** Natural gas is a naturally occurring hydrocarbon gas mixture consisting primarily of methane. By heating $NaHCO_3$, $CO_2$ is produced.

$$2NaHCO_3 \longrightarrow Na_2CO_3 + CO_2 + H_2O$$

Chalk, marble and limestone all three mainly consist of $CaCO_3$. Solid $CO_2$ is used as dry ice as it sublimes directly to gas without leaving any residue.

**30. (b)** Luminous zone, is the yellow zone, where incomplete combustion takes place because in this zone, the combustible vapours do not get sufficient oxygen to burn. Thus when a glass plate is introduced in luminous zone some unburnt carbon particles remain and cause black deposition.

## BIOLOGY

**33. (a)** Buffer stock refers to the grains stocked for emergencies. It ensures the availability of grains in the condition of shortfall in production in a particular year due to monsoon failure, flood, earthquake etc.

**35. (a)** In an integrated cultivation, crops are cultivated along with livestock.

**36. (c)** Virus is a particle that is too small to be seen with a light microscope or to be trapped by filters but is capable of independent metabolism and reproduction only within a living cell. It consists of a core of nucleic acid (DNA or RNA) surrounded by a protein coat. Thus they are also called as infectious nucleoprotein particles.

**37. (b)** Fungi grow best when there is warmth and enough moisture. If the bread is placed in moist temperature then there would be white, black and greenish patches of mould on it.

**38. (d)** IUCN is International Union of Conservation of Nature and Natural Resources which is now called World Conservation Union (WCU). It maintains a red data book or red list which is a catalogue of taxa facing risk of extinction. The purpose of IUCN's red list is:
  (i) to develop awareness about the importance of threatened biodiversity.
  (ii) identification and documentation of endangered species
  (iii) providing a global index of the decline of biodiversity.

**39. (b)** is the correct answer because a marine biome is contrasted to a freshwater biome by the amount of dissolved salt found in the water. In marine biomes there is much more dissolved salt found in the water than in freshwater biomes.
  (a) is not correct because the amount of sunlight that strikes a given surface area of water will vary in both marine and freshwater biomes.
  (c) is not correct because the amount of algae found in the water can be both high and low in freshwater and marine biomes.
  (d) is not correct because the temperature of the water can be both high and low in freshwater and marine biomes.

**41. (c)** Lysosomes are membrane bound cell organelles which contain hydrolytic enzymes. They are the organelles which digest various materials by using hydrolytic enzymes contained within. They are also called 'suicide bags of cell' because if they burst, the enzymes released will digest the whole cell.

**42. (d)** Cell wall may be present both in prokaryotic cell and eukaryotic plant cell. In prokaryotes, cell wall is made up of peptidoglycan.

Peptidoglycan is also called murein or mucopeptide. In eukaryotes, cell wall is made up of cellulose. Prokaryotes also lack a true nucleus (*pro* = before/primitive + *karyon* = nucleus). Their genetic material is not enclosed by an envelope but lies freely in cytoplasm. However, it is compactly coiled up and lies in a region called nucleoid. On the other hand, eukaryotes possess true nucleus. (*eu* = true + *karyon* = nucleus). They have spherical nucleus bound by double-membraned nuclear envelope. It encloses chromatin fibres (containing genetic material) and a round body called nucleolus.

**43. (d)** *Hydra* reproduce by budding. In *Hydra*, a small bulge appears from the lower part of the body. This grows into a bud, detaches from parent body and develops into a young *Hydra*.

**45. (d)** Placenta connects the foetus with uterine wall. Oxygen and essential nutrients are supplied to foetus from maternal blood. Excretory products and $CO_2$ are excreted out through it.

**46. (b)** During proliferative phase, proliferation of the uterine wall occurs. The uterine wall becomes thicker by cell division.

It takes about 6-13 days.

**47. (d)** Hormones are informational molecules secreted by the endocrine glands. They do not act as enzymes since they do not catalyse specific chemical reactions. Unlike enzymes, they are not catalytic molecules at all. They may influence the synthesis, activation or inhibition of some enzymes in their target organs. Again, unlike enzymes, all hormones are not proteins - some hormones are macromolecular proteins or large peptides (e.g. pancreatic and anterior pituitary hormones), but some others are only small peptides (e.g. posterior pituitary hormones), some are modified amino acids (e.g. thyroid hormones), some are amines (e.g. adrenal medulla hormones) and still others are steroids (e.g. gonadal and adrenal cortical hormones). So hormones differ from enzymes, both in action, and chemical nature.

**48. (c)** Chlorofluorocarbons (CFCs) are the gases which are released from air conditioners, refrigerators, aerosols sprays, etc. CFCs damage the ozone layer of the atmosphere. This can lead to skin cancer, diseases of the eye and can even cause damage to plants.

**49. (a)** Acid rain is a rain that is usually acidic or having low pH. Acid rain is caused by emission of sulphur dioxide and nitrogen oxides which react with water molecules in the atmosphere to produce acids. During rain, these acids come down on earth in the form of acid rain causing damage to plants, animals and monuments.

**50. (c)** CFC is strong enemy of ozone and causes depletion of ozone layer.

## MOCK TEST-2

### ANSWER KEY

| 1. | (c) | 11. | (d) | 21. | (a) | 31. | (a) | 41. | (b) |
|---|---|---|---|---|---|---|---|---|---|
| 2. | (c) | 12. | (c) | 22. | (d) | 32. | (b) | 42. | (c) |
| 3. | (c) | 13. | (b) | 23. | (d) | 33. | (d) | 43. | (c) |
| 4. | (a) | 14. | (a) | 24. | (b) | 34. | (c) | 44. | (a) |
| 5. | (a) | 15. | (d) | 25. | (c) | 35. | (b) | 45. | (b) |
| 6. | (a) | 16. | (d) | 26. | (d) | 36. | (a) | 46. | (c) |
| 7. | (b) | 17. | (b) | 27. | (d) | 37. | (a) | 47. | (b) |
| 8. | (c) | 18. | (d) | 28. | (d) | 38. | (d) | 48. | (b) |
| 9. | (a) | 19. | (b) | 29. | (a) | 39. | (d) | 49. | (b) |
| 10. | (b) | 20. | (d) | 30. | (c) | 40. | (a) | 50. | (a) |

## PHYSICS

1. **(c)** There is no need of frictional force in case of hearing but other activities like walking, writing, speaking can't be possible without friction.

2. **(c)** A positively charged body has deficiency of electrons.

3. **(c)** Copper is a conductor and rest are insulator.

4. **(a)** Time period is as follows : Neptune > New planet > Uranus

5. **(a)** Angle of incidence is equal to angle of reflection so eye should be kept at angle of reflection.

6. **(a)** Pressure with depth is given by
   P = hpg
   h-height from the top of the surface

8. **(c)** Rollers wheels in the shoes reduces friction and walking on the ground has high friction compared to roller wheels, therefore third statement is incorrect.

10. **(b)** Only A is correct

11. **(d)** Force is needed to produce accelaration.

12. **(c)** Chromium is used to make objects appear shining.

14. **(a)** Pressure = Force/Area = $\dfrac{F}{\pi r^2}$ on solving we get

$$= \dfrac{3.8N}{3.14 \times \left(0.9 \times 10^{-2}m\right)^2}$$

P = 14.9 KPa

15. **(d)** When negative charge is given to the sphere, electrons are put on it, and so its mass will increase.

16. **(d)** Conducts electric charge to the ground.

17. **(b)** Deviation at a plane mirror is
$180° - 2i = 180° - 2 \times 30° = 120°$

18. **(d)** Frictional force does not cause any repulsion.

19. **(b)** Constant force produce uniform motion.

## CHEMISTRY

**21. (a)** Plastics are made of long chains of molecules called polymers.

**22. (d)** Spontaneous combustion of coal dust has resulted in many disastrous fires in coal mine.

**23. (d)** All statements are correct.

**24. (b)** Thermoplastics can be deformed and remoulded easily thus (i) - thermoplastic. e.g., polyethylene, PVC etc. Thermosetting can not remoulded e.g., melamine, bakelite etc.

**25. (c)** (i) - (q), (ii) - (r), (iii) - (s), (iv) - (p)

**26. (d)** In a burning candle, there are both physical and chemical changes the melting of solid wax to form liquid wax and the evaporation of liquid wax to form wax vapour are physical change the burning of wax vapour is a chemical change.

**27. (d)** The given properties represent metals but potassium and sodium are soft metals thus can not be beaten into sheets thus X and Z are potassium and sodium. As W shows all three properties thus it is aluminium (a metal) and graphite is a non metal which conducts electricity (Y).

**29. (a)** As oil and gas are lighter than water thus these are present above water and do not mix with it.

**30. (c)** Synthetic fibres generate electric charge.

**31. (a)** Diagram (a) shows non-luminous flame.

## BIOLOGY

**35. (b)** The bacteria living within intestine are very helpful. They help in the digestion of food material and synthesize vitamin-B and vitamin-K in the intestine.

**37. (a)** Endemic species are those species which are confined to a particular area. This is due to a particular type of adaptation.

**38. (d)** The tundra is characterized by low temperatures and low precipitation.

**39. (d)** The plasma membrane is the outer covering of every cell. It is a bilipid membranous layer composed of protein and carbohydrates.

**40. (a)** A nerve cell is characterized by its long extension. It is very long, sometimes, reaching 90-100 cm.

**41. (b)** The male organ that helps in releasing sperms in female body is called penis. It is a muscular and erectile structure inside which urethra is present.

**42. (c)** Dr Ian Wilmut and his colleagues succeeded to develop a baby sheep-Dolly. It was done at Roslin Institute in Edinburgh (Scotland).

**43. (c)** Ovulation is the process in which ova are discharged by the rupture of follicles of ovary in females.

**44. (a)** The animals which excrete mainly uric acid are uricotelic. Uric acid can be stored or excreted in crystalline form.

**42. (b)** $A \rightarrow U, B \rightarrow S, C \rightarrow T, D \rightarrow Q, E \rightarrow P$

**46. (c)** Petroleum refineries are the source of sulphur dioxide emissions. Sulphur dioxide reacts with moisture to form sulphuric acid that causes acid rain e.g., Mathura Oil Refinery near Taj Mahal.

**47. (b)** Heat is a source of water pollution as high temperature of water reduces its dissolved oxygen resulting instant death of certain organisms, like fishes.

**48. (b)** Atmospheric $CO_2$ levels have increased by about 5%. $CO_2$ helps in maintaining the earth's heat balance by preventing part of the sun's reflected energy from returning back to space. With increased levels of $CO_2$, therefore, more energy is retained and the atmospheric temperature rises (global warming).

**49. (b)** Binary fission takes place in *Amoeba* to give rise to two daughter cells. Yeast reproduces by budding.

**50. (a)** Cell was discovered by Robert Hooke in 1665 and electron microscope was made by Knoll and Ruska in 1931.

Black reaction is a nervous tissue staining technique which was developed by Camillo Golgi but was extensively used by Cajal. This technique is also known as Golgi method or Golgi staining.

## MOCK TEST-3

| ANSWER KEY | | | | | | | | | |
|---|---|---|---|---|---|---|---|---|---|
| 1. | (d) | 11. | (a) | 21. | (b) | 31. | (d) | 41. | (b) |
| 2. | (c) | 12. | (c) | 22. | (d) | 32. | (d) | 42. | (c) |
| 3. | (d) | 13. | (d) | 23. | (d) | 33. | (d) | 43. | (d) |
| 4. | (a) | 14. | (a) | 24. | (c) | 34. | (a) | 44. | (d) |
| 5. | (a) | 15. | (d) | 25. | (b) | 35. | (b) | 45. | (d) |
| 6. | (c) | 16. | (c) | 26. | (b) | 36. | (d) | 46. | (d) |
| 7. | (c) | 17. | (b) | 27. | (a) | 37. | (c) | 47. | (d) |
| 8. | (b) | 18. | (a) | 28. | (a) | 38. | (a) | 48. | (d) |
| 9. | (d) | 19. | (a) | 29. | (c) | 39. | (a) | 49. | (b) |
| 10. | (c) | 20. | (c) | 30. | (c) | 40. | (c) | 50. | (d) |

### PHYSICS

1. **(d)** Electromagnet is not a source of electric current.

3. **(d)** Tsunami occur in sea and lightning in air.

4. **(a)** High frequency means high pitch and low frequency means low pitch.

6. **(c)** When we say sound travels it is actually the disturbance that travels in the medium.

8. **(b)** As sliding friction opposes motion on road.

9. **(d)** Electroplating waste cannot be disposed off easily without proper guidelines.

10. **(c)** If two mirrors are held perpendicular to each other then angle of reflection from second mirror = 90° − angle of incidence on the first mirror.

11. **(a)** $V = f \times \lambda$

   wavelength, $\lambda = \dfrac{v}{f} = \dfrac{320}{640} = 0.5\text{m}$

12. **(c)** Staying indoors away from metallic doors or windows.

13. **(d)** By electrostatic induction.

14. **(a)** Distilled water is a bad conductor of electricity.

15. **(d)** The angle of deviation is the angle between original path of the incident ray (the path it would have followed without any obstruction) and the reflected ray. In this case it is $50° + 50° = 100°$

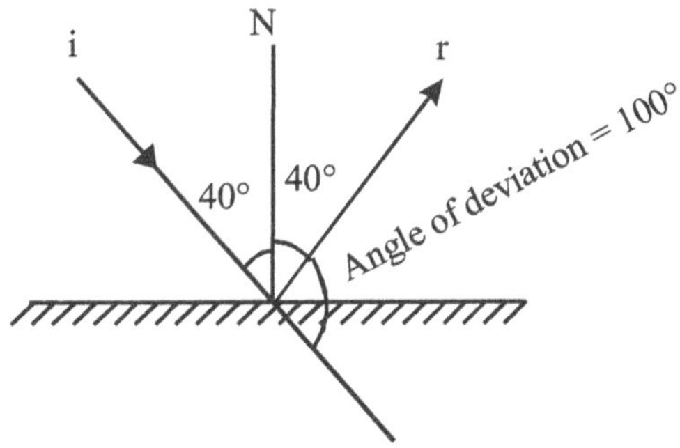


16. **(c)** Unbalanced force produces accelaration in a body.

**17. (b)** Object can be seen only when reflected light from the object reaches our eyes.

**18. (a)** Mass = Force/acceleration

$$=\frac{1}{9.8}=0.102\text{kg}$$
$$=102\text{g}$$

**19. (a)** When an axle rotates in a sleeve, the friction involved in the process is sliding friction.

### CHEMISTRY

**20. (c)** Tin (Sn); (It lies above copper in activity series).

**21. (b)** Butane can be easily compressed and liquified to be filled into cylinders.

**22. (d)** Synthetic fibres catch fire easily. Also they melt on heating and stick to the body of the person wearing it thus it is not advisable to wear synthetic clothes while working in a kitchen or bursting fire crackers.

**23. (d)** Kerosene is a fossil fuel since it is obtained from petroleum.

**24. (c)** Blackening of copper vessel from outside is due to improper combustion of fuel.

**26. (b)** More reactive metals can displace less reactive metals from their salt solutions and Fe is more reactive than Cu thus it displaces Cu from $CuSO_4$.

**27. (a)** X is coal and Y is coke.

**28. (a)** When the fuel burns rapidly and produces heat and light then the combustion is known as rapid combustion e.g., LPG.

The type of combustion in which a material suddenly bursts into flames, without the application of any apparent cause is called spontaneous combustion e.g., phosphorus burns in air at room temperature.

A combustion in which large amount of heat, light and sound is produced is known as explosion.

$NaHCO_3$ produces $CO_2$ near the fire.

$$2NaHCO_3 \longrightarrow Na_2CO_3 + CO_2 + H_2O$$

This $CO_2$ being heavier than oxygen, covers the fire like a blanket. Since the contact between oxygen and fire is cut off, the fire is controlled. Thus $NaHCO_3$ is used in fire extinguisher.

**29. (c)** In the fractional distillation of crude petroleum fractions with high boiling point condenses at the bottom of the column whereas fractions with low boiling point condenses at the top of the column.

**30. (c)** An alternative for expensive plastic recycling is developing of biodegradable plastics.

**31. (d)** Copper reacts with moist air to form a mixture of copper hydroxide and copper carbonate which is dull green in colour.

$$2Cu + \underbrace{H_2O + CO_2 + O_2}_{\text{Moist air}} \longrightarrow$$

$$\underbrace{Cu(OH)_2 + CuCO_3}_{\text{Greenish layer}}$$

## BIOLOGY

**32. (d)** Organic farming is a farming system in which organic manures, biofertilizers, biopesticides etc. are used with minimal or no use of chemical fertilizers, pesticides etc. By organic farming healthy plants can be grown while enhancing the sustainability and health of soil. This farming system is more ecofriendly and less expensive than the agriculture system using chemicals.

**34. (a)** The correct sequence of steps to develop a new plant variety is –

(i) Development of gene variation → (ii) selection → (iii) Evaluation → (iv) multiplication of improved seeds → (v) Distribution of improved seeds.

**37. (c)** Drying is a common method of food preservation but it is not implied in seafood industry. It is so because drying destroys taste, texture and aroma of sea food. Salting and freezing are commonly used for preservation of sea food.

**38. (a)** The cell walls of bacteria are rigid, porous, box like structures which provide physical protection to the cell. The rigid, covalently linked framework surrounding the bacterial cell is actually one large molecule, a complex polysaccharide-peptide called a peptidoglycan.

**39. (a)** White blood cells are the battling blood cells. Whenever a germ or infection enters the body, their number increases significantly to fight the infectious agents. Some infectious agents destruct the RBC, leading to anaemia.

**41. (b)** The picture given in the question is of tiger. Forest is a natural habitat of such animals. They depend upon forests, both for food and shelter. Food chains operating in forest ecosystem ensure the flow of energy and matter from producers to consumers. If forests will be cleared then the food chain will get disturbed. The number of herbivores will decline in the absence of vegetation which will eventually affect the number of carnivores like tigers, who depend upon herbivores for their food requirements.

Moreover, tigers hide themselves behind trees and thick bushes for protection and for hunting prey.

**42. (c)** When the number of a given species declines due to habitat change, then the species is categorized as vulnerable. Endangered species draws the attention for protection. Critically endangered species includes those animals whose number has gone down to initially low levels. Extinct means no existance at present on the earth.

**43. (d)**

| Organelle | Function | Presence |
|---|---|---|
| Ribosome | Site of protein synthesis | Plant & animal cells |
| Mitochondria | Site of respiration | Plant & animal cells |
| Chloroplast | Site of photosynthesis | Plant cell |

**44. (d)** Nucleus contains genetic material enclosed by nuclear envelope. Nucleolus is a part of the nucleus. It is the site of ribosomal RNAs (rRNA) synthesis. The genetic material is also found in mitochondria and chloroplasts.

**45. (d)** Some women are unable to have babies because their fallopian tubes are blocked. This prevents the ova being fertilized as the male gamete from the father cannot come in contact with female gamete of mother. This problem can be overcome through test tube baby technology. In this technique, freshly matured ova collected from a woman's ovaries by using a special syringe and semen from the man are kept in an incubator (*in vitro*). The sperms fertilize the ova to form an embryo. After a week, the embryo thus formed is then inserted into the woman's womb where the embryo gets implanted and develops into a baby in about nine months. The baby thus produced is called test tube baby. This technique was first successfully introduced in humans in 1978 and is called *in vitro* fertilization (IVF).

**46. (d)** In cockroaches, after fertilization eggs become surrounded by the secretions of collaterial glands, which harden to form an egg case or ootheca. 16 eggs are arranged in two rows in one ootheca. The 16 nymphs come out from an ootheca.

**47. (d)** Moulting is the process of periodic shedding of outermost dead skin layer. In insects like silkworm, cockroach etc., moulting is essential for their growth. Moulting is also observed in snakes. In birds and mammals seasonal loss of hair, fur and feather is also known as moulting.

**48. (d)** Global warming phenomenon occurs due to greenhouse effect. Global warming causes an increase in the sea level by melting of ice at mountain peaks. It will result in changes in weather and precipitation patterns leading to decrease in food production by plants.

**49. (b)** Mostly air pollution takes place due to burning of fossil fuels. By the use of renewable energy and catalytic converters in the vehicles, air pollution can be reduced.

**50. (d)** Air pollution affects our atmosphere surrounding the earth. It causes weather change, decreases the rate of photosynthesis, creates the problem of respiratory tract. The cause of air pollution is the burning of fossil fuels.

## MOCK TEST-4

### ANSWER KEY

| | | | | | | | | | |
|---|---|---|---|---|---|---|---|---|---|
| 1 | (a) | 11 | (c) | 21 | (c) | 31 | (a) | 41 | (b) |
| 2 | (c) | 12 | (c) | 22 | (b) | 32 | (b) | 42 | (a) |
| 3 | (d) | 13 | (a) | 23 | (b) | 33 | (d) | 43 | (d) |
| 4 | (b) | 14 | (a) | 24 | (c) | 34 | (a) | 44 | (b) |
| 5 | (a) | 15 | (c) | 25 | (b) | 35 | (c) | 45 | (b) |
| 6 | (a) | 16 | (b) | 26 | (d) | 36 | (a) | 46 | (a) |
| 7 | (c) | 17 | (a) | 27 | (b) | 37 | (b) | 47 | (d) |
| 8 | (d) | 18 | (a) | 28 | (c) | 38 | (a) | 48 | (b) |
| 9 | (a) | 19 | (b) | 29 | (d) | 39 | (b) | 49 | (a) |
| 10 | (c) | 20 | (b) | 30 | (a) | 40 | (a) | 50 | (d) |

## PHYSICS

1. **(a)** Friction is the opposing force due to which a body comes to rest.

2. **(c)** Pressure will become 4 times i.e.,

$$\text{Pressure} = \frac{\text{Force}}{\text{Area}}$$

4. **(b)** Amber when rubbed with wool transfer of charge takes place and spark is produced.

5. **(a)** Spillting of white light into seven colours is called dispersion.

6. **(a)** We can see only that part of the moon which reflects light towards us.

7. **(c)** Sound wave is an longitudinal wave having compression and rarefaction.

8. **(d)** Pressure in a liquid increases with depth.

9. **(a)** We move faster on roller-skates than on shoes as they have rollers which reduces friction.

10. **(c)** Force is necessary to change the shape, size state of rest or motion of a body.

11. **(c)** The sound could not be heard anymore

12. **(c)** Force of friction is independent of area of contact.

13. **(a)** B and C are at same height so pressure at both points will be same.

14. **(a)** A → R, B → P, C → S; D → Q

15. **(c)** When a body is stationary then net force acting on it is zero.

16. **(b)** Oil decreases the friction.

17. **(a)** Tsunami and Landslide occur on land which may happen because of earthquake.

18. **(a)** The force of friction between two bodies is parallel to the contact surfaces.

19. **(b)** $\text{mass} = \dfrac{\text{force}}{\text{acceleration}} = \dfrac{5 \times 10^5}{980} \simeq 500\,\text{g}$

## CHEMISTRY

**20. (b)** (i) - (q), (ii) - (r), (iii) - (t), (iv) - (p)

**21. (c)** The process of eating away of metals layer by layer due to formation of metal compound on surface is called corrosion.

**22. (b)** Due to non-availability of oxygen, charcoal stops burning.

**23. (b)** Polytetrafluoroethene is resistant to heat and other chemicals and does not stick to water and oil hence it is used to coat non-stick pans.

**24. (c)** Yellowing and blackening of Taj Mahal at Agra is due to $SO_2$ and other pollutants released by Mathura refinery.

**25. (b)** Spontaneous combustion takes place without any external source of heat.

**26. (d)** Coke is an almost pure form of the carbon.

**27. (b)** Outermost zone of candle flame is non-luminous it is poorly visible and is slightly blue. It is the hottest part of the flame.

**28. (c)** The fibres which we get from natural resources are called natural fibres like, cellulose, jute, cotton etc. Platics are produced by human these are not obtained from nature thus, their sources are artificial e.g. thermoplastics, thermosettings etc.

Polythene is an example of thermoplastic.

**29. (d)** All the given statements are correct.

**30. (a)** Coal tar has highest boiling point and petrol has lowest boiling point.

**31. (a)** Rusting of iron takes place only in presence of oxygen and waters vapour. In fig. C rusting is not possible. In fig. B, boiling water has no oxygen.

## BIOLOGY

**32. (b)** Sulphur dioxide and nitrogen dioxide are the pollutants which are causes marble cancer. These pollutants are emitted from various industries. They react with water vapour present in the atmosphere and produce compounds like sulphuric acid and nitric acid. Such acids when come down on earth surface alongwith rain, they make the rain acidic. Acid rain corrodes marble and affects the beauty of various monuments made of marble.

**33. (d)** Many plants, such as garlic, undergo a type of asexual reproduction known as fragmentation, in which parts of the parent plant break off and form mature plants.

**35. (c)** At menopause, no estrogen is secreted by the ovaries and thus no new follicles and hence no ovulation occurs, therefore, menstruation stops.

**36. (a)** *Amoeba* reproduces by binary fission creating daughter cells which are smaller than parent cells. Budding takes place in yeast, the buds are smaller than the parent yeast.

**37. (b)** Gestation does not follow if the egg is not fertilized. Gestation is the period between fertilization and the birth of the baby.

**38. (a)** Organelles are components present in the cytoplasm of a cell. Protoplasm is the living substance in the cell. Chlorophyll is present in the green part of the plant which is essential for the precess of photosynthesis.

Tissues are the group of cells having same structure and function. Organs are the structures which carry out a specific function. Vacuoles are found in the cytoplasm showing empty structure.

**39. (b)** The correct sequence of the steps for the preparation of a temporary mount of human cheek cells are as follows –

(i) Rinsing the mouth with fresh water and disinfectant solution.

(ii) Taking scraping from inner side of the cheek and spreading it on a clean slide.

(iii) Adding two or three drops of methylene blue.

(iv) Putting a drop of glycerene on the material.

**40. (a)** Lysosomes → Intracellular digestion

Mitochondria → Intracellular respiration

Microtubules → Intracellular movement

Golgi complex → cell secretion

**41. (b)** Dodo is an extinct species. It was flightless bird endemic to Indian Ocean island of Mauritius. Dodo got extinct in 17th century. Its flightlessness made it easy for humans to kill it, moreover, introduction of exotic species of animals including dogs, pigs, cats, rats, etc. by humans into the island became the reason of its extinction.

**42. (a)** Chipko-movement originated in 1970s in a small hilly village of the upper reaches of Himalayas. Tribal people of Tehri-Garhwal district of Uttarakhand realized the importance of forest. Under the leadership of Shri Sunderlal Bahuguna this movement spread to all nearby areas. The five Fs which forests give us are food, fodder, fuel, fibre and fertilizer trees.

**43. (d)** Among the given options, dinosaur, dodo, passenger pigeon and white tailed mongoose all are extinct animals.

**44. (b)** Ram found many similar plants in the forest because they are of same species and capable of interbreeding which lead to increase in their number at that particular area.

**45. (b)** Ammonification is the process of formation of ammonia. Nitrification involves production of nitrites $(NO_2^-)$ and nitrates $(NO_3^-)$. Nitrites are formed first which may be converted to nitrates.

**46. (a)** *Rhizopus* - bread mould, *Saprolegnia* - water moulds, *Puccinia* - Rust fungi, *Peziza* - Cup fungi, *Penicillium* - Blue or green moulds.

**47. (d)** Hoe (P), is a simple tool which is used for removing weeds and for loosening the soil. It consists of long rod made up of wood or iron. A strong, broad and bent plate of iron is fixed to one of its ends which works like a blade. Cultivator (Q), is attached to a tractor. Such tractor-driven cultivators save labour and time. Seed drill (R) is a modern tool, used for sowing with the help of tractors. This tool sows seed in a uniform manner at proper distances and depths. It also ensures that seeds get covered with soil after sowing. Manually, cutting of crops (harvesting) is done by sickle (S). It is a curved, sharp knife with a wooden handle.

**50. (d)** The correct sequence is as follows – maturation of egg $\rightarrow$ release of egg $\rightarrow$ fertilization of egg $\rightarrow$ embedding of embryo in thickened uterine wall.

## MOCK TEST-5

### ANSWER KEY

| 1 | (b) | 11 | (c) | 21 | (d) | 31 | (a) | 41 | (b) |
|---|-----|----|-----|----|-----|----|-----|----|-----|
| 2 | (d) | 12 | (a) | 22 | (c) | 32 | (a) | 42 | (b) |
| 3 | (d) | 13 | (c) | 23 | (a) | 33 | (c) | 43 | (b) |
| 4 | (d) | 14 | (a) | 24 | (b) | 34 | (a) | 44 | (c) |
| 5 | (c) | 15 | (c) | 25 | (c) | 35 | (c) | 45 | (b) |
| 6 | (d) | 16 | (d) | 26 | (a) | 36 | (b) | 46 | (b) |
| 7 | (c) | 17 | (c) | 27 | (c) | 37 | (c) | 47 | (b) |
| 8 | (c) | 18 | (c) | 28 | (b) | 38 | (d) | 48 | (b) |
| 9 | (c) | 19 | (d) | 29 | (b) | 39 | (c) | 49 | (d) |
| 10 | (a) | 20 | (a) | 30 | (d) | 40 | (d) | 50 | (d) |

## PHYSICS

1. **(b)** If the final rays are converging we have a real image

5. **(c)** short wave, long wave

6. **(d)** Plane mirror forms virtual and erect images.

7. **(c)** Constellation is a group of stars e.g. ursa major, ursa minor.

8. **(c)** Talcum powder decreases friction and rest increases friction.

9. **(c)** Muddy surface and brick surface have high friction coefficient.

10. **(a)** To hear a distinct echo, the minimum distance of a reflecting surface should be 17 meters.

11. **(c)** A coin stops because of frictional force which acts in opposite direction.

12. **(a)** Force = mass × acceleration

14. **(a)** Frictional force will be equal to the applied force and in opposite directions.

15. **(c)** Here,

$$a = \frac{v - u}{t}$$

$$a = \frac{5 - 0}{2}$$

$$a = 2.5 \text{ m/s}^2$$

Now, F = m × a

F = 60 × 2.5

F = 150 N

16. **(d)** Air also have friction which resists motion.

18. **(c)** Impure metal.

19. **(d)** Speed greater than speed of sound is called supersonic speed.

## CHEMISTRY

**20. (a)** Rayon is used for making automobile tyre cords.

Nylon also used for making tyre cords.

**21. (d)** Fossil fuels are obtained from dead remains of living organisms.

**22. (c)** Sodium and Potassium being very reactive are stored in kerosene.

**23. (a)** As it is clear from the experiment that wire $a$ can tolerate maximum weight that means wire $a$ is strongest thus $a$ is nylon because it is strongest fibre even stronger than steel wire. Wool is stronger than cotton thus $b$ is wool and cotton can tolerate minimum weight thus $c$ is cotton.

**24. (b)** Al and Zn react with sodium hydroxide to evolve hydrogen.
$$2Al(s) + 2NaOH(aq) + 2H_2O(l)$$
$$\rightarrow 2NaAlO_2(aq) + 3H_2(g)$$
$$Zn(s) + 2NaOH(aq) + 2H_2O(l) \rightarrow$$
$$Na_2Zn(OH)_4(aq) + H_2(g)$$

**25. (c)** The substance that have very low ignition temperature and can easily catch fire with a flame is called inflammable substances.

**26. (a)** O, H, N and S are present in small amounts in coal along with carbon.

**27. (c)** Coal is made up of carbon which is a non-metal and is brittle.

**28. (b)** A - (r), B - (s), C - (p), D - (q)

**29. (b)** Water increases the ignition temperature of an object.

**30. (d)** Copper is less reactive than sodium, hence, no reaction will take place. Aluminium is less reactive than magnesium, hence, no reaction takes place. Silver is less reactive than iron, hence, no reaction takes place. Only in (d), copper is more reactive than silver, hence, displacement reaction takes place.

**31. (a)** Natural gas can be easily transported through pipes.

## BIOLOGY

**32. (a)** Net primary productivity (NPP) measures the amount of matter produced that is available for heterotrophs.

**33. (c)** The leguminous and non-leguminous crops are grown alternately in the same field for fulfilling the need of nutrients. This type of agricultural method is essential to maintain the fertility of soil.

**34. (a)** *Rhizobium* — Nitrogen fixation

Organic manure — Animal excreta, cow dung and plant wastes

Threshing — Separation of grain from chaff

Seed drill — Sowing of seeds

Leguminous plants —Root nodules

**35. (c)** In ruminants like cow, cellulose constitutes a major part of their food as they chew raw vegetables and other plant products. The bacteria present in their stomach secrete certain enzymes which help in the digestion of cellulose. Digestion of starch starts in mouth where it is acted upon by an enzyme called salivary amylase present in saliva.

Influenza, commonly referred to as flu is caused by an RNA virus called influenza A virus. Wax and honey are two different products obtained from bees. Wax is formed by worker bees from eight wax-producing abdominal glands whereas, they make honey from nectar of flowers by the process of regurgitation. They collect and swallow nectar of flowers. It mixes with the proteins and chemicals present in the stomach of bees and gets converted into honey. The bees take it out and store in beehives.

Black Minorca is a breed of chicken which originated in Spain.

**36. (b)** Unicellular algae — *Chlamydomonas*

Filamentous algae — *Spirogyra*

Colonial algae — *Volvox*

Multicellular algae — *Sargassum*.

**38. (d)** Bharatpur National Park, also known as Keoladeo Ghana National Park is situated in Rajasthan.

**39. (c)** World forest day is celebrated on $21^{st}$ March to spread the awareness among people about the importance of forest.

**40. (d)** Marbled cat is a small wild cat of south and south-east Asia. Since 2002, it has been listed as vulnerable by IUCN (International Union of Conservation of Nature and National Resources). Asiatic lion is one of the 5 major big cats found in India. The only place in the wild where this species is found is Gir forest of Gujarat, India. Indian elephant is native to mainland Asia. Since 1986, it has been listed as endangered by IUCN. Bengal fox (also known as the Indian fox), is endemic to Indian subcontinent and is found from the Himalayan foothills through Southern India and from southern and Eastern

Pakistan to Eastern India. Indian rhinoceros is also called Asian one-horned rhinoceros and is found in parts of North-Eastern India and on protected areas in Jarai of Nepal. Asian wild ass also called Khur is native of Southern Asia. From 1958-1960, wild ass became victim of disease known as surra, which caused a dramatic decline in its population in India.

41. **(b)** Endoplasmic — Transport of
Reticulum     substances
Golgi complex — Secretion of
              chemicals
Mitochondria — Powerhouse
              of cells
Vacuole     — Storage
              organelle.

42. **(b)** Diffusion involves movement of molecules from their higher concentration to their lower concentration. Osmosis is a special case of diffusion in which selectively permeable membrane is involved. Unicellular freshwater organisms and most plants tend to gain water through osmosis. Osmosis can be of two types endosmosis (water moves into cell) and exosmosis (water moves out of the cell). Endosmosis occurs when a cell is placed in hypotonic solution and exosmosis occurs when a cell is placed in a hypertonic solution.

43. **(b)** In the given figure, mitochondria are highest in number. Among P, Q, R and S, P is a microvilus (*plural-*microvilli) which serves as an extension of cell membrane and increases the cell surface area. Q is nucleus that contains DNA which is the carrier of herditary information. S is vacuole and R is mitochondrion which breaks down glucose and provides energy.

45. **(b)** Edward Jenner, also known as father of immunology prepared the small pox vaccine. Chromosomes are related with heredity because they carry the genetic characters from one generation to the next. Hydra reproduces by the budding method.

46. **(b)** (1) The pituitary gland is located at the base of the brain, it is called the 'master gland' because it produces hormones that control several other endocrine glands.

(2) Thyroid gland secretes thyroxine hormone.

(3) Adrenal glands are found as a pair, one on top of each kidney.

(4) Pancreas secretes **insulin** which regulates sugar level in blood.

(5) Testes secrete male hormone – **testosterone**.

**47. (b)** Methane ($CH_4$), carbon dioxide ($CO_2$), chlorofluoro-carbon (CFC) and nitrogen oxide ($N_2O$) are some greenhouse gases. Among them, percentage greenhouse effect of $CO_2$ is highest (about 60%). Effect of $N_2O$ is 6%, of CFCs is about 14% and of $CH_4$ is about 20%. Thus, in the given figure X is $CO_2$, Y is $N_2O$, Z is CFCs and W is $CH_4$.

**48. (b)** Particulate matter — Air pollutants
Oil spills — Physical water pollutants
Detergents — Chemical water pollutants
Plastics — Non degradable soil pollutants
Domestic wastes —
Degradable soil pollutants.

**49. (d)** The first menstrual flow is called menarche while at the age of 45-50 years the menstrual cycle stops, this stoppage of menstruation, that is called menopause. The reproductive age of human female is in between menarche to menopause while in human male reproductive age starts from puberty to death.

**50. (d)** During puberty, hormones bring about changes in the body of girls. Girls start ovulation and development of secondary sexual characters take place e.g., enlargement of breast, broadening of hips, hair growth in pubic and armpit regions etc.

# GENERAL KNOWLEDGE

## MOCK TEST-1

### ANSWER KEY

| 1 | (d) | 6 | (b) | 11 | (d) | 16 | (a) | 21 | (a) |
|---|-----|---|-----|----|-----|----|-----|----|-----|
| 2 | (c) | 7 | (c) | 12 | (a) | 17 | (c) | 22 | (c) |
| 3 | (b) | 8 | (b) | 13 | (d) | 18 | (b) | 23 | (c) |
| 4 | (d) | 9 | (c) | 14 | (b) | 19 | (a) | 24 | (a) |
| 5 | (c) | 10 | (c) | 15 | (b) | 20 | (b) | 25 | (b) |

1. **(d)** Sutta Pitaka deals with philosophy and psychology and lays down methods for training the mind.

   Abhidhamma Pitaka is the third and latest of the Pali canonical texts recognized in the early Buddhist Theravada tradition.

   Its compilation is dated to the third Buddhist Council, held during the reign of the Mauryan emperor Asoka, that is,. third century BC.

8. **(b)** Nasik Conspiracy Case

10. **(c)** Rock Edict XII

11. **(d)** 31st Constitutional Amendment Act, 1973

16. **(a)** Full form of 4G is 4th Generation.

This term is used in telecommunication.

17. **(c)** National Highway 223

18. **(b)** Geeta Phogat won gold medal in wrestling at the Common Wealth Games in 2010.

19. **(a)** The Chishti Order is a Sufi order which arose from Chisht, a small town near Herat, in western Afghanistan. It was founded by Abu Ishaq Shami in about 930 CE. Before returning to western Asia, he trained and deputed the son of local emir, Abu Ahmad Abdal, under whose leadership, the Chishtiyya flourished as a regional mystical order. Moinuddin Chishti is credited with laying its foundations in

India. Other famous saints of the Chishti Order are Qutbuddin Bakhtiar Kaki, Fariduddin Ganjshakar, Nizamuddin Auliya and Alauddin Ali Ahmed Sabir Kalyari.

**20. (b)** 24th April

**21. (a)** Yisrael Kristal, 113-year old, the world's oldest man who lived through both World Wars, passed away in Haifa, Israel on August 11, 2017.

**22. (c)** Blood Moon. It lasted for 1 hour and 42 minutes and 57 seconds. It was considered as the 21st century's longest lunar eclipse. The longest total lunar eclipse of the last century happened on 16 July 2000, lasting nearly four minutes longer, at 1 hour and 46.4 minutes. The next such phenomenon can be witnessed on June 9, 2123 according to a National Geographic report.

**23. (c)** The Bhadra Wildlife Sanctuary (BWS) is a protected area and a Project Tiger, tiger reserve located 38 km northwest of Chikkamagaluru town in Karnataka.

**24. (a)** The Punjab government has recently launched its flagship 'Apni Gaddi Apna Rozgar' scheme for jobless youth.

**25. (b)** Two Indians, Bharat Vatwani and Sonam Wangchuk are named among the six winners of the prestigious Ramon Magsaysay Award for the year 2018. The Ramon Magsaysay Award Foundation stated in its citation that Vatwani is being recognised for his tremendous courage and healing compassion in embracing India's mentally-afflicted destitutes. Wangchuk has been recognised for his uniquely systematic, collaborative and community-driven reform of learning systems in remote northern India, improving the life opportunities of Ladakhi youth in Jammu and Kashmir. The others award winners are from Cambodia, East Timor, Philippines and Vietnam. The

Magsaysay Award winners will each receive a certificate, a medallion bearing the image of the late Filipino leader Ramon Magsaysay, and a cash prize. They will be conferred with the Magsaysay Award during a formal presentation ceremony at the Cultural Centre in the Philippines on August 31, 2018. The award is often referred to as the Asian version of the Nobel Prize.

## MOCK TEST-2

### ANSWER KEY

| 1 | (b) | 6 | (c) | 11 | (c) | 16 | (c) | 21 | (d) |
|---|-----|---|-----|----|-----|----|-----|----|-----|
| 2 | (c) | 7 | (c) | 12 | (a) | 17 | (b) | 22 | (a) |
| 3 | (b) | 8 | (c) | 13 | (c) | 18 | (c) | 23 | (b) |
| 4 | (b) | 9 | (b) | 14 | (b) | 19 | (a) | 24 | (c) |
| 5 | (d) | 10 | (a) | 15 | (a) | 20 | (c) | 25 | (a) |

1. **(b)** The Andes of South America

3. **(b)** Breadfruit is rich in starch and is eaten baked or boiled.

5. **(d)** All the animals are endemic to Pachmarhi Biosphere Reserve.

6. **(c)** Robert Hooke in 1665 observed the cell in a thin slice of cork and coined the term 'cell'.

8. **(c)** The telecommunication satellite INSAT-2E was launched from Kourou.

9. **(b)** Swami Vivekananda founded the Ramkrishna Mission.

11. **(c)** The name of the earth has been derived from Germanic.

12. **(a)** The Madhya Pradesh government will observed the 2018 Independence Day eve as Shahid Samman Divas to honour martyrs. The decision to this effect was taken at a cabinet meeting in Bhopal on July 30, 2018. According to official information, it will be a comprehensive program and spread across all the villages, blocks and districts of Madhya Pradesh, where rallies were organized to mark the day. The martyrs were paid homage and the relatives of the martyrs will also be honoured on the day. Ministers, members of Parliament and state legislative assembly and chief Minister himself will meet family members of martyrs on the occasion to express gratitude for supreme sacrifice done by their near and dear for the nation.

14. **(b)** Rukmini Devi is a Bharatanatyam dancer.

16. **(c)** Indian space agency ISRO is set to open a 100 acre space park in Bengaluru where

private industry players will be setting up facilities for making subsystems and components for satellites. This is going to be the country's first park.

**19. (a)** Homi J. Bhabha is called the "Father of Indian nuclear power' and was the founding director of the Tata Institute of Fundamental Research.

**20. (c)** The generally accepted period of Indus Valley Civilization is 2300-1750 B.C.

**21. (d)** Milk contains lactose, hence should not be consumed in case of lactose intolerance.

**22. (a)** The voice of the bird 'Red' in the movie 'Angry Birds' is given by Jason Sudeikis.

**23. (b)** Indian junior judokas won a gold and three bronze medals in the 2017 Commonwealth Youth Games being held in Nassau, Bahamas.

**24. (c)** Desert National Park (DNP) is located near Jaisalmer, Rajasthan and covers an area of 3162 km$^2$.

**25. (a)** On July 22, the official mascots for the Tokyo 2020 Olympic and Paralympic Games have been unveiled during a ceremony in the Japanese capital Tokyo. The Olympic mascot "Miraitowa" is a blue-checked pointy-eared figure, which fuses the Japanese words 'mirai', which means future, and 'towa', which means eternity. Its Paralympic counterpart "Someity" is derived from a type of cherry blossom 'Somei-yoshino'. It is represented as a pink-checked and wears a cape and is sounds similar to English phrase "So mighty". The Tokyo Olympics are schedule to run from July 24 to August 9, 2020. The Paralympics will take place between August 25 and September 6.

## MOCK TEST-3

| ANSWER KEY |||||||||
|---|---|---|---|---|---|---|---|---|---|
| 1 | (b) | 6 | (d) | 11 | (c) | 16 | (a) | 21 | (c) |
| 2 | (a) | 7 | (a) | 12 | (a) | 17 | (a) | 22 | (b) |
| 3 | (d) | 8 | (c) | 13 | (b) | 18 | (d) | 23 | (c) |
| 4 | (a) | 9 | (d) | 14 | (b) | 19 | (b) | 24 | (c) |
| 5 | (d) | 10 | (d) | 15 | (d) | 20 | (a) | 25 | (b) |

1. **(b)** Orangutan lives in the forest of Sumatra and Borneo in Southeast Asia.

4. **(a)** During digestion, the food undergoes many chemical reactions and changes into new products.

5. **(d)** Carbon dioxide and methane is released from permafrost after its melting.

6. **(d)** Shri Devendra Jhajharia, Paralympics double gold medallist is releated to Javelin.

12. **(a)** Ernest Hemingway has written the novel 'The Old Man and the Sea'.

14. **(b)** Dr. B.R. Ambedkar belonged to a Marathi-speaking dalit family. A lawyer and economist, he is best known as the Father of the Indian Constitution. Both Prime Minister Nehru and Deputy Prime Minister Vallabhbhai Patel were against the creation of linguistic states. Potti Siriamulu, was the Gandhian leader who died fasting for a separate state for Telugu. Speakers Krishna Menon led the Indian delegation to the UN between 1952 along with Nehru.

15. **(d)** Gopalkrishna Gandhi, the former West Bengal governor, has been selected for 2018 Rajiv Gandhi Sadbhavana Award for his outstanding contribution towards the promotion of communal harmony, peace and goodwill. The award was presented to him at a special ceremony on held at Jawahar Bhawan. The award, which carries a citation and cash amount of Rs 10 lakh, is given on the occasion of the birthday

of former prime minister Rajiv Gandhi. It was instituted to commemorate the lasting contribution made by him to promote peace, communal harmony and fight against violence.

**17. (a)** George Campos is a famous Mexican football player who is known for playing risky shots.

**18. (d)** The 102$^{nd}$ session of Indian National Congress was held at Mumbai University. The theme was "Science and Technology for Human Development".

**20. (a)** Apsara is the first nuclear research reactor not only in India but also in the whole of Asia.

**21. (c)** Mangalyaan is called 'The Super Smart Spacecraft'. It was launched on 5 November 2013.

**22. (b)** The term "debited" is used in bank statement when money is withdrawn from the account.

**23. (c)** Robert Millikan

**24. (c)** The Murlen National Park is located at Champhai district in Mizoram and cover an area of 200 square kilometers.

**25. (b)** Kuchipudi

## MOCK TEST-4

### ANSWER KEY

| 1 | (c) | 9 | (b) | 17 | (c) | 25 | (c) | 33 | (c) |
|---|-----|----|-----|----|-----|----|-----|----|-----|
| 2 | (d) | 10 | (a) | 18 | (c) | 26 | (b) | 34 | (a) |
| 3 | (c) | 11 | (b) | 19 | (c) | 27 | (c) | 35 | (b) |
| 4 | (b) | 12 | (c) | 20 | (d) | 28 | (a) | 36 | (c) |
| 5 | (a) | 13 | (d) | 21 | (a) | 29 | (c) | 37 | (b) |
| 6 | (a) | 14 | (c) | 22 | (b) | 30 | (a) | 38 | (b) |
| 7 | (b) | 15 | (a) | 23 | (a) | 31 | (c) | 39 | (d) |
| 8 | (c) | 16 | (b) | 24 | (d) | 32 | (b) | 40 | (a) |

1. **(c)** reduce high blood pressure

4. **(b)** Graphite which is crystalline form of carbon and iodine are the only two non-metals that have shining lustrous surfaces.

10. **(a)** Pulmonary artery

12. **(c)** The Government of Odisha has launched a 360 degree nation-wide publicity campaign "Heartbeats for Hockey" to attract fans for 2018 men's hockey World Cup. The movement attempts to get India behind the game by way of music, entertainment, fashion, pure sport and panel discussions. Each time, anyone holds the custom-made hockey stick, named 'Heart Beat', their heart beat will be recorded as a pledge to support hockey

14. **(c)** In 1976, the Congress Party set up the Sardar Swaran Singh Committee to make recommendations about fundamental duties.

15. **(a)** Jupiter has 63 moons and Saturn has 61 moons.

20. **(d)** Pulitzer Prize was established in 1917

21. **(a)** Eminent Konkani writer Mahabaleshwar Sail has been honoured with the Saraswati Samman 2016 for his novel Hawthan

23. **(a)** The museum for all former Prime Ministers of India will be constructed in the Teen Murti Bhavan complex that houses the Nehru Memorial Museum

and Library (NMML) in New Delhi. The decision was taken at the 43rd annual general meeting of the NMML chaired by Union Home Minister Rajnath Singh on July 26, 2018. The Teen Murti Bhavan complex is spread over 25 acres and the present museum for Jawaharlal Nehru occupied half an acre. The new museum would be constructed at a cost of Rs 270 crore and will be separate from the existing structure of the Nehru Memorial.

**24. (d)** Lithosphere is the domain which provides us land, settlements, grassland and mineral wealth.

**26. (b)** The World Youth Skills Day (WYSD) is observed every year on July 15 to call for increased prospects for youth to gain access to quality training and skills development. The purpose of the day is to spread awareness on the importance of youth developing skill development. The theme of 2018 is "Improving the image

of TVET (Technical & Vocational Education and Training)".

**29. (c)** Mohenjodero was located on banks of river Indus. Harappa on Ravi. Chanhudaro is in Pakistan now. Lothal was on mouth of Gulf of Cambay.

**35. (b)** This desert is blocked from moisture on both sides by the Andes mountains and by the Chilean Coast Range. A coastal inversion layer created by the cold Humboldt Current and the anticyclone of the Pacific is essential to keep the climate of the Atacama dry. Some parts of this desert have never received any rain.

**36. (c)** The National Gandhi Museum is located in New Delhi which showcases the life and principles of Mahatma Gandhi.

**37. (b)** Liu Xiaobo, the Chinese Nobel Peace Prize laureate and democracy campaigner, has died of multiple organ failure while under guard at a hospital in Shenyang, China on July 13, 2017.

**38. (b)** The book "Narendra Modi: The Making of a Legend" has been written by Bindeshwar Pathak, the Sulabh International founder and a Padma Bhushan recipient.

**39. (d)** Lilly Singh, an Indian-origin Canadian YouTube star, was the new UNICEF's Global Goodwill Ambassador at a special event in New Delhi.

**40. (a)** International UN Peacekeeper's Day is celebrated world over on 29 May to honour the fallen peacekeepers and to pay tribute to those who served or are still serving in UN peacekeeping missions.

The theme for the 2017 International Day of UN Peacekeepers is "Investing in Peace Around the World".

# MOCK TEST-5

| | | | | | | | | | |
|---|---|---|---|---|---|---|---|---|---|
| **ANSWERS KEY** | | | | | | | | | |
| 1 | (b) | 9 | (b) | 17 | (d) | 25 | (c) | 33 | (b) |
| 2 | (b) | 10 | (b) | 18 | (a) | 26 | (b) | 34 | (c) |
| 3 | (b) | 11 | (b) | 19 | (c) | 27 | (c) | 35 | (b) |
| 4 | (d) | 12 | (d) | 20 | (c) | 28 | (a) | 36 | (b) |
| 5 | (c) | 13 | (a) | 21 | (b) | 29 | (d) | 37 | (b) |
| 6 | (a) | 14 | (c) | 22 | (c) | 30 | (b) | 38 | (a) |
| 7 | (a) | 15 | (d) | 23 | (b) | 31 | (c) | 39 | (b) |
| 8 | (c) | 16 | (d) | 24 | (b) | 32 | (d) | 40 | (d) |

**2.** **(b)** The Bhitarkanika National Park (BNP) of Odisha has become the largest habitat of the endangered estuarine crocodiles in India with a record number of their nesting sites spotted in it. Recently, the enumerators have spotted 101 nests of crocodile in Kanika, Gahirmatha, Mahakalapada and Rajnagar wildlife forest range divisions under the park. As per the January 2018 crocodile census report, the water bodies of Bhitarkanika are home to 1,698 saltwater crocodiles. Estuarine crocodiles are also found in West Bengal's Sundarban areas having the country's largest mangrove cover. Besides, the mangrove wetlands in Andaman Islands are home to these species, but those cannot match the density and population of crocodile available in the wild habitats of Bhitarkanik National Park (BNP).

**6.** **(a)** Land provides us plants which fulfils over 95% of our requirement.

**8.** **(c)** Aditya-L1

**9.** **(b)** Venus is the brightest planet

**10.** **(b)** It involves setting down of heavier components of mixture.

**12.** **(d)** Judicial Review

**13.** **(a)** Fresco

**15.** **(d)** is the correct answer because the specific protease enzyme that is used to break down the organic molecule protein is called pepsin. (1) is not correct because lipids are broken down by lipases. (2) is not correct because carbohydrates are broken down by amylases. (3) is not correct because water is not chemically broken down in the stomach.

**16. (d)** Kapil Dev

**19. (c)** Uttar Pradesh Government has launched ganga Hariteema Yojana (also known as Ganga ... The scheme aims at enhancing green cover in catchment areas of river Ganga and control land erosion.

**21. (b)** The earth is inclined at 96½° with its orbital plane.

**22. (c)** Sri Lanka and Maldives are the non-neighbouring islands across the sea to South Africa. Whereas Andaman and Nicobar Islands are a part of India.

**24. (b)** Veld tropical grasslands are found in south Africa.

**27. (c)** West Bengal govt. has launched Rupashree Scheme to empower adolescent girls. Subsequently, girls will get Rs. 25,000 as one time assistance at the time of their marriage after attaining the age of 18 years. This scheme will benefit around 6 lakh girls across the state.The primary objective of this scheme is to help girls belonging to the economically weaker families and make them self-dependent

**28. (a)** [Goa]Under the system, fingerprints of the voters would be recorded by finger print reading machines along with their photographs by the web cameras fitted to computers.

**32. (d)** The 15th Asia Media Summit (AMS-2018) was held in New Delhi on May 10-12 with theme "Telling our Stories- Asia and More". The summit provided a unique opportunity for broadcasters in Asia to share their thoughts on broadcasting and information. It was organised by Asia-Pacific

Institute for Broadcasting Development (AIBD) in collaboration with its partners and international organisations

**37. (b)** The Grizzled Squirrel Wildlife Sanctuary (GSWS) is located in Virudhunagar and Madurai districts of Tamil Nadu.

**38. (a)** The Indian Space Research Organisation (ISRO) has successfully launched the navigation satellite IRNSS-1I into the orbit with the help of PSLV-C41 launch vehicle from the Satish Dhawan Space Centre (SDSC) at Sriharikota in Andhra Pradesh on April 12, 2018. IRNSS-1I is the 8th such satellite to be a part of the NavIC navigation satellite constellation. It is expected to replace IRNSS-1A, the first of the seven navigation satellites, which was rendered ineffective after its three rubidium atomic clocks failed

**39. (b)** In Uttar Pradesh, the iconic Mughalsarai junction has been formally renamed Deen Dayal Upadhyay (DDU), who was found dead in mysterious circumstances near the station in February 1968. The station is more than 150 years old and one of the busiest railway stations in India.

**40. (c)** Vinesh Phogat

# LOGICAL REASONING

## MOCK TEST-1

### ANSWER KEY

| 1. | (a) | 6. | (c) | 11. | (b) | 16. | (c) | 21. | (a) |
|---|---|---|---|---|---|---|---|---|---|
| 2. | (c) | 7. | (a) | 12. | (d) | 17. | (b) | 22. | (b) |
| 3. | (d) | 8. | (c) | 13. | (a) | 18. | (c) | 23. | (b) |
| 4. | (b) | 9. | (a) | 14. | (b) | 19. | (a) | 24. | (c) |
| 5. | (d) | 10. | (d) | 15. | (a) | 20. | (a) | 25. | (a) |

**1. (a)** The rule is +11, +22, +44, +88, +176

The next number is 178 + 176 = 354.

**2. (c)** First letter : +2, +3, +4, +5, etc.

Second letter: $-2, -3, -4, -5$, etc

**3. (d)** Clearly, we have :

COMPREHENSION

$\rightarrow$ (COM) (PREHENS) (ION)

$\rightarrow$ MOCIONSNEHERP

The middle letter is the seventh letter, which is S.

**4. (b)** POLICE

**5. (d)** In all other pairs, first is used to hold the second.

**6. (c)** If 63 is changed to 62, differences become 10, 20, 30, 40 which is a pattern of uniform increase.

**7. (a)** As,

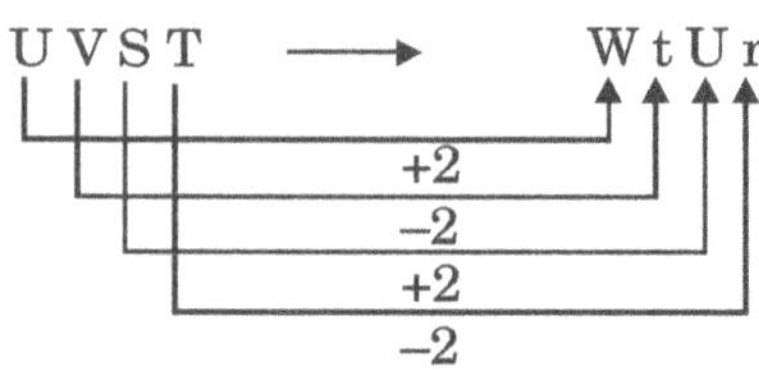


In the same way,

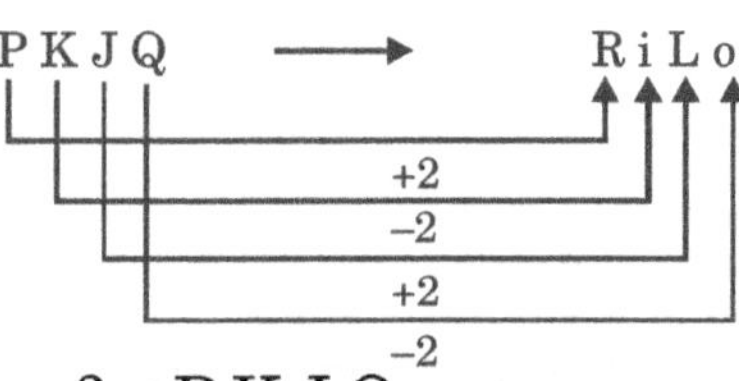


$\therefore$ ? = P K J Q

**8. (c)** Race causes fatigue and fast causes hunger.

**9. (a)** Just add '1' in the total number of each word

viz, DRIVER is formed of six letters hence

6 + 1 = 7, etc.

**10. (d)**
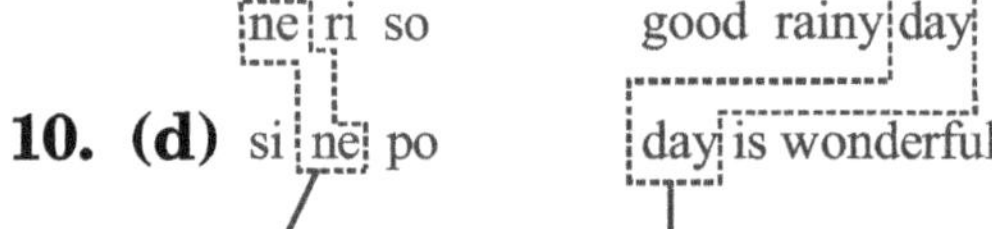


ne is common    day is common

$\Rightarrow$ ne means day

Again ;
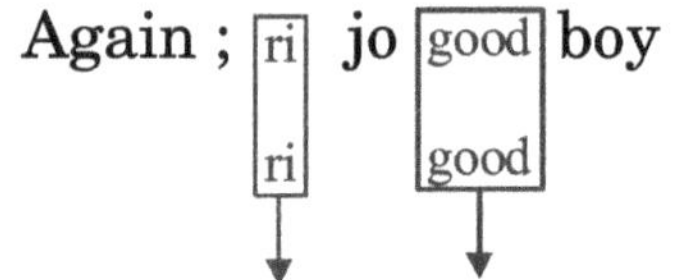


ne      so     rainy day

ri is common, good is common

$\Rightarrow$ ri mean good.

Thus, so means rainy.

**11. (b)** Sarita rank from the bottom = $(43 + 1) - 27 = 17$.

**12. (d)** In each step, the center smaller element moves 90° ACW and topmost element gets shaded.

**13. (a)** Ears alternate in shape between horizontal and diagonal positions, shading in the larger circles is vertical to the right and horizontal at the top.

**14. (b)** P is the daughter of V, who is spouse of T. T is the daughter of S. So, T is the mother and V is the father of P. Therefore, S is the grandfather of P.

**15. (a)** R and S are brother Q is the child of R and T is the child of S. So, cousin of Q. is T.

**16. (c)** The rule is: $2\ 1\ 3 = 2^2\ 1\ 3^2 = 4\ 1\ 9$; $3\ 2\ 2 = 3^2\ 2\ 2^2 = 924$; $4\ 1\ 5 = 4^2\ 1\ 5^2 = 16\ 1\ 25$
$\therefore\ 2\ 1\ 5 = 2^2\ 1\ 5^2 = 4\ 1\ 25$

**17. (b)**

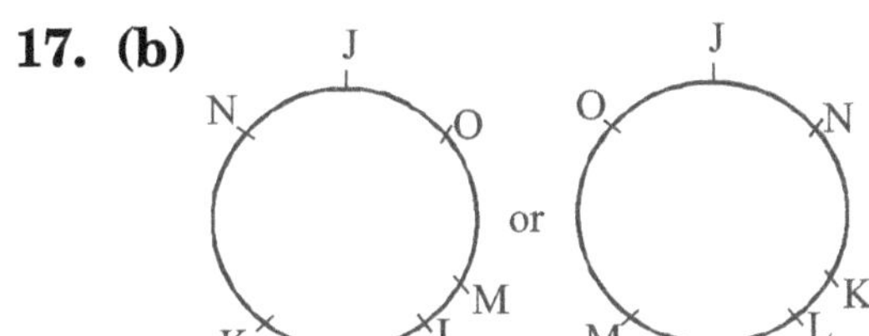


Hence, O is the opposite of K.

**18. (c)** Crows come under the class Aves. Cow is a mammal.

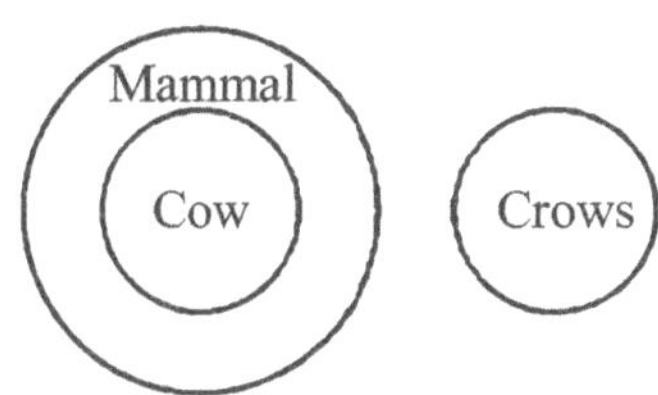


**19. (a)**

| Persons | Numbers | | | | | | |
|---|---|---|---|---|---|---|---|
| | 3 | 5 | 6 | 7 | 8 | 11 | 17 |
| Educated | ✓ | ✗ | ✗ | ✗ | ✓ | ✓ | ✗ |
| Employed | ✓ | ✓ | ✓ | ✓ | ✗ | ✗ | ✗ |
| Poor | ✓ | ✓ | ✓ | ✗ | ✗ | ✓ | ✓ |

Number of educated youth are poor = $11 + 3 = 14$

**22. (b)**

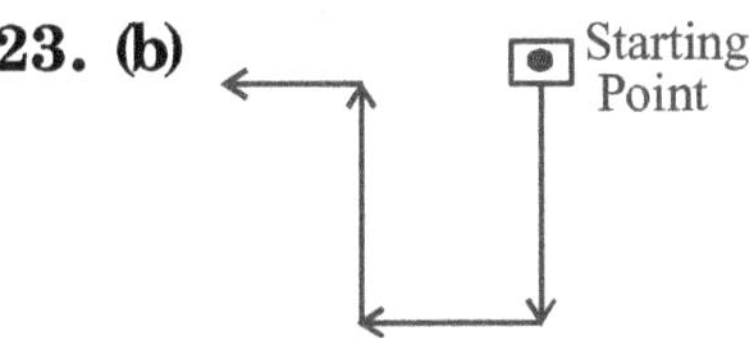

$6 + 18 = 24$ → Here $18 = 6 \times 3$
$24 + 36 = 60$ → Here $36 = 6 \times 6$  $+3$
$60 + 60 = 120$ → Here $60 = 6 \times 10$  $+4$
$120 + 90 = 210$ → Here $90 = 6 \times 15$  $+5$
$210 + 126 = \boxed{336}$ → Here $126 = 6 \times 21$  $+6$

**23. (b)**

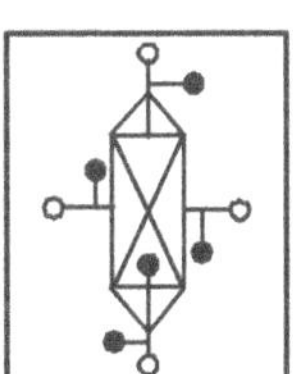


**24. (c)** $16 \div 64 - 8 \times 4 + 2$
$\Rightarrow 16 + 64 \div 8 - 4 \times 2$
$\Rightarrow 16 + 8 - 4 \times 2$
$\Rightarrow 16 + 8 - 8 \Rightarrow 16$

**25. (a)** In water image upside becomes downside.

## MOCK TEST-2

| ANSWER KEY | | | | | | | | | |
|---|---|---|---|---|---|---|---|---|---|
| 1. | (d) | 6. | (b) | 11. | (a) | 16. | (c) | 21. | (d) |
| 2. | (d) | 7. | (c) | 12. | (b) | 17. | (d) | 22. | (a) |
| 3. | (a) | 8. | (c) | 13. | (d) | 18. | (c) | 23. | (d) |
| 4. | (c) | 9. | (d) | 14. | (d) | 19. | (b) | 24. | (c) |
| 5. | (b) | 10. | (a) | 15. | (d) | 20. | (b) | 25. | (d) |

**1.** **(d)** The numbers 1, 2, 5 and 6 are on the adjacent faces of number 3. Therefore, the number 4 lies opposite 3.
The numbers 3, 4 and 6 can not be on the faces opposite to 1. Therefore, 5 lies opposite 1.
Now, 2 lies opposite 6.

**2.** **(d)**

| Regions → | 1 | 2 | 4 | 6 | 7 | 8 | 9 | 10 |
|---|---|---|---|---|---|---|---|---|
| Persons ↓ | | | | | | | | |
| Boys □ | ✓ | ✓ | × | × | × | × | ✓ | × |
| Girls △ | × | × | ✓ | × | × | ✓ | × | × |
| Sober ○ | × | ✓ | ✓ | ✓ | ✓ | × | × | × |
| Cricketer ▭ | ✓ | ✓ | × | ✓ | × | × | × | ✓ |

Region 2 presents the boys who are cricketer and sober.

**3.** **(a)** Day before yesterday was Sunday. Therefore, today is Tuesday.
Day after tomorrow will be Thursday.
Thursday + 3 = Sunday

**4.** **(c)**

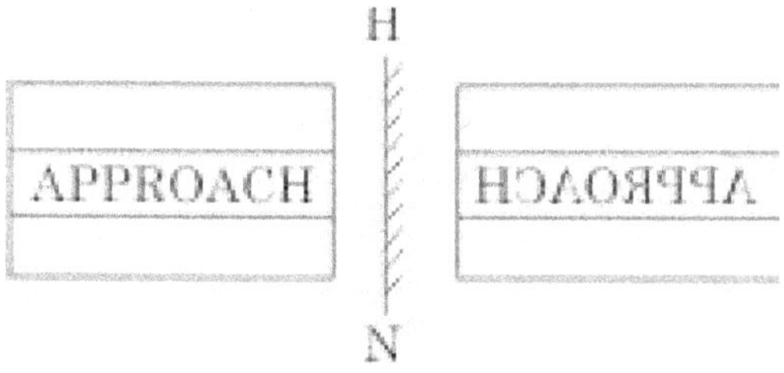


**5.** **(b)**

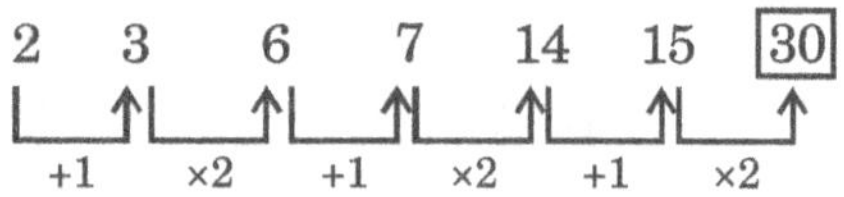


**6.** **(b)**

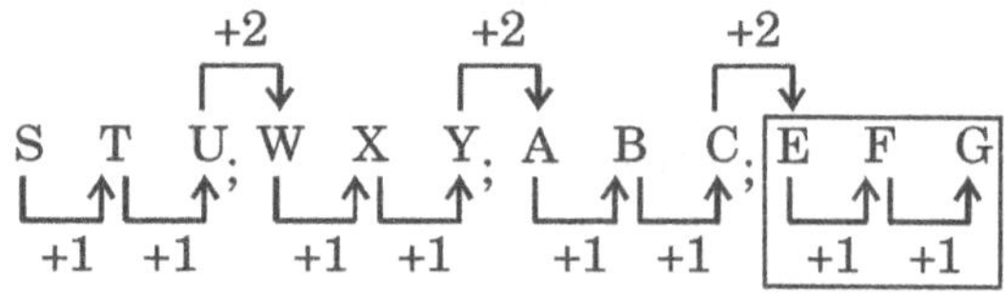


**7.** **(c)** The second column number is the product of first and third column

25 = 5 × 5

49 = 7 × 7

[36] = 6 × 6

**8.** **(c)** Moving clockwise, the terms are :

5 × 2 + 2 = 12

12 × 2 + 2 = 26

26 × 2 + 2 = 54

54 × 2 + 2 = 110

So, missing number

= 110 × 2 + 2 = [222]

**9.** **(d)**

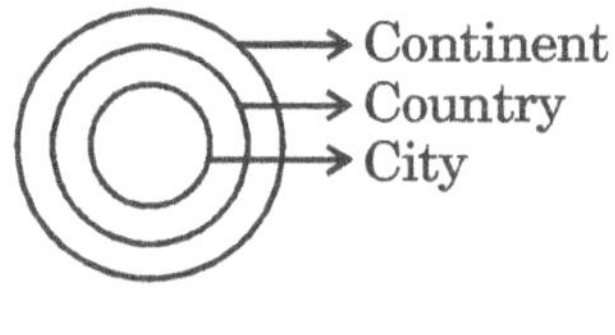


**10.** **(a)**

**11. (a)** After interchanging sign–
$$10 \times 5 \div 5 - 5 + 5 = 10 \times 1 - 5 + 5$$
$$= 10 - 5 + 5$$
$$= 15 - 5 = 10$$

**12. (b)** Suppose the age of Salim is x years
Age of Raju = x + 1 year
Age of Smith = x + 2 years
Age of Veni = x + 3 years
Therefore, Salim is the youngest of all.

**13. (d)**

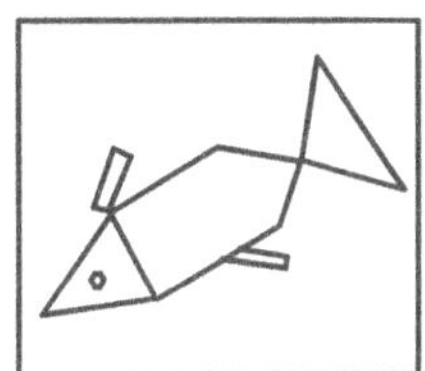

**14. (d)** A man + his wife = 1 + 1 = 2
His three sons + their wives = 3 + 3 = 6
Three children in each one's family = 3 × 3 = 9
Total members = 2 + 6 + 9 = 17

**15. (d)** $V \xrightarrow{+1} W \xrightarrow{+2} Y$

$Q \xrightarrow{+1} R \xrightarrow{+2} T$

$L \xrightarrow{+1} M \xrightarrow{+2} O$

But,

$J \xrightarrow{+1} K \xrightarrow{+1} L$

**16. (c)** Except the number pair 30 – 50, all other numbers pairs has ratio $= \dfrac{3}{4}$

**17. (d)** Standing arrangement : (facing south)

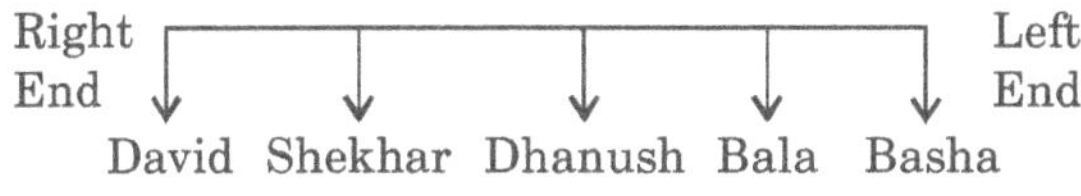

Hence, Dhanush is standing at the middle of the row.

**18. (c)** All the components of Question Figure are present in Answer Figure (c)

**21. (d)** As, S  E    A  S    O  N    A  L

E  S    S  A    N  O    L  A

Therefore,

S  E   P  A   R  A   T  E

E  S   A  P   A  R   E  T

**22. (a)** As,

F   L   A   T   T   E   R
↓   ↓   ↓   ↓   ↓   ↓   ↓
7   2   3   8   8   5   9

and,

M   O   T   H   E   R
↓   ↓   ↓   ↓   ↓   ↓
4   6   8   1   5   9

Therefore,

M   A   M   M   O   T   H
↓   ↓   ↓   ↓   ↓   ↓   ↓
4   3   4   4   6   8   1

**23. (d)** According to dictionary, order is : Bandage, Bangle, Bank, Banquet, Bantam.

**24. (c)** 'T' is not appearing in the word 'REASONABLE'. Hence BRAIN cannot formed from the given word.

**25. (d)** As, cube is 3-D of square. Similarly, sphere is 3-D of circle.

## MOCK TEST-3

### ANSWER KEY

| 1. | (c) | 6. | (d) | 11. | (b) | 16. | (b) | 21. | (c) |
|----|-----|-----|-----|-----|-----|-----|-----|-----|-----|
| 2. | (c) | 7. | (a) | 12. | (d) | 17. | (b) | 22. | (b) |
| 3. | (d) | 8. | (c) | 13. | (d) | 18. | (b) | 23. | (d) |
| 4. | (a) | 9. | (a) | 14. | (c) | 19. | (a) | 24. | (c) |
| 5. | (c) | 10. | (b) | 15. | (d) | 20. | (c) | 25. | (a) |

**1.** **(c)** First letter : +2, +3, +4, +5 etc.
Second letter : –2, –3, –4, –5 etc.

**2.** **(c)** +1, +2, +3, +4 in letters; +3, +5, +7, +9 in numbers.

**3.** **(d)** The new letter sequence is EDRPSEISNO.
The seventh letter from the right is P.

D E P R E S S I O N

1 2 3 4 5 6 7 8 9 10

**4.** **(a)** Arranging the words in alphabetical order, we have Random, Restrict, Robber, Rocket.
So, the word in the 2nd position is Restrict and the correct answer is (a)

**5.** **(c)** Deepak's new position is 22nd from left. But it is the same as Madhu's earlier position i.e. 12th from the right.
∴ there are (22 + 12 – 1) i.e. 33 boys in the row.

**6.** **(d)**
1.

Mili ──(Sister)──→ Ajay ──(Brother)──→ Vijay ──(daughter)──→
Mehul

2. Sanjay ──(brother)──→ Rahul

There are two sets of relationship information given is incomplete and no relation can be established between the two sets.

**7.** **(a)** Father's wife means mother ; mother's only son means himself and thus the girls is the daughter of the man.

**8.** **(c)** (12 km + 5 km = 17 km)

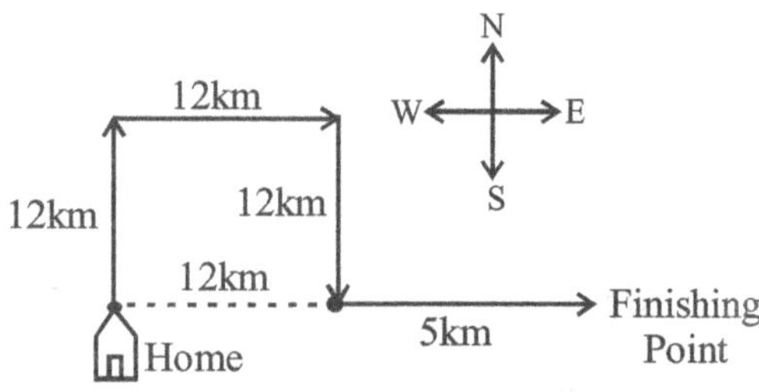


**9.** **(a)** From the relationship given in the question, we observe that each of the objects carries something in common to one another. A Tennis fan can be a cricket player as well as student. Hence, diagram (a) represents this relationship.

**10.** **(b)** We have (56 + 15) – (22 + 8) = 41, (46 + 9) – (10 + 6) = 39
So, missing number = (34 + 11) – (14 + 6) = 25.

**11. (b)** The sum of the two numbers in the upper part is 7 times the number in the lower part.
So, missing number
$= (89 + 16) \div 7 = 15$

**12. (d)** In each step, the shaded portion and small dot move 90° CW and inside dots take new place alternately.

**13. (d)** 1, 8, 9 are figures bisected by a straight line
4, 6, 7 are figures having an extended arm
2, 3, 5 are figures intersected by a line.
Thus the given figure containing nine figures may be divided into three pairs : (1, 8, 9), (4, 6, 7) and (2, 3, 5).
Hence the answer is (d).

**14. (c)** When this figure is folded to form a cube then the face bearing three dots will lie opposite the face bearing five dots.

**15. (d)** We have three squares with vertical and horizontal sides. Each such square has $1^2 + 2^2 = 5$ squares in it. Thus, there are 15 such squares.
In addition, we have two obliquely placed squares.
Hence, total no. of squares = 17

**16. (b)** $L \Rightarrow 12 + 8 = 20$
$E \Rightarrow 5 + 8 = 13$
$A \Rightarrow 1 + 8 = 9$
$D \Rightarrow 4 + 8 = 12$

$E \Rightarrow 5 + 8 = 13$
$R \Rightarrow 18 + 8 = 26$
Therefore,
$L \Rightarrow 12 + 8 = 20$
$I \Rightarrow 9 + 8 = 17$
$G \Rightarrow 7 + 8 = 15$
$H \Rightarrow 8 + 8 = 16$
$T \Rightarrow 20 + 8 = 28$

**17. (b)** Naresh is $17^{th}$ from left and $22^{nd}$ from the right.
So, total number of students in the line = $17 + 22 - 1 = 38$

**19. (a)**

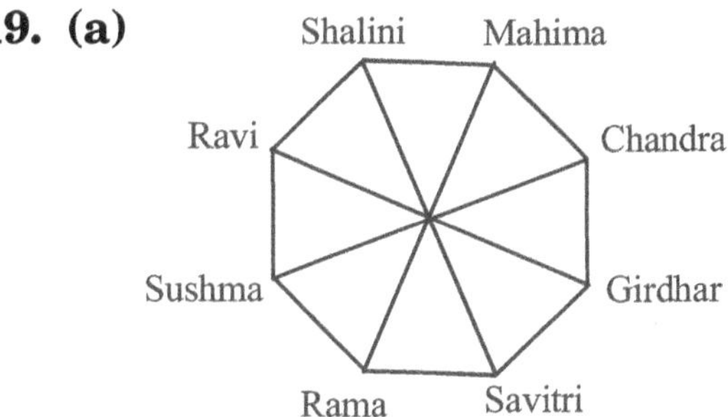


Ravi is to the right of Shalini.

**20. (c)** Metre is a unit of length likewise watt is a unit of power.

**21. (c)** The relationship is x : x (x + 1)

**22. (b)** Option (b) is complete the questions figure completely.

**25. (a)**

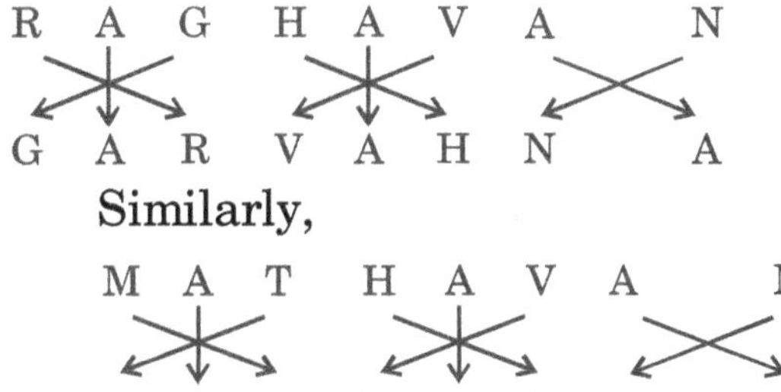


Similarly,

## MOCK TEST-4

### ANSWER KEY

| | | | | | | | | | |
|---|---|---|---|---|---|---|---|---|---|
| 1. | (b) | 9. | (b) | 17. | (d) | 25. | (d) | 33. | (d) |
| 2. | (c) | 10. | (b) | 18. | (d) | 26. | (d) | 34. | (b) |
| 3. | (c) | 11. | (b) | 19. | (c) | 27. | (d) | 35. | (b) |
| 4. | (d) | 12. | (b) | 20. | (b) | 28. | (b) | 36. | (d) |
| 5. | (c) | 13. | (a) | 21. | (a) | 29. | (b) | 37. | (d) |
| 6. | (d) | 14. | (d) | 22. | (b) | 30. | (d) | 38. | (d) |
| 7. | (a) | 15. | (c) | 23. | (c) | 31. | (c) | 39. | (a) |
| 8. | (b) | 16. | (b) | 24. | (b) | 32. | (d) | 40. | (c) |

1. **(b)** $\times 2 \pm 1$. Thus $53 \times 2 + 1 = 107$

2. **(c)** $P \to R \to T \to V \to X$
   $3 \to 5 \to 8 \to 12 \to 17$
   $C \to F \to I \to L \to O$

3. **(c)**

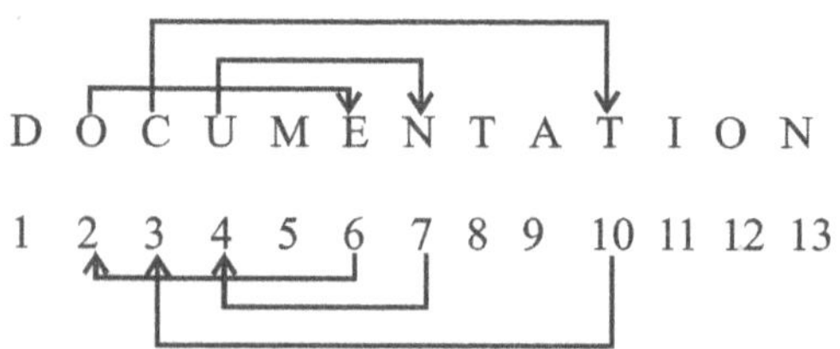

4. **(d)** Clearly, the given letters, when arranged in the order 5, 1, 2, 3, 4 from the word 'TRACE'.

7. **(a)** In other pairs, only one vowel is used

8. **(b)** All except lotus grows on land while lotus grows in water.

9. **(b)** In all other numbers, the sum of the digits is 17.

10. **(b)** The letters are consecutive and written in reverse order.

11. **(b)** Tie is worn in the neck and belt is worn on the waist.

12. **(b)** Sum of the digits of the first number is 2 more than the sum of the digits of the second number.

13. **(a)** In the given code 1 = A, 2 = B, 3 = C, ....... 24 = X, 25 = Y, 26 = X So, in FLOWER, F is coded as 6, L as 12, O as 15, W as 23, E as 5 and R as 18.

14. **(d)** 'BOSE' ; There is no 'S' in the given word.

15. **(c)** 'TRIBAL' is coded as 'TIRLBA' in the same way as 'RATIONAL' is coded as 'RTANIOLA'.

16. **(b)** From second and third statements it is gathered that 'Milk' is coded as 'sat'. From first and third statements, either of the two word 'is bringing' is coded as 'low' or 'ploy'. Hence, 'he' is coded as 'wis' from second statement.

17. **(d)** A teacher teaches in a class and as given 'teacher' is called 'clerk'. So a 'clerk' will teach in the class.

18. **(d)** Clearly, number of boys in a line
    $= 12 + 4 - 1 = 15$
    $\therefore$ Number of boys to be added
    $= 35 - 15 = 20$.

**19. (c)** If day before yesterday was Thursday, so today is Saturday. So tomorrow will be Sunday.

**20-22.** Information given in the questions that one of the two person at the extreme ends is intelligent and other one is fair, suggests two conditions as shown in fig. (1) and (2).

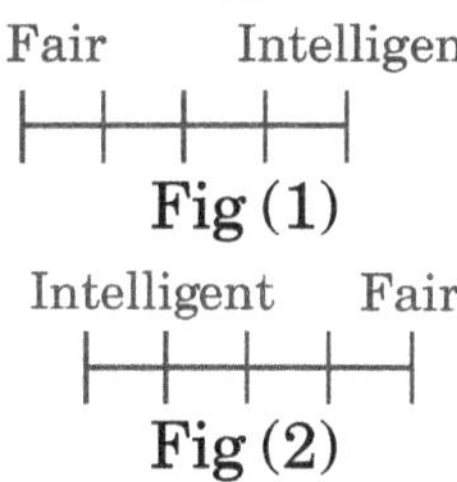


Information that a tall person is sitting to the left to the left of fair person rules out the possibility of fig. (1) as no person in fig.(1) can sit to the left of fair person. Therefore, only fig. (2) shows the correct positions of intelligent and fair persons. Now rest of the information regarding the position of other person can easily be inserted .The final ranking of their sitting arrangement is as shown in fig. (3).

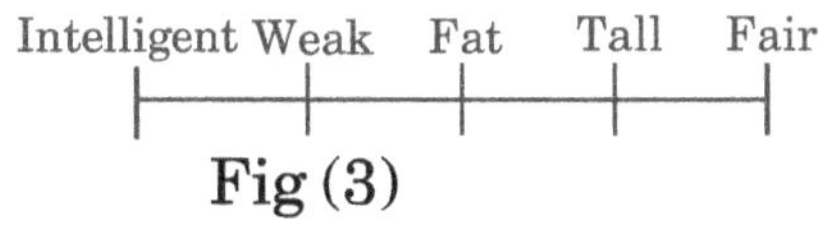


**23. (c)** P @ Q $ # T means P is the husband of Q who is the mother of M who is the father of T, i.e, is the father of T's father, i.e, P is T' paternal grandfather.

**24. (b)** R is the sister of H means R is the daughter of the father of H, i.e., R is the daughter of the husband (say D) of the mother (say F) of H i.e, R % D @ F $ H.

**25. (d)** C is B's daughter and D is B's son. So, D is the brother of C.E is a male married to C so, E is the husband of C, whose brother is D. Thus, D But D is the brother in-law of E.

**26. (d)** Using the correct symbols, we have

Given expression = 24 × 12 + 18 ÷ 9 = 288 + 2 = 290.

**27. (d)** The movements of the person are from A to F, as shown in fig.

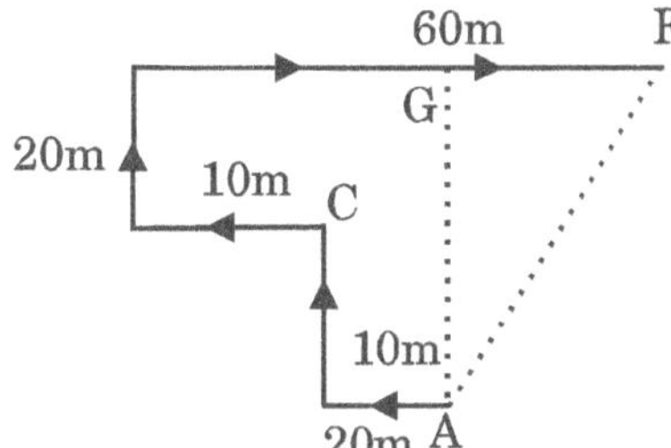


Clearly, the final position is F which is to the north east of the starting point A.

**28. (b)** Here, Ravi starts from home at A, moves 10 km southwards up to B, turns right and moves 10 km up to C, turns right again and moves 10 km up to D and finally turns left and moves 10 km up to E.

Thus, his distance from initial position A = AE

= AD + DE = BC + DE

= (5 + 10) km = 15 km.

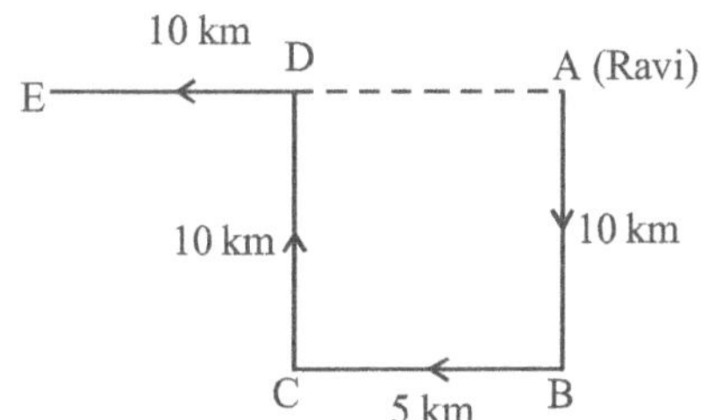

**29. (b)** Bidi smokers is a subset of smokers cancer patient may be a smoker, bidi smoker and non-smoker. Hence, third object shares a common relationship with first and second object as well.

**30. (d)** In fig. (A), $93 - (27 + 63) = 3$

In fig, (B), $79 - (38 + 37) = 4$

∴ In fig. (C), missing number

$= 67 - (16 + 42) = 9$

**31. (c)** The number inside the circle is equal to the difference between the sum of the numbers at the extremities of the horizontal diameter and the sum of numbers at the extremities of the vertical diameter.

In fig. (A), $(5 + 6) - (7 + 4) = 0$

In fig. (B), $(7 + 6) - (8 + 4) = 1$.

∴ In fig. (C) missing number

$= (11 + 2) - (0 + 2) = 11$

**32. (d)** This way, each row and column contains four white stars and five black stars.

**33. (d)** The dot in the top left-hand quarter moves backward and forward between two corners, as does the dot in the bottom left-hand quarter. The dot in the top right-hand quarter moves one corner counter-clockwise at each stage and the dot in the bottom right-hand quarter moves one corner clockwise.

**34. (b)**

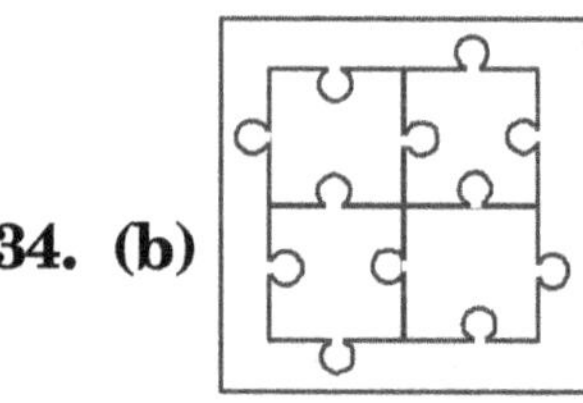

**38. (d)**

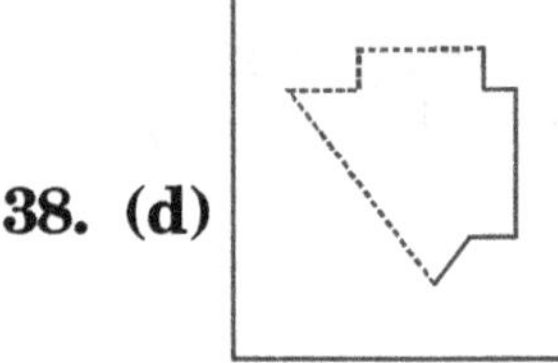

**39. (a)** In terms of weight :

Govind < Ashish; Mohit < Jack;

Jack < Pawan

and Pawan < Govind

⇒ The sequence is

Mohit < Jack < Pawan < Govind < Ashish

∴ Ashish is the heaviest.

**40. (c)** We can label the figure as shown.

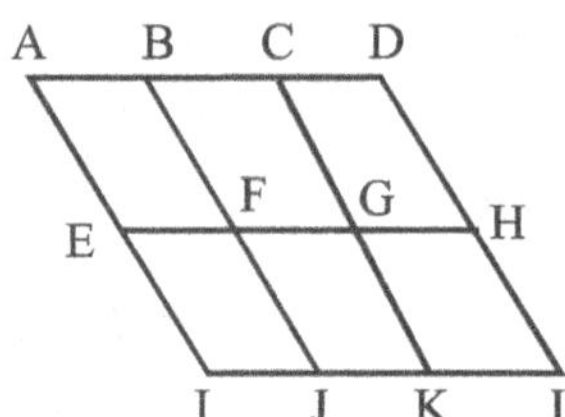

The simplest parallelogram are ABFE, BCGF, CDHG, EFJI, FGKJ and GHLK. These are 6 in number.

The parallelograms composed of two components each, are ACGE, BDHF, EGKI, FHLJ, ABJI, BCKJ and CDLK. Thus, there are 7 such parallelograms. The parallelogram composed of four components each are ACKI and BDLJ, i.e., 2 in number. There is only one parallelogram composed of six components, namely, ADLI. Thus, there are $6 + 7 + 2 + 1 = 16$ parallelograms in the figure.

## MOCK TEST-5

### ANSWER KEY

| | | | | | | | | | |
|---|---|---|---|---|---|---|---|---|---|
| 1. | (b) | 9. | (d) | 17. | (d) | 25. | (c) | 33. | (c) |
| 2. | (d) | 10. | (a) | 18. | (c) | 26. | (d) | 34. | (c) |
| 3. | (b) | 11. | (d) | 19. | (b) | 27. | (d) | 35. | (c) |
| 4. | (d) | 12. | (c) | 20. | (d) | 28. | (d) | 36. | (a) |
| 5. | (a) | 13. | (d) | 21. | (a) | 29. | (c) | 37. | (d) |
| 6. | (a) | 14. | (c) | 22. | (b) | 30. | (b) | 38. | (b) |
| 7. | (c) | 15. | (d) | 23. | (a) | 31. | (d) | 39. | (d) |
| 8. | (b) | 16. | (a) | 24. | (b) | 32. | (b) | 40. | (c) |

**1. (b)** By looking, the dice position, we can say that 2, 4, 5 and 6 are adjacent faces of 3. Therefore, if 1 number is at the bottom then 3 will be on the top.

**3. (b)** (a) BINARY can not be formed, there is no 'B' in the word DICTIONARY

(c) NATION can not be formed, as there is only one 'N' in the word DICTIONARY

(d) ADDITION can not be formed, as there is only one 'D' in the word DICTIONARY

**4. (d)**

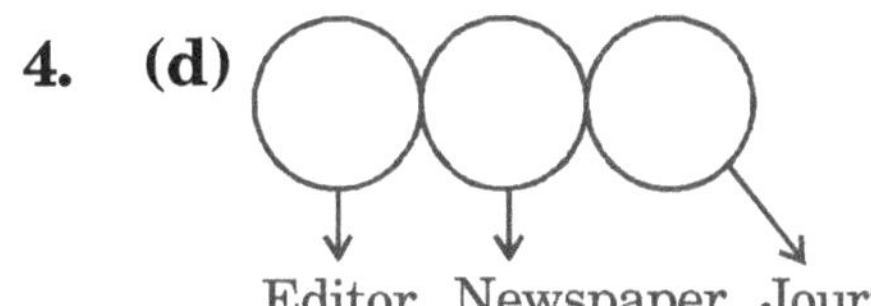


**5. (a)**

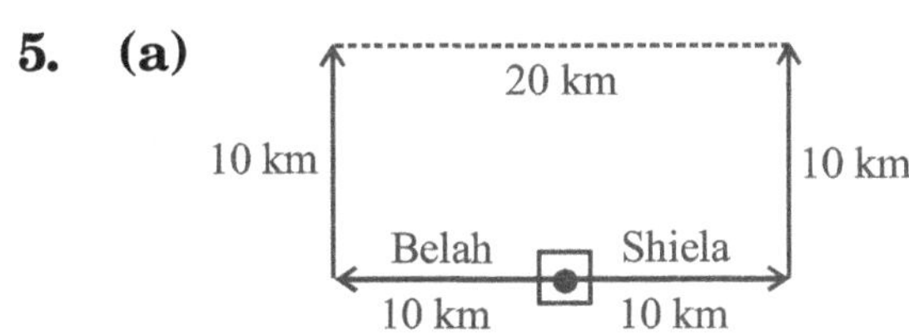


∴ Required distance
= 10 + 10 = 20 km

**6. (a)** Only 'S' can be prefixed to the given words.
New words are:
STILL, STABLE, SPILE, STAB, SPRING

**7. (c)** Dictionary order :
Command → Commerce
(1)            (6)
→ Commit → Conceive
(2)            (4)
→ Conduct → Connect
(5)            (3)

**8. (b)** Stomach is a part of body. Similarly, library has different kinds of books.

**9. (d)** As,

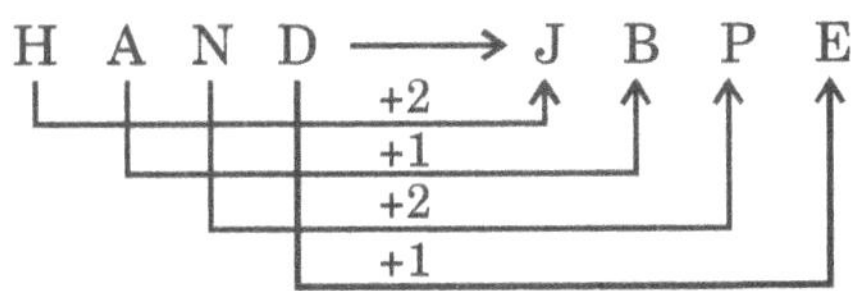


Similarly,

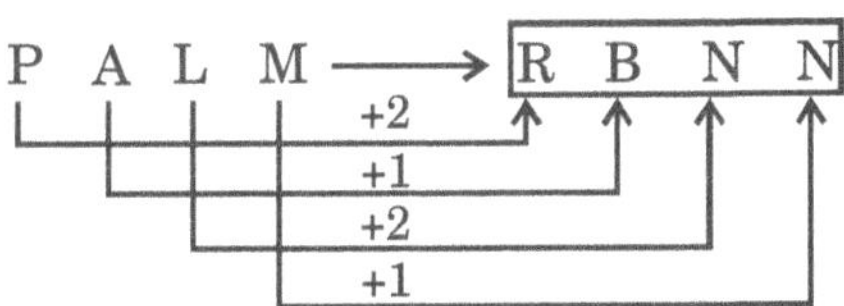


**10. (a)** As, 7 × 6 = 42
Similarly,
6 × 6 = 36

**12. (c)** Originally the colour of turmeric is yellow, here, yellow means red. So the colour of turmeric is red.

**14. (c)** All are parts of car.

**15. (d)** All are divisible by 5 except 256.

**16. (a)**

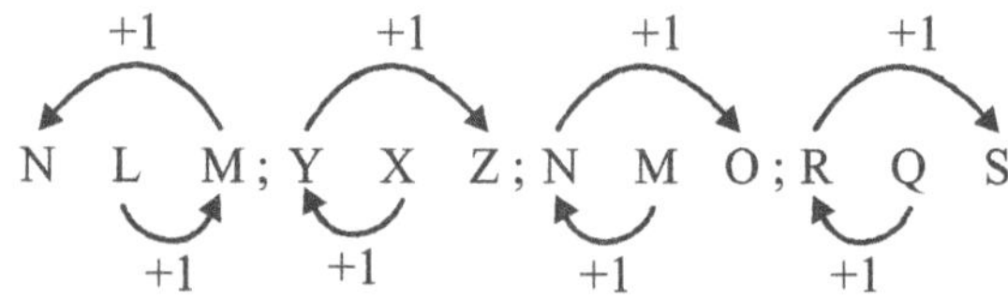


**17. (d)** Annual - 1 year  Monthly - 30 days
Weekly - 7 days  Biannual - 6 month
Fortnightly - 15 days.

**18. (c)** Water image of

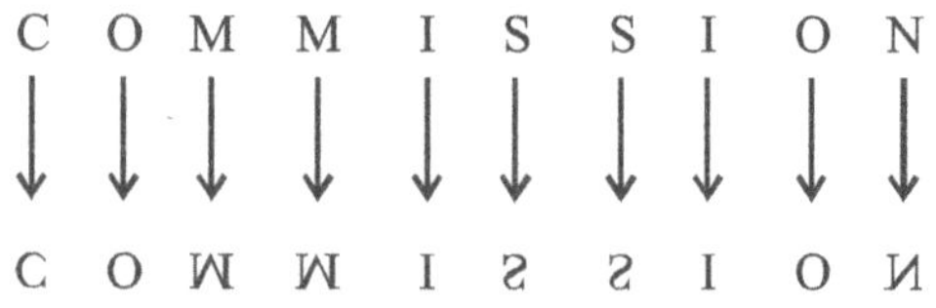

**19. (b)**

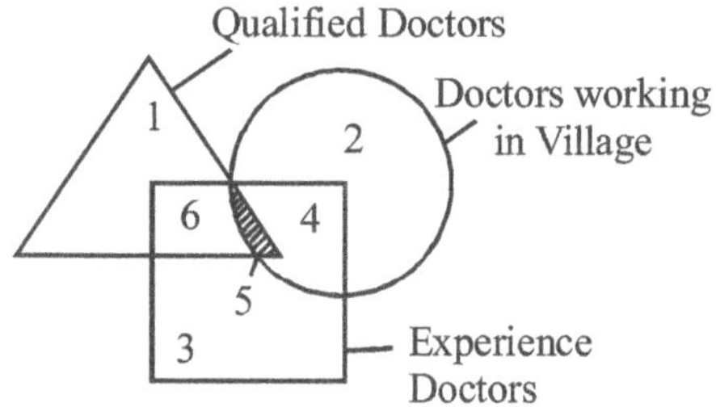


Hence, shaded portion in above diagram represents.
Qualified Experienced Doctors working in village i.e. 5.

**20. (d)**



Rani is facing towards East and Sarita is facing towards South.

**23. (a)** $5 + 2 - 12 \times 6 \div 2 = 10$
Can be written in original signs as
$5 \times 2 + 12 \div 6 - 2$
$= 10 + 2 - 2 = 10$

**24. (b)** Rewriting the expression 16 Q 12 P6R5S4 with original signs
$16 \times 12 \div 6 + 5 - 4$
$= 16 \times 2 + 5 - 4$
$= 32 + 1 = 33$

**25. (c)** $3 + 9 - 5 = 7, 2 + 8 - 6 = 4$
$4 + 7 - 5 = \textcircled{6}$

**26. (d)** $4 + 5 - 3 - 5 = 1$
$7 + 7 - 5 - 4 = 5$
$3 + 5 - 2 - 1 = \boxed{5}$

**27. (d)** Arranging digits according to question.
265, 178, 834, 357
Hence, third highest would be 265 and 8 be the sum of first and second digits of the number.

**28. (d)** Total number of students in the class = 45.
Neha's rank from first = 15$^{\text{th}}$

So number of students from the last = 45 − (1 + 14) = 30

So, Neha's rank from the last is 31st.

**29. (c)** Kathir > Ganesh > Raju > Apparu

Kathir is the senior most

**30. (b)**

$$7 \xrightarrow{+7} 14 \xrightarrow{+9} 23 \xrightarrow{+11} 34 \xrightarrow{+13} \boxed{47}$$

**31. (d)** $A \xrightarrow{+5} F \xrightarrow{+5} K \xrightarrow{+5} \boxed{P} \xrightarrow{+5} U$

$E \xrightarrow{+5} J \xrightarrow{+5} O \xrightarrow{+5} \boxed{T} \xrightarrow{+5} Y$

**Qs. 32-34.** The given information can be analyzed as under :

| | Hockey | Volley-ball | Base-ball | Cricket | Foot-ball |
|---|---|---|---|---|---|
| Ravi | √ | √ | √ | | |
| Kunal | √ | √ | | √ | |
| Sachin | √ | | √ | | √ |
| Gaurav | | √ | √ | √ | √ |
| Michael | | | √ | | √ |

**32. (b)** Kunal is good in Hockey, Cricket and Volleyball.

**33. (c)** Gaurav is good in Baseball, Cricket, Volleyball and Football.

**34. (c)** Ravi is good in Baseball, Volleyball and Hockey.

**35. (c)** 'S + Q' & 'P + S' means R is the grandfather of Q. Now P , R means P is daughter of R. This clearly means P is aunt of Q.

**36. (a)** P − R + Q, represents R is the father of Q, and P is the wife of R.

∴ P is the mother of Q

**37. (d)**

So, either F or B is facing A.

**38. (b)** C is facing D.

**39. (d)** The new sequence becomes 9 5 1 8 2 3 4 7 8 3 counting to the left, the seventh number is 8.

**40. (c)** In the first and the third statements '6' means 'is'. In the second and third statements we get '4' means 'colour'. Thus, in the third statement, '3' means 'fun'.

# CYBER

## MOCK TEST-1

| ANSWER KEY | | | | | | | | | |
|---|---|---|---|---|---|---|---|---|---|
| 1 | (a) | 6 | (d) | 11 | (b) | 16 | (c) | 21 | (c) |
| 2 | (b) | 7 | (d) | 12 | (c) | 17 | (a) | 22 | (a) |
| 3 | (c) | 8 | (a) | 13 | (c) | 18 | (d) | 23 | (d) |
| 4 | (d) | 9 | (a) | 14 | (d) | 19 | (c) | 24 | (a) |
| 5 | (a) | 10 | (c) | 15 | (c) | 20 | (b) | 25 | (c) |

**3.** **(c)** <hr> tag is used to put horizontal line.

## MOCK TEST-2

### ANSWER KEY

| 1 | (b) | 6 | (a) | 11 | (d) | 16 | (b) | 21 | (b) |
|---|-----|---|-----|----|-----|----|-----|----|-----|
| 2 | (a) | 7 | (b) | 12 | (c) | 17 | (c) | 22 | (b) |
| 3 | (a) | 8 | (c) | 13 | (b) | 18 | (b) | 23 | (a) |
| 4 | (a) | 9 | (b) | 14 | (a) | 19 | (b) | 24 | (b) |
| 5 | (d) | 10 | (c) | 15 | (d) | 20 | (b) | 25 | (b) |

1. **(b)** A common type of modem is one that turns the digital data of a computer into modulated electrical signal for transmission over telephone lines and demodulated by another modem at the receiver side to recover the digital data.

2. **(a)** SD stands for Secure Digital.

4. **(a)** The tool given in the question is of **Lasso** tool.

9. **(b)** Brain is a boot sector virus, infecting the first sector of floppies as they inserted into an infected computer. Brain is only a few kilobytes in size and most of it is located in sectors that are marked as "bad" in the FAT.

11. **(d)** A ring network is a network topology in which each node connects to exactly two other nodes, forming a single continuous pathway for signals through each node.

## MOCK TEST-3

| ANSWER KEY | | | | | | | | | |
|---|---|---|---|---|---|---|---|---|---|
| 1 | (c) | 6 | (c) | 11 | (c) | 16 | (d) | 21 | (c) |
| 2 | (a) | 7 | (d) | 12 | (a) | 17 | (c) | 22 | (b) |
| 3 | (a) | 8 | (d) | 13 | (c) | 18 | (c) | 23 | (c) |
| 4 | (b) | 9 | (b) | 14 | (b) | 19 | (d) | 24 | (c) |
| 5 | (d) | 10 | (a) | 15 | (a) | 20 | (d) | 25 | (d) |

**8. (a)** Option (a) is of Name manager. It is used to create, edit and delete names used in the workbook.

**11. (c)** Repeates are used in transmission systems to regenerate analog or digital signals distorted by transmission loss. Bridge is used to connect two segments of the same LAN.

**12. (a)** It includes Keynote, a presentation program; the word processing and desktop publishing application Pages; and and the the spreadsheet application Numbers.

# MOCK TEST-4

## ANSWER KEY

| | | | | | | | | | |
|---|---|---|---|---|---|---|---|---|---|
| 1. | (a) | 9. | (b) | 17. | (d) | 25. | (d) | 33. | (a) |
| 2. | (a) | 10. | (c) | 18. | (a) | 26. | (a) | 34. | (c) |
| 3. | (c) | 11. | (a) | 19. | (a) | 27. | (c) | 35. | (a) |
| 4. | (c) | 12. | (d) | 20. | (b) | 28. | (c) | 36. | (a) |
| 5. | (c) | 13. | (d) | 21. | (c) | 29. | (d) | 37. | (b) |
| 6. | (d) | 14. | (a) | 22. | (b) | 30. | (d) | 38. | (d) |
| 7. | (b) | 15. | (c) | 23. | (a) | 31. | (d) | 39. | (c) |
| 8. | (c) | 16. | (d) | 24. | (b) | 32. | (d) | 40. | (a) |

4. **(c)** Content Protection for Recordable Media and Pre–Recorded Media (CPRM/CPPM) is a mechanism for controlling the copying, moving and deletion of digital media on a host device, such as a personal computer, or other player.

7. **(b)** This 3D Rotation tool can be used on any movie clip instance to rotate and transform the symbol around x, y and z axes.

10. **(c)** The given icon is known as 'Compare'.

14. **(a)** =MIN (B2 : F2) will return, 32 as an output.

15. **(c)** Icon given in the question is of Macros. It can be accessed by hoing to : Create tab ® Macros & Code ® Macros

19. **(a)** TCP/IP stands for Transmission Control Protocol/Internet Protocol.

24. **(b)** Machine language.

25. **(d)** All of these

39. **(c)** American Standard Code for Information Interchange

## MOCK TEST-5

### ANSWER KEY

| | | | | | | | | | |
|---|---|---|---|---|---|---|---|---|---|
| **1** | **(c)** | **9** | **(c)** | **17** | **(d)** | **25** | **(d)** | **33** | **(a)** |
| **2** | **(a)** | **10** | **(b)** | **18** | **(d)** | **26** | **(b)** | **34** | **(d)** |
| **3** | **(a)** | **11** | **(c)** | **19** | **(a)** | **27** | **(d)** | **35** | **(b)** |
| **4** | **(c)** | **12** | **(d)** | **20** | **(d)** | **28** | **(b)** | **36** | **(c)** |
| **5** | **(b)** | **13** | **(a)** | **21** | **(d)** | **29** | **(a)** | **37** | **(a)** |
| **6** | **(c)** | **14** | **(c)** | **22** | **(a)** | **30** | **(b)** | **38** | **(c)** |
| **7** | **(d)** | **15** | **(a)** | **23** | **(a)** | **31** | **(b)** | **39** | **(a)** |
| **8** | **(a)** | **16** | **(d)** | **24** | **(a)** | **32** | **(a)** | **40** | **(a)** |

1. **(c)** operating systems e.g : Windows 7, Windows 8, Android, etc.

4. **(c)** PCMCIA is an organization consisting of some 500 companies that has developed a standard for small, credit card-sized devices, called PC cards.

5. **(b)** The <sub> tag defines subscript text. Subscript text appears half a character below the normal line, and is sometimes rendered in smaller font.

7. **(d)** The given tool is of Eyedropper tool.

8. **(a)** If the lines or shapes you want to select are located close to other lines, you may have difficulty selecting just the items you want with a rectangle. The lasso tool lets you create an irregular selection outline.

9. **(c)** Track changes is a way for Microsoft word to keep track of the changes you make to a document. You can then choose to accept or reject those changes.

14. **(c)** Causes of NULL error:
    - You may have used an incorrect range opertor.
    - Ranges do not intersect.

19. **(a)** Cookies is a small piece of data sent from a website and stored on the user's computer by the user's web broser while the user is browsing.

21. **(d)** FTP stands for File Transfer Protocol.